ALWAYS REFORMING

Explorations in Systematic Theology

EDITED BY A. T. B. McGowan

IVP Academic
An imprint of InterVarsity Press
Downers Grove, Illinois

InterVarsity Press
P.O. Box 1400, Downers Grove, IL 60515-1426
Internet: www.ivpress.com
E-mail: email@ivpress.com

InterVarsity Press® is the book-publishing division of InterVarsity Christian Fellowship/USA®, a student movement active on campus at hundreds of universities, colleges and schools of nursing in the United States of America, and a member movement of the International Fellowship of Evangelical Students. For information about local and regional activities, write Public Relations Dept., InterVarsity Christian Fellowship/USA, 6400 Schroeder Rd., P.O. Box 7895, Madison, WI 53707-7895, or visit the IVCF website at <www.intervarsity.org>.

Cover design: Cindy Kiple

Cover image: optic fiber ends: George Diebold Photography/Getty Images
pews: PhotoLink/Getty Images

ISBN 978-0-8308-2829-6

Printed in the United States of America ∞

Library of Congress Cataloging-in-Publication Data

A catalog record for this book is available from the Library of Congress.

P	18	17	16	15	14	13	12	11	10	9	8	7	6	5	4	3	2	1
Y	22	21	20	19	18	17	16	15	14	13	12	11	10	09	08	07		

CONTENTS

Contributors		7
Preface		9
Introduction		13
1.	The Trinity: Where Do We Go from Here? *Gerald Bray*	19
2.	Observations on the Future of System *Stephen Williams*	41
3.	Classical Christology's Future in Systematic Theology *Robert L. Reymond*	67
4.	On the Very Idea of a Theological System: An Essay in Aid of Triangulating Scripture, Church and World *Kevin J. Vanhoozer*	125
5.	The Atonement as Penal Substitution *A. T. B. McGowan*	183
6.	The Relationship between Biblical Theology and Systematic Theology *Richard C. Gamble*	211

7. Old Covenant, New Covenant   240
   Henri Blocher

8. Union with Christ: Some Biblical and Theological
   Reflections   271
   Richard B. Gaffin, Jr

9. Justification: The Ecumenical, Biblical and Theological
   Dimensions of Current Debates   289
   Cornelis P. Venema

10. The Doctrine of the Church in the Twenty-First Century   328
    Derek W. H. Thomas

    Index of Names   353
    Index of Biblical References   360

CONTRIBUTORS

Henri Blocher is Professor of Systematic Theology at the Faculté Libre de Théologie Évangélique, Vaux-sur-Seine, France and Gunther H. Knoedler Professor of Theology at Wheaton College, USA.

Gerald Bray is Anglican Professor of Divinity at Beeson Divinity School, Samford University, Birmingham, Alabama, USA.

John Frame is Professor of Systematic Theology and Philosophy at Reformed Theological Seminary, Orlando, USA.

Richard B. Gaffin, Jr is Professor of Biblical and Systematic Theology at Westminster Theological Seminary, Philadelphia, USA.

Richard C. Gamble is Professor of Systematic Theology at Reformed Presbyterian Theological Seminary, Pittsburgh, USA.

A. T. B. McGowan is Principal of Highland Theological College, Dingwall, Scotland, and Honorary Professor of Reformed Doctrine, University of Aberdeen.

Robert L. Reymond is Professor of Systematic Theology at Knox Theological Seminary, Fort Lauderdale, Florida, USA.

Derek W. H. Thomas is John E. Richards Professor of Practical and Systematic Theology at Reformed Theological Seminary, Jackson, Mississippi, USA.

Kevin J. Vanhoozer is Research Professor of Systematic Theology at Trinity Evangelical Divinity School, Deerfield, Illinois, USA.

Cornelis P. Venema is President and Professor of Doctrinal Studies at Mid-America Reformed Seminary, Dyer, Indiana, USA.

Stephen Williams is Professor of Systematic Theology at Union Theological College, Belfast, Northern Ireland.

PREFACE

I am thankful to editor Andrew McGowan for inviting me to present this fine group of essays to its readers. Reformed theology has often professed to be 'always reforming' (*semper reformanda*), but it has often been focused too much on its past achievements (*reformata*) at the expense of seeking new insight (*reformanda*). So I am delighted to see this book, and I am enthusiastic about the perspective set forth by McGowan's introduction.

Nobody knows what theology, even Reformed theology, will be like in the future. So this book is not a series of predictions. Rather, these discussions of the future are *normative*. The authors tell us not what Reformed theology will be like in the future, but what it *ought* to be like. They identify problems to be solved, opportunities to be seized, resources to be appropriated, dangers to be avoided.

One major topic of interest to them is the nature of systematic theology as a discipline. Is there a 'system' of Christian truth that theologians can discern? If so, what is the relation of that system to the biblical text? The answers do not seem as obvious today as they may have seemed a hundred years ago. Stephen Williams explores in this regard how the search for logically consistent formulations can lead us away from the 'wider system' of Scripture and of the life-context of biblical teaching. He also warns us against theologies too narrowly focused on defending the distinctives of a particular denomination or tradition. Gamble and Bray recommend basing systematics more closely on biblical theology.[1] Vanhoozer recommends a method of 'triangulation', in which we learn from God by correlating Scripture, church and world, participating with them in the 'theodrama' of salvation.

I do appreciate the attempts of Williams and Vanhoozer to make systematic theology less of an abstract conceptual theory, and more of a guide to the Christian life. So I have defined theology as 'the application of the Word of God by persons to all areas of life'.[2] Exegetical theology applies specific passages, biblical theology, the history of redemption, and systematics to the Bible as a whole. So Robert Reymond identifies the typical question of the systematic theologian, 'What does the whole Bible teach about such and such a topic?' But that teaching is always applicatory. It is the *didachē* or *didaskalia* of Paul's pastoral epistles; that is, to be 'healthy' (*hygiainos*), conducive to spiritual health (1 Tim. 1:10; 2 Tim. 4:3; Titus 1:9; 2:1). The questions of systematics guide not only theory, but all other sorts of practice as well, so that we find systematics not only in the tomes of professional scholars, but also in Sunday school materials for 11-year-olds, in laypersons' conferences, in sermons. And all Christians are systematic theologians when they take God's Word into their hearts and lives.

As a long-time triangulator, I share Vanhoozer's concerns about maintaining the primacy of Scripture alongside the vast complexity of other factors that go into human knowledge, even of the Scriptures. I applaud his rich discussion of this complexity. But I worry that in the triangulation literature, the

---

1. My good friend Richard Gamble accuses me of relating orthodox biblical theology too closely to liberalism in my *Doctrine of God* (Phillipsburg: P. & R., 2002), p. 197. I reply that he exaggerates the force of my comparison: (1) I referred to 'some', not all, biblical theologians in the passage he discusses, and (2) my comparison is only with regard to theological *emphasis*, not with regard to any specific doctrinal issues. I think it overstates the matter to say that I am here creating a 'guilt by association' or that I have been uncharitable. In fact, I am very enthusiastic about biblical theology as one of many ways of appropriating biblical truth, and I say so plainly on pp. 7–8 of the volume. If anyone wants to discuss my view in a serious way, they would be wise (and charitable) to look at my systematic statement of it rather than such incidental references as the above. That statement is in *Doctrine of the Knowledge of God* (Phillipsburg: P. & R., 1987), pp. 207–212. See also Chapter 16 of my forthcoming *Doctrine of the Christian Life.*

2. *Doctrine of the Knowledge*, p. 81. Readers of these essays should note that this definition of theology has a future orientation, as well as a foundation in biblical authority. Theology takes the unchanging Word of God and applies it to each new situation as it arises.

complexity may drown out the simplicity. The simplicity is that we hear the Word of God and do it, that we obey God rather than man. Given that triangulation is the key to our understanding and use of Scripture, that process ought to lead us back to the Bible, where we can say, 'Here God is speaking.' If hermeneutical complexity makes it too difficult for us ever to say this, then it has become too complex.

It is an essential of the Christian faith that believers are able to distinguish the Word of God from the word of man. History has shown that Christians have often erred in making this distinction by oversimplified exegesis. Triangulators (again, me among them) show how we cannot understand or properly use biblical texts without relating them to ancient language and culture, church creeds and tradition, our present community and the working of the Spirit in our heart. But if this process works properly, it must bring us to a place where we can say, 'Thus says the Lord,' even against ancient and modern culture, against our present community, and even against church creeds and tradition.

Certainly, there are many passages and teachings of Scripture that we can understand and affirm without much hermeneutical sophistication. Scripture teaches plainly that God created the world, that he values righteousness, that he hates murder and adultery, that he sent his Son to die for sinners, that he raised Jesus from the dead. In conflict with those who deny such teachings, we must not allow ourselves to be silenced by scepticism about what the Bible really means or how many factors must be related to other factors. Rather, our message should be loud and clear.

That clarity should be our goal, even as we explore more complicated issues like the Trinity, the nature of the atonement and so on. We must exegete responsibly, using all the tools at our disposal, doing our best to relate everything to everything else, taking into account the dramatic structure of Scripture, the communal nature of theology, and the spiritual maturity needed for interpretation. But this process should not leave us hanging – it should bring us to a point of confidence, where we can set forth God's words against the errors of sinners.

I have so far been speaking of confidence about theological propositions, and I am fully aware that the Bible, and theology rightly done, are more than merely propositional. Theology is the whole theodrama, in which we participate. But our roles in that drama, our living before God and one another, also require confidence. Our use of Scripture should energize our decisions and actions, not throw us into confusion.

Much as we try to see theological propositions in a larger perspective, however, they continue to play a large role in the life of the church, so that disagreements about them threaten the peace and unity of God's people. So we need to continue to devote attention to them. Thus many essays in this volume deal with specific theological issues: the Trinity, Christology, the atonement, old and new covenants, union with Christ, justification and the church. It is significant that three of these, on the covenants, union with Christ and justification, deal with a potentially divisive debate in American Presbyterianism today.

Here I find Gaffin's treatment especially illuminating on the question of whether God imputes the righteousness of Christ to the believer. Whether or not Scripture specifically refers to such imputation, it is clearly implicit in our union with Christ. Remember that 'imputation' means to reckon the righteousness or guilt of one person to another. But to be one with Christ is certainly to have his righteousness as our own. In him we become the righteousness of God (2 Cor. 5:21). Far from rendering imputation unnecessary, union with Christ is impossible without imputation, and vice versa. I am convinced that the church will make no progress on the justification issue until this point is fully understood and appreciated.

I could say much more by way of interaction with these insightful and wise authors, but my job is to whet the reader's appetite, and I hope that job is done. To read this book is not only to recall how rich a resource Reformed theology has been in the past, but to anticipate even more rich blessings from it in the future. May God use this book as a tool for continuing reformation.

John Frame

INTRODUCTION

A. T. B. McGowan

Although the Reformation took place in the sixteenth century, it is important to understand that this was the beginning of something and not the end. The Reformed churches affirmed the need to be *semper reformanda* (always reforming). Unfortunately, this commitment to continuing reformation has not been faithfully and consistently maintained over the centuries. At one end of the theological spectrum, some have invoked *semper reformanda* in order to justify abandoning the core of Reformation theology and departing from received orthodoxy. At the other end of the spectrum, some have forgotten about *semper reformanda* in their progress towards a rigid confessionalism, giving the impression that the final codification of truth has already taken place and that there is no further need for reformation. Between these two extremes, there is a vital task to be performed by the church in every generation; namely, to subject its beliefs and practices to the renewed scrutiny of Holy Scripture. In doing so, the church must restate the truth of Scripture in ways that faithfully communicate the gospel, advance the mission of the church and address the issues that men, women and children are facing day by day as they seek to follow Christ and witness to him. To be engaged constantly in this process of reforming is important for a number of reasons:

1. *God speaks today.* If we believe that God lives and speaks today, then we must always be listening and reforming. Some evangelicals have made the mistake of sinking into an unfortunate biblicism which at times gives the

impression that God, having given us the Scriptures, is no longer required (nor indeed expected) to speak today. A proper understanding of the relationship between Scripture and revelation will expect God to continue to speak, by his Spirit, through his Word. If we believe this, then we shall continue to search the Scriptures and will, in our theology, take account of what we learn.

2. *Theologians make mistakes!* Theology is written by human beings and human beings make mistakes. As evangelicals, we have often been good at pointing out the mistakes of others but bad at admitting mistakes ourselves. Do we really imagine that we have all of the truth? A study of church history and of the history of theology is a good cure for any such confident assertion. One has only to trace the doctrine of the Trinity or Christology through the early centuries of the church to see the various steps (forward and back) before the church came to a settled mind on these great doctrines. Even to trace the development of trinitarian theology in the Latin west from Tertullian to Augustine demonstrates a number of false moves and wrong turns. Can we really imagine that all theological issues are now settled once and for all?

3. *New issues require new thinking.* The sixteenth-century Reformation and the theology that developed from it was a movement rather than a completed event. For example, John Calvin lived and died prior to the debates about Arminianism, Amyraldianism and limited atonement. Those who followed Calvin developed his theology in various ways. Very often they asked different questions because they were dealing with issues to which he was a stranger. Sometimes the theological development within the movement was in line with his thinking, a natural development. At other times, his followers have taken the view that he was mistaken or had not gone far enough.

In our twenty-first century we face many complex issues, which earlier generations have not been required to face and it will not do merely to restate old ideas in the old familiar words and try to hide away from the modern world. It simply is not an option to create little communities of people who attempt to live as people did in earlier centuries, using seventeenth-century language and seventeenth-century Bibles and circling the wagons against the outside world. Apart from anything else, we do our children a serious disservice if we fail to address the issues that present the most serious challenges to their remaining in our churches.

What are we to say about cloning, about various forms of genetic engineering, about globalization and about world poverty? How are we to maintain the uniqueness of Christ in the face of pluralism? How are we to affirm truth in a postmodern world, which is committed to relativism? How can we stand firm for Christ against a plethora of religions and philosophies in a politically correct world, where it may soon be illegal to deny categorically the truth claims of other religions?

As a student in the early 1980s, I was hugely impressed and influenced by Francis Schaeffer. Here was a man who tried to engage with the world in which he was living. He examined the work of the philosophers, politicians, novelists, artists and others who had rejected Christianity and he tried hard to understand them properly. In doing so, he pointed out their presuppositions and ultimately the problems and inadequacies in their thought. That is the kind of work we must be doing in our generation.

4. *Scripture must have priority over Confessions.* One way in which we can be 'always reforming' is to review and rewrite our Confessions. Have you ever considered it astonishing that the Confessions to which most twenty-first-century denominations swear allegiance are those of the seventeenth century? In my view, the authors of those Confessions would be horrified to think that we had not updated them to deal with modern theological problems and heresies. The main concerns of those Confessions were the errors of late medieval Catholicism. For the past 150 years, the main opponent of evangelical Christianity has been liberal theology. That type of theology is more or less dead now but it has been replaced by many others, such as feminist and postmodern theologies, and none of them is dealt with in the Confessions and Catechisms we use in our churches.

Please do not misunderstand me. I am happy to affirm my belief in the core theology of the *Westminster Confession of Faith* (which is the Confession of Faith of my church, the Church of Scotland), but I also believe that it is time for new Confessions, which speak to the issues of today. The *Scots Confession* filled a significant role in my country from 1560 until 1647. It was then replaced, not because it was found to be wrong but because many issues had arisen in the interim period with which the *Scots Confession* did not deal. Similarly, today, we need new Confessions that will hold to the central theological affirmations of the old Confessions but which will apply that theology to the issues of today.

The key point, of course, is that Confessions must never take priority over Scripture. There is, in many evangelical circles, an unfortunate and increasing tendency to put tradition (in the form of Confessions) on a par with Scripture, an error that evangelicals often impute to Catholic theologians. In certain circles, to suggest that the Westminster Divines made mistakes is almost tantamount to heresy! A *semper reformanda* approach is vital if we are to avoid giving Confessions priority over Scripture. The great Reformed Confessions of the seventeenth century were undoubtedly a high point of the movement, involving a certain codification of the stage the tradition had then reached. Unfortunately, many still try to make decisions in respect of modern theological controversies by asking what the Westminster Divines said on the matter, instead of asking what the Scripture says. This has often led to priority being given to Confession rather than Scripture in settling debates.

5. *The right of private judgment.* In the work of *semper reformanda* there must be trust and a certain respect for the right of private judgment. In other words, if the church is going to take reformation seriously, we must encourage people to think 'out of the box'. Sometimes a scholar, in studying the Scriptures, may discover a theme that is new and perhaps needs exploration. Someone might decide to challenge a long-held and well-established doctrine and suggest that we must view the matter in a different light. Scholars must have the freedom to do this, within the constraints of the faith of the church.

In some circles today, when anyone seeks to explore a new idea or restate an old one in new words, there is an immediate rush to judgment. Often this approach amounts to theological bullying and oppression, leading to a situation where scholars do not feel free to go where they believe God through his Word is leading them, for fear that they will be declared heretics before they have even had time to explore the matter properly. In some situations, people run to the church courts and demand an ecclesiastical 'trial', where the more sensible approach would be to take a good long time to think and pray and study God's Word. Sometimes the pressure is more subtle, with younger scholars being advised to avoid certain issues or certain positions 'for the sake of their career'. This is a deeply regrettable and unfortunate situation. Evangelical scholars must have the courage of their convictions and be prepared to challenge (where necessary) the Creeds, Confessions and practices of the churches.

Having presented the arguments in favour of taking a *semper reformanda* approach, however, let me now indicate the parameters within which this should take place.

1. *Theology is the servant of Scripture.* One of the key marks of evangelical theology is a commitment to the authority of Scripture. Although I am arguing that theologians should challenge, question, reform and rethink established theological perspectives, this must be done on the basis of Scripture. Nothing I have said should be taken to imply that some external authority, secular presupposition, autonomous reason or anti-supernaturalist world-view can be the basis for proper theological reflection and statement. We must be centred upon God speaking to us through his Word.

2. *Theology takes place in the context of the church.* Theology can never be anything other than the theology of the church. When Karl Barth restarted his theological work, after an initial publication, he changed the title from *Christian Dogmatics* to *Church Dogmatics*. That was a vital move. The only theology worthy of the name is church theology, theology carried out in the context of a wor-

shipping community. The notion of a 'freelance theologian' is simply a contradiction in terms.

3. *Theology did not begin with us.* There must be a careful balance in our approach to the theme of 'always reforming'. On the one hand, there must be respect for the tradition but, on the other hand, we must avoid total submission to it. One should always think very carefully before departing from something the entire church has held to for many centuries, while at the same time one must remember that no Creed or Council or Colloquy is necessarily the final word. It is very easy to become an iconoclast and to make one's name by casually dismissing doctrines to which the church has given universal consent for centuries – many a PhD was thus made! On the other hand, it is equally easy to be paralysed by the fear of what others might think should we dare to challenge even one line of Nicaea or Chalcedon.

4. *The manner of* semper reformanda. Above all, it is important that we engage in the process of *semper reformanda* in a proper spirit and manner. There are personal qualities that ought to be seen in every theologian. The Scriptures tell us that when we disagree with our brothers and sisters we should do so graciously, gently, with a prayerful concern for the weaker brother, regarding others as better than ourselves. We should have regard to our own weaknesses, prejudices and inadequacy and seek to avoid pride, dissension and a contentious spirit. Why is it that so often in theological controversy people seem to be angry? It is dreadfully simple to dress up our own arrogance and pride in the guise of 'defending the cause of the gospel'. Rather, under the authority of God, speaking by Word and Spirit, the theologian should engage both subject and colleagues with intellectual rigour (there is no excuse for carelessness or laziness) and a prayerful spirit. There should be a real exhibition of kindness and love towards others, especially those with whom we disagree. If we engage in the theological enterprise in this way, it will be for our own good and for the good of the church.

The task ahead

This book, then, is an exercise in *semper reformanda*. Each contributor was asked to take a different theme, doctrine or subject area within the discipline of systematic theology. The task was then to assess the current state of scholarship in that area, before indicating areas where further work, development, restatement or clarification is required. For example, do we need to restate a doctrine that is in danger of being neglected or denied? Or is there a need to revisit a doctrine and look again at its formulation, where perhaps as evangelicals we may have been working with a weak or inadequate expression of the truth? Are there areas that have not been properly tackled and where much more work needs to be done? Are there areas where we simply have to hold up our hands and admit that we have been quite wrong?

The contributors are all scholars whose background is within the Reformed tradition, albeit from a range of denominations and nationalities. It is to be hoped, however, that what we have to say will be broadly of interest to anyone with an interest in systematic theology. Overall, the book is intended to make a positive contribution to evangelical scholarship, by helping to identify problems, dangers and exciting new possibilities. Above all, we want to help set an agenda for future work and scholarship.

Given this remit, it should be clear that there are several things that we are not trying to do. First, we are not trying to provide a definitive statement of each doctrine covered in these chapters. Rather, we are engaged in some exploration. Second, we are not trying to cover every doctrine that might be found in a volume of systematic theology. There are many topics that are not covered and that we would like to have explored, were it not for the overall constraints upon the size of this volume. What we have done is to explore a number of doctrines and themes, some of which have been at the heart of recent theological debates in evangelical theology. If the book is felt to have been useful, there is scope for other subjects to be given a similar treatment. It should also be noted that the order of chapters is not crucial. Rather than cluster all of the methodological and programmatic chapters at the beginning before moving on to the various doctrinal chapters, I have chosen to intermingle them.

Let me conclude by thanking all of the contributors for their willingness to participate in this volume and for their kindness in getting manuscripts to me in good time. May I also thank John Frame for agreeing to write the preface and Phil Duce of IVP for encouraging me to take on this project in the first place.

1. THE TRINITY: WHERE DO WE GO FROM HERE?

Gerald Bray

The twentieth-century revolution

Anyone embarking on a course of theological study a century ago would have found it surprising if the doctrine of the Trinity had figured very prominently in the curriculum. Of course, it would have been visible, as it still is, in the traditional hymns and liturgies of the church, but it would probably not have had much more than a formal presence in systematic theology and it would have intruded scarcely at all into biblical studies. No mainline denomination would have gone so far as to deny the doctrine altogether, but many church leaders would have been hard pressed to explain what it meant and the general approach would have been to consign it to the realm of the traditional – a doctrine inherited from the early church, but with dubious links to the Bible and of little practical importance for the Christian life. Had they enquired more deeply, students of that era would have discovered that much of that attitude towards the doctrine could have been traced back to the work of Friedrich Schleiermacher (1768–1834), who had placed the Trinity at the end of his systematic theology, almost as an afterthought, and considered it to be a theological opinion (*theologoumenon*) rather than an essential doctrine of the church.[1]

---

1. In this, Schleiermacher was only following a much older tradition, which can be

In his eyes, a Unitarian could be just as good a Christian as anyone else, and it would not be unfair to say that most Protestant pastors of the time probably agreed with him.[2] Even those who would have rejected Unitarianism as a theory (probably the vast majority) did not usually consider the matter to be of such fundamental importance that failure to agree about the Trinity would necessarily have put those who rejected it outside the bounds of the Christian church.

Attitudes of this kind remained common for much of the twentieth century, and they can still be found in some places, particularly among pastors who have no idea how to preach the doctrine and so avoid it as much as they can. But if the legacy of Schleiermacher is still alive and well in many pulpits, it must also be said that it is increasingly out of tune with the mainstream of Christian theological thought. One of the more remarkable developments of the past century, and especially of the last decade or two, is the astonishing way in which the doctrine of the Trinity, seemingly so at odds with the secular, multifaith approach to modern life, has returned to the very centre of Christian theological thought. So true is this that it is now almost impossible to pick up a book in any area of theology (with the notable exception of biblical studies) without finding at least a chapter devoted to examining the trinitarian dimension of whatever it is the book is about. As a result, it is probably true to say that more has been written on the subject of the Trinity in the past twenty years than in the rest of Christian history put together, and that dimensions of the doctrine that previously were scarcely suspected have become major subjects of discussion and debate.

Furthermore, it is also true to say that this modern interest in the Trinity is shared more or less equally by all the major Christian traditions. Roman Catholics have written about it at length, and the re-emergence of Eastern Orthodoxy as a significant player on the world theological scene has been

---

traced back to people like Michael Servetus and the Socinians of the sixteenth century. The difference is that whereas they were regarded as heretics, Schleiermacher was a leading theologian in a prominent German university.

2. See F. Schleiermacher, *The Christian Faith* (Edinburgh: T. & T. Clark, 1989), §172.2, p. 749: 'it is natural that people who cannot reconcile themselves to the difficulties and imperfections that cling to the formulae current in Trinitarian doctrine should say that they repudiate everything connected with it, whereas in point of fact their piety is by no means lacking in the specifically Christian stamp. This is the case often enough at the present moment not only in the Unitarian societies of England and America, but also among the scattered opponents of the doctrine of the Trinity in our own country.'

closely associated with its distinctive trinitarian doctrine, which is more widely accepted among non-Orthodox Western Christians than it has ever been before. Protestants have scarcely lagged behind; indeed, there are good reasons for claiming that it was within the Reformed tradition (in particular) that the modern flourishing of the doctrine began, and among the Reformed that it has been most rigorously pursued at all levels. The main reason for saying this is that virtually everyone now agrees that the prominence of the doctrine of the Trinity in modern theology is the legacy of Karl Barth (1886–1968) more than of anyone else. Barth had been educated in the Schleiermacherian tradition at Berlin, and it was in reaction to that tradition that he almost completely inverted the priorities of systematic theology. What for Schleiermacher had been an appendix, for Barth became the central theme of his dogmatics – a standpoint that has now gained all but universal acceptance right across the Christian world.

More important still, Barth did not merely resurrect a doctrine and leave it fundamentally unchanged from its ancient moorings. Although he clearly stood in the Augustinian tradition, which he was prepared to defend against the Eastern Orthodox alternative when the occasion arose,[3] his developed doctrine was quite different from anything Augustine or Calvin would have said. Where the Eastern Orthodox built their doctrine of the Trinity around the person of the Father, and the Augustinian doctrine saw it fulfilled in the person of the Holy Spirit, Barth made Jesus Christ the touchstone of all his theological thought. That in turn allowed him to focus on the principle of revelation as the basic framework within which the doctrine of the Trinity ought to be developed. In Barth's view, the Father and the Holy Spirit can only be known as they have been revealed to us in and through the Son, whose person and work remained for him the keystone of all theology. So true is this of Barth that he has often been accused of Christomonism – the belief that Christ is all there is to say about God, and also of modalism, the ancient heresy according to which the three 'persons' of the Trinity were no more than roles being acted out by the one God in different historical and revelational circumstances. It is now generally agreed that these accusations are extreme and unfair, but the fact that they could be made at all shows how difficult it has been for theologians to appreciate what an original and profound theological voice Barth's was.[4]

---

3. K. Barth, *Church Dogmatics*, 4 vols. (Edinburgh: T. & T. Clark, 1936–62), I/1, pp. 541–557.

4. For a recent assessment of Barth's trinitarian theology, see V.-M. Kärkkäinen, *The Doctrine of God: A Global Introduction* (Grand Rapids: Baker, 2004), pp. 125–130.

Barth's influence extended far beyond his own Reformed circles, but it was there, as much as anywhere, that his deepest impact was made. Opinions differ over how far Barth was followed in detail, and there are some things, like his spirited defence of the double procession of the Holy Spirit (*Filioque*), which have been all but repudiated by a number of later Reformed theologians, but it is fair to say that, whatever these latter have made of their Barthian inheritance, they have all agreed with him that the Trinity must be placed at the very centre of the Christian theological enterprise. Even if this were all that Barth managed to achieve, it would still be enough to make him the most significant and influential Reformed thinker of the twentieth century and the ultimate source of the current preoccupation with trinitarian doctrine in every major branch of the Christian church.

The achievements of modern trinitarian theology

What has modern trinitarian theology actually achieved? At one level, it is fair to say that it has forced theologians to take the ancient Christian theological tradition more seriously than had been the case for most of the nineteenth century. Augustine and the Cappadocians, for example, are once again living voices in theology, and they have been supplemented by a number of medieval thinkers – Anselm, Richard of St Victor and Gregory Palamas – who were little studied and in some cases scarcely known before. Theologians today have a much better sense than their grandfathers did of the ecumenical dimension of trinitarian faith, and of the complex ramifications which that has. They feel freer than they have ever done before to explore aspects of the doctrine that have been underemphasized – in particular, ideas associated with the mystical tradition of Eastern Orthodox theology, which had previously been unknown or ignored. They work in an integrated ecumenical environment in which every major Christian tradition must be given due consideration, and in which alternatives to their own approach have to be addressed as being potentially creative and not simply dismissed as misguided or downright heretical. So much is this now the case that it is increasingly difficult to identify any one approach as characteristically 'Catholic' or 'Reformed'. The Eastern tradition remains more immediately identifiable, partly because its differences from the West are more fundamental, and partly because few if any Eastern Orthodox theologians are genuinely open to any potential insights from Western trinitarian theology. On the other hand, the widespread willingness of Westerners to take the Eastern tradition seriously means that the latter has made an important contribution to ecumenical thought and helped to blur the distinctive lines of traditional Western theology.

One result of this is that it can now safely be said that the concept of 'person' has re-established itself in theological discourse and is increasingly widely regarded as the key to all creative theological development. Barth might have been surprised by this; he disliked the term 'person' and tried (unsuccessfully) to replace it with 'mode of being' (*Seinsweise*), a term with unfortunate associations which he was forced to refute in later life – not altogether happily. But whatever hesitations there may have been a generation ago, 'person' is now almost universally accepted as the word of choice to describe the quality of being common to all three members of the Trinity and it seems unlikely that it will be dislodged from this exalted position any time soon. Concomitant with this has been the apparent eclipse of the basically philosophical concept of 'substance'. This has been a long time coming, and it may not be definitive, but for the moment at least, it seems possible to say that the notion that God is a 'substance' somehow distinct from his three persons has been rejected, mainly on the grounds that the unity of God cannot be depersonalized, nor can there be a fourth 'thing' in him that can be conceptualized as such.

The apparent fate of the term 'substance' is a reminder that one of the most striking phenomena of the late twentieth century has been the apparent demise of traditional philosophical theology, not least in the Roman Catholic Church which had previously done so much to sustain it. There are a number of reasons for this, among them a growing realization that the Bible presents an essentially personal, and therefore non-philosophical, picture of God, who cannot be abstracted away into set categories derived ultimately from Aristotle. Another reason is that so much modern philosophy has either imploded into deconstructionism or some similarly self-destructive ideology, or else has become secularized and has lost the interest in metaphysical questions that previously brought it so near to theology in its concerns. Either way, it seems that at long last Christian theology has been liberated from its real or imagined captivity to alien philosophical systems, and this has brought the concept of divine personhood to the fore in a new and often compelling way. As the search for absolutes has given way to the exploration of relativity, so too the concept of a distant Deity has been replaced in many quarters by a God who relates to us in a personal way. He himself is a community of personal relations, and the message of the Christian gospel is that he wants us to enter into communion with him in that way also.

The priority of the persons leads naturally to a strong emphasis on relationships, and it is fair to say that modern theology has developed the notion of divine community, or communion, to a degree previously unknown. Particularly significant in recent years has been the way in which this idea has been extended and applied to human relationships, so that it is now common to find doctrines of the church and of marriage (to name but two obvious examples) that are rooted in a trinitarian understanding of the Godhead. Leaving aside the particular emphases of individual theologians, it seems fair to say that it is now no longer possible to develop a credible doctrine of the Trinity that does not take pastoral considerations like the above into account. In other words, the doctrine can no longer be treated as a theoretical abstraction with little relevance to the Christian life, but must rather be seen as a fundamental underpinning of all pastoral practice. If this is true, it is especially significant in a secular age where the general tendency is to reduce all religions to a single category and regard them as basically interchangeable. A trinitarian faith would not only exclude traditional Unitarians, but also Jews, Muslims and followers of other faiths that do not share this particular understanding of the Deity. That in turn is bound to have the most serious consequences for interfaith dialogue, which can hardly get very far as long as Christians insist on the centrality of the Trinity for their *practice* (as well as for their belief, of course).

The renewed emphasis on divine personhood has also had important consequences for the doctrine of the Holy Spirit. In traditional Augustinian thought, the Spirit is the bond of love uniting the Father and the Son, and there is a constant temptation to downgrade him to the status of a less than fully personal force. Accusations of that kind have always been denied, but it is hard to claim that they have been fully overcome, and the precise nature of the Holy Spirit's personhood remains somewhat underdeveloped in Western theology. Now that personal relations seem to have replaced divine substance as the locus of God's inner unity, this tendency to ignore or diminish the Spirit can no longer be maintained. The result has been a new concentration on his place within the Godhead and a new appreciation of his distinctive role in furthering the inner unity of the divine persons. It may still be possible to refer to him as the bond of love between the Father and the Son, but if so, this expression must now be carefully explained so as to avoid any suggestion that he is thereby being depersonalized.

Examination of the personal relations within the Godhead inevitably raises the great unfinished business of ancient trinitarian thought – the question of the double procession of the Holy Spirit, usually abbreviated in theological jargon as the *Filioque* controversy. Modern ecumenical discussions have made it clear that the Eastern Orthodox churches will never accept this, since rejection of it is now a fundamental part of their identity, but dialogue with them has reopened the question in the West, where the Augustinian position has been challenged from many different angles. It is still too early to say what the ultimate outcome of this will be, but it is at least clear that the procession of the Holy Spirit must figure more prominently than it has usually done in the past in any modern trinitarian theology.

A further aspect of this is the renewed emphasis on the mutual sharing of tasks and responsibilities within the Godhead. Classical theology has always resisted the temptation to reduce the distinction of the divine persons to their respective functions, as if the words Father, Son and Holy Spirit could be replaced by Creator, Redeemer and Sanctifier, or some equivalent terminology. It has always been recognized that each of the persons is in some sense Creator, Redeemer and Sanctifier, because the work of God cannot be neatly divided in that way. But it has also been understood that the way in which these functions have been fulfilled has varied according to the person concerned. In particular, it has always been agreed that only the Son became incarnate and died on the cross for our salvation, even if the other two persons were somehow present and involved in these events. In the twentieth century this question was reopened, particularly with respect to the question of divine suffering, and some have claimed that Christ's death on the cross was not unique to him – the entire Godhead participated in some mysterious way in that suffering and sacrifice. It is not necessary to adopt all (or any) of the conclusions of these theologians to recognize that a meaningful modern trinitarian theology must take into account the ways in which the work of the individual persons intersects and bears witness to the fundamental unity of God.

This in turn has led to a new discussion of the ways in which the traditional attributes of God ought to be understood. Does the coinherence (*perichoresis*) of the divine persons mean that the incarnation of the Son has somehow modified or discredited such traditional notions as divine 'impassibility'? To what extent, if at all, does a Christological focus alter our perceptions of who and what God really is? There is considerable debate about these issues today, and it would be wrong to suggest that one view has managed to hold the field against its rivals, but no-one can now doubt that the questions must be asked and an attempt (at least) made to answer them.

In all these and other matters, we are justified in concluding that the modern theological discussion of the Trinity has broken new ground, which cannot now be surrendered. It is important to differentiate here between theories that have been propounded about the divine relations (which are tentative and subject to revision as new thinking is applied to them) and the issues themselves, which will not go away. Most earlier trinitarianism either did not discuss these issues at all, or did so in a limited or fundamentally different way, which can no longer be accepted at face value or without serious qualification. It is in this sense that we are entitled to speak of the *achievement* of modern trinitarian thought. It raises new questions and formulates old ones in a new way, though whether it has succeeded in providing the right (or even adequate) answers is another question.

The limitations of modern trinitarian thought

Before proceeding to outline a possible trinitarian programme for theologians in the Reformed tradition, it might be worthwhile to consider, however briefly, some of the limitations of recent trinitarian thought, so as to get a more rounded picture of the current theological scene. Foremost among them must surely be the virtual absence of serious consideration of the Bible as the source of trinitarian doctrine. It is easy to understand why modern theologians are wary of seeing the Trinity in the Old Testament in the way that Augustine and even Calvin were prepared to do. We are more conscious than they were of the nature of historical development, and are disinclined to resort to allegorical or other 'spiritual' forms of interpretation in order to get the Trinity out of verses like Isaiah 6:3 or Genesis 1:26. But having said that, too many modern trinitarian theologians have been content to remain Schleiermacherians when it comes to the Bible, and serious studies of the doctrine as it is found in the New Testament remain exceedingly rare. In spite of everything, it is still possible to claim that the Trinity is somehow a non- or post-biblical theological development, an assertion that (if accepted) is bound to compromise it in the eyes of people wedded to *sola Scriptura* as the basis of their theology. Whatever the merits of the ancient creeds may be, Reformed theologians cannot be content to regard them as supplements to the Bible, which, for some reason, has failed to explain this particular part of Christian teaching adequately, and the persistence of this notion must therefore be regarded as one of the principal weaknesses of recent trinitarian thought.

Another weakness is the tendency of modern theology to abandon classical theological distinctions and categories in a way that leads to confusion rather than to deeper understanding. It is all very well to say that the being of God is an impenetrable mystery, but this truth should not be used as a means of obscuring important affirmations we must make of him. The whole impassibility debate suffers from an unwillingness, and perhaps even an inability, to make an adequate distinction between the persons and the nature of God. Classical theology has always said that the Son of God suffered and died on the cross, but *in his human nature*, which was alone capable of undergoing suffering and death. Failure to maintain this difference between person and nature has in some cases led to a situation in which divine suffering is portrayed in such a way as almost to preclude the possibility of divine victory over suffering. It is one thing to empathize with a victim, but if this goes to the point where the empathizer is reduced to the victim's helpless condition (on the ground that otherwise total identification with the victim would not have taken place), the possibility of salvation is removed and the gospel disappears.

Confusion over theological categories inevitably leads to confusion of vocabulary and meaning, and this too must be regarded as a weakness of modern trinitarian theology. This is particularly obvious when it comes to the question of divine 'substance', where the rejection of this notion too often occurs without any serious analysis of either the reasons for it or of the consequences that result from it. However we describe him, God will always remain an objective being of some kind, and a word will have to be found that can convey this without falling into any of the standard philosophical traps. Whether the coinherence of the persons is an adequate replacement for the notion of divine substance is highly uncertain, and it is somewhat worrying to find theologians making such assumptions without examining the ramifications that they might have. In some cases, one suspects that the desire to be original and creative has obscured the need for clarity and precision, particularly if that brings us back to all-too-familiar concepts from which we have been trying to escape.

Linked to this is a tendency to lapse into an ideology that can be made to sound plausible and relevant because of an apparent similarity of vocabulary, but that is in fact quite different. A clear case of this is the 'equality' that exists among the persons of the Trinity and that feminists claim for human relationships on the same basis, so that male and female become 'equal' just as the Father and the Son are 'equal'.[5] Without wishing to deny that inner-trinitarian relationships have something to say about human ones, we must nevertheless recognize that it is a verbal sleight of hand to connect the two things by lumping them together under a generic concept like 'equality'. The New Testament does not do this; when a divine analogy for husband and wife is expressed, it is the relationship between Christ and the church that comes to the fore, not the relationship between the Father and the Son – and no-one would claim that Christ and the church are 'equal' in the way the Father and Son are! Unfortunately, the urge to find the Trinity everywhere has sometimes led to shoddy thinking and false analogies that hinder our understanding of the Trinity, instead of promoting it in the way the theologians who do this kind of thing want.

Another recurring weakness of modern trinitarian thought is the tendency of many theologians to advocate a particular line of development that obliges

---

5. See M. Volf, *After Our Likeness* (Grand Rapids: Eerdmans, 1998), pp. 2–4.

them to discount something else of equal importance in the inherited tradition. This is most obvious at the present time in the rather uncritical way in which many people have embraced Eastern Orthodox theology – or at least the version of this that such interpreters as John Zizioulas and the late Vladimir Lossky have presented. This has led to an apparent rediscovery of such figures as Gregory Palamas (c. 1296–1359), though it is highly questionable how many of those who claim his legacy have any real understanding of his thought, or of the context in which Palamas was writing. This would matter less if it were not accompanied, as it too often is, with a rejection of such giants as Augustine, Anselm and Thomas Aquinas. If appreciation of the Eastern tradition leads to a devaluation of the Western one, there will be trouble ahead, because the Western tradition has its own integrity and validity, which cannot simply be overturned by a somewhat spurious appeal to Byzantium. Sooner or later, the weaknesses of the Eastern approach will be exposed, and the Western alternative will return with a vengeance to reclaim its traditional place in our theology.

Somewhat different from this, but equally one-sided, is a certain tendency to 'discover' the trinitarian teaching of a particular individual like Richard of St Victor or Jonathan Edwards, and promote it as if it were something unique – a claim that would no doubt have surprised, and perhaps distressed, the people about whom it is made. Here we are entering the dangerous territory of the theological fad, and we must be careful not to single out particular individuals for special mention, either positive or negative, when in fact they represent an ongoing tradition to which they may have made an interesting, but ultimately not very original contribution. Difficult and demanding though the task is, we need to consider our theological inheritance as a unity, and not seek to create divisions in it that may correspond to some ecclesiastical allegiance or temperamental preference today, but that subtly distorts the reality of theological evolution over the centuries and inadvertently deprives us of an important part of our inheritance.

The challenges to Reformed theologians

We can now begin to consider the challenges the current state of trinitarian theology poses for theologians in the Reformed tradition.[6] It is obvious that

---

6. Defining 'Reformed' is difficult, but broadly speaking, it would include most of English-speaking Christianity as well as the kind of Protestantism developed in France, Switzerland and the Netherlands. Germany is mixed, as are most Eastern

the Trinity is not a distinctive of Reformed theology as such, and Reformed theologians engage in discussion and debate with a wide range of thinkers from across the entire spectrum of Christianity. It is no longer possible to construct a trinitarian theology that can claim to be exclusively Reformed, nor is it desirable to do so. The Trinity is of all doctrines the one that most clearly links us to Christians of every tradition, and an understanding of it that failed to do this would be suspect from the start. On the other hand, it is fair to say that certain *emphases* characterize Reformed thinking, and Reformed theologians have a duty to offer these for the consideration of the wider Christian world. Indeed, it may not be too much to say that the Reformed approach to the Trinity can provide a bridge between the classical Augustinianism of the Western churches and the newly rediscovered mystical theology of the Eastern church. It can hardly be an accident that Reformed theologians of the stature of Thomas Torrance, Jürgen Moltmann and the late Colin Gunton have shown themselves so open to receiving the insights of the Eastern Orthodox tradition, while at the same time remaining firmly anchored in the Augustinian West and fully appreciative of Karl Barth's contribution to its continuing theological vigour. Serious engagement with the East may be a recent development, but there are indications even in the theology of John Calvin that point towards an openness in that direction,[7] and it may well be that there is something inherent in the Reformed tradition since the sixteenth century that makes it peculiarly able to reach out to the East in ways that might be able to bridge the gap between what appear to be two irreconcilable theological positions.

The first challenge, then, that faces the Reformed theologian when confronting the doctrine of the Trinity is that of creating a viable synthesis that can serve as a bridge to reconcile what have become two opposed ways of looking at the Trinity. Reformed theologians will surely agree with the Eastern Orthodox that God must be understood primarily as a communion of persons whose unity is manifested in complete coinherence; this was the teaching of John Calvin, which was brilliantly expounded by B. B. Warfield at a time when neither Calvin nor the Trinity were popular subjects of theological discourse.[8]

European countries where Protestants exist, though Hungarian Protestantism has a clearly Reformed heritage. Reformed Protestants are further subdivided into Calvinists (conservatives) and Arminians (liberals), but this distinction is less important in trinitarian thought than elsewhere.

7. See, e.g., J. Calvin, *Institutes of the Christian Religion* 1.13.5.

8. B. B. Warfield, 'Calvin's Doctrine of the Trinity', *Works*, 10 vols. (New York: Oxford University Press, 1931), vol. 5, pp. 189–284.

At the same time, they will also agree with Augustine's belief that God is a God of love, and that this love is perfectly manifested in the Trinity of his own being. They have no interest or desire to set the Cappadocians against Augustine, as if there is some deep incompatibility between them, nor are they concerned to defend medieval Scholastics against late Byzantine mystics, even though they were more obviously in conflict with one another and have left a thorny legacy that is unlikely to be resolved within the terms in which that conflict was originally defined.

The second great challenge that faces Reformed theologians is the need to ground trinitarian doctrine firmly in biblical theology. It is impossible for discussion of this doctrine to advance very far without a thorough study of its New Testament roots. It may also be possible for Reformed theologians to re-examine the question of a trinitarian presence in the Old Testament, but it is unlikely that this will get us very far and perhaps the best thing is to admit that, whatever suggestive allusions might be hidden in certain Old Testament verses, there is nothing that can justify the developed trinitarian teaching that Augustine based on Genesis 1:26 and the Eastern church 'discovered' in Genesis 18. This can best be done by accepting Barth's assertion that the Trinity is revealed to us in the teaching and work of Jesus Christ, without which it has no context in which to develop.

That of course raises the enormous challenge posed by the question of how the God of the Old Testament is related to the God of Jesus Christ in the New. That the two are identical has always been a mainstay of Orthodox Christianity, but in trinitarian terms the question arises as to whether the God of the Old Testament can be equated with the trinitarian Father, or whether he has to be regarded as being in some sense the Trinity as a whole. To put it a different way, was the God who spoke to Abraham and Moses the Father of Jesus Christ, or was he the undifferentiated Trinity, in whom Father, Son and Holy Spirit appear as one? It is surprising how this ancient question, which constantly rears its head in theological discussions of all kinds even today, has received so little serious attention from theologians in recent years. However complicated it may be, and difficult to resolve as it most certainly is, this question will not go away and needs to be addressed with the utmost care by Reformed theologians (as well as by others) engaged in serious trinitarian thinking.

One obvious issue at stake is the link between the two Testaments, a subject in which Reformed theologians may almost be said to have specialized in the past. A covenant theology implies a personal relationship with God even in Old Testament times, and this has been a constant theme of the Reformed — there is one covenant in two dispensations, one people of God united in the faith of Abraham, and so on. But would Abraham have understood the

Trinity? There is no reason to think so, and plenty of evidence that he would not have. Does this mean that the Father revealed himself to the patriarchs, but that the Son and the Holy Spirit remained hidden, or at least undefined in their relationship with the ancient Israelites? The snag here is that they never called God 'Father', and when Jesus used this term – and taught his disciples to do the same – he provoked a scandal among the Jews of his time (John 5:18). At most then, if the Jews worshipped the person of the Father, they did so unwittingly, which in turn raises the question of the nature of the divine self-disclosure in the Old Testament. Why would the Father not have revealed his most characteristic attribute to his own people, when he was perfectly pre-pared to communicate his name (Yahweh) to them (Exod. 3:14)?

These and other difficulties make it preferable to argue that the God of the Old Testament is the undifferentiated Trinity, but that in turn requires a detailed analysis of the data of his self-revelation that can substantiate this claim and relate it to the New Testament. Can it be said, for example, that although the Jewish people could not distinguish the three persons of the Trinity in the way that Christians can, they nevertheless had direct contact with God in his fullness, and that the voice which spoke to them out of the cloud and fire was the voice of the Father? In the Gospels it at least *seems* as if Jesus is revealing the Father to his disciples, and that he assumed they would equate the latter with the God of the Torah. Is this in fact the case, or was Jesus merely adopting that perspective in order to lead his followers into a deeper under-standing, which would include himself and the Holy Spirit in the divine mystery that they claimed to know as Yahweh?

It will be seen from questions like these that the formal abandonment of the concept of 'substance' does not remove the ancient question of the rela-tionship of the One to the Three in God, but gives it a new urgency. The days when the One could be described as the sum of the Trinity's common prop-erties and the Three as the persons may have gone, but the problem of the divine unity acquires a new urgency because of this. Can it be located in one of the persons, and if so, is that person the Father? This has long been the assumption of Eastern Orthodox theology, and it has been vigorously pro-moted in recent years by John Zizioulas.[9] It has much to commend it and is certainly worthy of the most careful consideration, but can it be accepted without qualification? Or do we have to look for something more subtle, a form of *perichoresis* in which no one of the persons stands out in opposition to the others, but in which all three speak with a single, undifferentiated voice?

---

9. See his influential *Being as Communion* (Crestwood, N.Y.: St Vladimir's Press, 1985).

Here is a matter that demands the urgent attention of Reformed theologians everywhere, and not least of those with particular expertise in biblical studies. One of the great weaknesses of modern orthodox theology is its reluctance (or inability) to come to terms with the Bible independently of the witness of the Church Fathers, which they take to be definitive in matters of Scriptural interpretation.[10] Theologians in the Reformed tradition have a real contribution to make here, especially if they can accept the witness of the Church Fathers and follow their lead in making the Bible and the Bible alone the source of their theological knowledge and reflection.

The problem of divine unity in Trinity also raises the important question of the divine attributes, which have taken quite a battering in recent years from the exponents of process theology and its foster child, so-called 'open theism'. If we are not to think in abstract terms of 'substance', how are we to understand the attributes of God, some of which at least, all Christians continue to affirm in one way or another? For example, nobody will deny that God is invisible, eternal and holy, but what do these words actually mean? In particular, how does the incarnation of the Son touch on them? Can one person of the Godhead become visible, mortal and even unholy (in the sense that he became sin for us, 2 Cor. 5:21), while the others remain just as they always were? Or does their mutual indwelling demand that in some mysterious way, they must all be present in the Son's incarnation? Furthermore, does the Son's passion mean that certain divine attributes, like immutability and impassibility, can no longer be held by theologians once the concept of 'substance' has been abandoned? Have we perhaps moved to an altogether new plane of discourse, one in which terms applicable to an abstract thing like 'being' are no longer relevant when we are talking about a relational community of persons? In other words, while it may have made sense to say that God could not suffer any diminution in the power of his absolute, divine substance without ceasing to be himself, can we deny that the Father and the Holy Spirit in some way felt the sufferings of the Son as he died on the cross for our salvation?

Perhaps it is true that the abandonment of the concept of 'substance' is the final outworking of a biblical theology that was obscured for so many centuries by a Hellenized version of 'divinity', but if so, this needs to be demon-

---

10. The Fathers themselves, of course, did not do this; they were avid readers and commentators of the Scriptures, and would probably have been dismayed to see later generations put them on a par with the authority they constantly cited in their defence.

strated by a much more careful and nuanced analysis than one typically finds among process or 'open' theologians. It is true that many ancient writers thought of 'God' primarily as a 'substance', of which the three persons were individual manifestations (*hypostases*), but it is also true that they experienced acute theological trouble until they were finally able to recognize that it was the three persons who possessed their common substance and not the substance that determined the limitations of their actions. This realization occurred in the debates over the nature of the Son's incarnation, as it became clear that the only way to resolve these was to say that a divine person in effect possessed two substances (natures), neither of which was able to interfere with or cancel out the other. The Son could become a man as a divine person, and his divine substance could not stand in the way of this, as it would surely have done if it had controlled the actions available to the divine person. To put it simply, the Son could not have become visible if his divine nature had made that impossible. It was precisely because his divine nature could not prevent his divine person from acting in complete freedom that the Son was able to acquire a second nature and become a man in the fullest sense of the word.

The theological revolution that put the persons in control of their substance can therefore be traced back at least as far as the council of Chalcedon (451) and perhaps even further, to the writings of the Cappadocian Fathers in the late fourth century. But it was a revolution that did not fully take root for many centuries, as the ongoing monothelete controversy in the East demonstrates. In the West, it was still a factor at the time of the Reformation, when it was necessary to reject the medieval doctrine of transubstantiation in order to reaffirm the primacy of personal relationships in God.[11] The most recent developments in this area therefore have a long pedigree, and it is the responsibility of modern theologians to demonstrate how their own assertions about divine 'substance' tie in with what has always lain at the heart of the orthodox tradition of theology. We may express it in a different way today, and perhaps we may have reached a point where we can analyse the divine self-revelation in a manner more consistent with the overall tenor of the biblical witness, but we must always remember that our faith is one with that of the saints in every age, and that if we are privileged to state certain aspects of that faith more clearly

---

11. This is what the sixteenth-century eucharistic controversies were really all about. The so-called 'receptionist' position held by the Reformed, according to which it is the faith of the recipient and not the transubstantiation of the elements by the priest that guarantees the 'real presence' of Christ in the sacrament, is just another way of saying this.

we are not authorized to reject their legacy merely because they represent an earlier phase of theological development.

Another area in which Reformed theologians can make a useful contribution to the development of trinitarian theology is that of definitions and boundaries. It is very good to see a growing awareness among theologians generally that everything is interconnected, and that Christian belief in the Trinity will have profound implications for pastoral practice, worship and every other aspect of theology. But it must also be said that a good deal of what we are seeing is a somewhat crude application of this principle to the subject at hand, and not a deep reflection on precisely how the Trinity affects the matter in question. This is probably most obvious (and most potentially dangerous) in the area of relationships. When church membership or matrimony start to be interpreted in trinitarian terms, questions must be asked about the way in which this doctrine is being applied. There has been a long history of attempts to find what are known as 'vestiges of the Trinity' (*vestigia Trinitatis*) in creation, of which undoubtedly the most sophisticated was Augustine's famous 'discovery' of the Trinity in the mind of man.[12] Something similar seems to be happening today, as one theologian after another discovers a trinitarian pattern in almost every facet of human life, whether it is immediately obvious or not.

The problem here is that the Trinity is about relationships within the Godhead, and these are undoubtedly connected with our human capacity for relationship, a capacity which is inherent in the fact that we have been created in the image and likeness of God (Gen. 1:26). Stated more simply, we are called to love God as he loves us, and in the light of that love, to love one another as we love ourselves. There is nothing wrong with this of course, but theologians have to point out that 'love' is a somewhat amorphous concept and that it is not a case in which 'one size fits all'. The essence of love is that we should adopt an attitude appropriate to the nature of the relationship we have with other people. An individual is called to love his or her parents in one way, spouse in another way, children in another way and so on. The same individual must also love neighbours, colleagues, fellow church members and complete strangers – all in ways that reflect the nature of the relationship concerned. Confusion in this area is potentially disastrous, as for example, when a person loves a colleague as if he or she were a spouse and so on.

The love of the persons of the Trinity for each other is absolute and perfect, because the persons are themselves absolute and perfect. If their mutual love were anything less than that, it would not be adequate and therefore it would

---

12. See, e.g., Augustine, *De Trinitate* 9.

not be appropriate to the nature of their relationship. When it comes to created beings, however, things are somewhat more complicated. The persons of the Trinity love human beings as human beings – that is, within the limitations the creation imposes on humanity. Similarly, human beings are called upon to love God, but we can do so only within the framework of our created nature, which is inadequate for the purpose, and which is why we need a heavenly mediator, whom God has provided for us in his Son, Jesus Christ. Our love for other people must be guided by the nature of our relationship to them, and we have also to accept the fact that it can never be perfect, because neither we nor they are perfect. Our limitations and imperfections make it extremely difficult to use the Trinity as a model for these relationships, and we must be extremely careful when we hear people describing marriage or church membership as somehow reflecting the communion of the Triune God. There may be some truth in it, but it is probably not what the person saying such a thing means by the statement. The danger is that most people who talk like this are probably idealizing their conceptions of human relationships, making more of them than they are and therefore (perhaps inadvertently) demanding more from them than they are able to give.

Modelling human relationships directly on the Trinity is a recipe for failure, because those relationships are different – even though the concept of relationship itself is one that is shared between them! Distinctions of this kind need to be maintained for the integrity of both trinitarian and human relationships, and, in the present theological climate, this will probably mean rolling back some of the suggestions that have been made and establishing boundaries that at first sight may seem to be excluding the Trinity from consideration. As long as this is seen for what it is – correcting an imbalance, rather than denying any trinitarian connection – this a healthy and necessary reaction, which theologians must promote in order to further our understanding of the doctrine's true place in our life and ethics.

One area that requires special consideration here is what is now called 'spiritual formation'. The popular belief that Reformed Christians are 'all head and no heart', the increasingly widespread assumption that to be 'filled with the Spirit' means to be a charismatic, and the dominance of Catholic thought in the field of 'spirituality' have all conspired to put Reformed theologians in a particularly difficult position here, and yet this area is perhaps the most vital of all. The doctrine of the Trinity grew out of the early Christians' experience of God, which included prayer, meditation and even ecstatic experiences at least as much as it did theological argument and discussion. It is quite clear from the New Testament that God cannot be known apart from spiritual experience; as the apostle Paul put it, 'God has sent the Spirit of his Son into our hearts, crying, "Abba! Father!"' (Gal. 4:6, ESV). No theological reconstruction of the doctrine of the Trinity can afford to neglect this dimension, nor indeed can it be relegated to a secondary place at the end of a detailed examination of the subject – an appendix in effect to the real meat of the message. On the contrary, it *is* the meat of the message, and to forget that is to misconstrue everything the Bible teaches us about our Lord and Saviour. Classical Reformed theology – the theology of John Calvin, Samuel Rutherford, Jonathan Edwards and Charles Hodge – knew that perfectly well and had no difficulty putting it into practice. Modern Reformed theologians have never denied it, and there are examples of men like the late Dr Martyn Lloyd-Jones who have exemplified it in practice. But it would be myopic in the extreme to deny that there is a popular perception abroad that the Reformed and the spiritually minded live in two different worlds, and issuing denials of this is simply not enough. The theologians must demonstrate in their teaching and by their behaviour that this dichotomy is a false one, and that only when the two things march in tandem will either of them carry conviction in the church at large.

This brings us naturally to the last but also the most difficult aspect of the doctrine that Reformed theologians must address afresh. This is what is generally known as the 'work of the Holy Spirit'. Modern theology and modern church life both refuse to allow any theologian to ignore or downplay the part the Holy Spirit plays in the Christian life, and we must be deeply grateful for this. However, it must also be recognized that the Holy Spirit has always posed a peculiar problem for Western trinitarianism, with its deeply Augustinian tinge, and also that the 'work of the Holy Spirit' is the theological rubric under which almost all the present divisions among Christians can be located. This is true not only of the classical division between Roman Catholics and Protestants, but also within the Protestant world, between liberals and conservatives on the one hand, and between charismatics and non-charismatics on the other. Failure to recognize this merely compounds the difficulty and is arguably responsible for the failure of so many ecumenical initiatives, which tend to treat of relatively superficial matters and fail to get to grips with the underlying causes of division. Long discussions about the ministry and the sacraments mean little and get nowhere if the fundamental question of the work of the Holy Spirit in and through these things is not adequately addressed.

To take but a simple, common example – does baptism suffice to make a person a Christian, or is something else required for the sacrament to achieve its intended purpose? This is not really a question about the rite of baptism, but about the work of the Holy Spirit in relation to it, and therefore about the link between a particular ecclesiastical act and the trinitarian God. For baptism is not primarily intended to represent union with the Holy Spirit; it is rather

union with Christ, by the Holy Spirit, and through union with Christ, reconciliation to God the Father that is at stake here. Does baptism produce this (as
Roman Catholics assert) or proclaim it (as Protestants believe)? If the latter,
does it proclaim it in expectation of future fulfilment (as in infant baptism) or
only as a witness to something already attained (as in believers' baptism)?

These questions may seem to be a long way from trinitarian theology as
such, but in fact are closely connected to it and heavily dependent on it. The
work of the Holy Spirit, even more than the work of the Father or of the Son,
is trinitarian in character, because the Holy Spirit comes to bring the entire
Trinity to bear on our lives (John 14:16–23). To say this is not to detract from
the detailed concerns that something like the sacrament of baptism is bound
to raise, but rather to assert that these concerns have to be seen against the
wider backdrop of the trinitarian God to whom the sacrament bears witness
(Matt. 28:19). Trinitarian theology must always be integrative in its approach
to Christian faith and practice, since it touches on every aspect of them. At the
same time, it must retain its own integrity and not allow itself to be swallowed
up by any one concern, however important or valid that might be. In the end
it is all a question of balance, and Reformed theologians, if they are true to
their heritage, ought to be as well placed as any others to provide this essential
ingredient of all enduring theology.

Summary and conclusion

What can we say then, by way of summary and conclusion? It may seem somewhat artificial to produce a checklist of desiderata for a future Reformed doctrine of the Trinity, but our examination of the current theological scene
imposes certain requirements that anyone setting out to provide us with such
a thing ought to take into serious consideration.

First, a future Reformed trinitarian theology must be solidly biblical. There is no point
writing about this doctrine if all we have to say is that it is essentially a post-
biblical development. If that were the case, it could hardly be central for
Christian faith and practice and would be no more binding on a Protestant,
committed to the principle of *sola Scriptura*, than anything else that cannot be
traced back to the New Testament. The teaching of the Bible on this subject
is profound and inclusive of everything we need to know about it, and it is
incumbent upon Reformed theologians, in particular, to bring this out and to
apply it to their theological construction. A biblical approach will also have
another salutary effect on the end result – it will prevent the theologian from
indulging in the sort of speculation that arises from an oversystematized

approach to theology. There are many things about God we cannot know and are not meant to know, but the Bible presents a coherent picture of him, and it is this we are called to bring out in our work. Furthermore, it is the application of a truly biblical theology to the doctrine of the Trinity that will finally decide the question of whether we need a concept of divine 'substance' or not. The current emphasis on personal relationships within the Godhead, bound together by mutual coinherence is certainly justifiable by an appeal to Scripture, though the case for saying this has yet to be made in detail, and on that point we may be confident that an examination of the biblical data will yield positive and encouraging results. The real issue here is whether the Bible also forces us to move into a more abstract realm, that of 'being' and 'nature', which cannot be separated from personal knowledge but cannot be conflated with it either. In other words, the relationship between the persons and their attributes has once again become a leading theological question, and only a careful exegesis of the relevant passages of Scripture will really help us to determine how we should express this in the future.

Secondly, a future Reformed trinitarian theology must be integrative of different theological traditions. Reformed theologians cannot afford to be sectarian in their approach to this doctrine, because it is one that is shared by all Christians, and any discussion of the subject is bound to raise issues that will directly affect one aspect of the ecumenical enterprise or another. We must face the fact that the Reformed tradition is a branch of Western Christianity, deeply imbued with Augustinianism and for that reason closer to Roman Catholicism than to Eastern Orthodoxy. This is a matter of historical fact, which it would be idle to deny and foolish to ignore. Progress in ecumenical relations will not be made by renouncing this inheritance; rather, it must be reviewed, critically examined and integrated into a new synthesis that can perhaps move us on to a deeper union of Christians. The willingness most Reformed theologians have shown to treat Eastern Orthodox trinitarianism sympathetically is to be welcomed, and we must never forget that the main reason for this springs from the depths of the Reformed tradition itself, which carries in it elements that reach out and connect with the Eastern approach. At the same time, we must not embrace it uncritically, merely in the interests of church unity. The Orthodox are not ready to budge in their theology; to them, the notion of integrating Western insights into their theology is at best strange and at worst heretical. As Reformed Christians, we must perform the delicate task of reaching out to them sympathetically without being seduced into accepting their point of view without reservation, since it too, is only a part of a greater truth. The Orthodox will not like this, but perhaps future generations of Eastern Christians will eventually come to see that it was the right course to follow after all, and that their particular insights can be accepted without compromise into a wider and deeper understanding of the doctrine.

Thirdly, a future Reformed trinitarian theology must seek definition and clarity as far as possible. It is all very well to speak of God as a mystery, but we are called to examine the revelation we have been given, and that requires careful and precise definition. We must try to outline trinitarian relations as they are and find the right way to connect them with wider ecclesiastical concerns. All theology is internally related, but what is said about the Trinity cannot be applied without modification to anything or everything else. Here the theologian will be forced to roll back some of the 'progress' registered in recent books on the subject, a task that is also unlikely to win him many friends, but which is essential if the doctrine is to maintain its own integrity and inner coherence.

Fourthly, a future Reformed trinitarian theology must re-examine the divine attributes in relation to the concept of mutual coinherence. However the problem of divine 'substance' is eventually resolved, it is essential that the divine attributes be reconsidered in the light of inner-trinitarian relations, and their meaning adjusted as necessary to fit this new context. The vagaries of 'open theism' are a reminder to us of what can happen if this is not done, and we must be on our guard against allowing so jejune and superficial an approach to the doctrine of God to take hold in the Christian church merely because the latter has been fed an inadequate understanding of the Trinity in the past. Failure to deal adequately with every aspect of this doctrine is almost bound to lead to aberrations of this kind, and we must be on our guard to do all that we can to see that it does not happen again, and that the bad influence of what has recently occurred can be counteracted as quickly and as thoroughly as possible.

Fifthly, a future Reformed trinitarian theology must be deeply spiritual in its approach. This is inherent in the biblical nature of the discipline, but it needs to be brought out as specifically as possible. Reformed theologians must accept that their bad reputation in the area of spirituality is not entirely without foundation, and do something to correct it. This does not mean that high academic standards must be sacrificed; on the other hand, it does imply that whatever we say should be capable of being put into immediate practice by ordinary Christians in their everyday lives. Too many people are befuddled by what they see as the abstractions of trinitarian doctrine, and this problem must be directly addressed in any future theology.

Sixthly, a future Reformed trinitarian theology must show how the work of the different persons relates to the Trinity as a whole. This is particularly urgent when it comes to the question of the work of the Holy Spirit, which in itself integrates the other two persons and lies at the heart of most of the disagreements that have divided Western Christians since the Reformation. It is probably true that a

bold assertion of Reformed claims in this area will have the effect of entrench-
ing these divisions still further, at least in the short term, but this may be necessary if there is ever to be a serious discussion of the issues involved.
Certainly, it can be said with complete assurance that failure to address these
concerns will lead to ecumenical disaster, as it already has done in several cases,
and we are fooling ourselves if we think otherwise.

Such a checklist cannot claim to be exhaustive, but it is hard to see how
anyone embarking on a trinitarian theology today can avoid addressing these
questions at least, whatever else it might be desirable to include in addition. We
must hope and pray that a younger generation of theologians will be motivated
to take on the task, and in the process perhaps make enduring sense of the
remarkable explosion of interest in the Trinity that has so characterized the
past few decades.

© Gerald Bray, 2006

2. OBSERVATIONS ON THE FUTURE OF SYSTEM

Stephen Williams

The debate over open theism is much more than a rerun of the Calvinist–Arminian dispute. Yet, during the course of it, that old chestnut keeps bobbing up to the surface. Will it always be with us in the Reformed tradition? Perhaps so, but that is a frustrating thought at best and it is natural to wonder whether its perennial possibility means that there is something in our approach to the issues that is amiss. My objective in this chapter is to use this particular controversy as a jumping-off point to address modestly one aspect of the question of theological method, specifically the question of system and systematic theology. To those who will groan at the prospect, wearily reflecting that such a project promises to enmesh us in the past and scarcely open up any future, let me say, please bear with me for a while. The prospect of re-covering Calvinist–Arminian terrain wearies me as well, whether or not it should. However, my direct concern is with theological method and not with the substantive issue.[1] What are or should we be up to in 'systematic theology'? If I remain desperately traditional in my approach to this question, it is because the focus of this chapter is somewhat ad hoc in the

---

1. Broad and interesting hermeneutical issues arise in connection with the Calvinist–Arminian debate: see Douglas Jacobsen, 'The Calvinist–Arminian Dialectic in Evangelical Hermeneutics', *Christian Scholar's Review* 23 (1993), pp. 72–89.

light of ecclesially deep divisions that are socially significant. Yet I hope that the investigation will be of intrinsic value in relation to its subject matter.[2]

First guidance: Simeon

Two hundred years ago, the Anglican evangelical Charles Simeon penned highly interesting and instructive prefaces to two homiletical works, the *Helps to Composition or Five Hundred Skeletons of Sermons* and the *Horae Homileticae or Discourses (in the Form of Sermons) upon The Whole Scriptures*.[3] He wrote at a time when the Calvinist–Arminian battle had been raging fiercely, occasioning considerable intra-evangelical bitterness. His remarks on theological method were directed to this battle, but apply more widely; indeed, they are not primarily remarks on theological method, but advice from a preacher to preachers that touches on theological method.[4] Simeon's worry was that biblical texts were being used in the pulpits to support one of the rival systems. The effect, he maintained, was that Scripture itself was downgraded; what it is saying and why, its wording and force, get lost in the cause of presenting a systematically consistent theological scheme that favours one or the other party. In the course of making his plea, Simeon included the following observations:

1. It is not the preacher's task to reconcile truths of apparently opposite tendency, but to preach them in all their particular force. Two things must be borne in mind. First, different truths are appropriately applied to different human circumstances, for example the assurance that God will keep believers by his grace and the warning to believers lest they fall away from grace. Secondly, different truths that appear to conflict systematically are reconcilable in religious experience, for instance that my will is truly free and that God sovereignly disposes of it.

---

2. I have benefited from exchanges with Kevin Vanhoozer as we prepared our respective contributions to this volume. The reader will decide, but our thinking appears to be harmonious when our interests overlap and nowhere dissonant where they do not. His is the more forward-looking; mine the rather more conventional approach . . . ad hoc!

3. Published respectively in Cambridge (1801) and London (1819).

4. A fuller account of Simeon's position, whose context is rather wider, is found in 'Notes on Calvinism and Arminianism', in A. W. Brown, *Recollections of Simeon's Conversation Parties* (London: Hamilton, Adams, 1863), pp. 267–288.

2. Different truths are particularly reconcilable in the experience of prayer.

Pious men, both of the Calvinistic and Arminian persuasion, approximate very nearly when they are upon their knees before God in prayer; – the devout Arminian then acknowledging his total dependence upon God, as strongly as the most confirmed Calvinist; and the Calvinist acknowledging his responsibility to God, and his obligation to exertion, in terms as decisive as the most determined Arminian.[5]

3. There is a system in Scripture, but Simeon

is persuaded that neither Calvinists nor Arminians are in *exclusive* possession of that system. He [Simeon] is disposed to think that the Scripture system, be it what it may, is of a broader and more comprehensive character than some very exact and dogmatical theologians are inclined to allow . . . There is not a decided Calvinist or Arminian in the world, who equally approves of the whole of Scripture . . . There is not a determined votary of either system who, if he had been in the company of St. Paul, whilst he was writing his different Epistles, would not have recommended him to alter one or other of his expressions.[6]

4. There are fundamental principles that must govern the elaboration of doctrinal schemes, guaranteeing whose observance is more important than adjudicating the detail of such schemes. In a lengthy footnote, Simeon describes an encounter between a young Calvinist interlocutor and an ageing Arminian leader. The Calvinist asks the questions. (I insert 'Q.' and 'A.' for convenience; the whole is an extended quotation.)

Q. Do you feel yourself a depraved creature, so depraved, that you would never have thought of turning unto God, if God had not first put it into your heart?

---

5. Simeon, *Horae Homileticae*, p. 7. Simeon adds that 'that which both these individuals are upon their knees, it is the wish of the author to become in his writings'.

6. Elsewhere, Simeon writes that 'the Bible has no system as such'; what reconciliation there is of theological truths awaits eschatological revelation: see Brown, *Recollections*, pp. 269–270. For a repetition here of the point about Calvinists and Arminians wishing 'for some texts to be expunged from Scripture', see p. 274 and the lively remark that a 'strong Calvinist looks on statements like that of Paul's possibly becoming a castaway (1 Cor.ix.27) as a dog looks on a hedge-hog: he knows not what to do with it' (p. 269).

A. Yes, I do indeed.

Q. Do you utterly despair of recommending yourself to God by any thing that you can do, and look for salvation solely through the blood and righteousness of Christ?

A. Yes, solely through Christ.

Q. Supposing you were at first saved by Christ, are you now somehow or other to save yourself afterwards by your own works?

A. No, I must be saved by Christ from first to last.

Q. Allowing then that you were first turned by the grace of God, are you not in some way or other to keep yourself by your own power?

A. No.

Q. What then, are you to be upheld every hour and every moment by God . . . ?

A. Yes, altogether.

Q. And is your hope in the grace and mercy of God to preserve you unto his heavenly kingdom?

A. Yes, I have no hope but in him.

The young Calvinist concludes:

Then, Sir, with your leave, I will put up my dagger again; for this is all my Calvinism; this is my election, my justification by faith, my final perseverance; it is, in substance, all that I hold, and as I hold it; and therefore, if you please, instead of searching out terms and phrases to be a ground of contention between us, we will cordially unite in those things wherein we agree.[7]

Simeon retains the anonymity of the dialogue partners, but we know that he himself was the young Calvinist, and John Wesley, the ageing Arminian.[8]

In the course of making the observations reported above, Simeon is not always persuasive:

Can any man doubt one moment whether he be a free agent or not? he may as well doubt his own existence. On the other hand, will any man who has the smallest spark of humility, affirm that he has 'made himself to differ; and that he has something which he has not received' from a superior power?[9]

---

7. Simeon, *Helps to Composition*, pp. vii–viii.

8. Hugh Evan Hopkins, *Charles Simeon of Cambridge* (London: Hodder & Stoughton, 1977), pp. 174–175.

9. Simeon, *Helps to Composition*, p. vi.

Simeon was right on that second question: a religious consciousness of humility rooted in a knowledge that God is our creator and redeemer will ascribe everything to God, nothing to self. But the case with 'freedom' is more elusive than Simeon apparently supposes. Freedom has different forms and degrees; it comprises different elements in relation to believer and unbeliever; putative experience or knowledge of it might turn out to be strictly experience or awareness of responsibility, rather than of freedom, from which freedom may be – rightly or wrongly – inferred. Again, Simeon asks:

> Does not every man feel within himself a liableness; yea, a proneness to fall . . . that there is corruption enough within him . . . eternally to destroy his soul? On the other hand, who that is holding on in the ways of righteousness, does not daily ascribe his steadfastness to the influences of that grace, which he received from God; and look daily to God for more grace, in order that he may be kept by *his* power through faith unto salvation?[10]

But the contrast Simeon really wants to advertise is not exactly described here; it is really the contrast between believing that we *can* fall away for ever and believing that God has *promised* that we *shall not*.

I do not, therefore, wish to endorse everything in Simeon's description or application of the principles he wants to advance. However, I am not interested in a critical reading of Simeon.[11] Rather, I wish to derive from him something that I take to be instructive on the question of system and systematic theology. The following four theses are proposed on the basis of Simeon's selected observations.

1. *Convictions cohere in a religious context whose coherence is difficult to describe in a speculative context. Theology should be more interested in the former than in the latter.* In the reference that he makes to prayer, mentioned in '2' above, Simeon implicitly distinguished between what we say to God in prayer and what we say about God, prayer and everything else, on paper. This properly invites consideration of the relation between the *lex orandi* and *lex credendi* and how it worked in the earliest formation of Christian doctrine, but I am noting instead the distinction between a religious and a speculative context for doctrinal thought. 'Religious context' is a cold and rather abstract way of identifying the scene of

---

10. Ibid, p. vii.

11. The 'Notes on Calvinism and Arminianism', Brown, *Recollections*, in any case provide a fuller account for such purposes than the remarks on homiletics. They are well worth the reading, even if they contain contentious things.

prayer wherein the whole person is engaged. By 'speculative context' I mean
neither to speak tendentiously of all reflection that is apart from prayer nor to
refer to a theology grounded in speculative reason *instead of* in Scripture. I have
in mind a speculative theology grounded in Scripture and not in reason, yet
remaining 'speculative' in its attempt to harmonize apparently discrepant doctrinal claims so that the context of the endeavour is speculative. What exactly
is in mind and what is supposed to be wrong with it?

In his controversy with Latomus, Luther submitted a point of the first
importance:

> Let us take St. Paul or Peter as they pray, preach or do some other good work. If it is
> a good work without sin and entirely faultless, they could stand with appropriate
> humility before God and speak in this fashion: 'Lord God, behold this good work
> which I have done through the help of Thy grace. There is in it neither fault nor any
> sin, nor does it need Thy forgiving mercy. I do not ask this, as I want Thee to judge it
> with Thy strictest and truest judgments. In my work, I can glory before Thee, because
> Thou canst not condemn it without denying Thyself. The need for mercy which, as
> Thy petition teaches, forgives the trespass [i.e. as in the Lord's Prayer] in this deed is
> cancelled, for there is here only the justice which crowns it.' Latomus, doesn't this
> make you shudder and sweat?[12]

Luther was not only establishing a substantive point in relation to the doctrine
of justification.[13] He was instructing us on the subject of context and norm

---

12. *Contra Latomum*, in *Luther's Works*, ed. J. Pelikan and H. T. Lehmann (Philadelphia:
    Muhlenberg, 1958), vol. 32, p. 190. Wesley appears to walk on the border of this
    conviction, for he is willing to surrender his doctrine of Christian perfection for the
    sake of maintaining the permanent importance of atonement for sin in the
    Christian life, yet is it a permanent sense of 'forgiving mercy' along Luther's lines?
    See *The Works of John Wesley* (Grand Rapids: Baker, 1996), vol. 11, p. 418. The
    question is not a snide way of suggesting that the answer must be no.

13. Substantively, the difference between a Lutheran or Protestant and Tridentine
    position comes to clear light: compare chapters 7 and 16 of the decrees on
    justification: Norman Tanner, ed., *Decrees of the Ecumenical Councils* (London: Sheed
    & Ward, 1990), vol. 2, pp. 671–681. Alister McGrath refers to this work as 'perhaps
    the most impressive of Luther's early works', but his description of it in terms of
    the distinction between forgiving grace and the gift of the Spirit does not rightly
    capture what is going on in it: *Iustitia Dei: A History of the Doctrine of Justification from
    1500 to the Present Day* (Cambridge: Cambridge University Press, 1993), p. 11.

of authentic theological discourse. The context is *coram Deo*, 'before God'; the norm is what is confessed there. Formulating the theological dynamics of *simul iustus et peccator* (at the same time justified and sinner) and applying it to act as well as to person may be difficult, and Luther's demonstrations of how the taint of sin clings to even the purest of human actions are not always persuasive.[14] But the point is that what is given in experience and rooted in Scripture can be grasped with a conviction that is much firmer than one that is consequent on the success of a strict systematic formulation of the matter. This raises the question of what kind of *intellectus* (understanding) interests theology as it reflects on *fides* (faith). In particular, it forces attention to the question of the place of philosophical reasoning in theology.

'Philosophical reasoning' is a phrase that picks out two things. First, there is the speculative endeavour to ferret out comprehension of theological truth in such a way that we reach out far beyond what is confessed; *intellectus* far outstrips *fides* and the concepts entertained become overwhelmingly intellectually interesting. Of course, the task of logical comprehension of what is believed is both necessary and wholesome. Believing divine truth to be good and holy, we seek, through understanding, to grasp something of its goodness, holiness and depth in order better to praise, serve and commend. The spirit of Anselm's *Cur Deus Homo* or Aquinas' *Summa Theologiae* is not impugned. But the profoundly salutary feature of such works lies in their fusion of religious sensibility and philosophical acuity; better, obedience of mind is driven by the love of God, more on the surface in Anselm than in Aquinas. Today, however, those who adopt the speculative habits of such as Anselm or Aquinas – we shall not haul in Scotus or Ockham – characteristically do not display their religious sensibility; it is not, that is, on the surface, where it should be.[15] This state of affairs is not doing theology much good, as far as I can judge, though there is some unevenness in the picture. When contemporary theological reflection gets caught up in a systematic exercise that makes philosophical demands, its term easily becomes the deliverances of a fallible system rather than the truth revealed by an infallible God.

Secondly, we note the more narrowly technical operations of logical reasoning – argument, inference, entailment. It would unjustly skew the issue to refer

---

14. E.g. in relation to the hermeneutics governing the exegesis of Eccl. 7:20 and 1 Kgs 8:46 in *Contra Latomum*.

15. Obviously, to say this is not to judge anyone's heart. Actually, Paul Wadell, following Josef Pieper, is among those who note that Aquinas 'harbored an extreme suspicion of systems', *Summa Theologiae* notwithstanding: *The Primacy of Love: An Introduction to the Ethics of Thomas Aquinas* (New York: Paulist Press, 1992), p. 28.

to such logical operations of 'philosophical reason' as though they were inter-lopers in the realm of theology. Despite questions attending the philosophy of logic and the cultural distinctives of Western forms of thought, let me assume, at least *ad hominem*, that certain basic rules of logic – of inference, entailment, contradiction – apply to certain standard prosaic forms of theological dis-course, as they do to certain standard prosaic forms of non-theological dis-course. But the development of analytic philosophy in the English-speaking world, including its use in Reformed circles, has resulted in the heightened sub-jection of theological truth to technical, logical treatment. Theologically, there is a very severely limited gain to this. More, it is foolish to make anything reli-giously significant hang on the precision of analytic reasoning at this level, for one false step in logic ruins everything and it is only the arrogant or the ignor-ant who will be confident that such a step is being avoided.[16]

In the context of the Calvinist–Arminian debate recycled in the context of open theism, take a claim on which theological opponents often agree: divine foreknowledge of all future human actions and libertarian human free will cannot coexist, for a person cannot be free to do that which God knows that he or she will not do. But supposing I dissent, insisting that God can foreknow that I shall freely drink coffee. In such a case, to say 'Necessarily, I shall freely drink coffee' is not to say that I shall drink coffee necessarily. I am free to drink tea instead and thus free to do that which God knows that I shall not do, in terms of my power. It is not that I cannot do what God knows that I shall not do; it is simply that I never shall do it. Does the argu-ment work? That can be decided only by logical analysis, but it would be foolish to make my convictions about the compatibility or otherwise of divine foreknowledge with libertarian freedom depend on the outcome of such analysis. If this is the case when there is agreement that the logic is faulty (Calvinists maintain incompatibility and reject libertarian freedom, while open theists maintain incompatibility and reject foreknowledge), how much more precarious are those arguments where protagonists disagree on the validity of the reasoning.[17]

---

16. The eventual outcome of confidence would be what Nicholas Lash, in a different context, describes as 'cataphatic cockiness': *The Beginning and End of 'Religion'* (Cambridge: Cambridge University Press, 1996), p. 170.

17. This is a slightly condensed version of an already condensed argument in Stephen N. Williams, 'More on Open Theism', *Scottish Bulletin of Evangelical Theology* 22.1 (2004), pp. 32–50, which contained an unfortunate typographical error that spoiled the argument, corrected in *Scottish Bulletin of Evangelical Theology* 22.2 (2004), p. 132.

If nothing religiously significant depends on whether or not this reasoning is valid, we must ask, why engage in it at all? It is possible to give a positive answer. Cognate exercises might, in principle, perform an apologetic role in a cultural context that features professional, academic, non-Christian or conflicting Christian philosophies or philosophical theologies. They might protect against the charge of manifest contradiction or show that theological tenets are not demonstrably incoherent. But they will do very little to advance theological understanding as such. When substantive convictions of faith ground the exercise of such philosophical demonstration and the proponent of the demonstration comes to recognize a logical flaw in it, more often than not the argument is reformulated. Why? Because the conviction is both gained and sustained apart from the formulation of the argument.

Theological reflection should be more interested in getting to the religious depth of what is disclosed to religious consciousness than in the logical constructions of speculative reason.[18] 'Thought is surrounded by a halo', Wittgenstein remarked, understanding logic as its essence.[19] P. T. Forsyth exemplifies the attitude I have in mind in his advocacy of a kenotic understanding of incarnation: 'The science of it can wait, but the religion cannot.'[20]

2. *Biblical theology is less about the mutual relation of doctrines than about the relation of particular doctrines to life. Systematic theology should follow its lead.* From what has been said above, it may seem that reservations about philosophical reason threaten the systematic enterprise, which relies on at least rudimentary philosophical reasoning to construct a system at all. At best, it will be said, the structural sinews of systematic theology are being weakened. Is that so? The question that arises here concerns the nature of system.

There is a striking contrast between one standard approach to systematic theology and the way theological truth is laid out in Scripture itself. The systematic theologian is a person thinking thoughts and organizing concepts: how does A relate to B, C and D and, if I connect A and D in this way or that, does it require the modification of B and actually threaten C altogether? In contrast, Scripture characteristically relates A to life, B to life and so with C and D. Where we are trying to interrelate particular truths systematically, Scripture relates them severally and particularly to life. This representation of

---

18. This may sound like the language of Schleiermacher, but I am not adopting his philosophy of religion.

19. *Philosophical Investigations* (Oxford: Blackwell, 1958), para. 97.

20. *The Person and Place of Jesus Christ* (London: Hodder & Stoughton, 1909), p. 294. Of course, I am not interested here in taking sides on the debate over kenosis.

the biblical picture must be modified, of course. It is not as though the Bible is a collection of atomistic truths, severally and distinctly related to life. Neither is it proposed that Hebrews or Romans, for example, should be stripped of any title to being systematic theologies, at least under some description of that phrase, interrelating truths.[21] But scriptural writings show more interest in establishing such truths as those of divine sovereignty and human responsibility or the divine promise to keep us and the human ability to forfeit what is vouchsafed, than the mutual relationship of the truths in each of these pairs. Of course, that does not per se dictate the course of systematic theology. What we are theologically called to do with the whole corpus of Scripture post-biblically is not identical with what Paul and others were called to do theologically within its pages. Nevertheless, we might ask whether there is anything instructive about the biblical state of affairs as regards the enterprise of systematic theology.

Systematic exactitude in describing the interrelation of concepts of the kind instantiated above is certainly no prerequisite for the proper and effective use of the Bible in the church and world. The Pentateuchal rendering of the theme of covenant provides a case in point. What exactly is unconditionally and irrevocably promised by God to Abraham's posterity? What role does faith play? Is the stability of the covenant or any significant element in it conditional on the exercise of faith? Or is obedient response to the claims of the covenant a requirement rather than being in any way its condition? And what is the difference between a condition and a requirement? It is possible to attempt some answers to these questions by an induction of the Pentateuchal data, but the actual history of Israel, including in the New Testament, and its New Testament interpretation more safely answer them than any amount of attention devoted to the semantics or logic of the Pentateuchal accounts, despite the importance of getting the semantics right. Even in the light of that New Testament history and its interpretation, we shall differ on how the questions should be answered and might conclude that we can as little be definitive in our systematic constructions when it comes to cognate issues arising in relation to the church, rather than to Israel.

Obedient response to the word of God is not contingent on systematic explication. We must act along the lines of how the leaders of Israel acted in

---

21. Of course, what constitutes a systematic theology in this connection is largely a matter of definition: the earliest 'dogmatics' of the Reformation, Melanchthon's *Loci Communes*, was modelled on Romans and yet was arguably not strictly a work of systematic theology.

their day and appropriately apply to the various particular occasions of our lives what Scripture tells us about divine sovereignty and human responsibility, its promises and its warnings. 'For the desponding and broken-hearted sinner, here is a salvation not depending on his own merits, or his own feeble effort. For the sluggish, or confident, or easily quieted conscience, here is a salvation which we must work out . . . '[22] Such applications should doubtless issue from a maximally comprehensive grasp of the interrelationship of every strand in Scripture. However, it is significant that the coherence of Scriptural teachings, warnings and promises can be experienced in an obedient life when systematic reason is bound to be somewhat speculative in its synthetic construction. In the Christian life, there need be no tension between confessing my responsibility when I have sinned, without blaming God, and thanking him when I have resisted sin, without the faintest trace of self-congratulation or sense of paying even a peppercorn.[23] We may come up with a systematic account of the conceptual logic of that coherence that we find satisfying or convincing, but the coherence is far more safely realized, experienced and tested in life than in formal statement.

To put it like this is to leave the door wide open for philosophical accounts that have had considerable exposure over recent years and may be deservedly persuasive in their own philosophical right. Prominent among these is the 'speech-act' investigation of what words do and the challenge to assumptions about the informative function of certain statements.[24] At a deeper level, we are in the neighbourhood of the Wittgensteinian insistence that the meanings of words lie in their use and that the meaning of a concept is given in its role in shaping a form of life. There is plenty of mileage in these proposals and they steer us along a road that is theologically profitable both generally and on

---

22. Simeon in Brown, *Recollections*, p. 269. Colin Gunton puts it thus: 'Systematic theology is . . . when rightly understood, dedicated to thinking in as orderly a way as possible *from* the Christian gospel and to the situation in which it is set, rather than in the construction of systems,' 'Rose', p. 22 (see last note on p. 66 of this volume).

23. The reference is to Richard Baxter's celebrated remark, but I make no assumptions here about the exact context or detailed substance of this theological averment.

24. Kevin Vanhoozer has done much distinguished work on speech-acts in relation to Scripture and doctrine, although we should note a recent challenge by Stanley E. Porter, 'Hermeneutics, Biblical Interpretation, and Theology: Hunch, Holy Spirit, or Hard Work?', in I. Howard Marshall, *Beyond the Bible: Moving From Scripture to Theology* (Grand Rapids: Baker, 2004), pp. 117–118.

the point under present consideration.[25] If I do not explore them, it is because I want to keep within the boundaries of a more immediately theological proposal rather than give it philosophical wings. If Simeon has encouraged us to rivet theology to preaching, the upshot of what we have just been saying is that it must also be riveted to pastoral concerns. Life, rather than thought, is the zone where coherence is demonstrated.

Ellen Charry has sought to impress on us the pastoral function of Christian doctrine.[26] Surveying key theologians from Paul to Calvin, she sets off their conception of the business of theology, which is the edification and transformation of the faithful through the knowledge of God, against the fact that sapience (*sapientia*) has been widely disregarded in favour of the purely intellectual and propositional preoccupation with truth that gained increasing hold in the West after the seventeenth century. Her insistence on the pastoral function of Christian doctrines, both as a past reality and as a present desideratum, prompts two comments.[27]

First, the knowledge of God is not related to our obedience simply as means to end. It actually grows from obedience. 'Whoever has my commands and obeys them, he is the one who loves me. He who loves me will be loved by my Father, and I too will love him *and show myself to him*.'[28]

---

25. For a Wittgensteinian perspective, see Paul Holmer, *The Grammar of Faith* (San Francisco: Harper & Row, 1978), especially ch. 7. Note too John H. Whittaker, *Matters of Faith and Matters of Principle: Religious Truth Claims and their Logic* (San Antonio: Trinity University Press, 1981), especially pp. 87–89. Fruitful comments by the maestro are found in *Philosophical Investigations*, no. 574 ('The concepts of believing, expecting, hoping are less distantly related to one another than they are to the concept of thinking'), and Part II, iv, on religion, picture and doctrine ('And it is the service which is the point'). Wittgenstein once made the extremely instructive remark that his thinking was Hebraic: see 'Some Notes on Conversations', in Rush Rhees, *Recollections of Wittgenstein* (Oxford: Oxford University Press, 1984).

26. E. Charry, *By the Renewing of your Mind: The Pastoral Function of Christian Doctrine* (Oxford: Oxford University Press, 1997).

27. In the context of our interest in the Reformed tradition, note Charry's conviction that even those who acknowledge that Calvin conceives the point of theology to be the transformation of life do not always grasp how the moral power of the theological enterprise means much more to Calvin than systematic coherence: see Charry, ch. 9. This is not the place to comment on her contention.

28. John 14:21 (New International Version), taking *emphanizein* in its broad sense. Italics obviously mine.

Theological reflection is substantially changed and deepened as we grow and according to growth. The obvious danger of a *theologia regenitorum* has always been that of making piety a kind of measurement of theological competence and of deflecting attention away from that which is the proper 'object' of our attention to the subject who is attending to it. But everything has its dangers and such a danger is no argument against the fundamental truth in the position: a theologian is a disciple with a particular vocation and cannot discharge that vocation effectively without growth in discipleship. God does not cast many theological pearls of the kingdom before the intellectual herd of swine.[29] I say this as one who has usually missed the point rather that one who has attained.

Secondly, when we are through with reading Charry's account of Paul, Matthew, Athanasius, Basil, Augustine, Anselm, Aquinas, Julian and Calvin, we ask ourselves, who is qualified to expound Christian doctrine? Our exemplars here are not academic theologians in the modern sense of that term and if they could never be academic theologians anyway, precisely because the 'academic theologian' *is* a modern character, the question remains of how much doctrinal illumination is to be expected from their ranks.[30] Did not Luther remark somewhere that one could not expound Romans properly unless one had been a pastor, a *gubernator ecclesiae*, for twenty years? So reflection on the coherence of doctrine in and with life raises far-reaching questions about practice and practitioners alike, in systematic theology.[31]

3. *There may be a 'wider system'; if so, it must be adumbrated in relation to biblical literary genres and the economy of salvation.* What follows from the above? The abandonment of system? Not necessarily: perhaps the outcome of these considerations should be that we think of 'system' in a 'wider' sense; Simeon explicitly said that he believed that there was a wider system in Scripture than

---

29. I hope that it goes without saying what this biblical reference is *not* implying!

30. I do not mean to suggest a determinate starting point for a theology of the academy, relatively or completely detached from the church at some stage after the point at which Charry breaks off. The origin of the university in the Middle Ages, Aristotelianism and Abelard all play a significant part in the story.

31. Lest there be misunderstanding, I reflect here on my own competence more than that of others. I was ordained a quarter of a century ago to a seminary teaching and not to a pastoral position. I have sought to make preaching and pastoral interest central over these years in the hope that Calvin would *just about* grant that I was, *in principle*, qualified to be a systematic theologian in a sense of the phrase that he would have accepted positively.

the Calvinist or Arminian. I am not directly addressing that particular dispute, but let it be clear that, as far as I am concerned, the first port of call for any venture to revise our notions of system or their content is renewed exegesis of Scripture, not an independent theory about how doctrine should work, and examples of this can be drawn from passages that bear on the Calvinist–Arminian difference. So, for instance, we might be impressed by the fact that the letter to the Hebrews views salvation in terms of corporate deliverance from Egypt all the way through the wilderness to the promised land, so that the individual who 'falls away' is modelled on the disobedient Israelites *in via* in the wilderness; the issue of whether someone personally regenerated can 'fall away' permanently from salvation does not arise here. Again, we might be impressed by the fact that, in Romans 9 – 11, Paul does not identify those who are rejected in God's historical purposes as those who are foreordained to personal damnation, nor guarantee that every individual among those who are the elect in God's purposes will not be cut off in the eschatological consummation of those purposes. I am not concerned here with whether these 'impressions' are right or wrong and certainly not suggesting that they are new. My only point is that I should want exegesis first to dictate what may or may not be said about a 'wider system' than the Calvinist or Arminian one, granted the assumption of the normative authority of the biblical text in theology and the fundamental nature of the hermeneutical question that underlies exegetical practice. Barth, treating the question of system, said, 'Essentially, dogmatic method consists in this openness to receive new truth and only in this.'[32] Certainly, ongoing exegesis must keep the question of the nature and possibility of 'system' open.

So are we to move, provisionally, in the direction of a 'wider system', or a different notion of 'system', in consequence of what I have said about how convictions cohere in life even when their systematic coherence is elusive or contentious? Hitherto, my argument has required no definition of what is meant by 'system' or 'systematic'. Nor do I propose one now. The phenomenon in mind is, generally speaking, recognizable enough: the elaboration of doctrine in the form of a rationally consistent propositionally interlocking structure.[33] Questions about the 'rational' and the 'propositional' have been in

---

32. *Church Dogmatics* (Edinburgh: T. & T. Clark, 1956), I/2, p. 867. One way or another, the point has been sustained in his volumes ever since Barth said that dogmatic work 'cannot aim to be a system of truth': *Church Dogmatics* (Edinburgh: T. & T. Clark, 1975), I/1, p. 79.

33. We can provisionally accept the broad description of system in Gunton, 'Rose',

the air for a long time, routinely connected with the question of tacit or explicit Enlightenment norms for the execution of the theological task and their perceived shortcomings. I do not want to rehearse these here. A 'system' of some kind, whether or not called by that name, is unavoidable. We aspire to think consistently; reason is the instrument of consistent thought; propositional form is its grammatical expression. But from the standpoint of the Scriptures to which Simeon's thought and, I hope, my own are directed, the most significant challenge to the systematic habit, as it has widely developed, lies in the genre of the Hebrew literature of the Old Testament and the religious thought-forms contained within its pages. What does all this do to enterprises that typically go under the rubric of 'systematic theology'?

We enter here rich, absorbing and very nourishing pastures. Much has been gained in twentieth-century New Testament studies from the growing appreciation of the Jewish background and flavour of the New Testament. It is hard to announce categorically that this has not yet had much of an impact on systematic theology because so much goes on under the title of 'systematic theology' or of 'theology', 'doctrine' or 'dogmatics' that it is neither possible nor desirable to keep up with what is abroad all over the world under its banner. But there surely remains much land to be possessed. How Hebrew 'works'; what the relation is between linguistic structures and conceptual structures; whether such a linguistic/conceptual distinction is already dangerous; whether the Old Testament modes of religious expression are meant to constrain the exercise of post-biblical systematic theology, on the assumption that they are also somewhat operative in the New Testament, written in Greek – all this seems to me essential for us to figure out in thinking about the future of systematic theology. One worrying feature of the contributions to open theism on the part of their main proponents (Clark Pinnock, John Sanders and Greg Boyd) is the lack of attention to Hebrew, in particular, given their use of Old Testament texts. In fairness to them, not only have their respondents often repaid them in kind, they also do make reference to Old Testament scholars to whom they would doubtless wish to hand the baton when such subjects come up for discussion. However, arguments about analogy, anthropomorphism and metaphysical predication

---

wherein it now has 'come to denote the logical constructions that systematic theologies and philosophies attempt' (p. 15). Nothing in this chapter hangs on a definition of system; I am more interested in the discipline that we call 'systematic theology' than in whether what we do or should do should or should not be called 'systematic'.

sometimes give the impression that the Hebrew Scripture was written in post-Lockean English.[34]

Many things that could and should be said on this subject cannot be treated in a short chapter and this author would be entirely incompetent to treat many of them at all. However, there is a further potential constraint on systematic theology on the surface of Scripture due to the broadly narrative structure of the canon of Old and New Testaments or, more accurately, the overarching narrative/history context within which everything written has its plenary intelligibility. The narrative is the narrative of the mighty acts of God in creation, providence, election, deliverance, redemption, reconciliation and consummation, including the shadow side of all this. The letters to the Hebrews and to the Romans, mentioned earlier, presumably the most 'systematic' contributions to the New Testament, are oriented to the exposition of *Heilsgeschichte* (salvation history). In Hebrews, high-priestly atonement is treated because the church of Jesus Christ is engaged in a mighty historical exodus, in the course of which sanctification and sprinkling take place, as in the wilderness, and the conscience of *homo viator* (the pilgrim traveller) is cleansed in order that we may participate in the journey to the city that has foundations, a journey on which Abraham started us out. If we are stretching things here, neglecting the question of 'realized' elements in the eschatology of Hebrews, the picture is certainly clear in Romans. 'Systematic' attention is given not to the relation of human and divine in Jesus (1:3–4) but to the significance of the provision made by a gospel announced in time because it proclaims a deed accomplishment in time; to the shape of a life lived since that time in relation to a law given before that time and to a liberation of creation that lies ahead; to an election, rejection and reconciliation that explains what is happening in history now that Israel and church are distinguishable entities.

What are the implications of these rudimentary and familiar reminders? I do not want to draw conclusions rigorously; indeed, that would be completely unwarranted solely on the basis of what has been said hitherto. However, let me at least make a suggestion. Systematic theology is frequently concerned

---

34. This is emphatically not to say that all contributions that do not closely attend to genre are thereby devalued; for an important discussion see, e.g., Michael S. Horton, 'Hellenistic or Hebrew? Open Theism and Reformed Theological Method', in John Piper, Justin Taylor and Paul Kjoss Helseth, eds., *Beyond the Bounds: Open Theism and the Undermining of Biblical Christianity* (Wheaton, Ill.: Crossway, 2003), pp. 204–212.

both with such things as the essential relations of the persons in the Trinity and things like the sanctification of the believer through Christ. The scriptural material directly encourages systematic reflection on the latter, but scarcely on the former. The latter is concerned with salvation and with history. Although the same is true of the former in relation to the economy, the internal relations of Father, Son and Spirit per se are not revealed and do not belong to us (Deut. 29:29). I am not inferring that no theological reflection of any kind for any purpose be given to those relations.[35] However, it may not be of the kind that can be usefully incorporated into or laid out in a system.[36] With sanctification in the economy things are different. Whether or not, with Simeon, we think that the Bible will yield a 'wider' system, a biblical orientation for the systematic task at least suggests a distinction in the kinds of subject profitably explored in their 'systematic' interconnections.

From the point of view of a historical interest in the Reformed tradition, there is plenty to occupy us here; indeed, I am not touching in this chapter on anything that has not come up in that tradition.[37] Deeper-lying still is the contribution of Irenaeus. In relation to more recent times, however, systematic theologians are surely well advised to come to better terms with the legacy of Oscar Cullmann's work.[38] Cullmann has frequently not had a good press, but not only is Cullmann's emphasis on history, in my view, defensible; he rightly challenged systematic theologians with his expression of surprise that they had done little or nothing with Christ as 'Son of Man' or with those Christological

---

35. Though Emil Brunner has a strong argument that must be reckoned with in *The Christian Doctrine of God: Dogmatics* (London: Lutterworth, 1949), vol. 1. In this chapter, I echo much that is said in the 'Prolegomena' to that volume, on 'The Basis and Task of Dogmatics'.

36. What really needs exploration here is the patristic distinction between 'theology' and the 'economy', especially in the Greek Fathers.

37. Of particular interest here are Cocceius, Burman and John Owen. The whole of Richard A. Muller's *Post-Reformation Dogmatics: Prolegomena to Theology* (Grand Rapids: Baker, 2003), vol. 1, is exceedingly important and relevant for our discussions throughout this chapter. See too Robert D. Preus, *The Theology of Post-Reformation Lutheranism*. Vol. 1: *A Study of Theological Prolegomena* (St Louis: Concordia, 1970).

38. I believe that I have the support of Robert W. Yarbrough on this point in particular, whether or not he is happy with the way I have arrived at it. I am grateful for his various contributions on Cullmann; see now Yarbrough's *The Salvation-Historical Fallacy? Reassessing the History of New Testament Theology* (Leiderdorp: Deo, 2004), pp. 213–260.

titles that 'refer to the present work of Jesus'.[39] Of course, reference to *Heilsgeschichte* as providing a focus for systematic thought cannot gloss over the potentially tricky question of the relation of historical narrative to historicity.[40] But we should not persist in the systematic task without engaging with precisely the significance of narrative form and of that question in all its trickiness. So our two points come together: the need to attend to literature and literary genre and the need to attend to the economy of salvation.[41]

4. *Simeon implies a distinction between doctrinal rules and doctrinal moves. It is a distinction that we need to deploy in the service of an ecumenical evangelical or Reformed theology.* In addressing the contentious issues between Calvinists and Arminians, Simeon invited us to consider thinking in terms of doctrinal rules and proposed the following: (1) we turn to God on account of his, not our own, initiative; (2) our righteousness is entirely of Christ; no work of ours savingly

---

39. Oscar Cullmann, *The Christology of the New Testament* (London: SCM, 1963), pp. 137, 192–193. N. T. Wright, *Jesus and the Victory of God* (London: SPCK, 1996), p. 614, is pretty scathing in his criticism of Cullmann's approach to Christology but I am not interested in defending him at this particular point. Although I believe that Richard Bauckham is unjustly harsh on Cullmann in his chapter 'Time and Eternity', in Bauckham, ed., *God Will Be All in All: The Eschatology of Jürgen Moltmann* (Edinburgh: T. & T. Clark, 1999), one might agree that Cullmann did not get the concept of 'time' sorted out properly, while believing he did get the concept of 'history' largely in place and that is the nerve of his enterprise. The kind of challenge to systematic theologians that Cullmann gives in *Christ and Time* (London: SCM, 1962), p. 26, n. 9, remains important. For his interest in Irenaeus and Cocceius, see pp. 56–57, followed up to some extent in *Salvation in History* (London: SCM, 1967). Re the organization of doctrinal reflection in relation to the economy, we might note a contribution here from an author who too easily slips by us these days: James Orr wrote an intriguing appendix on 'The Idea of the Kingdom of God' to *The Christian View of God and the World*, 2nd edn (Vancouver: Regent, 2002), and apostrophized that 'the time is not yet ripe for making it the one and all-inclusive notion in theology' (p. 404). However, this must be balanced against his other remarks.

40. See Robert Alter, *The Art of the Biblical Narrative* (New York: Basic, 1991). In Alter and Frank Kermode, *The Literary Guide to the Bible* (London: Collins, 1987), pp. 15ff., Alter voices his suspicion that the detailed understanding of the relation of fact and inventive freedom in Old Testament narrative may be irretrievably stymied. Again, I am not trying to adjudicate such a claim.

41. For why we might prefer 'economy' to 'narrative', see Gunton, 'Rose', p. 18. He nicely states what is the case with Irenaeus too (p. 9).

produces or contributes to it; (3) we are kept entirely by his, not at all by our own, power; (4) our hope of final perseverance is entirely placed in Christ. Again, I am not directly assessing these rules in particular. What matters is the notion that moves that we make within the body of doctrinal rules should not be the primary focus of our theological attention if theology is geared to worship, obedience, proclamation and service. The rules are what matter most.

In a game rules, but not moves, are prescribed. Some moves are better than others; some are dangerous and so must be discouraged, even if they are within the rules; some are brilliant; many are controversial. Theology can only be thought of as a game, in a non-trivializing sense, in certain analogical particulars and, in any case, there are games and games. But the distinction between rules and moves is helpful.[42] In systematic theology, the tendency has been to think in terms of making the precisely correct doctrinal moves. Now moves do matter: they may be outside the rules; only marginally within the rules; persistently deployed, they may call the rule into question. To emphasize rules rather than moves is not to relax one's intellectual grip on the subject matter of theology. But it might both redirect our theological attention and alter the mood of our theological engagement. Interest in the parameters, rather than detail, of theological construction, is sometimes rather spontaneously manifested.[43] However, there is an advantage to having a formal interest and taking formal note of the distinction between rules and moves. Some of what can be said under this rubric might be said under others, such as the rubric of a distinction between fundamental and non-fundamental articles. I am interested neither in the detailed defence of the comparative advantage of thinking in terms of rules and moves, nor in plotting the relation of this conceptuality to the fundamental/non-fundamental articles distinction. But there are at least three reasons for following Simeon's hint here.

First, some such distinction as he implies fits well with what has been argued hitherto. The way in which we customarily make doctrinal connections is often

---

42. I borrow here something of the terminology of George A. Lindbeck from his celebrated work *The Nature of Doctrine: Religion and Theology in a Postliberal Age* (Philadelphia: Westminster, 1984). My questions about what he does with rules are contained in 'Lindbeck's Regulative Christology', *Modern Theology* 4.2 (1988), pp. 173–186.

43. I hope that is a fair way of putting it in relation to I. Howard Marshall's approach to predestination in Romans: see his *New Testament Theology: Many Witnesses, One Gospel* (Leicester: IVP, 2004), pp. 334–335.

human, all too human, subject to revision, correction, change, dispute, ingenuity, error – none of which is attributable to that truth which comes from God and by which we are to live. A properly modest sense of our own fallibility should protect us from excessive systematic confidence. Secondly, a point that struck Abraham Kuyper should be taken to heart: Kuyper, as redoubtably Calvinistic as anyone that we shall find, apparently believed that a kind of erroneous creedal absolutism could characterize Reformation thought (e.g. as expressed in the Belgic Confession) as though everyone should think and believe in the same way, with no thought of ingrained pluriform diversity in the humanity that God created.[44] I mention this, however, as indicative of a strand in the Reformed tradition; apart from that, the point is pretty vacuous unless spelled out further. The third reason is, however, the one to which I draw particular attention. The distinction is ecumenically important. The well-being of the church is at stake. How so?

Reformed theology is a species of catholic theology, its confessions rooted in the trinitarian and Christological dogmas of the undivided church. When Calvin settles down to the ecclesiological discussion of Book IV in his *Institutes*, he shows how eager he is to establish that his reforming work stands in continuity with the teaching of the early church, unlike contemporary late-medieval Catholicism, on the points under consideration. Reformed theology is also a species of Protestant theology, sharing with the Lutheran tradition a formal principle, if it may be so described, of *sola Scriptura* and material principle of justification *sola fide*.[45] But in practice we easily mistake the relation of distinctives to essentials.

First, preoccupation with distinctives often marginalizes some essentials. Essential to Reformed theology is the belief that we should love our neighbour as ourselves and that God is triune. However, Reformed theology is not particularly associated with either of those beliefs. The former is confessed by non-Christian Jews, as well as non-Reformed Christians; the latter by non-Protestant, as well as Reformed, Christians. No-one in the Reformed tradition denies the centrality of the former; no comprehensive Reformed dogmatics neglects treatment of the latter. But because, historically, the Reformed tradition has been shaped from its inception by polemical relations with Catholicism, Lutheranism and Anabaptism, and because it has itself been con-

---

44. See, e.g., G. C. Berkouwer, *The Church* (Grand Rapids: Eerdmans, 1976), pp. 52–63.

45. We should maintain this irrespective of any intra-Protestant differences on Scripture, tradition and adiaphora, faith, law and sanctification.

stantly riven by doctrinal controversy, it has a polemical tendency to self-definition in terms that exalt the distinctives and play down common essentials. Thus, the shared confession that, in prayer, we are dependent on God, sadly occupies less theological attention than the precise and distinctive adumbration of the *ordo salutis* (order of salvation).

Secondly, distinctives come to be regarded as essentials. The biblical material (e.g. on the relation of divine–human action; on human freedom and responsibility; on God's determinations and on concurrence) is all rich, diverse and complex. Read against the background of centuries of controversy, one would have thought that many a reader – certainly, many an informed Western reader – would almost a priori allow that this data might be harmonized in different ways. A Reformed understanding of these and cognate matters might indeed be distinctive to that tradition, contributing to its distinctive identity. It might be defended as the most compelling interpretation of the biblical data – the best move within the rules. But the spirit that makes such distinctives Christian essentials is surely dangerous. Note that I refer to the 'spirit': it is impossible to discuss what should or should not be negotiable, what constitutes moves and what constitutes rules, in the abstract. We are at a rather stratospheric level of generality at the moment. But the concern is about a persistent tendency in Reformed circles – and others too, no doubt – to glorify the human understanding that interprets Scripture as much, in practice, as the divine Scriptures that ground understanding.

We are in a new world. The West is post- or ex- or anti-Christian in considerable measure, though there are marked differences between the United States and Western Europe, for example. In the early 1970s, Rahner could make the striking statement that 'even a baptised person is in many respects more "pagan" than ever anyone has been since Constantine'.[46] How this has come about is, in the nature of the case, a complex question, but the bitter and bloody controversies of the sixteenth and seventeenth centuries have played their role.[47] Those of us who do not believe that autonomous reason is the source or judge of religious truth or that moral action is the sole essential content of Christianity may, nevertheless, feel considerable sympathy for those who did come to think so in the wake and light of those centuries. The theological remedy today is not just to conduct our dogmatic disagreements

---

46. 'The Need for a Short Formula of Christian Faith', in K. Rahner, *Theological Investigations* (London: Darton, Longman & Todd, 1972), vol. 9, pp. 117–126.

47. See, e.g., Wolfhart Pannenberg, *Christianity in a Secularized World* (London: SCM, 1988), pp. 11ff.

more nicely than did our forefathers whenever their knockabout style became
too bruising. It is willingness to adjust our focus and ask not 'How can I defend
and promote Reformed theology against all-comers?' but 'What can Reformed
theology contribute to the universal Church of Jesus Christ, expanding in the
southern hemisphere, embattled in the northern?'[48] This is not to prescribe
indifference to those things that are cherished or regarded as true. But the
terms on which we appraise and correct ourselves, learn from others,
commend and promote what we regard as providentially preserved in our tradition will change. So will the focus and spirit of systematic theology. Unless
we let faithless fear get in the way, this will open the door to that substantive
self-correction for which we claim, as good Reformation Protestants, to be
constantly willing.

My modest proposal here is that to think of theologically trading in rules
rather than moves might be helpful. The more radical proposal is that, once
we do so, we might profitably consider abandoning talk of 'the Reformed
faith'. For the *fides qua creditor* (the faith by which we believe) is the gift of grace,
given to others in the one faith, under the one Lord, in the one faith, hope and
baptism, along with the Reformed. And the *fides quae creditur* (the faith which
we believe) are the rules that express the doctrine of the one church of Jesus
Christ, one beyond the bounds of the Reformed churches or communities.
In that perspective and in conjunction with the earlier theses, the
Calvinist–Arminian dispute, *inter alia*, might begin to look a little different.[49]

Second guidance: Berkouwer

Although, in line with the purpose of this volume, there has been consistent
allusion to the Reformed tradition, evidently my reflections rather hang on that
peg than constitute 'Reformed' reflections, as it were. In concluding, it may

---

48. Arminius's remarks on religious discord should be taken to heart here: see, e.g., the
    use he makes of the incident recorded in Plutarch in Jacobus Arminius, 'On
    Reconciling Religious Dissensions among Christians' (February 1606), in *Works*,
    tr. J. Nichols (London, 1825), vol. 1, p. 388. Note the attitude taken by Barth to
    Lutheran–Calvinist Christological differences in *Church Dogmatics*, I/2, pp. 170–171.
    For myself, I should wish to regard Melanchthon, Chemnitz and Gerhard as my
    'Fathers', and not just those of Lutherans.
49. Of course, 'Calvinism' and 'Arminianism' can mean different things in any
    case.

therefore be as well to indicate some more definite connection with Reformed theology. Although different candidates, going back to the beginning of that tradition, present themselves as possibilities for specific mention, if the finger of affinity points in any one direction, especially in modern theology, it probably signifies G. C. Berkouwer. Throughout his writings, he understands himself as standing in, expounding and defending the tradition of Calvin and confessional Calvinism, though his fidelity to these has been queried at some specific and significant points.[50]

Berkouwer announced his dogmatic method of correlation from the beginning of his multivolume dogmatic enterprise.[51] In insisting on the correlation of faith and revelation, Berkouwer repudiates the pretensions of speculation and logical systematization when they obscure the truth in Scripture that is given in revelation and received in faith. He is intellectually riveted to scriptural speech: 'Theology is not an excursion into the stratosphere that lies beyond the borders of faith's perspective. Beyond the word of Scripture we dare not go, in speech or in theological reflection . . . '[52] Naturally, Berkouwer's theological method is multidimensional. For example, at the specific and detailed end of things, he rejects the resolution of paradoxes by means of causal categories, whether applied to general accounts of the concurrence of divine and human agency or to more narrowly soteriological questions.[53] If excursion into such detail is out of place here, we must

---

50. Cornelius Van Til springs to mind: e.g. his *The Sovereignty of Grace: An Appraisal of G. C. Berkouwer's View of Dordt* (Phillipsburg: P. & R., 1969). Van Til sets the tone by declaring not only that the 'Church of Rome loved Aristotle almost as much as Christ', but that like 'the Church of Rome the Remonstrants too loved the freedom and autonomy of man almost as well as they loved Christ' (pp. 12–13). Such an identification of perceived theological error with spiritual unfaithfulness contrasts strikingly with Berkouwer's own attitude in theological debate, clear as he could be in riposte when it was needed.

51. See *Faith and Justification* (Grand Rapids: Eerdmans, 1954). There is a general account of this in Charles M. Cameron's monograph on Berkouwer, *The Problem of Polarization: An Approach Based on the Writings of G. C. Berkouwer* (Lampeter: Edwin Mellen, 1992).

52. Berkouwer, *Faith and Justification*, p. 160. However, these sentiments have to be interpreted in the overall context of Berkouwer's work.

53. On the former, see his eloquent chapter 'A Third Aspect?', in *The Providence of God* (Grand Rapids: Eerdmans, 1952); on the latter, see, e.g., *Faith and Perseverance* (Grand Rapids: Eerdmans, 1958), p. 98.

nevertheless go beyond attending to the general considerations that move Berkouwer, significant as they are: a sense of divine mystery and incomprehensibility or the orientation of theology to confession rather than system.[54] In our context, the most interesting remarks come in Berkouwer's volume *Divine Election*, to which I briefly turn.[55]

We recall Simeon's remarks on the attitude of Arminians in prayer and the subsequent reference to Luther's *coram Deo*. Berkouwer was struck by an observation that Bavinck made about Pelagianism that 'in doctrine one may be Pelagian, but in the practice of the Christian life, especially in prayer, every Christian is Augustinian, for then he declines all glory and gives all the honor to God alone'.[56] Berkouwer goes on to say that 'Bavinck wants to show that the main concern lies not with a number of logical conclusions drawn from a certain point of view, but that Pelagianism takes an irreligious position which comes into conflict with the nature of true Christian faith and prayer' and he remarks at the same time that 'there is something in it [Bavinck's argument] of Luther's *coram deo*'. More than 'something', surely: there is a great deal in it and Berkouwer himself elsewhere connects Luther's *simul iustus et peccator*, which we found closely connected with the *coram Deo* in Luther, with the scene of prayer.[57]

In his work on *Divine Election*, Berkouwer proceeds to explore the significance of *coram Deo*. It features in his treatment, for example, of 'Election and Rejection' in a discussion where he rejects the symmetry of predestination to life and predestination to death. More than one reason is given for the rejection and Berkouwer is ever, first and foremost, the exegete, but the deep methodological ground of his conviction is expressed in his conclusion, 'The dogmatician may not live secretly with a theory of parallelism or symmetry, as if he were allowed to work with other and deeper causes than those given to us in prayer, faith and confession of sins.'[58] The Confessions to which he appeals support him, he believes, but 'it is not sufficient merely to follow the Confessions. If anywhere, then here religious experience must become man's very own, if he would be kept from this abominable self-excuse' of making

---

54. Comparison with Brunner is fruitful here, both in detail (on causality) and more generally (on confession). Berkouwer engaged in more detail with Barth than with Brunner.

55. Grand Rapids: Eerdmans, 1960.

56. Ibid., p. 43. I am not tacitly equating Arminianism with Pelagianism.

57. Berkouwer, *The Church*, p. 353.

58. *Divine Election*, p. 216.

God's rejection of a person the explanatory device for sin and unbelief. A closed deterministic system has neglected the *coram Deo*.[59]

Again, the treatment of 'Election and the Certainty of Salvation', in the same volume, draws to its conclusion with observations on the *coram Deo* and its relevance to theological method.[60] Defending aspects of Van Ruler's thought on the *syllogismus practicus* (the conclusion of the argument from good works), Berkouwer insists that the 'conclusion is shaped through and on the basis of the *coram Deo*. It remains in the light of faith, prayer, and struggle.' Of course, Berkouwer concurs on the matter of theological principle, in words that echo or repeat what he has just said:

> It will always be necessary to distinguish between the conclusion, the syllogism, and any type of reasoning which operates independently of God's judgment over our lives. The conclusion can only have meaning and value through and on the basis of the *coram deo*. It remains in the light of faith, prayer, and struggle.[61]

My only objective here is to indicate resources and passages in Berkouwer that, I think, reflect some of the instincts that have informed my chapter.[62] Those within and without the Reformed tradition might profitably ponder the theological method that he deploys throughout his work in the interests of protecting biblical faith from the incursions of theological system. Berkouwer

---

59. Ibid., p. 201.
60. Cf. Berkouwer's *Faith and Perseverance* on correlation, confession, causation; the religious and the speculative; faith and system (e.g. pp. 98–100, 199, 226–227, 233–238).
61. *Divine Election*, p. 305.
62. I confess that I think it unfortunate when a respected fellow-contributor to the chapters in the present volume, Henri Blocher, speaks of Berkouwer's seduction by a '[milder] form of irrationalism': *Original Sin: Illuminating the Riddle* (Leicester: IVP, 1997), p. 109. Admittedly, Blocher makes the strict connection between the seduction and the irrationalism tentative, though he does not doubt that Berkouwer is guilty on both counts and admittedly he is directing his protest to one point, though it is a point that takes in Berkouwer's wider methodology. Nonetheless, I should myself say that it is no truer to say this of Berkouwer than to say of Blocher himself, in this fine work, that he has been seduced by a moderate form of rationalism. Berkouwer briefly speaks of original sin in particular elsewhere than in the volume Blocher has in mind; e.g. *The Church*, pp. 297–299.

finely exemplifies his stated conviction that the 'task of theology is to help preserve the doxology of dogma'.[63]

© Stephen Williams, 2006

---

63. *Half a Century of Theology: Movements and Motives* (Grand Rapids: Eerdmans, 1977),
    p. 216.

As Kevin Vanhoozer has written his chapter in memory of Stan Grenz, so I wish to
pay tribute to the memory of Colin Gunton, who wrote a distinguished essay, to
which I allude in this contribution, on the occasion of the launch of the *International
Journal of Systematic Theology* 1.1 (1999): 'A Rose by Any Other Name? From
"Christian Doctrine" to "Systematic Theology"'. We had our differences but
maintained our friendship in the theological task and service of the one Lord.

3. CLASSICAL CHRISTOLOGY'S FUTURE IN SYSTEMATIC THEOLOGY

Robert L. Reymond

Dan Brown's best-selling *The Da Vinci Code* represents Jesus as basically a man like other men. *The Myth of God Incarnate*,[1] Barbara Thiering's *Jesus the Man: A New Interpretation from the Dead Sea Scrolls*, A. N. Wilson's *Jesus*, John Selby Spong's *Born of a Woman: A Bishop Rethinks the Birth of Jesus*, John Dominic Crossan's *The Historical Jesus: The Life of a Mediterranean Jewish Peasant*, to name only five other works, as well as the radical conclusions of the Jesus Seminar[2]

---

1. A symposium of seven British theologians wrote *The Myth of God Incarnate* (Philadelphia: Westminster, 1977). In it they called upon the church to recognize that Jesus was originally 'a man approved by God' for a special role in the divine purpose and that the later conception of him as God incarnate is a mythological or poetic way of expressing this poetry to us – poetry, says John Hick the editor, that 'hardened into prose and escalated [Jesus] from a metaphorical son of God to a metaphysical God the Son' (p. 176).

2. Representing itself as part of the 'Quest of the Historical Jesus' movement, the Jesus Seminar, founded by Robert W. Funk in 1985 and chaired by Funk, John Dominic Crossan (who believes Jesus' body was never buried but was dumped in a trash heap and eaten by dogs and birds), and Marcus Borg, is a group of American New Testament scholars that meets twice a year to debate technical papers that have been circulated in advance. At the close of each debate on the agenda item the

and the modern 'Lesbian and Gay Jesus Movement' also do this. Even within respectable Academia serious questions are being raised in our generation about the Christ of classical Christology. For example, Raymond E. Brown, a Roman Catholic scholar, believes that while 'Incarnation is truly characteristic of Johannine Christology', it is 'quite uncharacteristic of about 90% of the rest of the NT', with this 90% reflecting 'other forms of NT theology'.[3] Brown's statement, if correct, would mean that the Christology enshrined in the creeds of the early church, particularly in the Definition of Chalcedon, would receive support from only about 10% of the New Testament with the other 90% neither recognizing nor claiming this creedal Christology as its own. Similarly, James D. G. Dunn, an alleged British evangelical, asserts, 'if we are to submit our speculation to the text and built our theology only with the bricks provided by careful exegesis we cannot say with any confidence that Jesus knew himself to be divine, the pre-existent Son of God'.[4]

In fact, Dunn can find an explicit statement of incarnation in *only one* passage in the New Testament – the so-called 'Logos Poem' of John 1:1–18.[5] And even that passage, Dunn notes, does not reflect Jesus' self-understanding but the theology of subsequent Christian reflection.[6] But if the full-blown incarnational Christology of John's Prologue is not so much the teaching

---

Fellows of the Seminar vote, using coloured beads, to indicate the degree of authenticity of Jesus' words and deeds. A *red* bead means Jesus undoubtedly said or did such-and-such or something like it, a *pink* bead means Jesus probably or might have said or done something like such-and-such, a *grey* bead means Jesus did not say or do such-and-such, but the idea or deed is close to what he might have said or done, and a *black* bead means Jesus did not say or do such-and-such; it is a later tradition. Of 1,500 reported sayings of Jesus that the Seminar examined, only 18% received a red or pink vote; of 176 reported deeds of Jesus that the Seminar examined, only 16% received red or pink votes. These are *radical* conclusions indeed! The Seminar, it is true, includes along with Jesus' sayings and deeds in the four canonical Gospels his sayings and deeds from the gnostic Gospel of Thomas (which fact in itself says a great deal about the Seminar's commitment to canonical truth), but its conclusions even so are still radical!

3. Raymond E. Brown, Review of I. Howard Marshall's *The Epistles of John* in the *New International Commentary on the New Testament* series, *Catholic Biblical Quarterly* 42.3 (July 1980), p. 413.

4. James D. G. Dunn, *Christology in the Making* (London: SCM, 1980), p. 28.

5. Ibid., p. 241.

6. Ibid., p. 30.

either of Jesus or of the rest of the New Testament as it is the product of the church's evolving reflection upon him over time, Dunn's contention, if correct, raises the question whether it should even be believed. Such representations, in my opinion, are reflections of our modern culture's sceptical, if not Arian,[7] bent concerning Jesus.

Of course, while I reject the Arian view of Jesus, neither I nor classical Christology deny for an instant that Jesus lived among men as a human being. He called himself (John 8:40) and was called by those who knew him a 'man' (*anthrōpos*) (Matt. 8:27; 26:72, 74; Mark 14:71; 15:39; Luke 23:4, 6, 14, 47; John 4:29; 5:12; 7:46; 9:11, 16, 24; 10:33; 11:47; 18:17, 29; 19:5).[8] But even as they did

---

7. Arianism, named for Arius, the North African churchman who espoused this teaching at the Council of Nicaea in AD 325, held that the Logos or Son of God was only a created being made out of nothing, first in the created order true enough but not divine, since 'there was [a time] when he was not', thereby denying the Son's unabridged deity. Arius' view was condemned at the Council of Nicaea. Today whoever denies the deity of Christ, such as the Unitarian and the Jehovah's Witness, may properly be said to be 'Arian' in his Christology.

8. Jesus is also called an *anēr* (man, male) (John 1:30; Acts 2:22; 17:31), and the author of Hebrews states that he 'shared our humanity' and was 'made like his brothers in every way' (Heb. 2:14, 17). Matthew traces his human lineage back to Abraham (Matt. 1:1–17), while Luke traces his lineage back to Adam (Luke 3:23–37). Luke also informs us that he was born during the reign of Caesar Augustus before Quirinius governed Syria (Luke 2:1–2) and that he conducted his earthly ministry during the reign of Tiberius Caesar when Pontius Pilate governed Judea, when Herod the tetrarch governed Galilee, and when Annas and Caiaphas were high priests in Jerusalem (Luke 3:1–2). John the Evangelist portrays him as one who grew weary from a journey, sat down at Jacob's well for a moment of respite, and asked for a drink of water to quench his thirst (John 4:6–7; see also Mark 4:37–38). People knew his adoptive father and his mother (John 1:45; 6:42; 7:27). He was troubled and perplexed in spirit as he was contemplating his impending death (John 12:27). Here is clearly a man for whom death was no friend, who instinctively recoiled against it as an enemy to be resisted.

Benjamin B. Warfield in his article 'On the Emotional Life of Our Lord', in *The Person and Work of Christ* (Philadelphia: P. & R., 1950), pp. 93–145, also shows that the Gospel narratives depict Jesus as a man who was subject to the full range of (sinless) human emotions – compassion or pity (Matt. 9:36; 14:14; Mark 1:41; Luke 7:13), mercy (Matt. 9:27; Mark 10:47–48; Luke 17:13), love (Mark 10:21; John 11:3, 5, 36), anger (Matt. 21:12–13; Mark 3:5; 11:15–17; Luke 19:45–46; John 2:14–16),

so, the question doubtless often intruded itself in their minds about 'what *kind* of man' he was and for good reason. For this man could and did still the wind and the stormy Sea of Galilee with a word (Matt. 8:27), walk on water, change water into wine, feed thousands with a child's lunch, heal the sick with a touch or a word, restore hearing to the deaf and sight to the blind, and raise the dead. Indeed, the Gospels ascribe a pervasive supernaturalism to both his person and his work, teaching that he was virginally conceived, performed mighty miracles, rose from the dead on the third day after his crucifixion, and ascended some days later into heaven. So it is quite natural for one to seek an explanation for this supernaturalistic side of his life. And while it is often explained away today as simply the language of mythology, such a conclusion the entire New Testament finds intolerable, ascribing to him as it does not only true manness but also true, unabridged, unqualified Godness. In sum, the New Testament portrait of Jesus is that of a two-natured person, and, accordingly, the Bible-believing part of the church has historically and classically borne witness to this two-natured Christ in its creeds and schools and from its church pulpits. As the answer to the *Westminster Shorter Catechism*, Question 21, declares, 'The only Redeemer of God's elect is the Lord Jesus Christ, who, being the eternal Son of God, became man, and so was, and continueth to be God and man, in two distinct natures, and one person, forever.'

In this single sentence is captured all the essential aspects of an orthodox classical Christology, declaring as it does

- that Jesus Christ was and is the eternal Son of God, the second person of the triune Godhead;
- that the eternal Son of God became man;
- that the eternal Son of God's becoming man in no way affected his deity in that he continued to be God;
- that the incarnated Son of God is now a two-natured single person; and
- that the eternal Son of God is and will continue to be this two-natured single person forever.

Jesus' humanity and historicity are rarely called into question today, but his deity and the supernaturalness surrounding him in the Gospels are regularly

---

indignation or irritation (Mark 10:14), joy (Luke 10:21; John 17:13), grief (Mark 3:5), perplexity (John 12:27), despondency, horror and distress (Matt. 26:37–38; Mark 14:34), and astonishment (Matt. 8:10; Mark 6:6; Luke 7:9). Clearly, Jesus was no docetic Christ.

explained away in one way or another as fraudulent mythology. Assuming then for our present purpose that which the world is willing to grant, namely, the historical existence of the first-century rabbi named Jesus of Nazareth, in this chapter I shall first present some of the New Testament evidence for Jesus' deity[9] and then enumerate some of the problems that yet remain to be resolved by the systematic theologian.

Some New Testament evidence for Jesus' deity

The biblical evidence for Jesus' deity includes Jesus' self-testimony in word and deed and the New Testament writers' united witness to his deity, especially their employment of *theos* (God) as a Christological title in John 20:28; Romans 9:5; Titus 2:13; Hebrews 1:8; 2 Peter 2:1; John 1:1; 1:18; and 1 John 5:20.

Jesus' self-testimony
James Dunn says that Jesus did not understand himself to be God. But did he? Because central to any answer to the question 'Who is Jesus?' is what Jesus believed and taught about himself and what he taught others to believe about him, I want to begin with the issue of Jesus' self-testimony. This should first be determined since the world, even the Christian world, should not ascribe to him, unless for the most unavoidable of reasons, opinions that he did not hold about himself, or deny to him, unless again for the most unavoidable of reasons, opinions that he did hold about himself.

Jesus' employment of the 'Son of Man' title
In the Gospels Jesus employs the title 'the Son of Man' as a self-designation eighty-two times. Assuming for good reason the authenticity of the Son of Man sayings as containing the *ipsissima vox Jesu* (very voice of Jesus),[10] the

---

9. I have argued the case for the Bible's 'revealedness', inspiration and inerrancy in my *A New Systematic Theology of the Christian Faith*, 2nd edn (Nashville: Thomas Nelson, 2002), pp. 3–126. For a much fuller presentation of the evidence for Jesus' deity see my *Jesus, Divine Messiah: The New and Old Testament Witness* (Ross-shire, Scotland: Mentor, 2003).

10. Because the dominical *logia* we shall be considering here are in Greek when, in fact, Jesus very likely spoke these *logia* originally in Aramaic, I recognize, when examining Jesus' self-testimony, that we are not working with the *ipsissima verba Jesu* (very words of Jesus). I shall assume, however, that we have in the four Evangelists' reports of

church of Jesus Christ has correctly understood the title itself, assuredly messianic (see Dan. 7:13[11]), as Jesus' way of laying public claim to his messianic investiture without having to use directly the title itself of 'the Christ' that would have fostered false expectations in the popular imagination.

Even a cursory examination of these sayings will bear out the title's transcendental implications. For example, in the Fourth Gospel the title 'connotes the heavenly, superhuman side of Jesus' mysterious existence',[12] expressing what is commonly called his pre-existence (John 3:13; 6:62). In his role as the Son of Man in the Synoptic Gospels Jesus claims to have the authority to forgive sins (Matt. 9:6; Mark 2:10; Luke 5:24) and to regulate even the observance of the divine ordinance of the Sabbath (Matt. 12:8; Mark 2:28; Luke 6:5) – clearly prerogatives of deity alone. As the Son of Man the angels are his (Matt. 13:41), implying his own super-angelic status and lordship over them. A man's eternal destiny turns on his relationship to him as the Son of Man, he taught, for unless the Son of Man gives a man life there is no life in him (John 6:53). As the Son of Man he would rise from the dead and be 'seated at the right hand of Power' (Matt. 26:64)[13] and be 'coming on the clouds of heaven with power and great glory' (Matt. 24:30; Mark 13:25; Luke 21:27). And when he comes, he declared, he would come with authority to execute judgment upon all men precisely because he is the Son of Man (John 5:27). Clearly, the Son of Man sayings embodied Jesus' conception of Messiahship that contain supernatural, even divine, characteristics. Warfield does not overstate the matter when he writes:

> It is . . . in the picture which Jesus Himself draws for us of the 'Son of Man' that we
> see His superhuman nature portrayed. For the figure thus brought before us is
> distinctly a superhuman one; one which is not only in the future to be seen sitting at

---

Jesus' self-testimony, as the essential and trustworthy equivalency of Jesus' original words, the *ipsissima vox Jesu*.

11. Commenting on the significance of Jesus' Son of Man title in his *The Self-Disclosure of Jesus* (Phillipsburg: P. & R., 1978), p. 254, Geerhardus Vos writes, 'In close adherence to the spirit of the scene in Daniel from which it was taken, it suggested a Messianic career in which, all of a sudden, without human interference or military conflict, through an immediate act of God, the highest dignity and power are conferred. The kingship here portrayed [in Daniel 7] is not only supernatural; it is "transcendental."'

12. Ibid., p. 239.

13. Unless stated otherwise, Bible quotations in this chapter are from the ESV.

the right hand of power and coming with the clouds of heaven . . . ; but which in the present world itself exercises functions which are truly divine, – for who is Lord of the Sabbath but the God who instituted it in commemoration of His own rest (Mark 2:28), and who can forgive sins but God only (2:10; see verse 7)? The assignment to the Son of Man of the functions of Judge of the world and the ascription to him of the right to forgive sins are, in each case, but another way of saying that He is a divine person; for these are divine acts.[14]

Jesus' employment of the 'Son [of the Father]' title in Matthew 11:25–27:

At that time Jesus said, 'I praise you, Father, Lord of heaven and earth, because you have hidden these things [about me] from the wise and learned, and revealed them to little children. Yes, Father, for this was your good pleasure. All things have been committed to me by my Father. No one knows the Son except the Father, and no one knows the Father except the Son and those to whom the Son chooses to reveal him.'[15]

By his assertions in these verses Jesus implicitly claims for himself a place of power and privilege as the 'Son' of the 'Father' that places him altogether on

---

14. Benjamin B. Warfield, *The Lord of Glory* (Grand Rapids: Baker, 1974), p. 41.

15. That theological quarter that rejects the ontological deity of Jesus Christ assails the authenticity of this passage for the following three reasons: First, the pericope has a 'Johannine ring' to it – K. A. von Hase speaks of it as a 'thunderbolt [meteor] from the Johannine heaven'; second, its content with its emphasis on knowledge appears to be a product of the Greek-speaking church; third, Jesus simply could not have made such absolute claims for himself. But its Johannine 'ring' in no way invalidates its authenticity unless one assumes as a canon of criticism that any Synoptic saying that sounds like something John might have written is *ipso facto* spurious. Moreover, the fact that this pericope's parallel is in Luke 10:21–22 places it in the critic's so-called 'Q' source and is thus guaranteed early dominical status on grounds recognized by the critical scholar. Too, it has no precise parallel in anything that John wrote. As for its so-called late Hellenistic emphasis on knowledge, in the light of the emphasis on knowledge in the Dead Sea Scrolls, one does not have to leave the Jewish milieu to account for this emphasis. Finally, it is nothing but bias that would deny these words to Jesus on the ground that he simply could not have made such claims for himself. Such bias must also assume that Jesus' frequent references to God as 'Father' and the other occurrences of the title 'Son' in the Synoptic tradition are likewise spurious.

the level of deity. By these assertions – assertions, by the way, that Benjamin B. Warfield declared constitute 'in some respects the most remarkable [utterance] in the whole compass of the four Gospels'[16] and that Geerhardus Vos judged to be 'by far the most important seat of the testimony which Jesus bears to his sonship' as well as being 'the culminating point of our Lord's self-disclosure in the Synoptics'[17] – by these assertions, I say, we are brought face to face with four great parallels that Jesus drew between God as 'the Father' and himself as the Father's 'Son' of Matthew 3:17 (Mark 1:11; Luke 3:22). The *unique* and *intimate* nature of the Father–Son relationship Jesus asserts here of himself – higher than which it is impossible to conceptualize unless it be in certain of the utterances of the Fourth Gospel, such as 'I and the Father are one' (10:30) – comes to expression precisely in terms of these four parallels.

The first parallel that Jesus draws is the *mutual absolute lordship that the Father and he the Son each possesses*, the Father's lordship expressed in Jesus' description of him in verse 25: 'Father, Lord of heaven and earth', his own lordship expressed in his words in verse 27: 'All things [in heaven and on earth] have been handed over to me by my Father.' (He makes the same claim in Matthew 28:18 when he states, 'All authority in heaven and on earth has been given to me.') Here Jesus claims to be, as a result of his Father's investing him with the messianic task, this planet's King of kings and Lord of lords, whose royal diadem out-rivals all the combined crowns and tiaras of all the kings and queens, of all the dictators and petty Caesars of this world. In a sentence, Jesus teaches that by virtue of his Father's investiture of the messianic office upon him he is in charge of all things!

The second parallel that he highlights is the *exclusive, mutual knowledge that the Father and he the Son each has of the other*. Jesus declares in verse 27, 'no one knows the Son except the Father, and no one knows the Father except the Son'. The first thing we note here is his dual employment of the same Greek verb (*epiginōskei*) to describe the Father's knowledge of the Son and the Son's knowledge of the Father, which verb with its attached preposition means 'knows exactly, completely, through and through'.[18] And the second thing to note is Jesus' emphasis upon the *exclusiveness* of this mutual knowledge reflected by his

---

16. Warfield, *Lord of Glory*, pp. 82–83; see also pp. 118–119.

17. Vos, *Self-Disclosure of Jesus*, p. 143.

18. W. Bauer, W. F. Arndt, F. W. Gingrich and F. W. Danker, *A Greek-English Lexicon of the New Testament and Other Early Christian Literature*, 2nd edn (Chicago: University Press, 1979), p. 291, 1a.

twice-used phrase, 'no one knows *except*' (*ei mē*).[19] Only a moment's reflection will show that the nature of this exclusive knowledge that Jesus claims to have lifts him above the sphere of the ordinary mortal and places him 'in a position, not of equality merely, but of absolute reciprocity and interpenetration of knowledge with the Father'.[20] Vos observes:

> That essential rather than acquired knowledge is meant follows ... from the correlation of the [parallel] clauses: the knowledge God has of Jesus cannot be acquired knowledge [it must, from the fact that it is God's knowledge, be direct, intuitive, and immediate – in a word, divine – knowledge, grounded in the fact that the Knower is divine[21]]; consequently the knowledge Jesus has of God cannot be acquired knowledge either [it too must be direct, intuitive, and immediate – in a word, divine – knowledge], for these two are placed entirely on a line. In other words, if the one is different from human knowledge, then the other must be so likewise.[22]

The only conclusion that this correlation of the two clauses justly warrants is, first, that God has his exclusive and penetrating knowledge of the Son because he is God, the Father of the Son, and, second, that Jesus has his exclusive and penetrating knowledge of the Father because he is God, the Son of the Father.

The third parallel, which rests upon the second, comes to focus in Jesus' assertion of *the mutual necessity of the Father and of him the Son each to reveal the other if men are ever to have an acquired saving knowledge of them*. This parallel is highlighted by Jesus' declaration in verse 25 that the Father had hidden (*ekrypsas*) from the spiritual 'know-it-alls' the mysteries of the Kingdom that are centred in him the Son and had revealed (*apekalypsas*) them to 'babies' such as Peter to whom Jesus would say in Matthew 16:17, 'flesh and blood has not revealed this to you, but my Father who is in heaven' (RSV), and his statement in verse 27 that 'no one

---

19. The exclusiveness of Jesus' knowledge is not invalidated by his following remark, 'and to whomever the Son wills to reveal him', since the very point of his statement is that other men must acquire their saving knowledge of the Father *from him*. They can acquire it *in no other way* (John 14:6), whereas his knowledge of the Father is intrinsic to the filial relationship he sustains to his Father.

20. Warfield, 'The Person of Christ According to the New Testament', in *The Person and Work of Christ*, p. 65.

21. See George Eldon Ladd, *A Theology of the New Testament* (Grand Rapids: Eerdmans, 1974), p. 166.

22. Vos, *Self-Disclosure of Jesus*, p. 149.

knows the Father except the Son and any one to whom the Son chooses to reveal [*apokalypsai*] him' (RSV). I call attention again to Jesus' dual employment here of the same Greek verb (*apokalyptō*) to describe the activities of the two: the Father reveals the Son; the Son reveals the Father.

The fourth parallel Jesus draws is that of *the mutual absolute sovereignty the Father and he the Son each exercises in dispensing his revelation of the other*. The Father's sovereignty in this regard is displayed in Jesus' words in verse 26, 'for this was your good pleasure [*eudokia*]'; the Son's sovereignty is displayed in his words in verse 27,'to whom the Son wills [*boulētai*] to reveal him'.[23]

A higher expression of parity between the Father and the Son with respect to the possession of the divine attribute of sovereignty in the dispensing of saving knowledge is inconceivable. Jesus teaches here that no sinful creature has a right to such revelation. If the creature ever learns about the Son it is because the Father has sovereignly determined in his grace to reveal him. If he ever learns about the Father it is because the Son has sovereignly determined in his grace to reveal him!

Warfield is surely justified when he summarizes Jesus' absolutely amazing utterance here in these words:

---

23. It was because of Jesus' claim to sole and unique knowledge of the Father that he issued the invitation that he did in 11:28, '[Therefore, in the light of my exclusive knowledge of the Father,] Come to me, all you who are weary and burdened, and I will give you rest.' His invitation provides the *formal* New Testament parallel to Yahweh's invitation in Isaiah 45:22:

> Yahweh invites in Isaiah 45:22, 'Turn to me, all the ends of the earth, and I will save you' (my tr.).
> Jesus invites in Matthew 11:28, 'Come to me, all you who are weary and burdened, and I will give you rest.'

Such a universal and unqualified invitation would be nothing less than grossly audacious – indeed, it would be indicative of delusions of grandeur – were it to come from the lips of any other person. No pastor, however great his gifts, abilities and fame, would ever dare to issue such an invitation. Nor would it ever enter his mind to do so. Were he to do so, the entire world would justly scoff at him and would rightly ask him, 'How do you have the temerity to issue such an invitation?' And if he continued to issue this invitation, the world would have the right to judge him to be insane. But such an invitation accords perfectly and appropriately with the claims Jesus made for himself in 11:27.

in it our Lord asserts for Himself a relation of practical equality with the Father, [who is] here described in most elevated terms as the 'Lord of heaven and earth' (v. 25). As the Father only can know the Son, so the Son only can know the Father: and others may know the Father only as He is revealed by the Son. That is, not merely is the Son the exclusive revealer of God, but the mutual knowledge of Father and Son is put on what seems very much a par. The Son can be known only by the Father in all that He is, as if His being were infinite and as such inscrutable to the finite intelligence; and His knowledge alone – again as if He were infinite in His attributes – is competent to compass the depths of the Father's infinite being. He who holds this relation to the Father cannot conceivably be a creature.[24]

Ned B. Stonehouse, professor of New Testament at Westminster Theological Seminary, in his *The Witness of Matthew and Mark to Christ*, similarly writes:

Here [in Matt. 11:25–27] Jesus claims such an exclusive knowledge of the Father, and a consequent exclusive right to reveal the Father (both corresponding with the Father's exclusive knowledge and revelation of the Son), that nothing less than an absolutely unique self-consciousness, on an equality with that of the Father, is involved.[25]

Also in his *The Witness of Luke to Christ* Stonehouse asserts:

Most clearly of all, perhaps, the claim to divine Sonship in a form excluding subordination altogether [of the Son to the Father] is found in Luke x. 22, which closely parallels Mt. xi. 27. The Son's knowledge of the Father and the Father's knowledge of the Son are set forth with such exact correspondence and reciprocity, and are moreover made the foundations of their respective sovereign revelational activity, that all subordination is excluded, and the passage constitutes an unambiguous claim of deity on the part of the Son.[26]

Jesus' use of 'Son' in the triune name of the baptismal formula of Matthew 28:19
This verse affords us entrance into the mind of the *risen* Jesus. I am particularly interested in the precise form of the baptismal formula. Jesus does not tell his church to baptize into the 'names' of the Father and the Son and the Holy Spirit,

---

24. Warfield, *Lord of Glory*, pp. 82–83; see also pp. 118–119.
25. Ned B. Stonehouse, *The Witness of Matthew and Mark to Christ* (Philadelphia: Presbyterian Guardian, 1944), p. 212.
26. Ned B. Stonehouse, *The Witness of Luke to Christ* (London: Tyndale, 1951), p. 167.

or into the name of the Father and into the name of the Son and into the name
of the Holy Spirit, or into the name of Father, Son and Holy Spirit (omitting
the three recurring articles). Rather, he instructs his church to baptize 'into *the*
name [singular] of *the* Father, and of *the* Son, and of *the* Holy Spirit', asserting
thereby first the unity of the three within the word 'name' and then stressing
the distinctness of the three by introducing each with the recurring article.

In the light of the fact that the word 'name' in Hebrew culture could refer
to the essence of a person and indeed stand in as a representative substitute
for the person (see Lev. 24:11; Deut. 28:58; Isa. 30:27; 59:19), the words 'the
name' here surely carry the connotation of deity inasmuch as it is the Father's
name and thus the Father's nature that is first mentioned. But it is precisely this
same 'name' that the Son (along with the Spirit) also possesses, thereby bringing the Son into the precincts of the divine name itself and evincing his equality with the Father in so far as his deity is concerned.

Jesus' claim to eternal pre-existence

For one who takes Jesus' words in John's Gospel at face value it is evident that
Jesus affirmed for himself both as the Son of God and as the Son of Man pre-
existence. Not only does he pray, 'Father, glorify me . . . with the glory that I
had with you *before* the world existed' (17:5, my italics), indeed, with 'my glory
that you have given me because you loved me *before* the foundation of the
world' (17:24, my italics), but he also declares, 'Before Abraham was, I am'
(8:58); 'No one has ascended into heaven except he who descended from
heaven, the Son of Man' (3:13); 'I have come down from heaven, not to do my
own will but the will of him who sent me' (6:38; see 6:33, 50, 58); '[No one] has
seen the Father except he who is from God' (6:46); 'what if you were to see the
Son of Man ascending to where he was before' (6:62); 'You are from below; I
am from above. You are of this world; I am not of this world' (8:23); 'I speak
of what I have seen with my Father' (8:38); 'I came out and came forth from
God' (8:42); 'the Father consecrated and sent [me, the Son of God] into the
world' (10:36); and 'I came from the Father and have come into the world'
(16:28; see 9:39; 12:46; 18:37).

These Johannine assertions clearly affirm pre-existence for Jesus, but in
what sense? In the divine sense or in the ideal, that is, 'foreknown' (by God)
sense? In the light of the literary device known as *inclusio* (inclusion), that is,
the placing both at the beginning and at the end of a literary piece, like bracket
signs, a thematic idea that everything that the author then inserts between
them he intends as support for his theme, Jesus' pre-existence here can only
be understood as affirming that John intended these dominical claims of pre-
existence as ascriptions of essential deity to Jesus. How does John begin his

Gospel? By declaring that Jesus as the Word 'was God' (1:1). How does he conclude his Gospel? By recording Thomas's ringing declaration '[You are] my Lord and my God' (20:28)! It is apparent that John's intention behind his reports of Jesus' claim of pre-existence, coming as they do between his thematic statements, has to be viewed, if the device of *inclusio* has any merit at all, as depicting a Jesus who, as God, possesses ontological deity.

Jesus' acts and attributes

During his earthly ministry Jesus performed mighty miracles of healing and exercised divine authority over the forces of nature,[27] he himself declaring in Matthew 11:4–5, 9:1–8, Mark 2:1–2, Luke 5:17–26, 7:22, and John 5:36, 10:24–37, 37–38, 14:11 that his mighty works authenticated his teaching and were themselves direct and immediate indications of the presence of the Messianic Age and his own divine glory as the Messianic King (John 2:11).

He also forgave sin (Matt. 9:2; Mark 2:5; Luke 5:20; 7:48), promised to hear and answer his disciples' prayers (John 14:13–14), accepted the adoration, worship and praise of men (Matt. 21:16; John 20:28), and portrayed himself as the proper object of men's saving trust (John 14:1).

Chief among his acts was his resurrection from the dead by his own power (John 2:19; 10:18), this historical event supported by the twin facts of his empty tomb and his fifteen post-crucifixion appearances (1) to the women who had left the tomb on that first Sunday morning after his crucifixion (Matt. 28:8–10), then in turn (2) to Mary Magdalene (John 20:10–18), (3) to Cleopas and the other (unnamed) disciple on the road to Emmaus that afternoon (Luke 24:13–35), (4) to Peter, no doubt also that same afternoon (Luke 24:34; 1 Cor. 15:5), (5) to the Ten (since Judas and Thomas were not present) – his *first* appearance to them as a group – in the upper room on the evening of that first Easter evening on which occasion Jesus invited them to touch him in order to satisfy themselves that it was really he who stood among them and then ate a piece of broiled fish in their presence as proof that his body was materially real (Luke 24:36–43; John 20:20–28; 1 Cor. 15:5), (6) to the Eleven, including Thomas – his *second* appearance to his disciples as a group a week later (John 20:26–29), (7) to the seven disciples by the Sea of Galilee – his *third* appearance to his disciples as a group (John 21:14) – on which occasion he prepared and ate breakfast with them and on which occasion Jesus also publicly reclaimed Peter (John 21:1–22), (8) to the Eleven again on a mountain in Galilee and quite possibly at this same

---

27. See my *Jesus, Divine Messiah*, pp. 259–262, for a complete list of Jesus' canonical miracles.

time to the five hundred disciples, many of whom were still alive as Paul wrote
1 Corinthians 15, on which occasion Jesus issued to them his Great
Commission (Matt. 28:16–20), (9) to James his half-brother (1 Cor. 15:7), (10)
to the Eleven again on the occasion of his ascension into heaven from the
Mount of Olives in Jerusalem (Luke 24:44–52; Acts 1:4–9; 1 Cor. 15:7), (11) to
Stephen at his stoning (Acts 7:55–56), (12) to Paul on the road to Damascus
(Acts 9:3–5; 22:6–8; 26:12–15), (13) to Ananias of Damascus (Acts 9:10), (14)
to Paul a second time on his first visit to Jerusalem three years after his conver-
sion (Acts 22:17–18), and (15) to John on the island of Patmos (Rev 1:9–17).

The probative significance of Jesus' resurrection as evidence for his deity is
declared by Paul in Romans 1:3–4: 'concerning [God's] Son, who was
descended from David according to the flesh and was declared to be the Son
of God in power according to the spirit of holiness by his resurrection from
the dead, Jesus Christ our Lord'.

The reader should note that Paul places between the bracketing phrases 'his
Son' and 'Jesus Christ our Lord', which in themselves suggest an incarnational
Christology, two participial clauses: 'was born . . .' and 'was declared to be . . .'
The former teaches that in one sense, that is, 'according to the flesh', Jesus had
a *historical beginning* when he was born to royal dignity in the Davidic line. Hence,
Jesus was the promised Davidic Messiah. The latter teaches that, in the sense
that he was not 'according to the flesh', Jesus' *historical establishment* as the Son of
God on his divine side[28] was demonstrated by his resurrection from the dead.
The relation of the two participial clauses then is that of *superimposition*, the first
clause teaching that God's Son was born as the Davidic Messiah with all the
glories that that birth to privilege entailed, the second clause teaching that

> the Messiahship, inexpressibly glorious as it is, does not exhaust the glory of Christ.
> He had a glory greater even than this. This was the beginning of His glory. He came
> into the world as the promised Messiah, and He went out of the world as the
> demonstrated Son of God. In these two things is summed up the majesty of His
> historical manifestation.[29]

He also claimed, as we have already seen, divine pre-existence as well as
sovereign omnipotence (Matt. 11:27; 28:18; John 5:21), omnipresence (Matt.
18:20), and omniscience (Matt. 11:27; John 1:48), attributes normally and

---

28. See my argument in ibid., pp. 379–384, for understanding 'according to the spirit of
    holiness' as a reference to Christ's divine nature.
29. Warfield, 'The Christ That Paul Preached', in *The Person and Work of Christ*, p. 80.

properly belonging to God alone. In making these claims he was claiming to be God incarnate.

The employment of *theos* (God) as a Christological title (treated in their chronological order)

Convinced as they all were that Jesus had in fact risen from the dead and that he had ascended to heaven as the rightful Lord of the universe, it is not at all surprising that we find Jesus' apostles willing to pray to him (2 Cor. 12:8–9), to declare his name as the name to be 'called upon' in the church (1 Cor. 1:2; Rom. 10:9–13), to couple him with God the Father as the co-sources of grace, mercy and peace (Gal. 1:3; 1 Thess. 1:1–2; Rom. 1:7 etc.), to apply Old Testament passages in which Yahweh is the subject directly to him (cf. Isa. 8:14 with Rom. 9:32, 33; Joel 2:32 and Rom. 10:12–13; Isa. 8:12ff. with 1 Pet. 3:14–15), to apply to him the term *kyrios* (Lord), which in the Septuagint is employed to translate the sacred name of Yahweh (*passim*), and more specifically, as we shall now see, even to employ *theos* (God) as a Christological title.

John 20:28

Exactly one week after Jesus' resurrection and in the presence of the other ten disciples, when confronted by the living Christ, Thomas gave instantaneous utterance to one of the great professions of Scripture, certainly the greatest of any in the Gospels: '[You are] my Lord and my God!'

What is the significance of Thomas's profession for the church? It means, first, that within a week of Jesus' resurrection, in the presence of the other disciples who were doubtless listening intently to their conversation and who would surely have learned from Thomas's words and Jesus' favourable response to them the appropriateness of doing so, a disciple for the first time did the unthinkable: *he employed with no qualification the word* theos, *'God', as a Christological title – unthinkable* because for a Jew to call his Master 'my God' would under any other circumstance have been regarded as blasphemy. Nevertheless, *this* disciple – the *least* likely of all the disciples to do so and the *last* one we would expect to do so – by his profession taught the church that it may use the same language when addressing Jesus that Old Testament Israel used when addressing Yahweh. For example, the psalmist says in

Psalm 35:23b: 'Contend for me, my God and Lord' (NIV).
Psalm 38:15, 21: 'I wait for you, O LORD; / you will answer, O Lord my God . . .
O LORD, do not forsake me; / be not far from me, O my God' (NIV).

It means, second, that one cannot legitimately argue as form-critical scholars do that the deification of Jesus was a late creation of the second- or third-century church, for as Raymond E. Brown states, these words in Thomas's mouth on this early occasion are 'textually secure'.[30] As such, Thomas's profession is the 'supreme christological pronouncement of the Fourth Gospel'.[31] Nor can one legitimately argue as Unitarians do that Thomas's entire utterance was an ejaculatory expression of astonishment addressed to God in heaven, or as the Jehovah's Witnesses do that only the first title, 'Lord', was addressed to Jesus while the second title, 'God', was addressed to God in heaven. Bruce M. Metzger of Princeton Seminary rightly observes, 'It is not permissible to divide Thomas' exclamation . . . Such a high-handed expedient overlooks the plain introductory words: "Thomas said *to him:* 'My Lord and my God.'"'[32]

Finally, it should not go unnoticed that John immediately follows Thomas's profession by his stated intention in writing his Gospel; namely, that his readers 'may believe that Jesus is the Christ [that is, the long-promised, long-awaited Messiah], the Son of God' (John 20:31). If John had intended by his title '*Son* of God' something less than an ascription of full deity to Jesus, it is odd that he would have brought this lesser title into such close proximity to Thomas's unqualified confession of Jesus' full, unabridged deity. Clearly, the only adequate explanation for the near juxtaposition of the two titles is that, while 'Son of God' distinguishes Jesus as the Son from God the Father, it does not distinguish him as God from God the Father. In sum, to be the Son of God in the sense John intended it of Jesus is just to say that Jesus as the Son of God is God the Son. If one does not say this, then one has no other alternative but to charge John with unforgivable ineptitude in bringing the two titles into immediate proximity with each other in the way he has done.

Romans 9:5

This verse most naturally reads, 'from whom [that is, the patriarchs] came the Messiah according to the flesh, who is over all, God blessed forever. Amen.'

---

30. Raymond E. Brown, 'Does the New Testament Call Jesus God?', *Theological Studies*
      26.4 (1965), p. 563.

31. Raymond E. Brown, *The Gospel According to John XIII–XXI*, Anchor Bible Series
      (Garden City, N.Y.: Doubleday, 1970), p. 1047.

32. Bruce M. Metzger, 'The Jehovah's Witnesses and Jesus Christ', *Theology Today* (April
      1953), p. 71, n. 13.

The *grammatical* demand of the verse would suggest that the articular present participle *ho ōn* (who is) introduces the relative clause that should be attached antecedently to the preceding *ho Christos* (the Christ). The *implicatory* demand of the verse flows from the presence of the words *to kata sarka* (so far as the flesh is concerned); that is to say, the Messiah is from the patriarchs so far as the flesh is concerned. But this raises the question 'In what sense is the Messiah not from the patriarchs?' the answer to which is supplied in the words that follow: 'who is over all, God blessed forever'.

Scholars who think that a reference to Christ as God here is an un-Pauline locution (but see Titus 2:13) either detach the last expression from the preceding words and construe it as a doxology ('May God be blessed forever!') or they detach the entire expression 'who is over all, God blessed forever' from the preceding words and again construe the clause as a doxology ('May he who is over all, even God, be blessed forever'). But if either of these detached clauses is in fact a doxology, a reversal of the word order of every other such doxology in the Bible (over thirty times in the Old Testament and twelve times in the New) occurs where the verbal adjective 'Blessed' always precedes the noun for God and never follows it as here. It is difficult to believe that Paul, whose ear for proper Hebraic and Hellenistic syntactical formulae was finely tuned, would violate the established formula for expressing praise to God, a formula that even he himself observes elsewhere (see Eph. 1:3; 2 Cor. 1:3). The second proposal, commended by the editors of the UBS New Testament, has an addiitional problem to address; namely, by disconnecting everything after *sarka* (flesh) and construing the disconnected portion as an independent ascription of praise to God it denies to the articular participle any real significance. Bruce M. Metzger highlights this failing:

> If . . . the clause [beginning with *ho ōn*] is taken as an asyndetic [unconnected] doxology to God, . . . the word *ōn* becomes superfluous, for 'he who is God over all' is most simply represented in Greek by *ho epi pantōn theos*. The presence of the participle suggests that the clause functions as a relative clause (not 'he who is . . .' but 'who is . . .'), and thus describes *ho Christos* as being 'God over all'.[33]

Nigel Turner also observes that detaching the words beginning with *ho ōn* from the preceding clause 'introduces asyndeton and there is no grammatical reason why a participle agreeing with "Messiah" should first be divorced

33. Bruce M. Metzger, 'The Punctuation of Romans 9:5', in *Christ and Spirit in the New Testament* (Cambridge: University Press, 1973), pp. 105–106.

from it and then be given the force of a wish, receiving a different person as its subject'.[34]

Actually, there is no justifiable reason for doubting that Paul in Romans 9:5, by his use of *theos* as a Christological title – surrounding it with the particular phrases that he employs – ascribes full deity to Christ who is *and abides as* (the force of the present participle) divine Lord over the universe, and who deserves eternal praise from all mankind.

Titus 2:13

When Paul wrote, 'while we wait for the blessed hope – the glorious appearing of our great God and Saviour, Jesus Christ' (NIV), did he intend to refer to one person (Christ) or to two persons (the Father and Christ)? What does grammatical exegesis demand? For the following five reasons I would urge that Paul intended his phrase 'our great God and Saviour' to refer to one person only – Christ.

First, it is the most natural way to render the Greek sentence. Indeed, more than one grammarian has observed that there would never have been any debate as to whether 'God' and 'Saviour' referred to the same person if the sentence had simply ended with 'Saviour'.

Second, the two nouns both stand under the regimen of the single definite article preceding 'God', indicating according to the Granville Sharp observation that the nouns are to be construed together, not separately; that is to say, they have a single referent. If Paul had intended two persons, he could have expressed this unambiguously by inserting an article before 'Saviour' and by writing 'our Saviour' after 'Jesus Christ'.

Third, never is the idea of 'appearing' associated with the Father; it is consistently employed to describe the return of Christ in glory. The *prima facie* conclusion is that 'the glorious appearing of our great God' refers to Christ's appearing and not to the Father's appearing.

Fourth, note has often been made of the fact that the terms *theos kai sōtēr* (god and saviour) were employed in combination together in second and first century BC secular literature to refer to single recipients of heathen worship such as Antiochus Epiphanes and Julius Caesar.[35]

Fifth, contrary to the oft-repeated assertion that the use of *theos* as a Christological title is an un-Pauline locution and thus the noun 'God' cannot

---

34. Nigel Turner, *Grammatical Insights into the New Testament* (Edinburgh: T. & T. Clark, 1965), p. 15.

35. See W. Dittenberger, *Sylloge Inscriptionum Graecarum*, 3rd edn (Hildesheim: Olms, 1960), p. 760.6 = 2nd edn, p. 347.6.

refer to Christ here, I would simply note that our exposition of Romans 9:5 demonstrated that this is not so. Grammatically, historically and biblically the evidence indicates that Paul intended in this verse to describe Christ, not just as our 'God and Saviour' but as our 'great God and Saviour'.

Hebrews 1:8

In this verse the author of Hebrews represents God as saying to his Son, 'Your throne, O God, will last for ever and ever' (NIV). The controversy here is whether *ho theos* is to be construed as a nominative ('God is your throne for ever and ever'), a predicate nominative ('Your throne is God for ever and ever') or a vocative that yields the translation given above. I believe that the writer applies Psalm 45:6 to Jesus in such a way that God addresses his Son directly as God in the ontological sense of the word. This position requires (1) that *ho theos* be construed as a vocative and (2) that the theotic character thus ascribed to Jesus must be understood ontologically and not functionally.

The fact that *ho theos* appears to be nominative in its inflected form means nothing. The so-called articular nominative with vocative force is a well-established idiom in classical Greek, the Septuagint and New Testament Greek. So the case of the noun must be established on other grounds than its case form. I believe that it is to be construed as a vocative for the following four reasons. First, the word order in Hebrews 1:8 most naturally suggests that *ho theos* is vocatival. A vocative immediately after 'Your throne' would be natural. But if *ho theos* were intended as the subject nominative ('God is your throne'), a translation that Nigel Turner regards as a 'grotesque interpretation',[36] it is more likely that *ho theos* would have appeared before 'your throne'. If it were intended as a predicate nominative ('Your throne is God'), a translation that Turner regards as 'only just conceivable',[37] it is more likely that *ho theos* would have been written anarthrously, appearing either before 'Your throne' or after 'for ever and ever'. Second, in the Septuagint of Psalm 45, the psalm that the author is citing, the king is addressed by the vocative *dynate* ('O Mighty One') in Psalm 45:4 and 45:6. This double use of the vocative heightens the probability, given the word order, that in the next verse *ho theos* should be rendered vocatively as 'O God'. Third, although 'about' or 'concerning' is probably the more accurate translation of the preposition *pros* in Hebrews 1:7, it is more likely that *pros* in Hebrews 1:8 should be translated 'to' in the light of the second

---

36. Turner, *Grammatical Insights into the New Testament*, p. 461.
37. Nigel Turner, *A Grammar of New Testament Greek* (Edinburgh: T. & T. Clark, 1965), vol. 3, p. 34.

person character of the quotation itself and on the analogy of the formula in Hebrews 1:13, 5:5 and 7:21. This would suggest that *ho theos* is vocatival. Fourth, the following quotation in Hebrews 1:10–12 (from Ps. 102:25–27) is connected by the simple *kai* (and) to the quotation under discussion in verses 8–9, indicating that it too stands under the governance of the words introducing verses 8–9. In the latter case the Son is clearly addressed as *kyrie* (O Lord). These four textual and syntactical features of the passage clearly indicate that *ho theos* should be construed vocativally, meaning that the author of Hebrews intended to represent God the Father as addressing the Son as 'God'.

I would suggest in the light of the entire context of Hebrews 1 that the Father addresses the Son as God in the ontological sense. This may be seen from the fact that, as a 'Son-revelation' and the final and supreme Word of God to humankind (Heb. 1:2), he is the Heir of all things and the Father's Agent in creating the universe. He abides as the perfect 'radiance' of God's glory and the exact imprint of his nature' (1:3). As God's Son he is superior to the angels, such that it is appropriate that they be commanded to worship him (1:6). He is the Yahweh and the Elohim of Psalm 102 who eternally existed before he created the heavens and the earth (1:10) and who remains eternally the same, though the creation will perish (1:11–12; see 13:8). Because he is all these things it is really adding nothing to what the author has said around the verse to understand him as describing the Son ontologically in the verse as God.

2 Peter 1:1

In his second letter Peter refers to Jesus as 'Jesus Christ' (1:1), 'the Lord and Saviour' (3:2), 'our Lord and Saviour Jesus Christ' (1:11; 2:20; 3:18), and quite interestingly, 'our God and Saviour Jesus Christ' (1:1) (NIV).

In this last reference we find Peter, like Thomas, Paul, and the author of Hebrews before him, employing *theos* as a Christological title. This assertion has not gone unchallenged, the alternative suggestion being that by *theos* Peter intended to refer to the Father. As earlier with Titus 2:13, the issue turns on the question whether by his phrase Peter intended to refer to two persons (the Father and Jesus) or to one person, Jesus only. For the following five reasons I would urge that he refers to Jesus alone:

First, it is the most natural way to read the Greek sentence. If Peter had intended to speak of two persons he could have expressed himself unambiguously by placing 'Saviour' after 'Jesus Christ' or by simply inserting an article before 'Saviour' in the present word order.

Second, as it is, both 'God' and 'Saviour' stand under the regimen of the single article before God, linking the two nouns together as referents to a single person. If one will translate *ho theos and patēr* in 1 Peter 1:3 by 'the God and Father' he should be willing to translate *ho theos and sōtēr* here by 'the God and Saviour'.

Third, five times in 2 Peter, including this one, Peter uses the word 'Saviour'. It is in every instance coupled with a preceding noun (the other four times always with *kyrios*) in precisely the same word order.

> 1:1: 'righteousness of the God of us and Saviour Jesus Christ'
>
> 1:11: 'kingdom of the Lord of us and Saviour Jesus Christ'
>
> 2:20: 'knowledge of the Lord of us and Saviour Jesus Christ'
>
> 3:4: 'commandment of the Lord and Saviour'
>
> 3:18: 'knowledge of the Lord of us and Saviour Jesus Christ'

In each of the last four instances 'Lord' and 'Saviour', standing under the regimen of the single article before 'Lord', indisputably refer to the same person. If we substitute the word *theos* for *kyrios* we have precisely the word order of 1:1: 'righteousness of the God of us and Saviour Jesus Christ'. In other words, the phrases of these verses are perfectly similar and must stand or fall together. The parallelism of word order between the phrase in 1:1 and the other four phrases, where only one person is intended, puts it beyond all reasonable doubt that one person is intended in 1:1 as well.

Fourth, Peter was present when Thomas confessed Jesus to be his 'Lord' and his 'God' (John 20:28). His knowledge of Thomas's confession and of Jesus' approval of it, would have removed any reticence on Peter's part, if he had any, to refer to Jesus here as our *theos*.

Fifth, Peter was also aware of Paul's letters, particularly his letter to the Romans (cf. 2:19 with Rom. 6:16, and 3:15 with Rom. 2:4; 9:22–23; 11:22–23). Almost certainly aware of Paul's reference to Christ as *theos* in Romans 9:5, and according scriptural status as he does to Paul's letters (3:16), again Peter would have seen nothing inappropriate or unscriptural in describing Jesus Christ as God.

We conclude then that 2 Peter 1:1 takes its place alongside Romans 9:5, Titus 2:13, Hebrews 1:8 as a verse in which Jesus is described as God by the use of *theos* as a Christological title.

John 1:1

John begins his Gospel with a remarkable statement about the Logos or 'Word'. What did he intend by this word? The Logos idea goes back to Heraclitus in the sixth century BC who taught that in the midst of the constant ebb and flow in the universe there is an eternal principle of order – the Logos – that makes the world an orderly cosmos. The Stoics employed the notion to solve the problem of dualism and to provide the basis for a rational moral life. Philo, for whom the Logos was both the divine pattern of the world and the power that fashioned it, employed the Logos as a means of mediation between God and the universe itself. The ideas of orderliness, the basis for rationality, the pattern and power that fashioned the world, the means of mediation, and God's word to his world are pregnant with implications for John's opening statement: 'In the beginning', he declares, 'was the Word' – the orderly, rational pattern and power that fashioned the world and that serves to bring God and man together. But John goes farther than any of these insights before him. As we shall see, in addition to understanding the Word as the rational Wisdom of God *he personalizes the Logos and incarnates him* (John 1:14). John deliberately repeats the term three times:

> In the beginning was the Word,
> and the Word was with God,
> and the Word was God.

Each time the term occurs in the nominative case and each time it occurs with *ēn*, the imperfect of *eimi* (to be). In the first clause John informs us that the Word was 'in the beginning', reminiscent of the same phrase in Genesis 1:1. In other words, in the beginning, at the time of the creation of the universe, the Word '[continuously] was' already – not 'came to be'. This is clear not only from the force of the imperfect tense of the verb but also from the fact that John 1:3 informs us that 'all things were made by him, and without him was nothing made that has been made', that is to say, the *being* of the Word pre-existed and antedated the *becoming* of all created things.

In the second clause the Word is both coordinated with God and distinguished in some sense from God as possessing an identity of its own. This sense may be discerned by comparing the phrase in John 1:2b, *ēn pros ton theon*, with its counterpart in 1 John 1:2 where we read that the Word that was 'from the beginning' (v. 1) 'was with the Father' (*ēn pros ton patera*). This implies that John intended by his word 'God' in John 1:1b God the Father. The Word that stands coordinate with God the Father is by clear implication then the pre-existent Son, suggesting that John is thinking of the Logos in personal terms.

The third clause now asserts the obvious: 'And the Word was God'. The fact that *theos* is anarthrous does not mean that it is to be construed qualitatively or adjectively; that is, 'divine', as Moffatt's translation renders it. No standard lexicon offers 'divine' as a meaning for *theos*, nor does the noun become an adjective when it sheds its article. If John had intended an adjectival sense he had an adjective, *theios*, ready at hand. Nor does the fact that *theos* is anarthrous mean that John intended indefiniteness, that is, 'a god', as the Jehovah's

Witnesses' *New World Translation* renders it, as is evident from the recurring instances of this anarthrous noun in John 1:6, 12, 13, 18 where in each case its referent is to God the Father.

By these three clauses John not only identifies the Word as 'God' and by so doing attributes to him the nature or essence of God, but when he also states in 1:2 that 'this one was in the beginning with God' and in 1:3 that 'through him all things were created', the conclusion is inevitable that John intended to teach that the Word is as ultimate as God as his distinctiveness as Son, while his distinctiveness as Son is as ultimate as his deity as God. When John then declared that this pre-existent, uncreated, personal Word who is God's Son 'became flesh' (1:14), he not only went beyond every earlier understanding of the Word but he also clearly intended to teach an incarnational Christology.

John 1:18

This verse confronts us with the problem of determining its original reading in the Greek text. Are we to read *ho monogenēs* (the unique one), *ho monogenēs huios* (the unique Son), *monogenēs theos* (unique God), or *ho monogenēs theos* (the unique God)? For reasons I have provided elsewhere,[38] I believe the fourth reading is the original reading and would translate it 'the unique [Son], [himself] God'. Giving full force to the present participle, *ho ōn* (who is continually) in the third line I would translate John 1:18 as follows:

> God [the Father] no man has seen at any time;
> The unique [Son], [himself] God,
> who is continually in the bosom of the Father –
> that one revealed him.

Very probably we have then in this concluding verse of John's Prologue another occurrence of *theos* as a Christological title, and the context clearly suggests that John regarded Jesus as the incarnate Son of God.

1 John 5:20

Translated literally, this verse reads, 'And we know that the Son of God has come, and he has given us understanding in order that we may know the True One. And we are in the True One in his Son Jesus Christ. This one is the true God and eternal life.' Did John intend by his 'This one is the true God' to refer to the Father or the Son? This is the issue before us.

---

38. See my *New Systematic Theology of the Christian Faith*, pp. 301–303.

A strong case can be made for understanding the Father as its referent, and fine exegetes have espoused this interpretation. But I believe that four grammatical considerations tell against it. First, the nearest possible antecedent to the demonstrative pronoun ('This one') is the immediately preceding phrase 'his Son Jesus Christ', and it is a generally sound exegetical principle to find the antecedent of a demonstrative pronoun in the nearest possible noun preceding it. Second, to choose the more distant antecedent – 'the True One' – injects a tautology into the verse for one does not need to be informed that the Father who has twice been identified as the 'True One' is 'the true God', whereas, by applying it to its nearer antecedent the thought is advanced and the tautology is avoided. Third, both the singular demonstrative pronoun ('This one') and the fact that 'true God' and 'eternal life' stand under the regimen of the single article before 'God', thereby binding the two predicates closely together, indicates that by the two terms John is thinking of one person. Because the Father is nowhere designated 'Eternal Life', whereas the Son is so designated in 1 John 1:2, these two combined predicates better fit the Son than the Father. Fourth, while John in John 17:3 describes the Father as 'the true God', he either describes Jesus or records that Jesus describes himself as 'the true Light' (John 1:9; 1 John 2:8), 'the true Bread' (John 6:32), 'the true Vine' (John 15:1), 'the true One' (Rev. 3:7; 19:11), 'the true Witness' (Rev. 3:14) and 'the true Sovereign' (Rev. 6:10). We have already seen that John is not hesitant to describe Jesus as God. So there is nothing to preclude his bringing together the adjective 'true' and the noun 'God' and applying them in their combined form to Jesus Christ, the view held by many equally fine interpreters. If this was his intention, then 1 John 5:20 is yet another verse in which *theos* is employed as a Christological title.

It was in the light of such biblical data as we have surveyed above and much more as well,[39] such as Paul's pericope in Colossians 1:15–20 and his statement in Colossians 2:9, that the Christians of the first five centuries – as monotheistic in their outlook as the ancient Israelites and who in fact believed that they were worshipping the God of Israel when they worshipped God the Father, God the Son and God the Holy Spirit – realized that they had to formulate their doctrine of God in trinitarian terms. That is to say, the early church's creedalized trinitarianism was a deduction from its conviction that Jesus Christ and the Holy Spirit were distinct divine persons. The formulating process itself, precipitated in the first three centuries particularly by the emergence of

---

39. See my *Jesus, Divine Messiah: The New and Old Testament Witness* (Ross-shire, Scotland: Mentor, 2003).

second-century Gnosticism and the Logos Christologies, by third-century Sabellianism, and by early fourth-century Arianism, brought the church to a very basic but real crystallization of the doctrine of the Trinity in the Nicene Creed of AD 325, a crystallization that it continued to refine, especially with regard to the person of God the Son, in the Nicaeno-Constantinopolitan Creed of AD 381, the fifth-century anti-Nestorian statement of the Council of Ephesus in AD 431, and the Definition of Chalcedon in AD 451 – this last document continuing to this day as 'the touchstone of Christological orthodoxy' and 'the supreme expression of an orthodox, biblical faith'.[40] Its most significant paragraph reads:

> In agreement, then, with the holy [Nicene] fathers we all unanimously teach that we should confess that our Lord Jesus Christ is one and the same Son; the same perfect in deity and the same perfect in manness, truly God and truly man, the same of a rational soul and body, consubstantial with the Father according to the deity and the same consubstantial with us according to the manness; like us according to all things except sin; begotten of the Father before the ages according to the deity and in the last days the same, for us and for our salvation, [born] of Mary the virgin, the *Theotokos* according to the manness; one and the same Christ, Son, Lord, only-begotten, being made known in two natures without confusion [*asynchytōs*], without change [*atreptōs*], without division [*adiairetōs*], without separation [*achōristōs*]; the distinction of the natures being by no means removed because of the union but rather the property of each nature being preserved and concurring in one person [*prosōpon*] and one *hypostasis*, not parted or divided into two persons but one and the same Son and only-begotten God, Word, the Lord Jesus Christ, as the prophets of old and the Lord Jesus Christ himself have taught us about him, and the [Nicene] Creed of our fathers has handed down.

Some problems in the doctrine of the Son's real incarnation

How are Christologies 'from above' to be harmonized with Christologies 'from below'?

The problem
Classical Christology has always been charged with being a Christology 'from above'; that is, its formulation begins with a Christ whose deity is already a

---

40. Gerald Bray, *Creeds, Councils and Christ* (Ross-shire, Scotland: Mentor, 1997), pp. 150, 162.

given, who already being God the Son became in the act of incarnation man. Such a Christology, it is maintained, always threatens the genuinely human existence of Jesus. Maurice Wiles puts the matter this way:

> throughout the long history of attempts to present a reasoned account of Christ as both fully human and fully divine, the church has never succeeded in offering a consistent or convincing picture. Most commonly it has been the humanity of Christ that has suffered; the picture presented has been a figure who cannot by our standards of judgment . . . be regarded as recognizably human.[41]

Better would it be, many suggest, if Christology would take its starting point in the human Jesus, that is, 'from below', and ascend by careful theologizing to whatever kind of affirmation of his divinity that that theologizing will consistently permit. Millard J. Erickson speaks of the alternative effort to integrate Christology 'from above' and Christology 'from below' as the 'Augustinian model' over against what he terms respectively as the 'fideistic' model in which one begins 'from above' with a Christ of the *kerygma* who is detached from history and the 'Thomistic' model in which one begins 'from below' with evidence that is then employed to interpret and integrate the data supplied by inquiry into the historical Jesus in order to demonstrate the supernatural character of Jesus.[42]

My solution

I think evangelicals must heed the implicit warning from those who prefer to begin 'from below' with the human Jesus and admit that it is altogether possible in their theologizing so to concentrate their attention on the deity of Christ that his humanness suffers eclipse in the church's witness and proclamation. The church must say 'Enough!' to such docetism wherever it appears and recognize that the *human* face of our sympathizing heavenly High Priest has a marvellous attractiveness about it (see *Belgic Confession*, Chapter 26).

It is also true that evangelicals may have been unduly hasty at times in 'beating the world over the head' with its biblical proof texts for the deity of Christ. They must reclaim lost high ground here by recognizing that there is something powerfully winsome and compelling about the man Jesus and his

---

41. Maurice Wiles, 'Christianity without Incarnation?' in John Hick, ed., *The Myth of God Incarnate* (Philadelphia: Westminster, 1977), p. 4.

42. Millard J. Erickson, *Christian Theology*, 2nd edn (Grand Rapids: Baker, 1998), pp. 682–691.

ethical teaching, his conflicts with temptation, his attitude towards human suffering and the felt alienation of human beings, and his sensitive views on life in this world in general as depicted in the Gospel narratives. The church can surely use Jesus' humanity to real apologetic value to define what true humanness is in a day when men feel 'dehumanized' in so many ways. After all, we must not overlook the fact that in the days of his earthly ministry men encountered and perceived Jesus first as a man (Phil. 2:8; Heb. 2:14–17). So there is something that can be said for a biblically oriented Christology 'from below' as long as it does not lose sight of everything else the New Testament teaches about him.

Beyond this, we must question the conclusions of any Christology 'from below' that claims to be the key for unlocking the real meaning of the human Jesus for us. We must ask, What are its underlying presuppositions? What philosophical, sociological, psychological and psychoanalytic theories are controlling it as it seeks to isolate out of the whole biblical picture of Jesus the 'truly scientific' elements of Jesus' humanness in order to build a Christology 'from below' that will also address the real needs of men? Indeed, we must ask, Do any of the diverse portraits of the Christ 'from below' proposed to date deserve our intellectual and religious allegiance? Are we to follow Bultmann's demythologized Jesus to 'authentic existence'? Or Tillich's Jesus as the 'Bearer of the New Being'? What about Rahner's Jesus as 'the unique, supreme case of the total actualization of human destiny'? Or Schoonenberg's Jesus as 'the embodiment of God's presence'? Or Schillebeeckx's Jesus as 'the revelation of the eschatological face of all humanity'? Or Goulder's Jesus as 'the man of universal destiny'? Or Lampe's Jesus as the 'supreme exemplar of perfect and unbroken response to the Father'? Where are we to pinpoint the uniqueness of Jesus' humanity? In his 'being for others', his 'being for God', his 'sinlessness', or what? Whatever one's answer here, every humanist Christologist 'from below' must be willing squarely to face the question, 'Does my Christology "from below" say enough, in the light of such biblical data as were presented in the first part of this chapter, to justify the church declaring him in its worship and its confessions to be both divine and human?' Every Christology 'from below' presupposes that there is some kind of continuity between the human and the divine in Jesus that can be displayed by means of the theologizing process that makes it possible to ascend in thought from reflecting in some fashion upon Jesus' humanity to his 'divinity' that requires the ascription of 'Godness' to him. However, the results thus far have been dismally meagre in this respect, since none of the representations of Jesus' 'divinity' by these constructions raises us up that high. Even his being the supreme revelation of God to man does not require that we believe, when we

reflect upon Jesus, that we are beholding God himself. Not even a real historical resurrection from the dead, based upon the fact of the empty tomb and
the subsequent post-crucifixion appearances, *requires* that one must necessarily ascribe ontological deity to him. Herein resides the fundamental problem
that every Christology 'from below' must honestly face: Does its construction
compel us to move beyond Jesus' humanness to Thomas's great confession of
John 20:28? Or does it offer to the church and so to the world a Jesus whose
'deity' in the final analysis is only his total dedication to God viewed in his
special mission from God or as the fullness of God's Spirit within him? The
church must seriously inquire whether such Christologies 'from below' do not
rule out at the outset, by their very methodologies, one alternative; namely, the
biblical ascription of ontological deity in the classical sense to him inasmuch
as one cannot ascend by induction from the finite to the infinite.

The church must clearly understand what is at stake when asked to grant
legitimacy to the modern efforts to explain Jesus 'from below', for if he is only,
after all, a man in these Christologies and their advocates urge that we should
worship him, that act of devotion constitutes idolatry and stands under biblical anathema. But if he is not only human but also God in the classical sense
and our theologizing either refuses to acknowledge him as such or fails to recognize him as such, that refusal or that failure constitutes either apostasy or
unbelief. And the Scriptures inform us in this latter case that only divine judgment awaits such recalcitrance (John 8:24).

While they may argue that classical Christology has insurmountable tensions and difficulties within it, Christologists 'from below' must face the fact
that their Christologies also have their own sets of tensions and problems. And
I for one prefer the tensions in classical Christology over their tensions. They
would do well to heed and to work within the constraints of the following
feature that Colin E. Gunton observes in the New Testament's depiction of
Jesus:

> amidst all the diversity of [the New Testament's] Christology one thing remains
> constant, and that is the refusal to abstract the historical events from their overall
> theological meaning. The historical man Jesus is never construed apart from his
> meaning as the presence of the eternal God in time. The New Testament . . . will not
> allow us to choose between time and eternity, immanence and transcendence, in our
> talk about Jesus. The two are always given together.[43]

---

43. Colin E. Gunton, *Yesterday and Today: A Study of Continuities in Christology* (Grand
Rapids: Eerdmans, 1983), p. 207.

So is there a sense in which we may legitimately hold to both kinds of Christology – that 'from below' and that 'from above' – in our systematic theologizing? I would say there is, but only in the sense clarified and illustrated by Benjamin B. Warfield many years ago:

> John's Gospel does not differ from the other Gospels as the Gospel of the divine Christ in contradistinction to the Gospels of the human Christ. All the Gospels are Gospels of the divine Christ . . . But John's Gospel differs from the other Gospels in taking from the divine Christ its starting point. The others begin on the plane of human life. John begins in the inter-relations of the divine persons in eternity.
>
> [The Synoptic Gospels] all begin with the man Jesus, whom they set forth as the Messiah in whom God has visited his people; or rather, as himself, God come to his people, according to his promise. The movement in them is from below upward . . . The movement in John, on the contrary, is from above downward. He takes his start from the Divine Word, and descends from him to the human Jesus in whom he was incarnated. This Jesus, says the others, is God. This God, says John, became Jesus.[44]

In sum, I would urge that our task as systematic theologians is simply that of listening as carefully as we can to Holy Scripture *in its entirety* and explicating all that we hear there about both Jesus' deity and humanness as faithfully as we can in order to benefit the church and to enhance the faithful propagation of the one true gospel. It is in his willingness to submit his mind to all that the Scriptures teach that the systematic theologian best emulates the example of his Lord, and it is in submission to Scripture that he best reflects that disciple character to which he has by grace been summoned.

How are 'functional' Christologies to be harmonized with 'ontological' Christologies?

The problem

Classical Christology is often charged with depicting Jesus only in ontological terms and not in the functional terms of the New Testament. What this means is that classical Christology is said to depict Christ in terms of what he is *in himself* (*in se*) rather then representing him, as the New Testament does, in terms of what he is *for us* (*pro nobis*). The functional Christologist contends that when

---

44. Benjamin B. Warfield, 'John's First Word', in John E. Meeter, ed., *Selected Shorter Writings of Benjamin B. Warfield* (Nutley, N.J.: P. & R., 1970), vol. 1, pp. 148–149.

the New Testament asks 'Who is Christ?' it never intends to ask exclusively or even primarily 'What is his nature?' but first of all 'What is his function?'

The early Fathers, it is alleged, influenced as they were by Aristotelian and Platonic categories of thought, in their conciliar descriptions of Christ unwittingly conceptualized the person of Christ in terms of 'natures'. As a result they viewed him in ontological categories as 'one person with two natures', rather than in the rich functional language of the theologies of the New Testament. The legacy of their efforts, it is alleged, is an unrelieved tension in the church's creedal portrayal of Christ that either threatens to rend asunder the unity of his person or places his essential man-ness in jeopardy. The Christ of Chalcedon, it is maintained, is neither descriptive of the Christ of the Gospels nor relevant in our times when people no longer think in ontological categories but rather in functional categories. In short, it is argued, classical Christology is both unreal and unintelligible because of its ontological conceptualization of Jesus.

My solution

I would counter this charge by first reminding the functional Christologist that the issues before the early councils were not 'What is Christ's function? What has he done for us?' Rather, they were faced by the questions 'Was the Logos created or uncreated?', 'How is it that the Father has a Son?' and 'How are we to relate the deity of the Logos to Jesus' man-ness so that justice is done to both?' I would also contend, against the notion that ontological considerations are 'Greek' and foreign to Hebraic thought, that the Jews of Jesus' day had a very good grasp of their God's ontological distinction over against his creation. It was precisely their knowledge of and conviction about the ontologically informed Creator–creature distinction that underlay their horror that a man standing in their midst would claim to be the Son of God in such a unique and essential sense that he made himself equal with God (John 5:17–18; see also John 8:58–59; 10:33; 19:7). For them this was blasphemy. And I would suggest that the reason for their hostility was grounded in Jesus' claim of ontological continuity between himself as God's Son and the Creator God as his Father. Still further, I would insist that it is superficial to suggest that people can forever be content only with questions concerning what Jesus does for them and never address the question of who he is ontologically. While it is doubtless true that often it was what the first disciples saw him do that drew them to him, very quickly they also began to speculate, in the light of what they saw him doing, about who he was. When his disciples saw him still the storm they did not ask, 'What does this mean for us?' Rather, they asked, 'Who is this, that even the wind and the sea obey him?' Matthew's report of their question is even more pointed: '*What kind of person* [*Potapos*] is this that even the wind and the sea obey him?'

In fact, Jesus himself did not allow his disciples merely to bask in the brilliance of his teaching and the wonder of his deeds. At the appropriate point in their education Jesus raised the questions 'Who do people say that I am?' and 'Who do *you* say that I am?' Peter responded with both a functional and an ontological answer: 'You are the Messiah [functional], the Son of the living God [ontological]!' (Matt. 16:13–16). That the second part of Peter's response contained ontological intention is apparent from Jesus' declaration that Peter was the blessed beneficiary of the Father's revelatory activity (see Matt. 11:27), a pronouncement hardly necessary if Peter were only confessing Jesus' messianic status, since this was a perception many others were entertaining about him as well (John 7:31). Jesus also forced the religious authorities of his day to face the ontological issue that later the Council of Nicaea in AD 325 would address when he asked them, 'What do you think of the Messiah? *Whose Son is he?*' When they replied that he was 'the son of David', Jesus asked them, 'How is it then that David, speaking by the Spirit, calls him "Lord"? For he says, "The Lord said to my Lord: / 'Sit at my right hand / until I put your enemies / under your feet."' If then David calls him "Lord", how can he be his son?' (Matt. 22:44–45, NIV). How indeed! If ever a question was designed to compel a consideration of ontological 'natures' this is it!

So whatever one may say about the concerns and interests of the New Testament witness to Jesus, the one thing one must not say is that the New Testament does not raise ontological questions concerning Christ's person. In fact, the New Testament presses the importance of the ontological issue by reporting that Jesus grounds a man's eternal destiny in a right view of *who he is*: 'If you do not believe that I am, you will indeed die in your sins' (John 8:24, NIV). So again, whatever else one may say about the concerns of the New Testament, he must not say that its interest in Jesus was purely functional and never ontological. I would even contend that the church at Nicaea was not in error when it declared of Christ that he was 'perfect in deity and perfect in man-ness, truly God and truly man . . . of the same essence with the Father according to deity and of the same essence with us according to man-ness'.

I do not intend, of course, to suggest for a moment that one should concern himself only with ontological issues when considering Christ. That would be tantamount to reducing Christ's salvific work to a narrowly conceived ontological Christology. But I do intend to erect a hedge against the other extreme that would, by means of a functional Christology, virtually reduce Christology to his salvific work. We must never forget that the biblical witness is interested in *both* the person *and* work of Christ. Both are essential to orthodoxy. Neither must be forgotten. Neither by itself yields an orthodox understanding of the New Testament picture of Christ.

When I wrote my *Jesus, Divine Messiah* some years ago, I was quite aware that I wrote as a systematic theologian and not as a New Testament scholar. Some New Testament scholars at the time judged that I had read the New Testament witness, particularly the Gospels, 'too flatly' at times, that I left no room for genuine differences between the Messiah in the Old Testament, the Christ of the Synoptics, the Christ of John's Gospel, the Christ of Paul's theology, and the Christ of the other witnesses in the New Testament. They said that I had failed to give sufficient place to the role that 'functional Christology' played in the 'development' of New Testament Christology as a whole. They thought that I had read the Gospels 'too historically' because I did not enter in any significant way into 'tradition criticism', a major interest in current New Testament research.

I shall now say that I had a twofold purpose for doing in the first part of this chapter the little bit of exegesis that I did about the evidence for Jesus' deity. I wanted not only to spell out again for the reader what he should believe about Jesus' deity but also to illustrate how the student of Scripture, not just systematic theologians but New Testament scholars as well, should go about the work of exegesis. So I reject the charges that some laid at my feet that as a systematic theologian I was reading the New Testament witness to Christ too flatly and did not do justice to the functional Christ of the New Testament. But I do want to assure my colleagues in the field of New Testament research that I hold no brief against any insights of functional Christology that can be *exegetically* sustained. But *they must be exegetically sustained!* For if these New Testament scholars may have been troubled because, in their opinion, I read the Scriptures 'too flatly' here or 'too historically' there in reaching my conclusions about Jesus in that volume, I must say that I too am troubled by what I see too often as a willingness of at least some New Testament scholars to postulate differences between and to impose 'functional' categories upon biblical statements where frankly I as a systematic theologian who also have a keen interest in and strong desire for careful exegesis, find no warrant for doing so. I would respectfully suggest that contemporary New Testament scholarship, even some *evangelical* New Testament scholarship, often reads the New Testament writers *too developmentally and functionally*. I would also suggest that New Testament scholarship, as the result of form criticism, redaction criticism and genre criticism, may be reading the Gospels today too much as if they were mere forms of ancient secular literature and losing sight of the fact that their authors, after all is said and done, intended their (inspired) accounts to be *historical* records of those aspects of the person and ministry of Jesus that were central to the apostolic witness and the proclamation of the gospel.

Of course, no knowledgeable person can or will deny that the New Testament writers expressed their Christological convictions in a variety of ways. And to the degree that their expressions and vocabularies vary, to that same degree there will be different nuances in some of their perceptions. In my opinion, however, when the New Testament writers are compared, the composite picture of Jesus that results from their combined apostolic voice (see 1 Cor. 15:11) only makes for a richer depiction of Jesus. This richness is what lies behind the fact that we have four canonical portrayals of Jesus' life, ministry and passion. But however much or little the New Testament writers differ in their nuanced perceptions of other things, such as the terms by which they represent the Messiah's salvific work (ransom, propitiation, reconciliation, redemption etc.), it is my conviction that they do not differ essentially in their basic perception of Jesus as the divine Messiah who by the act of incarnation came to earth to save sinners. I would argue that their writings indicate that they all wrote out of a deeply held conviction that Jesus of Nazareth was in fact the promised Messiah of the Old Testament, that he was God incarnate, that he was God in the same sense that Christians today would say that God the Father is God, and that they intended to communicate these basic perceptions of him to others. If I as a systematic theologian am wrong in this conviction, I want my error to be demonstrated to me by solid, careful exegesis of the biblical text. Such interdisciplinary dialogue can only result in a better, deeper and truer understanding of Jesus.

How are the methods of systematic theology and biblical theology to be harmonized with respect to Christology?

The problem

Systematic theology is that methodological approach to the study of the Bible that views the Holy Scripture as a *completed* revelation. The systematic theologian, attempting to answer the question 'What does the whole Bible teach about such and such a topic?' seeks to understand the plan, purpose and didactic intention of the divine mind revealed in sacred Scripture holistically, and to arrange that plan, purpose and didactic intention in orderly and coherent fashion as articles of the Christian faith. As he approaches Scripture he presumes as a given that he must take seriously the hermeneutical principle known as the 'analogy of Scripture' that insists that every Scripture text must be interpreted in the light of the entirety of Scripture. No Scripture text is to be read in isolation from the rest of the Bible.

Biblical theology, on the other hand, approaches Scripture as an *unfolding* revelation and seeks to interpret every Scripture text mainly, if not exclusively, within the historical context of the specific place in which it stands in the progressive unfolding of divine revelation. I have taught and practised both methods and appreciate the insights that both bring to the task of rightly interpreting the Scriptures.

Over the last couple of decades, however, the biblical theological method has more and more been overpowering the systematic theology method, its advocates urging that the biblical theological method is sensitive to the actual organic nature of the corpus of revelation while the systematic theology method imposes an extra-biblical structure on the revelation of the Scriptures. Walter C. Kaiser's book *Toward an Exegetical Theology: Biblical Exegesis for Preaching and Teaching*,[45] is a case in point. In the interest of giving the discipline of biblical theology its just due in the light of its vision of the progressiveness of revelation, Kaiser calls for a syntactical-theological method of exegesis composed of contextual, syntactical, verbal, theological and homiletical analyses of the biblical text. I commend him for his insistence that the task of the preacher is to discover the one intended meaning of the author in a given passage by means of sound canons of grammatical-historical hermeneutics. I also think that it is only positive gain when he urges the preacher to 'principlize' the author's intended meaning in timeless abiding truth to meet the contemporary church's current needs. But the area of his proposed methodology where I would contend that the church must *not* follow Kaiser is his insistence in many places[46] upon what he calls 'the analogy of (antecedent) Scripture'. What he means by this phrase is this: in determining the author's intended meaning in a given passage, *in no case* is the interpreter, in order to 'unpack the meaning or to enhance the usability of the individual text which is the object of [his] study',[47] to use teaching from a passage written or spoken later than the biblical statement being analysed. In arriving at the author's intended meaning, the exegete must restrict himself to a study of the passage itself and to 'affirmations found in passages that have *preceded* in time the passage under study'.[48] Kaiser's canon here, as I said, grows out of his concern to give the discipline of biblical theology its just

45. Walter C. Kaiser, Jr, *Toward an Exegetical Theology: Biblical Exegesis for Preaching and Teaching* (Grand Rapids: Baker, 1981).

46. E.g, ibid, pp. 82, 134–140.

47. Ibid., p. 140.

48. Ibid., p. 136 (emphasis original).

due in the light of its vision of the progressiveness of revelation. To permit subsequent revelation to determine a given earlier author's intention is to 'level off' the process of revelation in a way overly favourable to the interests of systematic theology.

My solution

Aside from the vexing fact that tells against Kaiser's hermeneutical canon that we just do not know for sure the chronological relationship that exists between some portions of Scripture,[49] and hence we could fail to use an antecedent bit of revelation or 'misappropriate' a subsequent piece of revelation for exegetical purposes. I would stress that there are Christological passages where clearly there is no way the exegete can discern what the author or speaker intended without the benefit of *subsequent* revelational insight. For example, apart from Peter's authoritative insight in Acts 2:24–31 into Psalm 16:9–11, there is no way, I would contend, that the exegete can discern, on the grounds allowed him by Kaiser, that David was not speaking of his own (and others') resurrection when he wrote Psalm 16, but that he wrote *specifically* and *exclusively* of the Messiah's resurrection. Grammatical-historical exegesis of Psalm 16 and comparison of this psalm with previous revelation simply will not yield the disclosure that David, 'Seeing what was ahead, he spoke of the resurrection of the Christ' (Acts 2:30, 31, NIV; cf. Paul's similar argument in Acts 13:34–35).

Another example: apart from John's later teaching in John 2:21, there is no way that the preacher can read Jesus' words 'Destroy this temple, and I will raise it in three days' (John 2:19, NIV) and know that it was his body to which Jesus referred. (It should be remembered that Christ's statement in John 2:19 was spoken some years before his resurrection and a good many years before John wrote his Gospel.)

One more example. Apart from the historical facts of the incarnation of God the Son and the special manifestation of God the Holy Spirit at Pentecost and then subsequent New Testament revelation, it is extremely doubtful that an exegete could discover all the balancing elements of the *doctrine* of the Trinity from the Old Testament alone, and yet I feel sure that Kaiser believes

---

49. E.g. was Obadiah written before or after Joel? Was Psalm 'x' written before or after Psalm 'y'? Was Mark written before or after Matthew? Was Colossians written before or after Ephesians? Was 2 Peter written before or after Jude? Was the Johannine literature written before or after the destruction of Jerusalem in AD 70?

that these elements are there and that the Old Testament intends to reveal the *fact* of the Trinity throughout (e.g. Gen. 1:26; Pss. 45:6; 110 etc.). I would urge, therefore, that we take seriously Warfield's (I believe, correct) insight that the Old Testament is like a room richly furnished but dimly lit. The New Testament does not bring 'furniture' into the Old Testament 'room' that was not there before, but it does illumine the 'room' so that we can see the 'furniture' that was there all the time and that was doubtless intended to be there all along by the Old Testament writer himself.

I agree with Kaiser, of course, that there can be an undisciplined employment of the New Testament to discern the intention of the Old. But I would suggest that Kaiser, by his canon of the 'analogy of (antecent) Scripture', has overreacted against what he discerns as one abuse and fallen into the ditch on the other side of the issue. I would urge, therefore, that the hermeneutical rules in both disciplines should be viewed as contributing to the task of biblical interpretation, but they must never be played off over against each other with one taking the position of first among equals. This means that while the exegete – be he or she systematician or biblical theologian – must surely first seek to understand every biblical statement within the historical period in which it occurs in the process of revelation (this is the 'historical' part of the classical 'grammatical-historical' method of exegesis); he must never conclude that he has properly understood a given author's intended meaning *until he has honoured the 'analogy of Scripture' and taken into account the teaching of the entire Scripture, especially the New Testament.* This is only urging an attitude in harmony with the time-honoured hermeneutical axioms 'The New is in the Old concealed; the Old is in the New revealed' and 'The New within the Old is latent; the Old within the New is patent.'

Was the Son always the Son of the Father or did he become the Son of God by his incarnation?

The problem

I can be brief here by employing one illustration of this problem. Palm Helm maintains that *all* the biblical, and especially the New Testament, data advancing the concept of Jesus' divine sonship are intended to reveal him in the economy of salvation and *not* as he is in himself; that is to say, that the Father's begetting of the Son and therefore the 'sonship' of the eternal Logos is a metaphor for his incarnation. He writes:

> I believe that the verses [regarding the relationship between Father and Son to
> which Roger Beckwith alludes such as John 1:3; 6:38; 10:36; 16:28; 17:5, 24; Col. 1:16;

Heb. 1:2; Rev. 3:14] may all be understood, without exception, in the references they make to 'Father' and 'Son', as reading back into the eternal relationships of the godhead what became true at the Incarnation.[50]

My solution

With Helm's argument I cannot agree. The persons of the Godhead have eternally existed within the ontological Trinity as the Father, the Son and the Holy Spirit. A couple of examples showing this, beyond those Beckwith advanced, will have to suffice.

A careful exposition of the word 'son' in the parable of the wicked farmers (Matt. 21:37; Mark 6; Luke 20:13) will show that Jesus represented himself as the Son *before* his mission and as God's beloved Son *whether he be sent or not*. As Vos writes:

> His being sent describes . . . his Messiahship, but this Messiahship was brought about precisely by the necessity for sending one who was the highest and dearest that the lord of the vineyard could delegate . . . The sonship, therefore, existed *antecedently* to the Messianic mission.[51]

This is also the case in Paul's use of the word 'Son' in Romans 1:3; 8:3, 32 and Galatians 4:4. These verses clearly suggest that the Son enjoyed an existence with God the Father prior to his being sent into the world on his mission of mercy and that in this pre-existent state he stood in a relation to the Father as the Father's unique Son (see also Col. 1:16–17 where the Son is said to be 'before all things').[52]

Then as we saw earlier, the Word that John 1:1 coordinates in the beginning with *God* before the creation of all things with its *pros ton theon* is in its counterpart in 1 John 1:2 coordinated in the beginning with the *Father* with its *pros ton patera*, showing that John was thinking of the Word who was in the beginning with God in John 1:1 in *personal* terms as the Son of the Father.

We systematicians should give careful thought to this issue, but I would urge here that we should not discard cavalierly the eternal sonship of the Son in favour of simply affirming the eternal existence of the Logos. For with the rejection of the Son's eternal sonship also goes the Father's eternal fatherhood

---

50. Paul Helm, 'Of God, and of the Holy Trinity: A Response to Dr. Beckwith', *Churchman* 115.4 (2001), p. 357.

51. Vos, *Self-Disclosure of Jesus*, pp. 162–163 (my emphasis).

52. See my fuller treatment of this matter in my *Jesus, Divine Messiah*, pp. 373–375.

with tragic results. With what are we then left in regard to distinguishing properties in the persons of the Godhead that will undergird classical trinitarianism?

Does the doctrine of the anhypostasia necessitate the conclusion that the Definition of Chalcedon is docetic or at least reductionistic in its representation of Christ's human nature?

The problem

Christological orthodoxy, represented by the Definition of Chalcedon, maintains that in the incarnation the Son of God, the second Person of the Godhead, already a self-conscious, self-determining person within the Godhead, took into union with himself not a human person but only a human nature.[53] This doctrine is known as the doctrine of the *anhypostasia* that literally means 'no person'. Critics of the Definition charge that it is docetic or at the very least reductionistic in that it denies to Christ's human nature a human personality. This charge deserves careful reflection and a studied response.

My solution

While it is true that the Fathers at Chalcedon taught that the Son of God did not take into union with himself a human person (if he had he would then have been two persons, but never does he say anything on the order of 'Truly, *we* say to you'). It is equally true that they never for a moment held that Jesus as a human being had an *impersonal* human nature. Jesus was personal as a man by virtue of the union of his human nature in the person of the Son. In other words, as a person the Son of God gave personal identity to the human nature he had assumed without losing or compromising his divine nature. Never for a moment did the man Jesus exist for a moment apart from the union of natures in the one divine person. This means that the man Jesus from the moment of conception was personal by virtue of the union of his human nature in the divine Son. David F. Wells states this well:

> The Definition asserted that it was to a human nature . . . rather than a person . . . that the divine Word was joined. This means that all of the human qualities and powers were present in Jesus, but that the ego, the self-conscious acting subject, was in fact a composite union of the human and the divine.[54]

---

53. By 'person' is meant a self-conscious, self-determining entity; by 'nature' is meant a complex of attributes that makes a thing what it is.

54. David F. Wells, *The Person of Christ* (Westchester, Ill.: Crossway, 1984), p. 108.

This explanation of the personality of the human nature of Jesus has come to be known as the nuanced doctrine of the *enhypostasia*; that is to say, in the incarnate Christ the humanity of Jesus that was indeed personal from the moment of its virginal conception derived its personality from its union in the person of the Son. This 'one person' teaching implies that there were not two 'self-consciousnesses' within Jesus. Prior to the incarnation he was self-consciously divine in the sense that he was in possession of the full complex of divine attributes. After and by virtue of the incarnation the Son was still self-consciously divine but now also consciously – not *self*-consciously – human as well. John Murray writes:

> We do not find our Lord speaking or acting in terms of merely human personality. In the various situations reported to us in the Gospel record, it is a striking fact that he identifies himself as one who sustains to the Father his unique relationship as the only-begotten Son, as the one whose self-identity, whose self, is conceived in such terms. It is indeed true that he speaks and acts as one who is human and intensely aware of his human identity. He shows the limitations inseparable from this identity, and also the limitations prescribed by the task given him to fulfill in human nature. But it is highly significant that in situations where his human identity, and the limitations incident to this identity and to his commission, are most in evidence, there appears the profound consciousness of his filial relationship and of his divine self-identity (see Matt. 24:36; 26:39, 42, 53; John 12:27. See also John 5:26, 27; 17:1; Rom. 1:3; Heb. 5:7–9; 1 John 1:7). In such contexts the experiences that were his, in virtue of being human, are consciously in the forefront in all the intensity of their being. But just then the consciousness of his intradivine Sonship is in the foreground as defining the person that he is. And the inference would seem to be that our Lord's *self*-identity and *self*-consciousness can never be thought of in terms of human nature alone. Personality cannot be predicated of him except as it draws within its scope his specifically divine identity. There are two centers of consciousness but not of self-consciousness.[55]

This is the best explanation I have ever read concerning this implication in the *anhypostasia*. But perhaps if contemporary systematic theologians would give more thought to this matter they could throw additional light on this surpassing mystery.

---

55. John Murray, 'The Person of Christ', in *Collected Writings of John Murray* (Edinburgh: Banner of Truth, 1977), vol. 2, pp. 137–138. See also his discussion of the *anhypostasia* in his review of D. M. Baillie's *God Was in Christ*, in *Collected Writings of John Murray*, vol. 3, pp. 342–343.

Did God the Son divest himself of any of his divine attributes when he became a man?

The problem

Even those who are most zealous to defend the altogether transcendent character of the Christmas miracle of the incarnation and the true deity and true humanity of Christ as these are defined by the Definition of Chalcedon have not always done so with doctrinal consistency. For example, classical Lutheranism affirms by means of its doctrine of the *communicatio idiomatum* (the communication of attributes) in the unity of the one person our Lord's divine nature at the virginal conception virtually 'divinized' his human nature by communicating its attributes to it. The human nature of Christ, after assuming divine dimensions by virtue of this communication of divine attributes to it, either hid or divested itself of its divine dimensions during the days of Christ's earthly ministry. At Christ's resurrection, Lutherans argue, his human nature began to manifest its divine dimensions, becoming thereby 'ubiquitous'; that is, capable of being *physically* present 'in, with and under' the elements of bread and wine on all the tables of Lutheranism at the same time. This Christological construction, in my opinion, is neither true to the Definition of Chalcedon that states with no equivocation that Christ was made known to us 'in two natures without confusion [*asynchytōs*], without change [*atreptōs*] . . . , the distinction of the natures being by no means removed because of the union but rather the property of each nature being preserved', nor does it 'form [any] part of Catholic Christianity'.[56]

The Lutheran construction is a form of kenosis[57] that pertains only to the 'divinized' *human* nature and only for a time. Another type of kenosis is a more serious deviation from classical Christology because it pertains to Christ's divine nature, asserting that God the Son 'emptied', that is, divested, himself of one or more of his divine attributes such as omnipresence and omniscience or of the use of these attributes when he assumed human flesh. This second kenotic view was first propounded by Gottfried Thomasius (1802–1975), a German Lutheran theologian, and it has been perpetuated

---

56. Charles Hodge, *Systematic Theology* (Grand Rapids: Eerdmans, 1952), vol. 2, p. 418.

57. The word 'kenosis' is from the Greek verb *kenoō* that appears in Philippians 2:7 in its inflected form *ekenōsen*, whose root meaning is 'to empty'. In this current context the term 'kenosis' designates those Christological constructions that maintain that God the Son 'emptied' himself in some sense of at least some of his divine attributes when he became a man.

with variations to this day. Unwittingly, even many evangelical theologians, pastors and laymen today describe the effect that the Son's assumption of human nature had upon his divine nature in kenotic terms. In his *Christian Theology* Millard J. Erickson argues that the Son of God emptied himself, not of the form of God, but of his equality with God (his Jewish adversaries certainly did not think this), accepting 'certain limitations upon the functioning of his divine attributes'. For example, though the Son 'still had the power to be everywhere . . . he was limited in the exercise of that power by possession of a human body'.[58]

In his *The Word Became Flesh* Erickson argues similarly, declaring that the restrictions imposed upon Christ's divinity by his human nature meant that he as God could be in only one physical place at a time. Christ made a voluntary decision, he argues, to limit the exercise of his omnipresence for a certain period of time. The voluntary character of his decision did not mean that he could have overridden his decision at any time. He had willed that from approximately 4 BC to AD 29 he would not have the free use of his omnipresence. It was not that he was pretending that he could not use it; *he really could not use it*. In like manner, when Jesus asked how long a child had suffered from a disease, or when he professed that he did not know the time of his second coming, he was not pretending ignorance. He as God really did not know. He had chosen to subject his omniscience to the veiling or cloaking effect of humanity. For that period of time, God the Son gave up his intuitive knowledge of many of the things that God knows.[59] Erickson acknowledges that his view is 'a species of kenotic theology', but in my *A New Systematic Theology of the Christian Faith*[60] I demonstrate exegetically that there is no basis in Philippians 2:6–7 for thinking that in the act of incarnation Christ 'emptied' himself of anything. The 'emptying' referred to there refers, not to his incarnation, but to his 'pouring himself out' in death in his role as our heavenly High Priest (see Isa. 53:12).[61] Erickson's entire argument is thus based on faulty exegesis.

---

58. Millard J. Erickson, *Christian Theology*, 2nd edn (Grand Rapids: Baker, 1984), pp. 751–752.

59. Millard J. Erickson, *The Word Became Flesh* (Grand Rapids: Baker, 1991), p. 549.

60. Robert L. Reymond, *A New Systematic Theology of the Christian Faith*, 2nd edn (Nashville: Thomas Nelson, 2002), pp. 253–265.

61. The pronoun *heauton* (himself) as the direct object of 'emptied' in Phil. 2:7 makes clear that Jesus did not empty himself *of* something. He 'emptied' *himself*; i.e. 'poured *himself* out' in death!

If Erickson, a reputable theologian, blunders in this way, it is not surprising when on several occasions I have asked gatherings of evangelical pastors the question 'After the incarnation had occurred, did the Second Person of the Godhead still possess and exercise the attribute of omnipresence, or was he confined to the human body he had assumed?' that many have opted for the latter construction: 'After all,' they say, 'is this not what the word "incarnation" means?' They did not seem to realize that the necessary implication of this choice is that in the incarnation God the Son divested himself of his attribute of being always and everywhere immediately present in his created universe.

My solution
Divine attributes are not characteristics that are separate and distinct from the divine essence so that God can set them aside as one might remove a pin from a pin cushion and still have an intact pin cushion or choose not to use some for a time. Rather, the divine essence is expressed precisely in the sum total of its attributes; indeed, his glory is just the inescapable weight of his entire divine essence. To hold that God the Son actually divested himself in his state of humiliation of even one divine attribute or of his use of one of his essential attributes is tantamount to saying that he who enfleshed himself in the incarnation, while perhaps more than man, is not quite God either. But as Bishop Moule once wrote, a saviour not quite God 'is a bridge broken at the farther end'.

The uniform representation of the New Testament and Chalcedonian Christology is that the incarnation was an act of *addition* rather than subtraction. Without ceasing to be all that he eternally and unchangeably is as God, the Son of God took into union with himself what he was not, making our human nature his very own. And during the days of his earthly ministry, though he displayed all the characteristics of humankind generally, sin excepted, he also claimed to be omnipresent (Matt. 18:20) and gave evidence of his omniscience (Matt. 11:27; John 1:47; 2:25; 4:29; 11:11–14). When he changed water into wine, John informs us that his disciples saw his glory, the glory of God's unique Son, himself God, who is in the bosom of the Father.

While we must not ascribe to Church Fathers, Councils or Creeds the same authority that we accord Scripture, it can at least be demonstrated that kenotic Christology was never a part of Christological orthodoxy. For example, Cyril of Alexandria who led the orthodox opposition against Nestorius at the Council of Ephesus in AD 431, wrote in a letter to Nestorius:

> [The eternal Word] subjected himself to birth for us, and came forth man from woman, *without casting off that which he was,* but although he assumed flesh and blood, *he remained what he was,* God in essence and in truth. Neither do we say that his flesh was

changed into the nature of divinity, nor that *the ineffable nature of the Word of God was laid aside for the nature of flesh; for he is unchanged and absolutely unchangeable*, being the same always, according to the Scriptures. For although visible and a child in swaddling clothes, and even in the bosom of his Virgin Mother, *he filled all creation*, and was a fellow-ruler with him who begat him, for the Godhead is without quantity and dimensions, and cannot have limits.[62]

Twenty years later, in AD 451, the Council of Chalcedon, whose creedal labours, as we have already observed, produced the Christological definition that fixed the boundaries of all future discussions, declared that Jesus Christ possessed

[two natures without confusion [*asynchytōs*], without change [*atreptōs*], without division [*adiairetōs*], without separation [*achōristōs*]; the distinction of the natures being by no means removed because of the union but rather the property of each nature being preserved.

Calvin was hardly being heterodox, then, as Lutherans contemptuously charge by their *extra-Calvinisticum* (Calvin's 'outside thing')[63] when he wrote:

Another absurdity . . . namely, that if the Word of God became incarnate, [he] must have been confined within the narrow prison of an earthly body, is sheer impudence! For even if the Word in his immeasurable essence united with the nature of man into one person, we do not imagine that he was confined therein. Here is something marvellous: the Son of God descended from heaven in such a way that, *without leaving heaven*, he willed to be born in the virgin's womb, to go about the earth, to hang upon the cross, yet *he continuously filled the earth even as he had done from the beginning*.[64]

Calvin's representation here is simply a restatement of Chalcedonian Christology at its best.

---

62. From 'The Epistle of Cyril to Nestorius with the XII Anathematisms', in Phillip Schaff and Henry Wace, eds., *A Select Library of Nicene and Post-Nicene Fathers of the Christian Church*, 2nd series (Grand Rapids: Eerdmans, 1956), vol. 14, p. 202 (my emphasis).

63. Because Lutherans contend that the human nature of Christ is ubiquitous and therefore is as 'omnipresent' as his divine nature, they will not allow his divine nature to be 'outside' his human nature.

64. John Calvin, *Institutes of the Christian Religion* 2.13.4 (my emphasis).

The *Heidelberg Catechism* grants explicit Reformed creedal status to this position when it declares in Question 49, 'Since [Christ's] Godhood is illimitable and omnipresent, it must follow that it is beyond the bounds of the human nature it has assumed, and yet none the less is in this human nature and remains personally united to it.'

It is clear, then, both from Scripture and from church history that kenotic Christology cannot claim to have the sanction of orthodoxy. In my opinion it is a blemish, if not acne, on the face of historic Christology and should be repudiated as a reductionistic heterodoxy respecting Christ's deity. This issue should be given much more thought than it receives today for the sake of the preservation of Chalcedonian Christology.

How can the one Christ be self-consciously infinite in knowledge as God and consciously finite in knowledge as man at the same time?

The problem

Christian orthodoxy has always held that the God of Holy Scripture is omniscient. That is to say, God's knowledge – intuited in the sense that he never had to learn anything through the learning process – encompasses all possible and actual knowable data. He knows to perfection and without qualification all things – all things visible and invisible in heaven and on earth; all spirits, thrones and dominions in heaven and in hell; all matters past, present and future; all the thoughts of every mind, all the words of every tongue and all the activities of every creature living and dead; all their purposes, all their plans, all their relationships, all their complicities and all their conspiracies; all physical and spiritual causes, all natural and supernatural forces, and all real and contingent motions; all mysteries and all unuttered secrets; all true propositions as true and all false propositions as false, all valid conclusions as valid and all invalid conclusions as invalid – and always has known them and always will know them. We must affirm this as true of God the Son, the second Person of the triune Godhead.

But if we take seriously the fact of Christ's humanity with all of its limitations then we must also affirm that he, as a man, was and continues to be finite in knowledge forever. As Warfield observed:

> [We have] never hesitated to face the fact [that all that man is, that Christ is to eternity] and [we] rejoice in it, with all its implications. With regard to knowledge, for example, [we have] not shrunk from recognizing that Christ, as man, had a finite knowledge and must continue to have a finite knowledge forever. Human nature is ever finite . . . and is no more capable of infinite *charismata*, than of the infinite *idiomata* or attributes of

the divine nature; so that it is certain that the knowledge of Christ's human nature is not and can never be the infinite wisdom of God itself. [We have] no reserves, therefore, in confessing the limitations of the knowledge of Christ as man, and no fear of overstating the perfection and completeness of his humanity.[65]

How is this possible? How can the one Person of Christ be, as God, self-consciously infinite in knowledge and also, as man, consciously finite in knowledge at the same time?

My solution

In one respect my solution is that there is no solution to this question, for it would appear that this is simply one of the elements of the altogether transcendent mystery intrinsic to the incarnation and an example of the kind of difficulty that has caused some people to stumble at the portrait that the Gospels draw of Christ. Some theologians have suggested the answer lies in the postulation of two 'levels' of consciousness in Jesus – a level of active consciousness at which level Jesus as a man developed in wisdom and knowledge as do other human beings and at which level he acknowledged ignorance of some things and another (subconscious?) level of awareness as the Son of God (in so far as the active level was concerned) at which level he knew all things. At any moment in his earthly existence, theoretically, he could have called up to his active level of consciousness any knowledge datum he desired from the infinite pool of divine knowledge that was his possession as God. But prior to the incarnation, in the eternal councils respecting his ministry on earth, it had been determined that he would hold in his active consciousness, with some few exceptions, only such information as is commonly available to other Spirit-led men. I am not completely convinced that this construction is the answer, since it does not explain how it is that Jesus clearly evidenced a sustained knowledge at the active level of his consciousness that he was divine.

Others have proposed a 'two mind' solution that may overcome this difficulty to some degree, postulating that the human mind of Christ did not have access to the divine mind unless the latter willed and permitted the former such access upon occasion. But this comes perilously close to over-turning the 'one person' character of Jesus.

Probably we shall never discover the true solution to this problem, as I already said. Of course, I would welcome any suggestion that would remove the difficulty, but I would counsel that, in removing this difficulty, the proposed

---

65. Warfield, *Selected Shorter Writings*, vol. 1, p. 162.

solution must not seize upon one series of qualities in Christ and make that
'the church's position' and discard the other series. We must always be willing
to go as far as Scripture goes with both series of qualities. For example, in the
Gospels Jesus

> is represented as not knowing this or that matter of fact (Mark 13:32), [but] he is
> equally represented as knowing all things (John 16:30; 21:17). If he is represented as
> acquiring information from without, asking questions and expressing surprise, he is
> equally represented as knowing without human information all that occurs or has
> occurred – the secret prayer of Nathaniel (John 1:47), the whole life of the Samaritan
> woman (John 4:29), the very thoughts of his enemies (Matt. 9:14), all that is in man
> (John 2:25). Nor are these two classes of facts kept separate – they are rather
> interlaced in the most amazing manner. If it is by human information that he is told
> of Lazarus' sickness (John 11:3, 6), it is on no human information that he knows him
> to be dead (John 11:11, 14); if he asks, 'Where have you laid him?' and weeps with the
> sorrowing sister, he knows from the beginning (John 11:11) what his might should
> accomplish for the assuagement of this grief.[66]

Doubtless, wisdom would dictate that we should go as far as Scripture goes
in such matters and when Scripture falls silent we should shut our mouths as
well. For one thing is certain: we cannot afford to lose either the man-ness in
the person of Jesus or the Godness in the person of Jesus, the reason being
that because he was man he was able to bear our sins in his own body on the
tree and pour out his blood in death at Calvary, and because he is God his
blood[67] has infinite value to save his own forever from all their sin.

How is the Son to be related to the Father in the Trinity?

The problem
By their creedal phrases 'begotten out of the Father', 'that is, out of the being of
the Father' (which Nicene phrase is replaced in the Niceno-Constantinopolitan
Creed of AD 381 by the phrase 'before all ages'), and 'God out of God, Light
out of Light, very God out of very God', the Nicene Fathers intended to teach,
first, that only God the Father is 'God in his own right',[68] second, that he is the

---

66. Warfield, 'The Human Development of Jesus', in *Selected Shorter Writings*, vol. 1, p. 163.

67. Acts 20:28 speaks of God's 'blood'.

68. Donald Macleod, *Behold Your God*, rev. edn (Ross-shire, Scotland: Christian Focus,
    1995), p. 200.

source of the Son, and third, that the Son derives his essential being as God from the Father through an eternal 'always continuing, never completed' act of begetting on the Father's part. They believed and taught that the Father, by his act of eternally generating the Son, is the 'beginning' (*archē*), the 'fountain' (*pēgē*) and the 'cause' (*aitia*) of the Son's essential deity (*theotēs*). That is to say, in the approving words of Roger Beckwith, 'central to the teaching of the Creeds' is the notion of 'an eternal impartation of the divine being and nature by the Father to the Son, whereby the Father is Father and the Son is Son'.[69] They also intended to teach that the Father (the later phrase 'and the Son' was added to the Creed here probably by the Third Council of Toledo in Spain in AD 589), by his act of eternally 'processing' the Spirit, is the 'beginning' (*archē*), the 'fountain' (*pēgē*) and the 'cause' (*aitia*) of the Spirit's essential deity (*theotēs*). They show no apparent awareness that such teaching by implication *denies to the Son and to the Spirit the attribute of self-existence* or aseity that is necessarily theirs as divine Persons of both the tri-personal Yahweh of the Old Testament and the triune God of the New Testament, and without which they could not be *theotic* at all inasmuch as self-existence is an essential attribute of deity.

The Nicene Fathers, of course, were satisfied that they had carefully guarded the full deity of the Son (and by extension the full deity of the Spirit) by their affirmation of the *homoousia*, and by their statement that the Son was 'begotten not created'. But their language, if not their theology, in spite of their commendable intention by it to distance the church from Sabellianism, suggests both the Son's subordination to the Father not only in modes of operation but also in a kind of *essential* subordination in that he is not God *a se* but God *out of* (*ek*) the Father by the latter's ever-continuing act of generation that in effect denies to the Son his *autotheotic* self-existence as God, and the Spirit's essential subordination to the Father (and the Son) in that he is not God *a se* but God by an ever- continuing procession from the Father (the *filioque* was added later) that in effect denies to the Spirit his *autotheotic* self-existence as God. The Nicene language also raises the basic *epistemological* problem of how an unbegotten, a begotten and a processing essence can be *simultaneously* the *same* essence, and the *theological* problem of how the one divine essence can be *simultaneously* unbegotten, begotten and processing, depending upon the Person of the Godhead being considered, without implying tritheism. In any event this became by and large the doctrine of the church and it went virtually unchallenged for well over a thousand years. Indeed, as Donald Macleod, professor of systematic theology

---

69. Roger Beckwith, 'The Calvinist Doctrine of the Trinity', *Churchman* 115.4 (2001), pp. 308–315.

at the Free Church of Scotland College in Edinburgh, observes, '[this] subor-
dinationist strain [implying tritheism] has continued right down to the present
day, even in orthodox Christology'.[70]

My solution

I stand with John Calvin who contended in the sixteenth century against all
subordination of the Son to the Father with respect to his divine essence (as
well as all subordination of the Spirit to the Father and the Son with respect
to his divine essence). While Calvin's trinitarian thought was not quite the total
innovation it is sometimes said to be since there were antecedents for it over
a millennium before him in the trinitarian constructions of some of the
ancient Fathers such as Gregory Nazianzus, Cyril of Alexandria and
Augustine of Hippo, Calvin did 'conceive more clearly and apply more purely
than had ever previously been done the principle of equalization in his
thought of the relation of the Persons to one another, and thereby . . . [his
view] marks an epoch in the history of the doctrine of the Trinity'.[71] By doing
so, in the words of Gerald Bray, Anglican Professor of Divinity at Beeson
Divinity School, Birmingham, Alabama, Calvin 'found the key to a more
deeply orthodox trinitarianism' that avoided 'any hint of causality in the terms
"generation" and "procession".'[72] While he was willing to hold that the Father
is the 'beginning of deity' within the Godhead (*Institutes* 1.13.23, 25), Calvin
explains that he means by the word 'beginning', not the Father's bestowing of
essence to the Son (*Institutes* 1.13.26), but rather 'in respect to order . . . the
beginning of divinity is in the Father' (*Institutes* 1.13.24, 26). That is to say, he
endorsed the doctrine of the Father's 'eternal generation' of the Son, not with
respect to his essence as deity, but with respect to his sonship that he derives
from the 'eternally generated' relationship in which he stands to the Father. In
sum, Calvin employed the doctrine to distinguish between the Father and the
Son with respect *to their order* within the Godhead, but he did not endorse the
doctrine as being true, as we just said, with respect to the Son's divine essence.
With respect to the Son's divine essence, Calvin argued, the Son is – and this
is the key to which Bray refers – *autotheotic*. And he repeatedly argues that the
Son is God *of himself* because Scripture names him Yahweh (*Institutes* 1.13.20,
23), an argument that Charles Hodge of Old Princeton found to be 'conclu-

---

70. Macleod, *Behold Your God*, p. 201.

71. Benjamin B. Warfield, 'Calvin's Doctrine of the Trinity', *The Works of Benjamin B.
    Warfield* (Grand Rapids: Baker, 1991), vol. 5, p. 230.

72. Gerald Bray, *The Doctrine of God* (Downers Grove: IVP, 1993), pp. 201, 204.

sive'.[73] Indeed, if the Son is not *auto*theotic, Calvin argued, he is not *theotic* at all. He concluded his exposition of the Trinity by declaring that the ancient speculation that the Father's eternal generation of the Son's essence as an *always* continuing process was 'of little profit', unnecessarily 'burdensome', 'useless trouble' and 'foolish', 'since it is clear', he states, 'that three persons have subsisted in God from eternity' (*Institutes* 1.13.29).

By his exposition of Scripture Calvin 'not only attacked all forms of Origenism [see *Institutes* 1.13.23–29], but also the Sabellianism latent in the Western tradition'.[74] And his successors at Geneva, as well as a mass of representative Reformed teachers of the period, followed Calvin's insights, all teaching that the Father, the Son and the Spirit are properly to be regarded as *autotheotic*, the three Persons being 'united with each other . . . by their mutual fellowship and coinherence – the Cappadocian doctrine of *perichoresis* in God, applied at the level of person, not essence',[75] which is to say as well that, even though the three Persons are 'of themselves' essentially, they do not possess the quality of aseity independently of each other which would suggest tritheism. Rather, they share the quality of aseity that inheres in the one undivided divine essence that each fully possesses. And while some Protestant churchmen such as George Bull and William Pearson wrote defences of the statements of the Nicene Creed, a good many Reformed theologians and pastors in more recent times have deemed it appropriate and necessary to follow Calvin's exposition. For example, Charles Hodge, professor of systematic theology at Princeton Seminary, taking exception, not to the facts themselves of the subordination of the Son and the Spirit to the Father and the Son's eternal generation, but to the Nicene Fathers' explanations of them,[76] declared that

---

73. Charles Hodge, *Systematic Theology* (Grand Rapids: Eerdmans, n. d.), vol. 1, p. 467.
74. Bray, *Doctrine of God*, p. 201. This latent Sabellianism is due to the influence, to varying degrees, of Neoplatonism in the tradition reflected in its reading back into the *ontological* Trinity the inter-trinitarian relations known to us from the economical Trinity's activities in the economy of redemption. On this influence of Neoplatonism on Nicene thought, see Bray's helpful comments in his *Doctrine of God*, pp. 28–35, 40–41, 158, 168–169.
75. Bray, *Doctrine of God*, p. 202.
76. Hodge, *Systematic Theology*, vol. 1, p. 468. Strangely, both Hodge (*Systematic Theology*, vol. 1, p. 462) and Warfield ('Calvin's Doctrine of the Trinity', *Works*, vol. 5, p. 250) draw a distinction between the Nicene Creed as such and the theology of the Nicene Fathers who produced it. By drawing this distinction they give their endorsement to the Creed as written, while at the same time calling into question

the fathers who framed [the Nicene] Creed, and those by whom it was defended, did go beyond [the] facts [of Scripture] concerning the Son's subordination to the Father as to the mode of subsistence . . . instead of leaving the matter where the Scriptures leave it, [they] undertake to explain what is meant by sonship, and teach that it means derivation of essence. The First Person of the Trinity is Father, because he communicates the essence of the Godhead to the Second Person; and the Second Person is Son, because he derives that essence from the First Person. This is what they mean by Eternal Generation. Concerning which it was taught [that] . . . the person of the Son is generated (*i.e.*, He becomes a person) by the communication to Him of the divine essence.[77]

With respect to the Reformers' attitude toward these Nicene affirmations, Hodge continues, 'The Reformers themselves were little inclined to enter into these speculations. They were especially repugnant to such minds as Luther's. He insisted on taking the Scriptural facts as they were, without any attempt at explanation . . .'

Calvin also was opposed to going beyond the simple statement of the Scriptures.[78] Benjamin B. Warfield, professor of polemic and didactic theology at Princeton Seminary, states in his elaborate article 'Calvin's Doctrine of the Trinity':

[Calvin] seems to have drawn back from the doctrine of 'eternal generation' *as it was expounded by the Nicene Fathers*. They were accustomed to explain 'eternal generation' (in accordance with its very nature as 'eternal'), not as something which has occurred once for all at some point of time in the past – however far back in the past – but as something which is always occurring, *a perpetual movement of the divine essence from the first Person to the second*, always complete, never completed. Calvin seems to have found this conception difficult, if not meaningless.[79]

---

some of the doctrinal thinking of the ancient Fathers that lay behind some of the Creed's particular formulations. I find this confusing, to say the least. A creed will normally *contain* the doctrine and *reflect* the theology of those who compose it. This means in the present case, in my opinion, that if they would be critical of the Nicene Fathers' doctrine in certain areas, as Hodge and Warfield are, they ought also to be equally critical of the formulations that are the products of that doctrine, should they appear in the Nicene Creed. Neither is willing to be consistent and thus do this.

77. Hodge, *Systematic Theology*, vol. 1, pp. 465, 468.
78. Ibid., p. 466.
79. Warfield, 'Calvin's Doctrine of the Trinity', *Works*, vol. 5, p. 247 (my emphasis).

As proof of his assertion, Warfield cites, as I did earlier, Calvin's closing words in *Institutes* 1.13.29.

Then in concert with the Nicene Fathers' opposition to the Arian heresy, Calvin found the notion that the Son's generation occurred punctiliarly, or once for all at some point of time, in the distant past equally abhorrent, for this would mean that before that point of time in the past he did not exist and that he had been created. The only alternative left is the one he himself espoused; namely, the simple affirmation that 'three persons have subsisted in God from eternity' (*Institutes* 1.13.29). By this his meaning appears to be, writes Warfield, that the Son's generation

> must have been completed from all eternity, since its product has existed complete from all eternity, and therefore it is meaningless to speak of it as continually proceeding. If this is the meaning of his remark, it is a definite rejection of the Nicene speculation of 'eternal generation'.[80]

Warfield continues:

> The principle of [Calvin's] doctrine of the Trinity was . . . the force of his conviction of the absolute equality of the Persons. The point of view which adjusted everything to the conception of 'generation' and 'procession' as worked out by the Nicene Fathers was entirely alien to him. The conception itself he found difficult, if not unthinkable; and although he admitted the facts of 'generation' and 'procession', he treated them as bare facts, and *refused to make them constitutive of the doctrine of the Trinity*. He rather adjusted everything to the absolute divinity of each Person, their community in the one only true Deity; and to this we cannot doubt that *he was ready not only to subordinate, but even to sacrifice, if need be, the entire body of Nicene speculation*. Moreover, it would seem at least doubtful if Calvin . . . thought of [the] begetting and procession as involving *any communication* of essence.[81]

Warfield notes further:

> the direct Scriptural proof which had been customarily relied upon for [the] establishment [of the Nicene Fathers' doctrine of 'eternal generation'], [Calvin] destroyed, refusing to rest a doctrinal determination on 'distorted texts'. He left, therefore, little Biblical evidence for the doctrine . . . , except what might be

---

80. Ibid, p. 248.
81. Ibid., pp. 257–258 (my emphasis).

inferred from the mere terms 'Father', 'Son', and 'Spirit',[82] and the general consideration that our own adoption into the relation of sons of God in Christ implies for him a Sonship of a higher and more immanent character, which is his by nature.[83]

Warfield is certainly correct to conclude that Calvin, while he rejected its speculative elaborations, held to the substantial core of the Nicene tradition.[84] I think it is in this sense that Calvin felt he could honestly write in *Institutes* 4.9.8, 'we willingly embrace and reverence as holy the early councils, such as those of Nicaea, Constantinople, Ephesus I, [and] Chalcedon . . . in so far as they relate to the teachings of faith'.[85]

And while it was never Calvin's intent to create a party – he simply wanted to reform the church by restoring a scriptural theology in it – Warfield observes that Calvin's treatment of the Trinity, nevertheless, marking as it did an epoch in church history,

> did not seem a matter of course when he first enunciated it. It roused opposition and created a party. But it did create a party: *and that party was shortly the Reformed Churches, of which it became characteristic that they held and taught the self-existence of Christ as God* and defended the application to Him of the term *autotheos*; that is to say, in the doctrine of the Trinity they laid the stress upon the equality of the Persons sharing the same essence, and thus set themselves with more or less absoluteness against all subordinationism in the explanation of the relations of the Persons to one another.[86]

The reader can now understand why Warfield strikingly acknowledges what for him are the following three causes for astonishment:

> We are *astonished* at the persistence of so large an infusion of the Nicene phraseology in the expositions of Augustine, after that phraseology had really been antiquated by his fundamental principle of equalization in his construction of the Trinitarian relations; we are *more astonished* at the effort which Calvin made to adduce Nicene

---

82. For these inferences see pp. 168–170.
83. Warfield, 'Calvin's Doctrine of the Trinity', *Works*, vol. 5, p. 278. See also vol. 5, p. 248, n. 86.
84. Ibid., p. 279.
85. Note Calvin's 'in so far as' qualification here.
86. Warfield, 'Calvin's Doctrine of the Trinity', *Works*, vol. 5, p. 251 (my emphasis).

support for his own conceptions; and we are *more astonished still* at the tenacity with which [Calvin's] followers cling to all the old speculations.[87]

In his article to which I previously referred, 'The Biblical Doctrine of the Trinity', Warfield summarized the history of the development of the Christian doctrine of the Trinity as follows (I shall place in bold the four significant names from this history as Warfield rehearsed it):

In the conflict between [the Logos-Christology and Monarchianism] the church gradually found its way . . . to a better and more well-balanced conception, until a real doctrine of the Trinity at length came to expression, particularly in the West, through the brilliant dialectic of **Tertullian**. It was thus ready at hand, when . . . the Logos-Christology . . . ran to seed in what is known as Arianism . . . and the church was thus prepared to assert its settled faith in a Triune God, one in being, but in whose unity there subsisted three consubstantial Persons. Under the leadership of **Athanasius** this doctrine was proclaimed as the faith of the church at the Council of Nicaea in 325 AD, and by his strenuous labors and those of 'the three great Cappadocians', the two Gregories and Basil, it gradually won its way to the actual acceptance of the entire church. It was at the hands of **Augustine**, however, a century later, that the doctrine thus received its most complete elaboration and most carefully grounded statement. In the form in which he gave it, and which is embodied in . . . the so-called Athanasian Creed, it has retained its place as the fit expression of the faith of the church as to the nature of its God until today. The language in which it is couched, even in this final declaration, still retained elements of speech which owe their origin to the modes of thought characteristic of the Logos-Christology of the second century, *fixed in the nomenclature of the church by the Nicene Creed of 325* AD, *though carefully guarded there against the subordinationism inherent in the Logos-Christology, and made the vehicle rather of the Nicene doctrines of the eternal generation of the Son and procession of the Spirit, with the consequent subordination of the Son and Spirit to the Father in modes of subsistence as well as of operation.* In the Athanasian Creed, however, the principle of equalization of the three Persons, which was already the dominant motive of the Nicene Creed – the *homoousia* – is so strongly emphasized as practically to push out of sight, if not quite out of existence, these remnant suggestions of derivation and subordination. It has been found necessary, nevertheless, from time to time, vigorously to reassert the principle of equalization, over against a tendency unduly to emphasize the elements of subordinationism which still hold place thus in the traditional language in which the church states its doctrine of the Trinity. In particular, it fell to **Calvin**, in the interest

87. Ibid., p. 279 (my emphasis).

of the true Deity of Christ – the constant motive of the whole body of Trinitarian thought – to reassert and make good the attribute of self-existence (*autotheotos*) for the Son. Thus Calvin takes his place alongside of Tertullian, Athanasius, and Augustine, as one of the chief contributors to the exact and vital statement of the Christian doctrine of the Triune God.[88]

A careful reading of this summary will show that Warfield believed, first, that the Nicene Creed, by its doctrines of the eternal generation of the Son and the procession of the Spirit, implies 'the consequent subordination of the Son and Spirit to the Father in modes of subsistence as well as of operation' as well as 'suggestions of derivation and subordination'; second, that Calvin, over against this subordination of the Son and the Spirit in subsistence to the Father, finally made good the attribute of the Son's (and the Spirit's) self-existence, thereby taking his place as the fourth major contributor to the exact statement of the doctrine of the Trinity; and third, that by so doing Calvin made a critical adjustment to the theological implications in the language of the Nicene Creed at the point of Nicaea's implied subordinationism of the Son by derivation from the Father.[89]

John Murray, professor of systematic theology at Westminster Seminary, states regarding the Nicene tradition's depiction of Christ, 'It had been Nicene tradition to embellish the doctrine . . . of Christ's Sonship with formulae

---

88. Warfield, 'The Biblical Doctrine of the Trinity', in *Biblical and Theological Studies*, pp. 58–59 (my bold).

89. Written as this article was in 1915 for *The International Standard Bible Encyclopedia*, whereas Warfield's earlier article 'Calvin's Doctrine of the Trinity' was written in 1909 for the *Princeton Theological Review* 7, pp. 553–652, I think we should assume that the later article also represents Warfield's mature thinking on the doctrine of the Trinity, only considered from the biblical perspective. I also think we should assume that Warfield's understanding of both Nicaea's doctrine of the Trinity and Calvin's understanding of Nicaea as he represents both in these two articles is essentially the same in both articles. I underscore this because Robert Letham, who has criticized my exposition of Calvin's trinitarianism, told me that he appreciated Warfield's exposition of Calvin's doctrine of the Trinity in the 1909 article but wished Warfield had never written what he did about Calvin's understanding of it in the 1915 article. By saying this Letham is implying that Warfield's understanding of Calvin's doctrine, or at least his expression of it, degenerated rather than matured with the passing of years. I would urge, however, that the 1915 article helps us better understand Warfield's intended exposition of Calvin's trinitarianism in the 1909 article.

beyond the warrant of Scripture.'[90] He also states regarding Calvin's view of the 'catholic' doctrine of the early Fathers' eternal generation of the Son:

> Students of historical theology are acquainted with the furore which Calvin's insistence upon the self-existence of the Son as to his deity aroused at the time of the Reformation. Calvin was too much of a student of Scripture to be content to follow the lines of what had been regarded as Nicene orthodoxy on this particular issue. He was too jealous for the implications of the *homoousion* clause of the Nicene Creed to be willing to accede to the interpretation which the Nicene Fathers, including Athanasius, placed upon another expression in the same creed, namely, 'very God of very God' (*theon alēthinon ek theou alēthinou*). No doubt this expression is repeated by orthodox people without any thought of suggesting what the evidence derived from the writings of the Nicene Fathers would indicate the intent to have been. This evidence shows that the meaning intended is that the Son derived his deity from the Father and that the Son was not therefore *autotheos*.[91] It was precisely this position that Calvin controverted with vigour. He maintained that as respects personal distinction the Son was of the Father but as respects deity he was self-existent (*ex se ipso*). *This position ran counter to the Nicene tradition.* Hence the indictments levelled against him. It is, however, to the credit of Calvin that he did not allow his own more sober thinking to be suppressed out of deference to an established pattern of thought when the latter did not commend itself by conformity to Scripture and was inimical to Christ's divine identity.[92]

Morton H. Smith, professor of systematic theology at Greenville Presbyterian Theological Seminary, South Carolina, states that the Nicene theologians taught that 'the Father is the beginning, the fountain, the cause, the principle of the being of the Son' and that 'the Son derives his essence from the Father by eternal and indefinable generation of divine essence from the Father to the Son'. He then notes:

> Calvin was the first one to challenge these . . . two speculations. He taught that the Son was *a se ipso* with regard to his deity. He did not derive his essence from the Father. There is no warrant in the Scripture for the subordination of the Son in his

---

90. John Murray, 'The Theology of the Westminster Confession of Faith', *Collected Writings of John Murray* (Edinburgh: Banner of Truth, 1982), vol. 4, p. 248.

91. See, e.g., Athanasius' *Expositio Fidei* where he clearly states that the Son derives his deity (*theotēs*) from the Father. See also his *De Decretis Nicaenae Synodi* §§3 and 19.

92. Murray, 'Systematic Theology', *Collected Writings*, vol. 4, p. 8 (my emphasis).

essence to the Father. The same may be said of the Holy Spirit. He is *a se ipso* as regards his essence.[93]

Finally, Donald Macleod laments the fact, as did Warfield, that 'the valuable work done by John Calvin in this area has been largely ignored',[94] observing:

> Subordinationism survived the introduction of the *filioque* as it had that of the *homoousion*, largely because the successors of the Nicene theologians were content to reproduce their language and sentiments uncritically . . . This stubborn residue of subordinationism provided the background to John Calvin's formulation of the doctrine of the Trinity . . . His whole concern is to maximize the equality between the Father and the Son, and he is ill at ease with any suggestion of subordination. While he retains some of the language of causality he denies that the Father is in any sense the *deificator* ('god-maker') of the Son. The Father gave the Son neither his being nor his divinity . . . [Because the Son and the Holy Spirit are both Yahweh] the essence of the Son and the Holy Spirit cannot be subordinate in any sense to the essence of the Father because it is one and the same essence, equally self-existent in each person. Consequently, such terms as 'begotten' and 'proceeding' apply only to the persons of the Son and the Spirit, not to their essence.[95]

I would urge, therefore, with Calvin and these cited theologians, that Christians should believe that God the Father is indeed 'the beginning of activity, and the fountain and wellspring of all things' (*Institutes* 1.13.18). But they should not believe that the Father, through an eternal act of begetting in the depth of the divine being that is *always* continuing, is begetting the Son's essential being as God out of his being, which act thereby 'puts this second person in possession of the whole divine essence'.[96] They should believe, rather, that the Son with respect to his essential being is wholly God of himself from all eternity, to whom as God the Son the Scriptures attribute 'wisdom, counsel, and the ordered disposition of all things' (*Institutes* 1.13.18). Of course, they should also believe that the Son as the second Person of the Godhead derives

93. Morton H. Smith, *Systematic Theology* (Greenville, S.C.: Greenville Seminary Press, 1994), vol. 1, p. 152.

94. Macleod, *Behold Your God*, p. 201. Macleod adds here the qualification 'apart from the prevalence of a certain suspicion that [Calvin] was unsound on the doctrine of the eternal sonship' (see his n. 39).

95. Donald Macleod, *The Person of Christ* (Downers Grove: IVP, 1998), pp. 149–151.

96. Louis Berkhof, *Systematic Theology* (Grand Rapids: Eerdmans, 1996), p. 94.

his incommunicable *hypostatic* identity from the 'generated' relation that he sustains 'before all ages' to God the Father, the first Person of the Godhead (what this 'generation' means beyond 'order' and the distinction just noted I cannot say and will not attempt to say), and that the Father by his incommunicable property as Father precedes the Son within the Godhead by reason of order.

I have mentioned only some of the problems that systematic theologians could and should give more thought to in our time. Other systematicians could surely mention still others. But whatever the problems are with which they wrestle, it is imperative that they keep certain essential facts before them. I began this chapter by observing that the cultural trend today in the field of Christology is towards Arianism, that is, towards a denial of the divine side of our Lord's dual life. The temptation will ever be with us, confronted as we are by the great incarnational mystery of the two-natured Christ, to deny one of the two series of biblical data teaching his two natures. But it is precisely this path of choosing only one series of data, taken by so many in the Christological controversies leading up to the Council of Chalcedon, that the Fathers of Chalcedon, desiring to be biblical, refused to take. As a result, the Definition of Chalcedon remains to this day a cherished heritage in the church. This Definition, writes Warfield,

> was not arrived at easily or without long and searching study of the Scripture material, and long and sharp controversy among conflicting constructions. Every other solution was tried and found wanting; in this solution the Church found at last rest, and in it she has rested until our own day. In it alone, it is not too much to say, can the varied representations of the Bible each find full justice, and all harmonious adjustment. If it be true, then all that is true of God may be attributed to Christ, and equally all that is true of man. Full account is taken of all the phenomena; violence is done to none. If it be not true, it is safe to say that the puzzle remains insoluble.[97]

This being so, the characterization of the Definition that one sometimes hears to the effect that with its four adverbs it is essentially negative in its teaching is surely inadequate if not totally erroneous. The Definition is quite positive in what it asserts about Christ, declaring that he is (1) one person who is (2) both truly divine by virtue of his deity and truly human by virtue of the virginal conception, who is also (3) both consubstantial with the Father

---

97. Warfield, 'The Human Development of Jesus', in *Selected Shorter Writings*, vol. 1, p. 165.

according to his deity and consubstantial with us according to his humanity, (4) with the distinction of his two natures being by no means taken away by their union in the unity of his person, but (5) the property of each nature being preserved and (6) concurring in one person, that is, in one subsistence. The 'four great negative Chalcedian adverbs' are only a small, though not an insignificant, part of the total Definition. And while they do indeed describe the relationship of the natures to one another in the one person in terms designating how the two natures are *not* to be related, they do so for the very positive reason of fending off all attempts to make the divine act of the incarnation 'transparent by categories in which the unity [of the Person] must yield to the duality [of the natures] or the duality [of the natures] to the unity [of the Person]'.[98] Of course, I do not intend to suggest that the Definition should be the terminal point in Christological reflection in the sense that further reflection on the implications of the incarnation is out of order. Dogma, however much revered and time-honoured, must be subject at all times to the Word of God, and it is uninterrupted research into Scripture that must ultimately guide the church. Consequently, the benchmark creedal declarations in the history of the church – even the Definition of Chalcedon – must never stifle continuing reflection upon Scripture to understand the incarnation and its Product better. But I would insist with Berkouwer that 'there is a "Halt!" at Chalcedon that will indeed continue to sound against every form of speculation that attempts to penetrate into this mystery [of the two-natured Christ] further than is warranted in the light of revelation'.[99]

Said another way, the Definition of Chalcedon, the product of the three major schools of Christological thought that had long struggled to understand him who was their Lord, does mark the terminal point, and legitimately so, of all speculation that would discard either its 'one Person' doctrine or its 'two natures' doctrine so as to eliminate the supernaturalness of the incarnation and the incarnate Christ, for it captures more accurately and more fully than any other single statement all that the Scriptures teach about him who stands at the centre of the Christian confession. I would submit that the systematic theologian of the twenty-first century must not discard lightly or cavalierly *without sound exegetical reasons* any of the lengthy and searching labour that the Definition of Chalcedon represents.

© Robert L. Reymond, 2006

98. Gerritt C. Berkouwer, *The Person of Christ* (Grand Rapids: Eerdmans, 1954), p. 95.
99. Ibid., p. 88.

4. ON THE VERY IDEA OF A THEOLOGICAL SYSTEM: AN ESSAY IN AID OF TRIANGULATING SCRIPTURE, CHURCH AND WORLD

Kevin J. Vanhoozer

Systematic theology is the cognitive enterprise that passionately seeks to know the God of the gospel and to demonstrate its understanding in forms of loving and obedient speech and practice. Scripture, the supreme authority that guides and governs the church's search for understanding, is the 'soul' of theology. As such, it animates the 'body' of theology in the church's performance of Scripture. Theological method pertains to how one actually moves from page to practice, from *sacra pagina* to *sacra doctrina*, from the biblical texts to patterns of ecclesial speaking, thinking and living. Two basic questions emerge: Should theologians build systems of doctrinal truth from Scripture and, if so, how? Is *systematic* theology biblical?

The standing of doctrine as truth is a perennial issue, and is fiercely contested on theology's Western front. Some critics maintain that conservative theology is guilty of unequally yoking the gospel to modern epistemology.[1]

---

1. In particular, to 'foundationalism', the theory 'that knowledge of the world rests on a foundation of indubitable beliefs from which further propositions can be inferred to produce a superstructure of known truths'. This, at least, is the definition given in Ted Honderich, ed., *The Oxford Companion to Philosophy* (Oxford: Oxford University Press, 1995), p. 289. In practice, however, the term 'foundationalism' is used in a variety of ways. We shall return to this matter in due course.

A second Western front – postmodernity – has now opened up. Reaction among evangelicals is, however, mixed: while some theologians train their guns on the postmodern, others seek diplomatic relations.

We begin with three anecdotes about systems – the first of several 'triangulations' that will help us to determine our fronts, allies and combatants with greater accuracy than the all too common two-party distinctions (e.g. conservative/liberal; modern/postmodern; foundationalist/non-foundationalist).

Introduction: three short stories about systems

In an intriguing footnote in his *The Symbolism of Evil*, Paul Ricoeur makes the following statement: 'That the theology of love cannot become a systematic theology appears evident.'[2] Ricoeur has other uncharacteristically harsh things to say about theology's penchant to drain away the rich surplus of Scripture's metaphorical and narrative meaning. It is because the systematician moves to concepts too hastily that Ricoeur advises the interpreter of Scripture to have the exegete rather than the theologian as partner.

Meanwhile, in a philosophical galaxy far, far away, Michael Dummett has asked, 'Can Analytical Philosophy Be Systematic, and Ought it to Be?'[3] Dummett writes in the analytic tradition, for which the object of philosophy is the analysis of thought, and the reality represented by thought, via an analysis of language: 'It is of the essence of thought, not merely to be communicable, but to be communicable, without residue, by means of language.'[4] Clearly, such a project is of interest to the theologian who seeks to know God's thoughts, and reality, through the language of the Bible. Philosophy has often served as handmaid to theology. It is therefore appropriate in the context of an essay on the future of systematic theology to inquire whether the latter will continue to require philosophy's services if, following Ricoeur, the task of theology is faith seeking understanding through biblical interpretation, particularly if this latter task inevitably involves linguistic and conceptual analysis. Can such an 'analytic theology' be systematic without importing certain philosophical presuppositions, say, about the nature of meaning and truth?

And so to our third story about systems of interpretation: '[I]f I have a

---

2. Paul Ricoeur, *The Symbolism of Evil* (Boston: Beacon, 1969), p. 326, n. 7.

3. In Kenneth Baynes, James Bohman and Thomas McCarthy, eds., *After Philosophy: End or Transformation?* (London: MIT Press, 1987), pp. 189–215.

4. Ibid., p. 195.

system, it is limited to a recognition of what Kierkegaard called the "infinite qualitative distinction" between time and eternity'.[5] So begins Barth's defence of his reading of the book of Romans. For Barth, the only assumption needed to do justice to the subject matter was the theological assumption 'that God is God'.[6] 'System' here means something like the procedure a gambler uses in placing his or her bets. Of course, the 'bet' in this instance is the wager of faith. Barth wagers everything on the premise that faith's search for understanding depends for its success on its ability, above all, to distinguish God from everything else in the world. Hans Frei rightly comments, however, that Barth does not reject conceptual analysis, or even formal categories such as meaning and truth, but believes that these must 'be governed by the specific theological issue at hand'.[7]

Is there a moral in these stories? At a minimum, theologians must be prepared to give an account of the 'system' that is within them – or rather, of the assumptions and procedures that govern their use and interpretation of the Bible. With this moral in mind we turn in the next section to examine three contemporary challenges to the very notion of 'systematic' theology. A description of the work of some contemporary theologians who represent distinct methodological trajectories follows. I then inquire whether and to what extent these proposals are susceptible to Donald Davidson's critique of conceptual schemes and to Bruce Marshall's critique of the epistemic dependency thesis, two critiques that allow us further to press home the key question *Can systematic theology be biblical and, if so, how?* The final section sets forth a constructive proposal for doing theology that integrates the best of the three previous approaches under the rubric of 'theodrama'. This involves revisiting the doctrine of Scripture and the nature of doctrine itself and of reorienting theology towards wisdom rather than mere theoretical knowledge. The conclusion returns to the question of the future of systems in theology and offers three theses towards a theodramatic systematics.

Prolegomena to any future systematics: three challenges

Etienne Gilson once described systems of medieval theology as 'cathedrals of the mind'. Like cathedrals, systematic theologies are summaries of the best of

---

5. Karl Barth, 'Preface to the Second Edition', *The Epistle to the Romans*, tr. Edwyn C. Hoskyns (Oxford: Oxford University Press, 1968), p. 10.

6. Ibid., p. 11.

7. Hans Frei, *Types of Christian Theology* (New Haven: Yale University Press, 1992), p. 41.

a particular civilization. But also like too many cathedrals, many systems have become ruins that are no longer fit to inhabit. What happened? Why are theologians (and others) saying such awful things about systems?

'Systematic theology is modern, and hence reductionist'

Beginning students of theology quickly learn that it is the *logos* of *theos*, reasoned discourse about God, that sets out the varied ideas of the Christian faith in a single, coherent and well-ordered presentation. A 'system' of theology here refers to the topical collection and exploration of the content of the Bible and the attempt to bring this content to bear on the contemporary situation. Systematic theology 'seeks to articulate the *content* of the gospel of Jesus Christ to the *context* of a particular culture'.[8]

'Systematics' an early modern literary genre? Biblical content and its standardized theological form

While it would be historically inaccurate to say that systematic theology is a modern development, it is equally mistaken to suggest that the shift from the medieval to the early modern world-view had no impact on the way in which theologians conceived their task.[9] The so-called Protestant scholastics of the seventeenth century sought to systematize Scripture by using reason to clarify and order its teaching. Francis Turretin, for example, formulated a system of 'right-doctrine'.[10]

Conservative evangelical theologians of the nineteenth and twentieth centuries followed suit, emphasizing the cognitive content – revealed truths – of Scripture in opposition to liberals who viewed the Bible as the symbolic expression of religious experience (Schleiermacher defines doctrines as 'religious feelings set forth in speech'). From the basic postulate that God reveals

---

8. David K. Clark, *To Know and Love God: Method for Theology* (Wheaton, Ill.: Crossway, 2003), p. 33.

9. See Nicholas Lash, who suggests that the word 'god' came to be used 'to name the ultimate explanation of the system of the world' (*Holiness, Speech, and Silence: Reflection on the Question of God* [Aldershot: Ashgate, 2005], p. 9). In short, 'god' becomes the key component in a metaphysical system. Lash also suggests that this shift – from worship to metaphysics – is accompanied by a shift in theology's voice, from second-person prayerful reflection to third-person theoretical description, and thus from dialogue to monologue.

10. Richard A. Muller, 'Scholasticism Protestant and Catholic: Francis Turretin on the Object and Principles of Theology', *Church History* 55.2 (June 1986), p. 205.

himself in Scripture, says Millard Erickson, 'we may proceed to elaborate an entire theological system by unfolding the contents of the Scriptures'.[11] Indeed, on one telling of the story, the 'standard' paradigm of evangelical theology is a rationalist approach that accepts the Bible as a book of propositional revelation – divinely communicated information – and uses reason to present these propositional truths in orderly fashion.[12]

According to this genealogy, a concern for right doctrine begat propositionalism: a focus on Scripture as a handbook of doctrine rather than a story of what God was doing in Jesus Christ. Carl F. H. Henry declares that 'God's revelation is rational communication conveyed in intelligible ideas and meaningful words, that is, in conceptual-verbal form.'[13] Such a view of revelation fits well with 'analytic theology'; namely, the attempt to clarify God's thoughts through an analysis (which includes both clarification and organization) of biblical language. One critic of this approach suggests that such a focus marks 'the triumph of the formal principle of evangelicalism over the material'.[14]

Others have wondered whether the Scripture principle has become unequally yoked with foundationalism, a distinctly modern epistemology.[15] To be sure, the church is built upon 'the foundation of the apostles and prophets, Christ Jesus himself being the cornerstone' (Eph. 2:20).[16] But is confessing Christ as the foundation of the faith the same thing as espousing an epistemological foundationalism for which biblical propositions are the brick and mortar with which to build one's theological tower? It is salutary to recall the second half of Paul's thought: 'Christ Jesus himself being the cornerstone, *in whom the whole structure is joined together*' (Eph. 2:21). The operative image here is

---

11. *Christian Theology*, 2nd edn (Grand Rapids: Baker, 1998), pp. 34–35.

12. So Stanley J. Grenz, *Renewing the Center: Evangelical Theology in a Post-Theological Era* (Grand Rapids: Baker, 2000), ch. 2, 'Scripture and the Genesis of the New Evangelicalism'.

13. *God, Revelation, and Authority* (Waco: Word, 1979), vol. 3, p. 248.

14. Grenz, *Renewing the Center*, p. 101.

15. Their name is Legion! Among the more influential such accounts are the following: Nancey Murphy, *Beyond Liberalism and Fundamentalism: How Modern and Postmodern Philosophy Set the Theological Agenda* (Valley Forge, Pa.: Trinity Press International, 1996), chs. 1, 4; Nicholas Wolterstorff, *Reason within the Bounds of Religion* (Grand Rapids: Eerdmans, 1976); Stanley J. Grenz and John R. Franke, *Beyond Foundationalism: Shaping Theology in a Postmodern Context* (Louisville: Westminster John Knox, 2001).

16. Bible quotations in this chapter are from the RSV.

not simply foundation but also coherence, the very notion to which the non-foundationalist appeals. Be that as it may, the question of whether being biblical in theology means building systems out of revealed propositions gains currency.

'Systematics' as ancient-modern violence? From theory to -ism

Some critics see systematic theology as the modern flowering of a theoretical impulse that began in ancient Greece. Carl Raschke, for example, calls for a 'dehellenizing' of evangelical faith and an undoing of theology's dependence on categories taken from secular philosophy.[17] The prime offender according to Raschke is the notion that knowledge is *theoria*, a kind of 'seeing' with the mind's eye, a metaphor that encourages us to think of knowing as a subject's seeing an object: 'The goal of thought is to obtain a clear and precise picture of what one is viewing.'[18] Postmodernity is a reaction to this ideal of theoretical knowledge and its key assumptions: (1) that we behold reality via a rationalistic induction (2) that language represents thought's apprehension of reality and that (3) that truth is the correspondence of thought and reality.

Raschke appeals to the Jewish philosopher Emmanuel Levinas and contrasts his postmodern biblical hermeneutic with what he takes to be the modernism of inerrantists. Levinas has argued that the subject–object dichotomy is itself intrinsically violent. He calls the attempt of knowing subjects theoretically to master the world of objects 'Greek-think' and goes on to accuse it of 'totalization'. Totalization is a matter not of saving but of razing the phenomena, of swallowing everything up into procrustean conceptual schemes in an effort to grasp things with 'our' categories. What this amounts to is an attempt to assimilate the 'other' violently to the 'same', that is, to our systems of thought: 'The labor of thought wins out over the otherness of things and men.'[19] Systematic theology thus becomes a violence we do to biblical things.

With Levinas, Raschke views the word not as a sign that indicates a thing but as a call from an other. The exegete is not dealing with an object, but an interlocutor.[20] For the subject matter of the Bible is ultimately Jesus Christ –

---

17. Carl Raschke, *The Next Reformation: Why Evangelicals Must Embrace Postmodernity* (Grand Rapids: Baker, 2004), pp. 131–134.

18. Ibid., p. 213.

19. Levinas, 'Ethics as First Philosophy', in Seán Hand, ed., *A Levinas Reader* (Oxford: Blackwell, 1989), p. 79.

20. We shall return to this theme below in the context of rehabilitating the historic Reformed emphasis on Word and Spirit.

a person, not a proposition – and what is at stake in reading the Bible is not mastering biblical propositions but engaging in personal dialogue: 'The idea of God as an entity knowable by propositional analysis is metaphysical, a survival of heathen philosophy.'[21] Raschke goes on to attack the 'heresy' of inerrancy for idolizing the text and for implying that readers can attain truth – the correspondence of word and thing – apart from the gracious illumining work of the Holy Spirit. It is the Hellenizers, says Raschke, who reduce *logos* to logic, saying to predication. For Raschke, the Logos is not representational (a content that can be stated) but vocative (a word of address): 'Truth is the intimacy of the interpersonal.'[22]

David Tracy's take on the *logos* of *theos* affords a similar way of viewing the relation of the modern and the postmodern. Modernity, he suggests, has developed and perfected its own characteristic form for naming and thinking God: the concept. In Tracy's words, 'What modernity provides for the naming of God . . . is a series of seemingly endless debates on the correct -ism, that is, the correct set of abstract propositions which name and think God.'[23] It is as if theologians ask of conceptual schemes what the disciples asked of Jesus: 'Are you the -ism that is to come, or shall we look for another?' (see Matt. 11:3).[24]

Postmodernity is the acknowledgment that there are other valid forms besides the concept for naming and thinking God that are proper to Christianity itself (e.g. the prophetic; the mystic). Hence Tracy's claim that *theos* ultimately upsets every *logos*. God is not a tame lion; no system can domesticate him. In Tracy's words, '*Theos* has returned to unsettle the dominance of the modern *logos*.'[25]

'*Systematic theology is Western, and hence imperialistic*'

Complaints that theology is modern necessarily overlap with the complaint that it is too Western. It is probably for this reason that many non-Western and

---

21. Raschke, *Next Reformation*, p. 119.
22. Ibid., p. 134.
23. David Tracy, 'Literary Theory and Naming God', *Journal of Religion* 74 (1994), p. 307.
24. Hegel is the prime example of this tendency. His attempt to systematize biblical religion consisted of translating Scripture's narrative *Vorstellung* (representation) into a consistent system of *Begriffe* (concepts).
25. 'The Return of God in Contemporary Theology', in his *On Naming the Present: God, Hermeneutics, and Church* (Maryknoll: Orbis, 1993), p. 37.

postmodern theologians raise the same complaints against traditional systematic theology. The focus of this double-barrelled criticism is the West's trust that following scientific methods and procedures will yield universally valid conclusions, whether about the natural world or the biblical text. The postmodern response to modernity's 'view from nowhere' is 'location, location, location': the situatedness of the theologian trumps his or her supposedly objective methodology. From this perspective, the history of Western theology is simply a series of 'local theologies'.[26]

The demographic shift of Christians away from Europe and North America towards the global south has been called the 'greatest single change that has come upon the Christian faith during the last century'.[27] Thanks to this demographic shift, and to the postmodern critique of universal reason, it is becoming increasingly apparent that theology is ineluctably tied to and rooted in particular social and cultural conditions. Hence, 'Context has . . . become primary for the theological task.'[28] Do systems neutralize contexts, or do contexts explode systems? Theology at present is pulled by two forces: a centripetal, catholic force and a centrifugal ethnic force. We have therefore to ask of the globalization of theology what cosmologists ask of the universe: will it keep expanding (into more and more locales) or will it collapse in upon itself?

Already theology has gained from the expanded conversation. Latin American liberation theologians, for example, have reminded us that theology involves much more than theoretical reflection. They have stressed the importance of praxis: of seeing, judging and acting in society in such a way that one contributes to the coming reign of God. Expanding the conversation to include theologians from other corners of the world will undoubtedly occasion similar insights. Craig Ott therefore calls for a 'globalizing' theology; that is, a way of doing theology that is intentionally informed by the diverse perspectives represented in the worldwide church on topics of relevance to the church's global situation.[29] Clearly, there is no 'one size fits all' systematic theology. Ott comments that, while certain creedal formulations are no less true

---

26. So Robert J. Schreiter, *Constructing Local Theologies* (Maryknoll: Orbis, 1985).

27. John Parratt, *An Introduction to Third World Theologies* (Cambridge: Cambridge University Press, 2004), p. 1.

28. Ibid., p. 8.

29. Craig Ott, 'Conclusion: Towards an Evangelical Globalizing of Theology', in Craig Ott and Harold Netland, eds., *Doing Theology in a Globalized World* (Grand Rapids: Baker, forthcoming).

in Africa or Asia than they are in Europe or North America, 'they are not necessarily equally *relevant, understandable* or *adequate* in all contexts'.[30] We are only
now beginning to sense what the implications of such insights might be for
doing systematic theology.[31]

'Systematic theology is wissenschaftlich, *and hence impractical'*
The criticism that systematic theology is *wissenschaftlich* – an academic special-
ization with scientific, methodical procedures for gaining knowledge – but
unrelated to the life of the church is connected to the fact it is modern and
Western. After all, nothing more characterizes the modern West than the
scientific method. The complaint that theology is too *wissenschaftlich* breaks
down into two further, more specific complaints.

'Systematic theology is an academic specialization'
No single recent work has elicited more discussion about the nature of theological education than Edward Farley's *Theologia*,[32] a book that chronicles the
fragmentation of what was once a united enterprise into four increasingly
autonomous theological specialities (biblical studies, dogmatics, church
history and practical theology): 'Once the theological school and the course of
theological study is thought of as a plurality of sciences, theology as a single
science (discipline) is lost.'[33]

In the early Christian centuries, *theologia* denoted a saving knowledge of
God and a mind illumined by and inclined towards God. Farley claims that the
impasse between this earlier pious knowledge of God and today's specialized
theological sciences has 'brought about . . . the abandonment of both for the
professional, strategy-oriented, programs of recent decades'.[34] Moreover, he
blames the Scripture principle (i.e. the belief that the Bible is the deposit of
divine revelation): 'For once theology is thought of as itself simply a deposit,
a collection of truths, the modern problem of building a bridge from those
truths to practical ends is created.'[35]

---

30. Ibid.
31. See my '"One Rule to Rule Them All"? Theological Method in an Era of World
    Christianity', in Ott and Netland, *Doing Theology*.
32. *Theologia: The Fragmentation and Unity of Theological Education* (Philadelphia: Fortress,
    1983).
33. Ibid., p. 42.
34. Ibid., p. 17.
35. Ibid., p. 61.

'Systematic theology is unimaginative, unspiritual and unrelated to life'
Perhaps the most common objection to systematic theology arises from the perceived (and often felt) disconnect between theory (*Wissenschaft*) and practice (real life). In the words of the would-be bishop of the emerging church, 'humans shall not live by systems and abstractions and principles alone, but also by stories and poetry and proverbs of mystery'.[36]

Brian Gerrish believes, with Farley, that the malaise in theological education at present stems from the tendency to confuse knowledge with information processing or the mastery of certain skills. Teachers need to focus on inculcating good habits of thought, and this means thinking 'more about the person who *has* the information and the skills, more about what it is that integrates the fields of study'.[37] According to Gerrish, the Reformed habit of mind, in contrast to the common stereotype of systematic theology, has always been practical: 'the good works of the theologian's mind are not just true thoughts, but thoughtful actions'.[38] For Calvin, the end of theology is not encyclopaedia but edification: 'Knowledge of God is not a theory but a praxis . . . of life under God and his will.'[39]

Miroslav Volf rightly says that 'at the heart of every good theology lies not simply a plausible intellectual vision but more important a compelling account of a way of life'.[40] The ultimate purpose of theology is not to produce pristine systems but 'to serve a way of life'.[41] To be precise, Christian theology serves the way of Christian discipleship by striving to understand God's own way in our world, what Barth calls 'the way of the Son into the far country'. In short, theology is the attempt to understand and respond to God's story. Only

---

36. Brian McLaren, *New Kind of Christian: A Tale of Two Friends on a Spiritual Journey* (San Francisco: Jossey-Bass, 2001), p. 159.

37. Brian Gerrish, 'Tradition in the Modern World: The Reformed Habit of Mind', in David Willis and Michael Welker, eds., *Toward the Future of Reformed Theology: Tasks, Topics, Traditions* (Grand Rapids: Eerdmans, 1999), p. 9. Cf. John Webster, in the same volume, who contrasts *Wissenschaft* with *Bildung*, where the former pertains to information and the latter to formation and transformation, 'Theological Theology', pp. 6–7.

38. Ibid., p. 17.

39. Jans-Joachim Kraus, 'The Contemporary Relevance of Calvin's Theology', in Willis and Welker, *Toward the Future of Reformed Theology*, p. 327.

40. 'Theology for a Way of Life', in Dorothy C. Bass and Miroslav Volf, eds., *Practicing Theology: Beliefs and Practices in Christian Life* (Grand Rapids: Eerdmans, 2002), p. 247.

41. Ibid., p. 247.

recently, since the 1980s, has systematic theology seriously grappled with the implications that Scripture is less a storehouse of facts than a realistic narrative that renders personal identity: of God, Jesus Christ and Christians.

Systematic theology cannot properly make sense of narrative with the tools of linguistic and conceptual analysis only. Reading Scripture theologically needs imagination, 'the faculty which makes sense of things, locating particular bits and pieces within larger patterns'.[42] Whereas analytic exegesis breaks Scripture up into fragments, the imagination is more synthetic; its business is to grasp the pattern of the whole. Moreover, to the extent that theology serves a way of life, imagination locates everyday reality within a biblical pattern, that is, if one is really going to *indwell* the world of the biblical text. To live so that the biblical world is one's primary interpretative framework is an imaginative, practical and spiritual enterprise.[43] As I argue below, facilitating *that* kind of interpretation is the true aim, and glory, of systematic theology.

A scientific theology 'according to the Scriptures'? Three contemporary trajectories

A comprehensive survey of how theology is now being done is beyond the scope of the present chapter. My immediate concern is with the way in which three contemporary theologians – Alister McGrath, Stanley Grenz, Donald Bloesch – respond to the charges lodged in the preceding section.[44] If I converse with these three trajectories, it is because they each display certain key insights that will be important to incorporate in any future systematics, and because they each represent a distinct position with regard to the relation between theological scheme and biblical content. Better: the challenge for future systematics will be to 'triangulate' their respective concerns: world (McGrath), worshipping community (Grenz) and Word (Bloesch).

You will know them by the company they keep. Theologians have had diverse disciplinary waltzing partners at different times, with philosophers dominating

---

42. Trevor Hart, 'Imagination and Responsible Reading', in Craig Bartholomew, Colin Greene and Karl Möller, eds., *Renewing Biblical Interpretation* (Grand Rapids: Zondervan, 2000), p. 319.

43. I understand spirituality not as some kind of ethereal existence but rather in terms of everyday life lived out of the desire to love, obey and glorify God.

44. Had time and space permitted, I would also have liked to examine the recent proposals of Richard Lints, David Clark and Michael Horton, among others.

their dance cards. Interestingly, each of the three theologians we shall consider lays claim to the status of science, and each displays an affinity with a previous theologian. McGrath dialogues with the natural sciences and thus recalls the theological method of Charles Hodge; Grenz works with the social sciences and thus bears an affinity to George Lindbeck; Bloesch works towards a properly theological science and thus follows Karl Barth.

Theology and the natural sciences

Charles Hodge: inductive exegesis

The opening line of Hodge's *Systematic Theology*[45] speaks volumes as to its location in the history of ideas: 'In every science there are two factors: facts and ideas; or facts and the mind.'[46] The Bible is not itself a science but is raw material: it is the theologian's 'storehouse of facts'.[47] The theologian stands to Scripture as the scientist does to nature. In each case, one begins by observing the facts (the method of induction) and then derives principles from the facts (the method of deduction): 'So the Bible contains the truths which the theologian has to collect, authenticate, arrange, and exhibit in their internal relation to each other.'[48] Theology is thus 'the exhibition of the facts of Scripture in their proper order and relation, with the principles or general truths involved in the facts themselves, and which pervade and harmonize the whole'.[49]

Hodge's rules of interpretation – taking words in their plain historical sense; interpreting Scripture with Scripture because it all ultimately is the work of one divine mind; seeking the guidance of the Holy Spirit – seem on the surface to be unexceptional with regard to the mainstream Protestant tradition. Upon closer inspection, however, Hodge's inductive method betrays certain tell-tale marks of its time, though this alone is hardly an argument against it. In particular, the method presupposes a subject–object dichotomy in which the interpreter's mind observes and analyses its object: the facts of the Bible.[50] The direction of theological reasoning is bottom-up: from biblical foundations to

45. Charles Hodge, *Systematic Theology*, vol. 1 (Grand Rapids: Eerdmans, 1979).

46. Ibid., p. 1.

47. Ibid., p. 10.

48. Ibid., p. 1.

49. Ibid., p. 19.

50. At the same time, 'The theologian . . . acknowledges that the Scriptures must be interpreted in accordance with established facts' (ibid., p. 57).

doctrinal formulation. The location or situation of the interpreter is irrelevant: the glory of the inductive method is that close observation allows the facts to emerge, regardless of who is doing the observing. Second, Hodge works with a dichotomy between fact and theory that has been called into question by philosophers of science who insist that data are always/already 'theory-laden'. Third, Hodge's decision to read the Bible as a book of divinely revealed facts predisposes him to focus on the Bible's content and to construe this content as propositional teaching. Such a focus on revealed content runs the risk of neglecting the larger canonical context and literary form of the biblical 'facts', perhaps the inevitable result of biblical empiricism.[51]

What complicates this description of Hodge's theological method is his well-known piety and his remarks concerning the role of the Holy Spirit. On the one hand, Hodge makes a strong case for the necessity of trusting our senses: because God has created us to know the world through our senses, 'Confidence in our senses is . . . one form of confidence in God.'[52] Moreover, all supernatural revelation is addressed to the senses: 'Those who heard Christ had to trust to their sense of hearing; those who read the Bible have to trust to their sense of sight.'[53] On the other hand, Hodge is well aware that there is a peculiarly religious experience, a spiritual 'sense', as it were, that he relates to the 'inward teaching' of the Holy Spirit.[54] Indeed, Hodge notes that the inward teaching of the Spirit is so powerful 'that it is no uncommon thing to find men having two theologies, – one of the intellect, another of the heart'.[55]

The question this raises for theological method is simply this: how do we attend to 'what God teaches'? Is 'what God teaches' – the facts in Scripture – in plain view of the theologian/scientist, or do we need the 'inner teacher' correctly to approach the biblical facts? Hodge would no doubt object to the hint of methodological bifurcation by urging us to 'prayerful induction' and perhaps this is the best we can do. Hodge's discussion nevertheless poses an important theological issue for his successors: is revelation – 'what God teaches' – *behind*

---

51. Empiricism is the epistemological theory which holds that knowledge comes through or is based on sense experience. Whereas most empiricists limit their sources to those sensations that come through the five physical senses, there is a sense in which we can extend it to biblical interpretation viewed as 'my experience of the biblical text'.

52. Hodge, *Systematic Theology*, vol. 1, p. 60.

53. Ibid.

54. Ibid., p. 16.

55. Ibid.

the text (e.g. in the history of Jesus Christ), *in* the text, what comes *through* the text, or is it somehow *behind, in, and through* the text, as I shall argue below?[56]

Alister McGrath: abductive metaphysics

Alister McGrath's recent three-volume work, *A Scientific Theology*, continues theology's dialogue with the natural sciences.[57] A scientific theology is 'a principled attempt to give an account of the reality of God, which it understands to be embedded at different levels in the world'.[58] With Hodge, McGrath believes there is a convergence between the way in which the scientific and theological communities develop their respective theories: 'Both the natural sciences and theology propose that development in theory is governed by attentiveness to reality.'[59] Against Hodge, McGrath acknowledges the failure of classical foundationalism as an account of science or of how we come to know reality.[60]

Although McGrath acknowledges twentieth-century criticisms of the inductive model, he insists that a scientific theology conceives itself as an a posteriori discipline. However, a *little* social constructivism is not necessarily a dangerous thing (to realism, that is). Theologians are not neutral observers, but bearers of a tradition-bound rationality. McGrath rejects both classic foundationalism (rationality is universal) and postmodern pragmatism (rationality is what you make of it) and instead opts for Alasdair MacIntyre's tradition-based reality (rationality is relative to community tradition, but some traditions are more explanatory than others).[61] McGrath points to Roy

---

56. Hodge sees the Spirit both as the revealer of all divine truth ('The doctrines of the Bible are called the things of the Spirit') and as the 'attender' of all divine truth 'by his power' (*Systematic Theology*, vol. 1, pp. 531–532). Subsequent theologians such as Barth have argued that the 'attending by his power' is itself an aspect of divine revelation.

57. In the opening volume of his trilogy McGrath says, 'A positive working relationship between Christian theology and the natural sciences is demanded by the Christian understanding of the nature of reality itself – an understanding which is grounded in the doctrine of creation' (*Nature* [Grand Rapids: Eerdmans, 2001], p. 21).

58. McGrath, *A Scientific Theology*. Vol. 2: *Reality* (Grand Rapids: Eerdmans, 2002), p. xi.

59. Ibid., p. 315.

60. Ibid., pp. 20–39.

61. McGrath defines classical foundationalism in terms of its three central assumptions, of which the first is most important for the purposes of the present chapter:
    (1) that there are foundational beliefs that guarantee their own truth, and which are

Bhaskar's critical realism as an approach that takes the social location of the observer seriously, but not so seriously that it abandons realism for a pure social constructivism.[62] A scientific theology maintains both the public accessibility of reality while recognizing the tradition-specific nature of the process of observing and interpreting reality.[63] Christians, for example, view the natural world *as* God's creation.

McGrath, like Hodge, is at pains to stress the continuity of theology's method with that of the natural sciences. He rightly resists the materialist temptation to reduce 'reality' to its physical components, preferring rather to speak of reality as stratified or composed of various layers. Just as, say, biology develops a vocabulary and principles for its unique level – organic life – so theology develops its distinct vocabulary and conceptuality with which to articulate the reality to which it particularly attends. Against Hodge, however, McGrath identifies the primary object of scientific theology not with the Bible as a storehouse of facts but with the revelation of God in the history of Jesus Christ.[64]

A truly scientific theology works with a posteriori ideas and criteria that emerge from an actual engagement with some aspect of reality: 'Each tradition or discipline potentially demands its own criteria of engagement. Methodology is ultimately dependent upon ontology.'[65] The matter of theology is God's revelation, but Christians hold that this is located 'in nature, in history, in personal experience, in the life of the church, and especially in Scripture ... each of these can be regarded as a "level of reality" open to investigation'.[66] Specifically, Christian theology is 'grounded in *a posteriori* reflection on the biblical witness to Christ, not derived from *a priori* ideas about God or

---

accessible to any rational person, irrespective of their historical or cultural context; (2) that further beliefs may be derived from these foundational beliefs; (3) the connection between these further and foundational beliefs is 'truth-preserving' (*Reality*, p. 21).

62. Ibid., p. xvi.

63. Ibid., p. 54.

64. In an important aside, McGrath notes that the correlation of roles between the pre-existent Christ, through whom all things were created, and the incarnate Christ, through whom all things have been made new, 'establishes a fundamental link between ... a natural and a systematic theology ... between the study of *nature* and the study of *Christ*' (*Reality*, p. 307).

65. Ibid., p. 118.

66. Ibid., p. 227.

humanity'.[67] Furthermore, because Christ is both the one through whom all things were made (the pre-existent *logos*) and the one in whom all things have been made new (the incarnate *logos*), there is a link 'between a natural and a systematic theology [and] between the study of *nature* and the study of *Christ*'.[68]

The final volume in McGrath's trilogy treats 'theory', understood as a communal beholding of an experienced reality. Here, too, McGrath wants to affirm both the realism of theology's object and the traditioned nature of theological reflection. Theories are not free creations of the human mind but accountable to the community's experience. Doctrines are 'the theological counterpart of scientific theories'[69] and, as such, articulate the community's response to the 'phenomena' of divine revelation.

As to the nature of the phenomenon or *datum* that is theology's object of enquiry, McGrath claims that the deposit of faith is 'a multilevelled reality, embracing a number of revelational strata', ranging from the biblical texts and patterns of worship to ideas and institutional structures.[70] A scientific theology will not seek to reduce all strata to a foundational level but will explicate each level in its own right. The method is not induction but abduction, an 'arguing backwards from what is accessible and may be observed in the present to what may be argued to lie behind it'.[71] Significantly, McGrath identifies theology's object as *past* revelation. We do not have direct access to this past revelation, but rather we know it 'primarily by its effects – by the impact it has had upon history, such as Scripture, various ecclesiastical institutions, and the liturgy'.[72]

What is crucial for McGrath is that the Christian community, and its ensuing tradition, was called into being by a series of historical events: 'From an orthodox perspective, the precipitating cause of Christian faith and Christian doctrine was and remains Jesus Christ.'[73] We know this history only through the testimonies of his words and deeds preserved in the New Testament. The basic

---

67. Ibid., p. 301.
68. Ibid., p. 309.
69. Alister McGrath, *A Scientific Theology*. Vol. 3: *Theory* (Grand Rapids: Eerdmans, 2003), p. xv.
70. Ibid., p. 145.
71. Ibid., p. 149.
72. Ibid., p. 153. McGrath cites Schleiermacher's attempt to trace present Christian experience back to the impact of Jesus on the original Christian community as an example of theological abduction.
73. Ibid., p. 176.

'fact' on which Christianity is based is the history of Jesus Christ, and this fact takes a narrative form in its biblical representation.[74] The biblical texts transmit the past to the present: 'The New Testament is essentially the repository of the formative and identity-giving traditions of the Christian community.'[75] The task of theology is to continue to transmit the church's identity-giving past to the present through the critical appropriation of tradition.[76]

What shall we say to this sophisticated prolegomenon to scientific theology? If it has a weakness, it lies not in its conception of science (there is much here to commend and critical realism is a vast improvement on Hodge!) but in its conception of theology's distinctive object. McGrath appears to be caught between a metaphysical rock and an epistemological hard place. On the one hand, he is a realist who identifies theology's object with the history of Jesus Christ, an 'extrasystemic' reality. On the other hand, there is no access to this reality except through the community's 'reception' of it (which includes its theory-making). Furthermore, McGrath counts this reception among the strata of revelation. In other words, the community's 'beholding' or experience of reality is itself part of the reality being described. Hence doctrine is not a summary of 'what God teaches' in Scripture, as it was for Hodge, so much as the community's articulation of what it has seen and experienced.[77] Revelation for McGrath embraces 'both the foundational events of the Christian faith . . . and their perceived significance'.[78] The goal remains metaphysics – saying who Jesus is – yet it is not altogether clear whether, or how, Scripture continues to function as supreme norm of the community's beholding and articulating.

What, then, is the nature and locus of theology's prime datum, divine revelation, vis-à-vis the work of theology? What precisely are Christian theologians to observe? If revelation embraces both the foundational events of the Christian faith (now inaccessible to us) and their perceived significance, how can we ever criticize the latter by the former and, if not by the former, then how? In the final analysis, it is not sufficiently clear whether Scripture has authority over other strata of revelation, what role appeals to Scripture play, or

---

74. Nancey Murphy classifies McGrath's work as a species of 'narrative foundationalism' (*Beyond Liberalism and Fundamentalism*, p. 19). Murphy is reacting primarily to McGrath's *Genesis of Doctrine*.

75. McGrath, *Theory*, p. 177.

76. Ibid., p. 183.

77. Ibid., p. 28.

78. Ibid., p. 190.

just how one actually appeals to Scripture.[79] One possible solution is to see Scripture itself as an authoritative communal beholding of divine reality in which the present-day church seeks faithfully to participate. At some point, however, McGrath has to answer the question 'Why *this* community's beholding?' In short, does the canonical testimony have its origins in God? Is Holy Scripture divine discourse, God's Word?

Theology and the social sciences

George Lindbeck: community-based rationality

George Lindbeck's influential proposal for Christian theology borrows more . from the social than the natural sciences and brings the believing community even more to the methodological fore than does McGrath. Lindbeck borrows from the later Wittgenstein and from the anthropologist Clifford Geertz, and thus comes at the question of the relation of language, experience and the world from a very different perspective than was typical of much modern philosophy and science. He self-consciously rejects foundationalist approaches that ground theology either in revealed propositions (conservative) or in religious experience (liberal).

Lindbeck's postliberal approach argues that religions resemble cultures in which language takes on meaning only in relation to certain forms of life. Doctrines are neither referential statements that describe some reality outside the culture, nor are they expressive statements that describe the way the members of a culture feel. Doctrines are rather grammatical rules that teach adherents how to speak and act with 'cultural correctness'. Lindbeck insists that these grammatical categories are not the result of but the *condition* for that culture's distinct kinds of cognition and experience. Doctrines are the rules for the 'game' of Christian living. As such, their truth is 'intra-systematic', a matter of what coheres with the life and language of the church.[80]

The Bible is not a handbook of theological grammar, nor even the primary source of correct Christian speech. On the contrary, it is the use of language that largely determines its meaning and, similarly, it is the use of Scripture in the church, not Scripture-in-itself, that is the primary theological datum. The

79. McGrath speaks of revelation as an 'explosion' (cf. the Big Bang!) that leaves behind a stratified crater, the deposit of faith. Significantly, however, the biblical text is only one of these strata, with tradition being a significant other (*Theory*, pp. 145–153).

80. George A. Lindbeck, *The Nature of Doctrine: Religion and Theology in a Postliberal Age* (Philadelphia: Westminster, 1984), p. 64.

task of theology is to describe Christian *language* in the context of the Christian *form of life*. The danger is that theology is no longer discourse about God, but dwindles into a kind of social anthropology or ethnography. Tradition is less a means of connecting to a metaphysical reality in the past (so McGrath on revelation) than it is a means of socialization into the present. Everything thus depends on belonging to the right community when ecclesiology becomes 'first theology', the source of theology's first principles. Indeed, some critics accuse Lindbeck of repeating Schleiermacher's error on a grander scale, making theology a kind of *corporate* expressivism.[81]

Stanley Grenz: eschatological socially constructed realism
In a flurry of books and articles that seek to revision and recentre evangelical theology, Stanley Grenz follows Lindbeck in giving pride of place to the social sciences as offering a new paradigm with which to find a third way beyond the modern polarization of conservative and liberal.[82] Sociologists of knowledge in the late twentieth century convincingly argued that the scientist can no longer be seen as a passive observer of data but as one who has always/already been socially formed, and hence one who approaches the data with pre-understanding. Not only is personal identity formed within social structures, then, but the very process of knowing and even experiencing the world 'can only occur within a conceptual framework, a framework mediated by the social community in which we participate'.[83] Grenz's aim is to wed postmodern insights concerning ways that language constructs reality with the distinctly Christian insight that the Holy Spirit is building a new, eschatological world in and through the Word.[84] He thus shares McGrath's desire to do justice to the role of social construction in theological theory-making, but not the latter's metaphysical sensibilities.

---

81. So Richard Heyduck, *The Recovery of Doctrine in the Contemporary Church: An Essay in Philosophical Ecclesiology* (Waco: Baylor University Press, 2002), p. 38. George Hunsinger calls Lindbeck a 'neoliberal' rather than a postliberal for the same reason. See his chapter in Kevin Vanhoozer, ed., *The Cambridge Companion to Postmodern Theology* (Cambridge: Cambridge University Press, 2003), pp. 42–57, esp. 44.

82. Grenz, *Renewing the Center*, pp. 235–248.

83. Grenz, *Revisioning Evangelical Theology: A Fresh Agenda for the 21st Century* (Downers Grove: IVP, 1993), pp. 73–74.

84. Grenz, 'Articulating the Christian Belief-Mosaic', in John Stackhouse, ed., *Evangelical Futures: A Conversation on Theological Method* (Grand Rapids: Baker; Leicester: Apollos, 2000), p. 109.

Theology's distinct object is neither God nor the Bible – these ways foundationalism lies – but rather the world-view of the community of faith, what
Grenz terms the community's interpretative framework or 'belief-mosaic' that
arises from the community identity-constituting shared biblical narrative:
'Taking Lindbeck's ideas a step further, we conclude that theology system-
atizes, explores and orders the community symbols and concepts into a unified
whole – that is, into a systematic conceptual framework.'[85] Grenz acknowledges that the church is 'basic' for theology, for without the church community there would be no mosaic of beliefs for theology to articulate.[86] What is
'basic' for Christian theology is the whole interconnected interpretative framework – the whole triangle of Scripture, tradition and contemporary cultural
experience that constitutes the Spirit's community-forming speaking.

Grenz likens doing theology to a three-way conversation between Scripture,
tradition and contemporary culture. The primary voice in this theological conversation belongs to the Bible. However, being biblical in Grenz's view has
nothing to do with a foundationalism in which Scripture provides revealed
propositional 'data' that are then worked into 'theory/doctrine' by individual
knowing subjects. It is precisely this way of doing theology that Grenz asso-
ciates with modernism and from which he seeks to liberate the church. Grenz
proposes instead to view Scripture as the 'instrumentality of the Spirit', the
means through which the Spirit brings about a new social construction: the
kingdom of God. This is Grenz's 'eschatological' variation on realism.[87]

Grenz has a theological reason for preferring social constructivism to
metaphysical realism. The purpose of the Spirit's speaking is not revelation
(reality-depicting) so much as sanctification (reality-making): reshaping the
people of God. The objectivity in which Grenz believes is not 'the world as it
is' but 'the world as it is becoming in Christ through the Spirit'. Truth, similarly, is less a matter of historical actuality than of future possibility. Given the
role of language in world-construction, Christians participate in this triune

---

85. Grenz, *Revisioning*, p. 78. The metaphor of 'mosaic', like Quine's 'web', stresses the
    interconnectedness of human beliefs. We accept a belief not because it is 'founded'
    on something more basic, but because it 'fits' or coheres with other held beliefs.
    Interdependence rather than dependence is the watchword for the relation of one
    belief to another.
86. Grenz, 'Articulating', p. 132.
87. See ibid., pp. 124–125. Grenz's emphasis on the Spirit's constructing a world inclines
    him to speak of the Bible in instrumental rather than communicative terms, and to
    emphasize perlocutions over illocutions.

work by inhabiting 'a present linguistic world that sees all reality from the per-spective of the future, real world that God is bringing to pass'.[88] Theology's articulations contribute to the identity-forming language by which Christians seek to align themselves with the future world God is now bringing about through the Spirit.

Scripture is the primary means through which the Spirit speaks and shapes, but tradition is the ongoing history of the effects of the Spirit's address. It is not enough, then, for theology to be 'canonic'; it must also be catholic. More controversially, Grenz argues that the Spirit's speaking is always contextual, and that the church must attend to 'the Spirit's voice in culture'.[89] To be sure, what the Spirit says in culture coheres with the Spirit's primary speaking through Scripture. Indeed, Grenz claims that the Bible, tradition and culture do not form three different moments of communication but that they are all 'ultimately one speaking'.[90]

If there is a problem with Grenz's proposal, it does not stem from his attempt to triangulate the biblical message, the theological heritage of the church, and the thought forms of the present historical-cultural context of the church, but from the way he does so. While he is right to worry that some con-servative approaches to the Bible and theology 'collapse the Spirit into the Bible',[91] his own approach risks collapsing the Bible into the Spirit's speaking through tradition and contemporary culture. Indeed, for Grenz the Bible itself represents 'the self-understanding of the community in which it developed'.[92] The contemporary community understands some things differently, thanks to its new historical-cultural context and to the Spirit speaking through tradition and contemporary culture. Hence Grenz can state that 'we must never conclude that exegesis alone can exhaust the Spirit's speaking to us through the text'.[93]

---

88. Ibid., p. 136.

89. Ibid., p. 128.

90. Ibid.

91. Grenz, *Revisioning*, p. 117.

92. Ibid., p. 121.

93. Grenz, *Beyond Foundationalism*, p. 74. Stephen J. Wellum worries that Grenz fails to distinguish between the Bible as the 'first order' authoritative and true discourse that anchors theology, and theology as 'second order' reflection. See Wellum, 'Postconservatism, Biblical Authority, and Reception Proposals for Re-doing Evangelical Theology: A Critical Analysis', in Millard Erickson, Paul Kjoss Helseth and Justin Taylor, eds., *Reclaiming the Center: Confronting Evangelical Accommodation in Postmodern Times* (Wheaton: Crossway, 2004), pp. 161–197, esp. 189.

Is anything in Scripture *fixed*, not subject to semantic and cultural drift? Yes, but for Grenz it is not the Bible's statements or truths in the first instance but the Bible's 'categories' – creation, the exodus, the cross.[94] These are the narrative footholds that establish and preserve the identity of the people of God. Theology's norming norm is the biblical message, which is not to be equated with the message 'behind' the text (e.g. authorial intention), or with the message 'of' the text (e.g. its immanent sense), but ultimately with the message 'in front of' the text; namely, the message the Spirit declares by appropriating the text.[95] To be sure, Grenz maintains that the Spirit's speaking is bound up with (but not bound by) the discourse of the original human authors. At the end of the day, however, he identifies theology's norming norm with 'the message the Spirit declares through the text'[96] and attempts to buttress his point about the theological interpretation of Scripture with references to Ricoeur's philosophical hermeneutics ('once it is written, a text takes on a life of its own'). Yet how can one determine what the Spirit is saying if and when his speaking goes beyond 'what is written'?

What Grenz most cares about is the Spirit's using Scripture to perform the perlocutionary act (the act achieved *by* speaking) of creating a world that is centred and joined together in Jesus. Theology is not to drain the text of its life and power by distilling a system of truths but is to serve the Spirit's 'world-formative act'. Grenz's emphasis in using the Bible in theology is less on knowing than it is on being: 'It is in our participation in the gathered community that we are most clearly a "people of the book." And it is here that the Spirit's voice speaking through scripture can be most clearly discerned.'[97]

There is much here to admire: the desire to interact with critics of modernity; the concern to reclaim the role of the Spirit for a doctrine of Scripture and a theological hermeneutic; the emphasis on participating in God's world-building project; and, especially in the light of the concern with theological method of the present chapter, the attempt to triangulate Scripture, tradition and contemporary culture. What is missing, however, is an adequate account of theology's

---

94. Grenz, *Revisioning*, p. 126.

95. Grenz and Franke, *Beyond Foundationalism*, p. 74. Grenz makes some serious missteps here with regard to his use of speech-act theory, suggesting that the 'Spirit speaking through the Scriptures' is a matter of his performing the illocutionary acts of 'addressing' and 'appropriating'. For a fuller development of this critique, see my *First Theology*, pp. 197–198.

96. Grenz, *Beyond Foundationalism*, p. 74.

97. Ibid., p. 92.

norming norm. Grenz's identification of the latter with the Spirit's speaking in and through Scripture, when combined with his contention that the Spirit's speaking goes beyond authorial discourse and may be heard in and through tradition and contemporary culture too, leaves him without a criterion for distinguishing between the Word of God and the hearing of the church, or between the gospel and its possible distortions in the community's understanding.[98]

Grenz's objections to theology's using the Bible as a deposit of propositional revelation seem to stem more from postmodern sensibilities than from any properly theological concerns. His main justification for revisioning evangelical theology is to point out the latter's indebtedness to foundationalism, which he sees as nothing more than a discredited modern epistemology. Not so our next two theologians, who object to identifying the Bible with divine revelation on purely *theological* grounds.

Theological science

Karl Barth: Word of God theology

A third trajectory eschews methods taken from other disciplines and focuses instead on letting theology's distinct subject matter dictate its approach. According to Karl Barth, modern theologians have been searching (in vain) for some theological foundation in something external to theology's own subject matter. Barth himself views the task of dogmatics as 'the criticism and correction of talk about God according to the criterion of the Church's own principle'.[99] If theology calls itself a science it is because, like other sciences, (1) it is a human concern with a definite object of knowledge, (2) it follows a definite and self-consistent path to knowledge and (3) it gives an account of this path to others.[100]

Everything thus hinges on one's account of theology's subject matter and, indeed, this is precisely the area of Barth's greatest contribution. As is well known, Barth identifies the object of theology as the Word of God. However, the 'object' of theology is in fact a 'subject': the living God in his (triune) self-revelation. It follows that, for Barth, the Word of God is much more than a

---

98. Similarly, Scott Smith fears that Grenz leaves himself with no way to check to see if the linguistic world of his own making corresponds with anything more than the way his local community views the world. See especially the essays by Wellum, Carson and Caneday in Erickson et al., *Reclaiming the Center*.

99. Barth, *CD* I/1, p. 6.

100. Ibid., pp. 7–8.

mere deposit of revealed information, waiting to be mined. No, the Word of God is a dynamic act of revelation that depends on the grace of a sovereign subject and is never wholly under human control, never able definitively to be pinned down. What theology (faith seeking understanding) is trying to understand is ultimately nothing less than the freedom of God encountering humanity as this has been expressed in Jesus Christ.

The Word of God is a free act of a sovereign subject: the Father making himself known, objectively (through the Son) and subjectively (through the Spirit). It is this conviction that explains Barth's reluctance to identify the Bible directly with the Word of God. He is unwilling to make an ontological postulate – that is, to identify the Bible with divine revelation – that in his eyes would actually deprive God of his freedom to reveal or not to reveal himself in and through Scripture. The Bible is for Barth a form of the Word of God thanks to its character as prophetic and apostolic witness to Jesus Christ. Without the Spirit's work, however, there is no guarantee that the Bible will indeed present Christ to a given reader. At the same time, it really is the Bible, and not simply the church's use of the Bible, that remains authoritative: 'the Bible . . . remains free in face of all interpretation'.[101]

Barth's antipathy for 'systematic' theology has nothing to do with his being postmodern, but everything to do with his construal of theology's subject matter: 'In rejecting systematisation, Barth is not rejecting God's "givenness" but specifying it.'[102] Again, the theological 'given' is not an object but *the event of God's freedom*: the person and history of Jesus Christ ('God with us'). At the heart of theology, then, is not a system of belief but a person whose being is his act: 'not a scheme, but a name, a set of actions'.[103]

Donald Bloesch: Word and Spirit theology
Donald Bloesch has broken ranks with recent evangelical theologians by writing a seven- rather than three-volume systematics, *Christian Foundations*. By 'foundations' Bloesch has in mind not a priori principles or self-evident truths but rather the mighty deeds of God in Israel and in Jesus Christ.[104] The first

---

101. Ibid., p. 259.

102. John Webster, 'Barth, Modernity and Postmodernity', in Christian Mostert and Geoff Thompson, eds., *Karl Barth: A Future for Postmodern Theology?* (Adelaide: Australian Theological Forum, 2000), p. 16.

103. Webster, 'Barth's Christology', in ibid., p. 48.

104. Donald G. Bloesch, *Holy Scripture: Revelation, Inspiration and Interpretation* (Downers Grove: IVP, 1994), p. 20.

volume, *A Theology of Word and Spirit,* treats questions of authority and method.[105] In denying that 'Word of God' refers to a book that receives its stamp of approval from the Spirit, Bloesch claims a pedigree that includes the magisterial Reformers as well as Barth.

Though he does not agree with all of Barth's conclusions, Bloesch believes that 'we need to take his way of doing theology' over that of liberals like Paul Tillich and conservatives like Carl Henry.[106] In particular, Bloesch follows Barth in viewing God's Word as referring not to the Scripture per se but to 'the living Word in its inseparable unity with Scripture and church proclamation as this is brought home to us by the Spirit in the awakening to faith'.[107] Theology's business is not that of systematizing a set of revealed propositions gleaned (abstracted!) from Scripture; it is rather a matter of bearing faithful witness to the truth of revelation that shines through Scripture.

The ampersand in Bloesch's title is there for a reason; it signals his desire to keep theology balanced by preserving a number of constitutive tensions: faith and reason; objectivity and subjectivity; the humanity and divinity of the Scriptures and so forth. The Word of God is 'both conceptual and personal, propositional and existential'.[108] The primary authority for theology is 'the voice of the living Christ'.[109] Bloesch dubs his approach 'fideistic revelationism' and says that 'the decision of faith is as important as the fact of revelation'.[110] Elsewhere Bloesch identifies the 'dialectical interplay between Word and Spirit' as an accurate description of his position.[111] 'Word and

---

105. Donald G. Bloesch, *A Theology of Word & Spirit: Authority and Method in Theology* (Downers Grove: IVP, 1992).

106. Ibid., p. 271.

107. Ibid., p. 14.

108. Ibid., p. 20. In similar fashion, dogma has a propositional dimension but ultimately transcends all propositional forms: '[Dogma] signifies the truth of what is expressed as opposed to the way in which it is expressed. Dogma must not be reduced to propositions as statements, but propositions can convey the truth of dogma . . . [dogma] is best described as a propositional-existential truth' (ibid., p. 274, n. 9). Even universal truths such as the Golden Rule do not constitute the Word of God for Bloesch, for God's Word 'is always a personal address' (*Holy Scripture*, p. 343, n. 106) that calls for personal decision.

109. Bloesch , *Theology of Word & Spirit*, p. 187.

110. Ibid., p. 21.

111. 'Donald Bloesch Responds', in Elmer M. Colyer, ed., *Evangelical Theology in Transition: Theologians in Dialogue with Donald Bloesch* (Downers Grove: IVP, 1999), p. 188.

Spirit' says it all: revelation is not simply propositional (textual) but existential (spiritual).

As to his doctrine of Scripture, one commentator states that 'it stands somewhere between the neo-orthodoxy of Barth and Brunner and the rationalist-propositional . . . biblicism of much contemporary evangelical thought'.[112] Concerning the latter, Bloesch pulls no punches: he believes that the bane of much modern evangelicalism is a rationalism which presupposes that the Word of God is directly available to human reason. Bloesch resembles Barth in distinguishing between the Word of God and the words of the Bible. He sets forth a sacramental understanding of the Bible, comparing the Bible to a light bulb and revelation – the Spirit's communicating the Word – to the light that shines through it. The Bible is 'a divinely prepared medium or channel of divine revelation rather than the revelation itself'.[113]

Bloesch distinguishes his own 'biblical evangelical' position from what he calls 'evangelical rationalism' or 'scholasticism'. The latter equates revelation with Scripture and so regards knowledge of God (the infinite) as something that human reason (the finite) can grasp through procedures of biblical interpretation. In contrast, Bloesch believes that knowledge of God is not possible apart from faith, which is the gift of the Holy Spirit. Only the Spirit can turn the *written* Word of God into the *living* Word of God, and only the latter really communicates the truth and power of Jesus Christ.[114] The Word of God cannot be reduced to rational statements: 'It is God in action, God speaking and humans hearing.'[115] Interestingly, Bloesch does Barth one better and proposes a *fourth* form of the Word of God in addition to Barth's three (Jesus Christ, Scripture, proclamation): the *inner* Word the Spirit ministers to our hearts.[116]

Clearly, Bloesch does not want to reduce the Word of God to words of the prophets and apostles. Their words 'correspond' to God's Word but they are not 'identical' with it.[117] But why not? What exactly does the Spirit add or do to the human words? The most charitable reading of Bloesch's position at this point suggests that the Spirit adds clarity and power. These provide the 'exist-

---

112. So Roger Olson, 'Locating Bloesch in the Evangelical Landscape', in Colyer, *Evangelical Theology in Transition*, p. 28.

113. Bloesch, *Holy Scripture*, p. 18.

114. Ibid., pp. 25–26.

115. Ibid., p. 48.

116. Bloesch, *Word & Spirit*, p. 191.

117. Bloesch, *Holy Scripture*, p. 26.

ential plus' to what would otherwise remain the inert semantics. 'Clarity' and 'power' ultimately amount to the presence of the living Word, Jesus Christ, the light both of the world and of the biblical words: 'The presence of the living Word in Holy Scripture is not an ontological necessity but a free decision of the God who acts and speaks.'[118] Bloesch advocates a 'historical-pneumatic hermeneutic that recognizes the dynamic unity of Word and Spirit.[119]

'Can you by exegeting find out God?' Bloesch thinks not. The task of biblical interpretation would indeed be easier, Bloesch notes, if we could simply equate the words of the Bible with revelation. Yet our final authority as theologians is 'not what the Bible says but what God says in the Bible'.[120] Bloesch here makes what he calls 'a clear-cut distinction' between the historical meaning of the text and its 'revelational' or 'spiritual' meaning.[121] The spiritual meaning is what the text assumes 'when the Spirit acts on it in bringing home its significance to people of faith'.[122] At this point, even Grenz displays some discomfort, wondering whether Bloesch has overcome a Nestorian-like tendency to let the human words and the divine Word drift apart.[123]

Reprise: shaking the biblical foundations

Thus far, then, we have seen that each of the three contemporary trajectories works with a certain conceptual distinction between the Bible and revelation. For McGrath, the history of Jesus Christ is the prime datum of theology. For Grenz and Bloesch, it is the Holy Spirit speaking 'in and through' the Scriptures. The salient point is that the Bible itself — the text and its verbal

---

118. Ibid.

119. Ibid., p. 200. Is there a stable sense in the human words of Scripture? It is not entirely clear how Bloesch would respond. At one point he sees that 'their meaning-content includes their significance for those who hear God's Word in every new situation' (*Holy Scripture*, p. 52). In the final analysis, Bloesch is much closer to Gadamer than to Hirsch (see *Holy Scripture*, p. 178).

120. Ibid., p. 60.

121. Ibid., p. 190.

122. Ibid. Bloesch says he agrees with Barth that the subject matter of the text 'controls' its meaning and our understanding of it. As to just what the text of the Bible is, there appears to be some confusion or at least ambiguity: 'The text is sovereign in its interpretation, because the text constitutes not only letter but spirit as well' (*Holy Scripture*, p. 201).

123. Grenz, '"Fideisitic Revelationism": Donald Bloesch's Antirationalist Theological Method', in Colyer, *Evangelical Theology in Transition*, p. 59.

meaning – no longer functions as the object of theology. None of our three case studies would be happy simply equating the Bible with the history of Jesus or with the Spirit's speaking. Strictly speaking, the Spirit's speaking – God's actually disclosing himself – is not a static 'given' but always a dynamic 'gift'. It follows for Grenz and Bloesch in particular, then, that the Spirit's speaking is not an 'object' to be observed and hence cannot serve as the 'foundation' of systematic theology.

All three agree that the classical foundationalist understanding of the relation of the Bible to theology has a twofold problem. First, it assumes that divine revelation is simply and objectively there, 'in' the text, a proposition conveyed by the human words themselves. Revelation, they contend, is not an inert object, however, but a living, dynamic, free divine address whereby God presents himself (the Son) through himself (the Spirit). Second, it assumes that theological knowledge is a kind of biblical empiricism, where everything begins (and ends?) with an individual's own reading experience. Modern (Cartesian) foundationalism introduced a first-person approach to epistemology where the basis of knowledge claims was in a person's own reasoning or experience. For John Locke, a belief is foundational if it is evident to the senses. Of course, in biblical interpretation it is not physical perception that counts, but rather 'semantic perception' – my experience of grammatical-historical (e.g. observable) meaning: 'my sense of what the Bible means'.

'Can you by exegeting find out God?' Ought we simply to equate an individual's experience of the text ('what I hear God saying') – whether this is viewed as a subject rigorously observing an object or as a fusion of horizons – with divine revelation itself ('what God says')? To hold that the interpreter's exegetical experience is an indubitable foundation for constructing a system of theology is to subscribe to what Wilfred Sellars calls the 'Myth of the Given';[124] namely, the myth that our sensory powers are incorrigible and independent of any prior cultural, linguistic, theoretical – or for that matter, systematic theological – frameworks for processing that experience.[125] Merold Westphal goes further, accusing classical foundationalism not only of subscribing to cleverly devised myths, but to heresy – Pelagianism, to be exact: 'Foundationalism itself is partly to be under-

---

124. In Sellars, 'Empiricism and the Philosophy of Mind', reprinted as ch. 5 in his *Science, Perception and Reality* (London: Routledge & Kegan Paul, 1963), pp. 127–196 (esp. pp. 169–170).

125. What is here being questioned is the adequacy of 'classical' or 'strong' foundationalism to serve as theology's epistemological handmaiden. Classical foundationalism is an account of how subjects come to know objects. As we have

stood as a sinfully arrogant attempt at methodological self-purification, void of contrition, confession, or dependence upon divine grace.'[126]

Theological systems and conceptual schemes: the Marshall–Davidson challenge

Philosophy has been notably absent from my account thus far. What has Athens to do with Jerusalem, the water of worldly wisdom with the wine of the wisdom from above? Thomas Aquinas responds to the objection that the Bible condemns those who mix water with wine by citing Jesus' miracle at the wedding at Cana: 'those who use the works of philosophers in sacred doctrine so as to bring them into the obedience of faith do not mix water with wine, but transform water into wine'.[127] Whether Bruce Marshall's appropriation of Donald Davidson's philosophy works such a miracle is a moot point. It suffices for my purposes to call attention to the Marshall–Davidson critique of methods that rely on evidentialism and conceptual schemes.

Davidson and the third dogma of empiricism
Why Donald Davidson? Davidson's work on meaning, truth and interpretation ranks among the high points of twentieth-century analytic philosophy.[128]

---

seen, this raises two issues: the nature of the object to be known; the relation between subject and object (and, as we shall see, whether the subject–object picture is itself able to account for faith getting understanding). For a description and critique of classical foundationalism, see W. Jay Wood, *Epistemology: Becoming Intellectually Virtuous* (Downers Grove: IVP, 1998), ch. 4. For other kinds of foundationalism, see Timm Triplett, 'Recent Work on Foundationalism', *American Philosophical Quarterly* 27 (1990), pp. 93–116. My own preference is for a modest, chastened, 'fallibilist' foundationalism in which one employs basic beliefs on a provisional basis. We begin not with indubitable foundations but with load-bearing frameworks that from time to time may need adjusting and repair.

126. Westphal, 'Taking St. Paul Seriously: Sin as an Epistemological Category', in Thomas P. Flint, ed., *Christian Philosophy* (Notre Dame: University of Notre Dame Press, 1990), p. 218.

127. Aquinas, *Expositio super librum Boethii De Trinitate* 2, 3, cited in Bruce D. Marshall, 'Theology after Cana', *Modern Theology* 16 (2000), p. 525.

128. William Taschek suggests that Davidson's overarching concern is 'to come to some sort of systematic understanding of the various factors that constitutively enter

Analytic philosophers deal with questions about the relationship of language, thought and the world, questions that, as we have seen, are the staple of theological method as well.

It is worth pausing a moment to reconsider philosophy's handmaiden role to systematic theology. Philosophers offer at least two very different kinds of 'service'. Continental philosophy has been the 'Mary' of systematics, offering large-scale ready-made metaphysical and epistemological conceptual packages for theological ideas. Analytic philosophers, by contrast, have played the more practical 'Martha' role, content with providing tools for cleaning up theological language and for tidying theology's conceptual house.[129] At first glance, there would seem to be a natural affinity between the philosophical method of analysis – analysing language to clarify thought – and grammatical-historical exegesis. In fact, the picture is more complicated. The so-called 'ideal-language' philosophers wanted to recast ordinary language into a more proper logical form in order to eliminate ambiguity. By contrast, ordinary-language philosophers advocated a deeper understanding of language as it is used in everyday life.[130]

To appreciate Davidson's contribution, we must first say a word about Willard Quine's attack on empiricism in his celebrated article 'Two Dogmas of Empiricism' (1951).[131] The relevance of this discussion is not hard to find if one keeps in mind what Hodge says about theological method as involving induction of biblical 'facts'.

The first dogma of empiricism is reductionism: the view that all the sentences of one area of discourse can be translated, without impoverishment,

---

into and control interpretation: the particular and distinctive way in which we do make sense of human thought and intentional action – including, importantly, speech' ('Making Sense of Others: Donald Davidson on Interpretation', *Harvard Review of Philosophy* 10 [2002], p. 28).

129. Augustine's comment on Mary and Martha is apt: 'Both occupations were good, but yet as to which was the better, what shall we say?' (cited in 'Martha', in David Lyle Jeffrey, ed., *Dictionary of Biblical Tradition in English Literature* [Grand Rapids: Eerdmans, 1992], p. 485).

130. It is significant that many of the analytic philosophers in the tradition of Frege harbour a *mistrust* of ordinary languages. The confusions of ordinary prose must undergo analysis – not Freudian but Fregean, which is to say, *logical* therapy. Frege believed that ordinary language was too ambiguous and imprecise, an assumption that eventually led to a totalitarianism of its own; namely, positivism.

131. In Willard Van Orman Quine, *From a Logical Point of View*, 2nd edn (New York: Harper & Row, 1961), pp. 20–46.

into the sentences of another area of discourse. Quine was thinking about the empiricists' tendency to reduce all meaningful sentences to reports about sensory experience. But it is equally reductionistic – a dogma of *biblical* empiricism – to suggest that biblical sentences can be translated without impoverishment into theological propositions. It is no coincidence that the harshest critics of foundationalism in theology (e.g. Nancey Murphy) have appealed precisely to Quine's holism; namely, to the idea that sentences make sense not by being anchored in some experience or fact but rather by being part of an interconnected 'web'. Quine also attacks a second dogma of empiricism; namely, the so-called analytic–synthetic distinction between sentences that are true by virtue of their meaning and sentences that are true because they correspond to certain facts. Perhaps the closest biblical-theological counterpart to this second dogma is what David Clark calls 'principlizing'; namely, the practice of separating universal principles from their disposable cultural husks.[132]

Davidson picks up where Quine left off and denounces a third dogma of empiricism; namely, the Kantian notion of conceptual schemes that organize and translate our raw, preconceptual sensory experiences. The dogma relies on the notion of an uninterpreted stock of experience or information that is then processed through one or another conceptual scheme. Conceptual schemes are ways of organizing experience: 'they are systems of categories that give form to the data of sensation; they are points of view from which individuals, cultures, or periods survey the passing scene'.[133] What George Lindbeck calls 'cultural-linguistic' frameworks work in much the same way for much the same reason. Indeed, the logical conclusion of the scheme–content dualism is something like Lindbeck's view, where all interpretation is relative to a cultural-linguistic framework that regulates the speech, action and thought of a given community at a particular place and time.[134]

What Davidson rejects is the dualism of scheme (organizing system) and content (that which awaits organization). Specifically, he rejects the idea that the mind works first by passively receiving data and then by processing this

---

132. Clark, *To Know and Love God,* p. 91.

133. Donald Davidson, *Inquiries into Truth and Interpretation,* 2nd edn (Oxford: Clarendon, 2001), p. 183.

134. Thomas Kent helpfully suggests that a conceptual scheme is roughly equivalent to a hermeneutic strategy, a theory for helping us to understand what others – in this case, the biblical authors – are saying ('Interpretation and Triangulation', in Reed Way Dasenbrock, ed., *Literary Theory after Davidson* [University Park, Pa.: Pennsylvania State University Press, 1993], p. 44).

data via a conceptual scheme. Conceptual schemes are in fact conceptual *screens* that create barriers between the subject's mind ('in here') and the external world ('out there'). The idea of a conceptual screen is precisely what invites scepticism, and not only about philosophy. The theologians we have just examined are equally suspicious of the dualism of 'exegetical scheme' and 'biblical content'.

Who subscribes to this third dogma of empiricism? Not only card-carrying empiricists, but a host of others as well: virtually all post-Kantian philosophers; most postmodernists; modern theologians searching for the right -ism; postliberal theologians who believe that we are trapped within incommensurable cultural-linguistic frameworks. Charles Hodge's approach seems to be another clear example of one who trades on the scheme–content dichotomy by distinguishing the facts (propositions) of the Bible and the laws and theorems (systems) that theologians devise to account for their relation.

Davidson's arguments against the idea of a conceptual scheme are too complex to rehearse here. Suffice it to say that he objects to the idea of conceptual schemes because it encourages both scepticism (about getting back to the given 'behind' the scheme) and relativism (i.e. the notion that meaning and truth are relative to a conceptual scheme). Furthermore, the notion that meaning and truth are determined by and captive to self-contained conceptual schemes subverts the possibility of translating from one language to another and undermines our ability to understand others.[135]

Theology under Marshall law: the epistemic primacy of the gospel
In his highly regarded monograph *Trinity and Truth*,[136] Bruce Marshall employs Davidson's critique of the scheme–content dichotomy to drive out a certain kind of foundationalism from theology's house. Everything hangs on what he calls the 'epistemic dependence thesis': 'The dependence thesis in theology is the view that a certain set of beliefs ("universal", "public", "*wissenschaftlich*" or whatever) is not only uniquely relevant to deciding about the truth of Christian beliefs, but has a fixed truth value.'[137] Theology becomes epistemically depen-

---

135. For the record, I am neither a son of Davidson nor a Davidsonian. Systematic theology should belong to no one philosopher or philosophy. What I take from Davidson is a fundamentally negative point (viz. his critique of empiricism) and a suggestion (about triangulation, on which see below). I have continuing reservations with regard to his holism and his way of going beyond realism.

136. Cambridge: Cambridge University Press, 2000.

137. Marshall, *Trinity and Truth*, p. 98.

dent, therefore, when it seeks to demonstrate the truth of Christian doctrine in terms of an extra-biblical conceptual scheme. One need not seek far for examples. Bultmann, for example, assumes the truth of existentialism in order to demonstrate the truth of Christian faith. Other theologians employ Neoplatonism, Marxism, process philosophy, Aristotelianism, feminism and a host of other conceptual schemes.

Those who hold the epistemic-dependence view wrongly assume that the meaning of Christian beliefs can be determined apart from any assessment of their truth. According to Marshall, however, it is impossible 'to hold for meaning while testing for truth . . . Our true commitments determine, on the whole, the meanings we assign to words.'[138] To employ a conceptual scheme that is generally assumed to be true may look, at first glance, like a promising apologetic strategy. What really happens is that the very beliefs we are trying to defend undergo a drastic reinterpretation: 'epistemic dependence as a view of justification in theology tends to go together with revisionism about the meaning of Christian claims'.[139] Bultmann's existential account of the cross and resurrection, for example, is actually a different story altogether.

Marshall puts forward an alternative proposal – call it the 'epistemic *independence* thesis'. This thesis states that theology must not interpret biblical narratives by means of some conceptual scheme but rather *begin* by assuming the truth of the biblical narratives as they stand. The narratives that identify Jesus are 'epistemic trump' and enjoy 'unrestricted epistemic primacy'.[140] No sentence that is inconsistent with the gospel can be true. With this thought, the tables of the temple of epistemology are truly overturned: instead of needing to explain the events of the Bible in terms of some conceptual scheme, these events themselves, thanks to their 'narrative emplotment', acquire explanatory power with respect to everything else, including epistemology![141] Indeed, for Marshall the explanatory or 'assimilative' power of biblical narrative is its own justification, giving an interesting new twist to the older notion of the self-attestation of Scripture.

What shall we now say about the three contemporary trajectories to theology we examined above? To what extent do they work with the scheme–content

---

138. Ibid.
139. Ibid., p. 99.
140. Ibid., p. 116.
141. For an example of how epistemology might look in terms of Christian doctrine (e.g. creation, fall, redemption), see my *The Drama of Doctrine: A Canonical-Linguistic Approach to Christian Theology* (Louisville: Westminster John Knox, 2005), ch. 9.

dichotomy that Davidson and Marshall have sought to overturn? It is important to keep in mind that there is probably no other single factor more responsible for the popular perception that theologians impose something foreign on the Bible than this biblical-content and theological-scheme dichotomy.

Even the default model of evangelical theology associated with Charles Hodge buys into the scheme–content dichotomy to the extent that it affirms the first dogma of empiricism; namely, that sentences in one kind of discourse (biblical) can be translated without significant loss into another kind of discourse (theological). Hodge's dogma of biblical empiricism is the belief that one can isolate and then abstract Scripture's revealed propositional content.[142] Bernard Ramm sees this attempt to translate the representational and figurative language of the Bible into the conceptual discourse of the theologian as a prime example of such reductionism: 'It is amazing how the current evangelical stress on propositional revelation is but an alternate version of this Hegelian theory of a pure conceptual language.'[143]

Whereas Hodge focuses on content, Grenz focuses on scheme. Grenz's notion of the socially constructed belief-mosaic is probably the closest analogue in theology to Davidson's conceptual schemes. Grenz buys into the general notion that the process of knowing and experiencing the world 'can only occur within a conceptual framework, a framework mediated by the social community in which we participate',[144] but then establishes an ecclesial franchise: the Christian belief-mosaic or web of belief.[145] The Bible is not a foundation for the ensuing theology but an important thread, along with tradition and culture, in the Christian web. As to epistemic primacy, it is hard to see how Grenz could assign this to anything other than the whole belief mosaic without falling into the very foundationalism from which he is trying to extricate evangelical theology.[146]

---

142. As to epistemic dependence, Marshall might say that Hodge ascribes primacy not to the biblical narratives and their way of making sense but to the inductive method itself, which is to say, human reason.

143. Bernard Ramm, *After Fundamentalism: The Future of Evangelical Theology* (New York: Harper & Row, 1983), p. 90.

144. Grenz, *Revisioning*, pp. 73–74.

145. Grenz equates the notion of a web of beliefs with that of a conceptual scheme ('Articulating', p. 114, n. 26).

146. To be fair, Grenz explicitly accords Scripture the role of 'primary voice' in the theological conversation ('Articulating', p. 124), yet it is not the text as such but the text as vehicle of the Spirit's speaking in the present that is ultimately authoritative.

Bloesch trades in a different kind of scheme–content dichotomy when he distinguishes between dogma and doctrine. Dogma is 'the divinely given content' apprehended by faith; it is God's own self-understanding.[147] Doctrine, by contrast is the (human) systematic articulation of the divinely given content: 'Doctrine is open to reformation and correct, but its dogmatic content is irrevocable and unalterable.'[148] This is similar to his dichotomy between two levels of meaning in Scripture: the historical (authorially intended) meaning of the written words and their 'spiritual' content or living Word. The biblical text here becomes the 'scheme' the Spirit uses to relate readers to the text's subject matter, the living Christ.[149]

Of the three theologians we have considered, McGrath is probably the least susceptible to the scheme–content dichotomy. Indeed, his central thesis is that theology is an a posteriori discipline, not one that approaches the data with an a priori conceptual scheme already in place. At the same time, he is aware of the tradition-bound nature of theological rationality. The question, therefore, is *bound by what?* Is McGrath's scientific theology an example of the epistemic dependency thesis or does it maintain the epistemic primacy of the Gospel narratives? This is a delicate query. As we have seen, Murphy views McGrath as a narrative foundationalist, because the narrative of Jesus is the form the basic datum – the history of Jesus – takes. However, McGrath is clear that Scripture itself is not the revealed datum but part of the community's articulation – theory – of what it has beheld. It would thus seem that the norm of theology sits, like the wizard of Oz, *behind* the canonical screen.

Understanding as triangulation

Theology is 'faith seeking understanding' (Anselm). This much is clear, and widely accepted. But what is understanding? It was Wilhelm Dilthey who distinguished between explanation in the natural sciences (a matter of determining causal laws) and understanding in the human sciences (a matter of discerning part–whole relations).[150] The human sciences seek to understand

---

147. Bloesch, *Theology of Word & Spirit*, p. 120.
148. Ibid.
149. Bloesch, *Holy Scripture*, p. 190.
150. *Das Verstehen* (Understanding) was for Dilthey a technical term for the method of the human sciences (e.g. history, psychology, sociology), which have as their aim a grasp of meaning – a product of a person's mental life – as it is manifested empirically in words and gestures. Pannenberg applies Dilthey's part–whole reasoning to theology by focusing on revelatory events in history in

but not necessarily to explain meaningful human action; they focus on the *semantics* rather than the physics, as it were, of personal behaviour. To be sure, Anselm's definition of theology pre-dates Dilthey's distinction by several centuries. Nevertheless, theology is arguably more interested in interpreting meaningful action – Scripture, for instance! – than in adducing causal explanations. The question before us is whether the subject–object dichotomy is the best way to account for how *understanding* takes place. This brings us back to Davidson; specifically, to his suggestion that understanding others is a *three* dimensional affair, a matter of 'triangulation'.[151]

Davidson views triangulation as an alternative to the subject–object model found in foundationalism and communitarianism alike.[152] Foundationalism works with a subject–object dichotomy that leaves the subject with the contents of his or her own mind only, unable to know whether one's experience and conceptual scheme really correspond to the world (or, we might add, to the Word) or not. Communitarianism too is subjective in the sense that members of a given interpretative community know only their community's own mind – their community's own conceptual scheme or cultural-linguistic framework. In both cases, the problem is determining how we can know a scheme is true to the content if we can never get outside our scheme to see the content as it is in itself. Wretched knower that I am! Who will deliver me from the prison-house of my own, or my own community's, mind? According to Davidson, only triangulation transcends the subject–object model of understanding.

---

his *Theology and the Philosophy of Science*. The present chapter argues, by way of contrast, that what theology primarily seeks to understand is God's self-communicative action in Christ as it is attested in God's self-communicative action in Scripture.

151. In the context of mathematics, triangulation refers to the process of locating unknown points by using known points and trigonometry; it helps us to navigate the seas and to survey landscapes. In the social sciences, triangulation refers to the use of more than a single method or perspective in order to gain depth in one's description or analysis. David Clark mentions Einstein as a triangulator who was in the habit of viewing truth from multiple angles by using various sets of assumptions (*To Know and Love God*, pp. 186–187).

152. For an attempt to use Davidson against communitarians like Stanley Fish, see Thomas Kent, 'Interpretation and Triangulation: A Davidsonian Critique of Reader-Oriented Literary Theory', in Dasenbrock, *Literary Theory after Davidson*, pp. 37–58.

Understanding requires three sorts of knowledge: of our own minds, of other minds and of the world.[153] But – and this is Davidson's key point – we have to work our way into the whole three-dimensional system at the same time. We know what our own words and concepts mean only by triangulating with other language users about our shared world: 'we cannot form concepts without communication, and communication requires triangulation'.[154] Real-world triangulation is Davidson's way out of scepticism; namely, the possibility that our conceptual schemes create an impassable barrier between subject and object, the 'in here' (of our minds) and the 'out there' (of the world).

Understanding is thus not a bilateral affair between subject and object, mind and world, interpreter and text. It takes three. We come to know our own minds – the meaning of the concepts we employ – only when we understand how others are using language in relation to the world too. Thought, language and intentional action are so inextricably interrelated that 'any attempt to understand one of them in isolation from the others is bound to fail'.[155] Triangulation coordinates beliefs, words and actions: 'interpreting an agent's intentions, his beliefs, and his words are parts of a single project'.[156]

Davidson contends that objectivity itself is ultimately a matter of interpersonal relations and communicative interaction: 'The ultimate source of both objectivity and communication is the triangle that, by relating speaker, interpreter, and the world, determines the contents of thought and speech.'[157] What connects or triangulates language, our beliefs and the world is *communicative action*. Understanding thus depends on two speakers coordinating their beliefs and practices with the world through communicative interaction, through *language*. *Triangulation is the project of coordinating subjectivity, objectivity and*

---

153. For Davidson, the triangle minimally consists of two people and the world. This triangle is reflected in the subtitle of the present chapter, where 'Scripture' serves as a cipher for 'the Spirit speaking in and through the Bible'.

154. Kent, 'Interpretation and Triangulation', p. 50.

155. Taschek, 'Making Sense of Others', p. 28.

156. Davidson, 'Radical Interpretation', in *Inquiries into Truth and Interpretation*, p. 127.

157. Davidson, 'The Structure and Content of Truth', *Journal of Philosophy* 87 (1990), p. 325. In the next section, I shall relate Davidson's point about communicative interaction to theology's subject matter: theodrama, the dialogical interaction between God and his covenant creatures.

intersubjectivity via communicative interaction. Indeed, communicative interaction with others in the world is what language *is*.[158] Let us call this Davidsonian account of how we understand the words, beliefs and actions of others 'general triangulation'.[159]

A few literary theorists have begun to work out the implications of Davidson's position for hermeneutics. One suggests that readers triangulate between 'what we know, what the text says, and what others say about it'.[160] Systematic theology, similarly, involves more than individual readers observing and processing biblical content with conceptual schemes. Theological understanding requires not two, but at least three, coordinates. The model of triangulation depicts the theologian not as an autonomous knowing subject but as a person in communicative interaction with others.[161] A theology with Reformed and evangelical sensibilities, however, will want to give 'what the text says', or rather, 'what God says in and through the biblical text', the privileged place in the triangle. Clearly, Davidson's proposals cannot simply be appropriated by theology *in toto*.

Back to Marshall and the question of epistemic primacy. Marshall suggests that the best way to identify a distinctly Christian system of beliefs 'is to attend to what the Christian community as a whole – the church – holds true, and the practices by which they do so'.[162] We discern what the most important identity-forming beliefs of the church are, not by looking at a book 'but at what

---

158. In my earlier work I tended to give the impression that communicative action was the work of autonomous speech agents. While I still believe that persons are communicative agents, with all the dignity and responsibility that such agency entails, the metaphor of triangulation better accounts for the irreducible social aspect of what we do with words.

159. I would be remiss if I did not point out a certain connection here with Jürgen Habermas's notion of communicative action. According to Habermas, every communicative act has propositional content, engages reality and establishes interpersonal relationships; and hence every communicative act (if it is to be rational) must fulfil three related validity conditions: sincerity, truth and appropriateness. See Habermas, 'What is Universal Pragmatics?', in *Communication and the Evolution of Society* (London: Heinemann, 1979), pp. 1–68.

160. Kent, 'Interpretation and Triangulation', p. 53.

161. It would be a mistake to equate Davidson's principle of intersubjectivity with, say, Fish's notion of consensus. Intersubjectivity does not necessarily mean agreement, but *engagement*.

162. Marshall, *Trinity and Truth*, p. 18.

the community *does*.[163] This is an eminently Davidsonian move for, as we have seen, thought, language and intentional action are parts of a single package. Marshall is not a pragmatist: church practices do not make 'Jesus is Lord' true, though they do serve to specify the meaning of the church's Christological confession. One of Marshall's most interesting suggestions is that the Spirit plays an epistemic role in shaping church practices so that Christian speech will indeed articulate true belief. In particular, the Spirit-wrought practice of Eucharistic worship teaches us 'to mean what we ought to believe'.[164] One cannot help but notice the triangulation (i.e. between words, beliefs, practices). But does any single point on the triangle enjoy epistemic primacy, and, if so, which one?

With the possible exception of Hodge, our three case studies in theological method are all aware of the need to move beyond the subject–object dichotomy (and hence beyond objectivism and relativism) by means of something like triangulation, though they do not explicitly call it that. Grenz comes closest, speaking explicitly of the 'three pillars' or norms of theology: the biblical message, the tradition of the church, the thought-forms of one's contemporary culture context.[165] An overemphasis on any one of these points leads to biblicism (fundamentalism), confessionalism or liberalism respectively.[166] Bloesch triangulates the Word of God somewhat differently, linking it to a divine event (revelation), a historically mediated text (the Bible) and an ecclesial activity (faith). Finally, McGrath proposes a procedure for doing justice to the real world, to tradition-bound rationality and to the history of Jesus Christ narrated in Scripture.

We have to press home the same question to each of our case studies as we did to Marshall: to which point on these respective triangles do we assign epistemic primacy? Not just any triangulation will do for a theology that affirms Scripture as its supreme authority. We must also keep in mind that theology's triangulation – faith's search for understanding – must correspond to faith's subject matter. Our systematic triangulation must therefore take two things into account: the epistemic primacy of the canonically attested gospel (the formal principle) and the nature of the gospel itself (the material principle). With regard to the latter, theology has to do primarily with God's salvific self-communication in the Son through the Spirit. Hence my thesis, to be

---

163. Ibid.
164. Ibid., p. 203.
165. Grenz, *Revisioning*, p. 93.
166. Ibid., p. 102.

developed below: *the best systematics is a matter of theodramatic triangulation with an authoritative script.*[167]

A future for theology: theodramatic triangulation

The bold contribution of a Reformed and evangelical theology lies in its resisting 'the many attempts to empty God's Word of its content and to bring it under the dominion of metaphysics, morality, mysticism, or the dictatorship of a "spirit of the age".'[168] Everything thus hinges on the Word of God: on its form and content, its nature and function, its locus and locution.

The Christian gospel is something God both says and does. It is not a philosophy, a system of morality nor an expression of human subjectivity, but a *theodrama*: God's words and deeds on the world stage with and for us, especially with respect to our creation and redemption as these are summed up in Jesus Christ. Drama involves both 'spoken action' and 'action that speaks'. The following proposal suggests what doing theology according to the Scriptures should look like if its method is adequate to its theodramatic matter. By way of anticipation, we can say that theodramatic understanding calls for a triangulation between words, God's Word and the world.

A future for theology sub specie theodramatis: *the material principle of systematics*
Bavinck rightly says of special revelation that 'God's word is an act, and his activity is speech.'[169] Dramatists have known for ages what speech act philosophy discovered only in the twentieth century; namely, that speaking is a form of acting: 'the particular vocation of theatre is to explore the consequences of this intuition that "to say is to do" and "to do is to say".'[170] The subject matter

---

167. The reader may be perplexed by the multiple triads I mention when speaking of triangulation. The central point to keep in mind is that triangulation involves communicative interaction: not simply a subject and an object but at least two subjects in interaction over something in the world.

168. David Willis and Michael Welker, 'Introduction', in Willis and Welker, eds., *Toward the Future of Reformed Theology* (Grand Rapids: Eerdmans, 1999), p. x.

169. Herman Bavinck, *Reformed Dogmatics*. Vol. 1: *Prolegomena* (Grand Rapids: Baker, 2003), p. 323.

170. Ross Chambers, 'Le Masque et le miroir: vers une théorie relationelle du théâtre', *Etudes littéraires* 13 (1980), p. 402.

of theology is God's drama: God's doing and God's saying things in the world to and for others. The theodrama begins with God bespeaking creation. The plot accelerates with God's promise to Abraham: 'I will make of you a great nation, and I will bless you . . . and by you all the families of the earth shall be blessed' (Gen. 12:2–3). It continues with God making good on his *promissio* thanks to the *missio* (sending) of Son and Spirit.

Humans have speaking and acting parts too. Theology involves making sense not only of what God has done but also of what we are to do in order to participate rightly in the action. And we must not forget that the triune God is active even in the process whereby humans come to know him. John Webster rightly observes that the distinctiveness of theology lies not simply in its posing ultimate questions, but rather 'in its invocation of God as agent in the intellectual practice of theology'.[171] Theology is a human endeavour (the drama of human knowing) that prays to be caught up in a prior divine endeavour (the drama of God making himself known).

It is perhaps worth pausing to consider theodrama as itself an instance of *triune* triangulation, for it is almost impossible, or at least ill-advised, to describe the way in which God reveals himself in terms of the subject–object dichotomy. Strictly speaking, God is not the 'object' of human experience or investigation.[172] The operative concept in theodrama, as in triangulation, is not 'subject and object' but *communicative interaction*. Consider the way God makes himself known. God's word came first to Abraham in the form of a promise, then to Israel through the law and the prophets, and finally to us in the person of Jesus Christ. God makes himself known to others by what he says *and does*. The incarnation is the supreme instance of God's communicative interaction with others, a matter not only of divine translation (of the substance of divinity into the form of humanity) but of divine triangulation: the Word speaking words, acting and suffering with and for others, in the world.

It is, therefore, but a small conceptual step from the notion of general to 'special' (e.g. theological) triangulation. There is, however, a significant difference: God's triangulation – his communicative interaction with others – are *covenantal* interactions, part of the broader economies of revelation and redemption. And, though these covenantal interactions are triangular,

---

171. Webster, 'Theological Theology', p. 18.
172. Recall the resistance of Grenz and Bloesch in particular to the idea that 'the Spirit speaking in the Scriptures' is an objective phenomenon or property of the biblical text. To make it so is to forego divine freedom and the element of living and personal divine address.

involving God's Word, the covenant community and their communicative interaction in the world, it does not follow that each point in the triangle carries equal weight in determining the other two. After all, covenantal interactions take place between lord and servants.

The crucial point is to acknowledge God's communicative prevenience. Without God's prior word and deed, theology would have no access to its object. Barth described God's self-communicative activity in trinitarian terms, involving Revealer, Revelation and Revealedness. To invoke theodrama is to view God's saying and doings more broadly. God is doing more than making himself known when he interacts covenantally with humanity. God promises, commands and consoles, thereby soliciting not only theoretical but practical knowledge, not only beliefs and thoughts but praise, obedience and friendship.

There is a strong link between viewing the subject matter of theology in theodramatic terms and viewing theological method in terms of triangulation. *Theodramatic understanding requires triangulation and theological triangulation is theodramatic.* (1) Theodramatic triangulation relates what God does in Christ, the Scriptures that present Christ, and the Word-and-Spirit-guided practices of the church, the body of Christ. The goal is so to triangulate divine and human action (including speech) with reality made new in Christ, so that the church today will know how to participate rightly in the ongoing drama of redemption. (2) The triangle of Christian understanding – its distinct system – is thoroughly theodramatic: the world is the stage of the theodrama; the words are those of the principal *dramatis personae*; the belief-practices that characterize the church are theodramatic belief-practices; belief-practices that are generated by and participate in the prior words and deeds of the triune God. In both cases, the operative concept is, once again, communicative interaction. Theology, then, is *faith seeking theodramatic understanding*: the attempt to appreciate more fully what God is saying and doing in Christ and what we, as members of Christ's church, must say, think and do in response. Theology triangulates (plots our itinerary, our 'walk') God's triangulation (incarnation, covenant) after him.

What the notion of 'drama' adds to propositions is the element of *embodied witness*. Now we can see why theology involves not only conceptual scheme but theodramatic practice; namely, the practice of knowing what to say, think and do as disciples of Jesus Christ. This is nothing less than a practice of biblical interpretation consisting of three moments: a pre-understanding of the theodramatic action, an analysis of the theodrama's normative specification or script (Scripture), and finally a performative understanding whereby the church demonstrates its understanding through fitting participation in the triune drama.

A future for Scripture sub specie theodramatis: the formal principle of systematics

How exactly might a theodramatic approach triangulate while still holding Scripture as the norming norm? Is it possible to ascribe epistemic primacy to Scripture without espousing a biblical empiricism or a rationalist foundationalism? We may recall that each of our three case studies had difficulty clearly identifying Scripture with the authoritative word of God. Some distinguished between the words of Scripture and the revealed word (Bloesch) or between the narratives of Scripture and the history of Jesus Christ (McGrath), while others virtually identified the word of God with the Spirit speaking through an ecclesial belief-mosaic made up of pieces from the Bible, tradition and culture alike (Grenz).

'Exegesis, exegesis, exegesis.' Barth's parting words to the church in Germany are well taken. But exegesis ultimately involves more than observation and deduction. Such a subject–object empiricism falls short of the communicative interaction required of the theological interpretation of Scripture. It was also Barth who claimed that exegesis was not simply a matter of discovering or replicating the contents of the author's mind, but engaging with authors in the matter of their discourse: 'The decisive prerequisite for the interpretation of a text for me therefore is participation in its *subject matter*.'[173] The church's script is not an end in itself but the royal road towards joining in on the theodramatic action. More to the point: the script is itself an element of that action, an element in what we might call the economy of triune communicative action.

Fully to appreciate how theology can triangulate while assigning epistemic primacy to the Bible obliges us to say more about what it means to affirm 'the Spirit speaking in (and through) the Scriptures'. Most importantly, we need to see that the Bible is the means and medium of God's communicative interaction with the church. Let us therefore acknowledge Scripture as dual-authored, human–divine discourse, where discourse is what someone (ultimately the Spirit) says to someone (ultimately the church) about something (ultimately Christ). Several things follow from looking at the Bible in theodramatic perspective (*sub specie theodramatis*) as 'Spirited' discourse.

First, the Bible is not merely an epistemological foundation – either a 'storehouse of facts' (Hodge) or a deposit of propositional revelation (Henry) –

---

173. Barth, Preface Draft II to the first edition of his *Römerbrief*, cited in Richard Burnett, *Karl Barth's Theological Exegesis* (Tübingen: Mohr Siebeck, 2001), p. 95.

whose objective content human knowing subjects then process intellectu-ally.[174] Its epistemic primacy stems rather from its nature as the church's author-itative script, the normative specification for interpreting what God is saying and doing in creation, in the history of Israel, and in Jesus Christ. It is a mistake to abstract Scripture from the drama of redemption and treat it as an autono-mous holy object. Scripture is correctly grasped only when viewed *sub specie theo-dramatis*; that is, in relation to the events it recounts, displays and enjoins.

Second, it is not simply the substance (*Sache*) of Scripture that is theodram-atic but also its form. The Bible is many-voiced – polyphonic – and not all the voices speak in the same way (or even in the same language!). Here too we see a difference between drama and narrative. Narratives are told by a story-teller and metanarratives are monologic epics: comprehensive stories told by an omniscient narrator with a single set of concepts and categories. The biblical theodrama, by contrast, is dialogical. While there is a unifying plot, there is no one voice, perspective or set of categories that alone articulates it.[175]

Third, the forms of Scripture are as theologically significant as its content. Stated differently, Scripture is not merely 'content' but also 'scheme': a *canon-ical* scheme. In Bavinck's words, directed largely against Hodge: 'Scripture does not give us data to interpret; it is itself the interpretation of reality, the shaper of a distinct worldview.'[176] Each of the Bible's literary genres represents a par-ticular type of communicative interaction. Genres do not merely transmit sense, but make sense. What gets communicated in narrative, for example, is not simply discrete events but a way of seeing diverse events as having a certain kind of wholeness (e.g. they all belong to the same plot). Similarly, each of the Bible's literary forms is a mode of cognition and experience.

We are now in a position to make a fourth and final point about Scripture *sub specie theodramatis*. Epistemic primacy belongs to the Word of God or, to be exact, to what the Westminster Confession of Faith terms 'the Holy Spirit speaking in the Scriptures'.[177] The attentive reader will at this point wonder

---

174. Carl F. H. Henry agrees with the early Clark Pinnock that the term 'propositional' – as in propositional revelation – rightly describes 'the conceptual truth-content extractable from Holy Scripture' (cited in Henry, *God, Revelation, and Authority*, vol. 3, p. 456).

175. In my view, God is the playwright who communicates his ideas via the many characters (viz. biblical authors) who have speaking parts. So, while there is a unified author (playwright), no one voice alone speaks for God.

176. Bavinck, *Reformed Dogmatics*, vol. 1, p. 354.

177. Westminster Confession of Faith, 1.10.

how my proposal differs from that of Grenz and Bloesch. They also hold Word and Spirit together; both advocate something like triangulation.[178] The difference between my proposal and theirs comes to light when we speak not of propositional but *prepositional* theology. In particular, everything hinges on how we parse the Spirit's speaking, using the prepositions 'in and through' the Scriptures.

Grenz and Bloesch are unwilling to assert that the Spirit speaks 'in' Scripture and leave it at that. To say that God's speaking is 'in' Scripture is to objectify it, they worry. If revelation is thought to be 'in' the text, then it appears to be up to us to get 'it' out. Furthermore, 'it' – the meaning extracted from the text and distilled into a pure theological proposition – inevitably becomes the foundation for a system of truths, the very rationalist picture they both reject. Grenz in particular favours the preposition 'through' because it affords more scope for the Spirit's dynamic involvement. It is most significant that *both Grenz and Bloesch locate the key action of the Spirit elsewhere than in the verbal form and content of the biblical discourse.* This is admittedly a subtle point, and I for one have no 'morbid craving for controversy and for disputes about words' (1 Tim. 6:4), especially when the words in question are prepositions (e.g. 'in', 'through')! Nevertheless, something important is at stake in the way we describe the relation of Word and Spirit.

Grenz and Bloesch are right to insist upon the work of the Holy Spirit in the reader's personal appropriation of God's Word, but they are wrong to view the Spirit's work as disconnected from words and from what I shall call 'communicative reason'. The problem with dissociating the 'pneumatic' meaning from the verbal meaning (Bloesch) or with viewing the Spirit's speaking as something over and above what exegesis can discern (Grenz) is that it turns the Spirit's communication into a form of causation. I believe, by way of contrast, that the Spirit's illumination is a matter of properly communicative, not causal, force.[179] There is an important difference, as Habermas has pointed

---

178. Bloesch posits the Bible, the community of faith, and the Spirit 'charging' the biblical words with the light and power of the living Christ; Grenz posits a mosaic made up of three voices: the Spirit speaking 'in and through' Scripture, the Spirit speaking through church tradition, and the Spirit speaking through contemporary culture.

179. I develop this point further in relation to the so-called 'effectual call' in my 'Effectual Call or Causal Effect? Summons, Sovereignty, and Supervenient Grace', in *First Theology: God, Scripture, and Hermeneutics* (Downers Grove: IVP, 2002), ch. 3, esp. pp. 117–123.

out, between speech acts that achieve their effects through communication and strategic acts that achieve their effects through brute force. The Spirit is no Sophist: the understanding that the Spirit's illumination brings about is the result of communicative rationality, not of causal coercion.[180]

We have already seen why Grenz and Bloesch resist unpacking their doctrine of the Word of God in terms of the preposition 'in' only; they refuse to objectify the dynamic divine address or to reduce God's free and personal self-revelation to a set of inert propositions. From what we have just said it should now be apparent why they also view the Spirit speaking 'through' the Scripture in terms of instrumental causality. However, 'instrumental causality' misunderstands the way the Spirit relates to Scripture as divine discourse (speech acts) that carry both propositional information ('matter') and illocutionary force ('energy'). Here the theologian could benefit from the secular illumination of philosophy and from certain conceptual distinctions that clarify what speakers and writers do with language.

An 'illocution' is what someone does *in* saying something. The 'perlocution', as the etymology suggests, is what someone does by or *through* saying something. Hence my suggestion: the Spirit's speaking 'in and through' the Scriptures is best understood in terms of the illocutions and perlocutions that attend locutions. The really important question concerns the status of perlocutions: are they strategic or communicative, effects of instrumental causality or of communicative rationality? Does the Spirit transform individuals, build up the church and construct a new eschatological world strategically – by raw power, as it were – or are these works themselves functions of what God says in Scripture? The way one answers this question will have a decisive bearing on how one understands the relation of Word and Spirit.

---

180. Interestingly, Davidson too may be susceptible to this critique to the extent that he sees the mind–world relation in terms of causation. Though Davidson recognizes the qualitative distinction between nature as a realm of causality and brute force on the one hand and the mind as the space of reason, freedom and choice, he nevertheless betrays a tendency, as did Quine before him, to see experience in terms of causation (e.g. the world 'causing' us to have sensations). The problem, however, is that causes and sensations are not reasons. Marshall, in similar fashion, speaks of the Spirit's leading us into all truth in terms of the Spirit's *causing* us to have certain beliefs. The question, however, is how something that is not in the realm of reason (e.g. cause) can justify belief. (I owe the material in this note to an unpublished paper by Adonis Vidu, 'Bruce D. Marshall and Realism'.)

Rightly relating illocutions to perlocutions is perhaps the best way to preserve the historic Reformed emphasis on the necessity of maintaining the integrity of Word and Spirit. The Spirit's speaking through the text (perlocutions) is intrinsically tied to the text's meaning (its locutions and illocutions) – to what God has said in inspiring, authorizing, commissioning and appropriating the human authorial discourse. The Spirit's work is to render the illocutions efficacious and to bring about further perlocutionary effects that are commensurate with those illocutions. In Calvin's words: God 'sent down the same Spirit by whose power he had dispensed the Word, to complete his work by the efficacious confirmation of the Word' (*Institutes* 1.9.3).

As the Spirit of perlocutionary power – or in Barth's terms, the 'Lord of the hearing' – the Spirit brings about a properly *textual* effect: understanding. Calvin concurs: faith 'is the principal work of the Holy Spirit' (*Institutes* 3.1.4) and the presence of faith – illumination – neither changes nor supplements the meaning of the text but rather enables those whom the Spirit illumines to recognize, feel and respond to the meaning and force of what is written: 'the Spirit [is] the inner teacher by whose effort the promise of salvation penetrates into our minds' (*Institutes* 3.1.4). Illumination refers not to some causal effect that has nothing to do with textual meaning, then, but to the right and proper outcome of communicative action. In short, what the Spirit does *through* the text is not unrelated to what the authors, human and divine, have said. As far as concerns the Spirit's speaking 'through' Scripture, then, we might say that the *message* is the medium.[181]

The Spirit speaking 'in and through' Scripture is the principle that holds theodramatic triangulation together, and this on two distinct levels. On the first, Davidsonian, level, the Spirit is active triangulating language, belief-practices and reality.[182] The formation of the canon was a result of the human authors' communicative interaction with the mighty acts of God and the Spirit's leading them to understand these acts truly. The Bible, then, is the result of *inspired* triangulation (Triangulation I). On a second level, the Spirit continues to be active in the contemporary church's attempts at theological

---

181. For a more developed treatment of these issues, see my 'From Speech Acts to Scripture Acts', in *First Theology*, ch. 6, esp. pp. 184–187 and 197–200. Other prepositions are also appropriate. Mark Bowald prefers 'in, with, and under' in order to signal a certain eucharistic resonance (point made in personal communication).

182. I call this the 'Davidsonian' level because *all* understanding involves communicative interaction that coordinates language, beliefs and the world.

triangulation (Triangulation II). The Spirit ministers reality – the truth of creation made new in Jesus Christ – through the inspired biblical discourse to the church in the world today. The Spirit speaking in and through Scripture *is* the crucial communicative interaction that coordinates biblical discourse, Christological subject matter, and the reception of this discourse on this matter by the interpretative church community.

If the Spirit speaking in and through the canonical script is indeed the locus of epistemic primacy, then a promising approach to theology (as faith seeking biblical understanding) is what I call the canonical-linguistic method. The implied contrast is with Lindbeck's cultural-linguistic approach. The change in terminology signals a change in priorities. What is ultimately authoritative for theology is God's discourse, not the community's interpretation. To put the point somewhat differently: canonical triangulation (Triangulation I) is the norm for ecclesial triangulation (Triangulation II). While both Scripture and the church's interpretation are components in the triune economy of communicative action, only the divine biblical discourse carries epistemic primacy. The church's interpretations and practices are corrigible; not so the divinely authored biblical discourse.[183]

It is important not to confuse canonical-linguistic exegesis with biblical empiricism. Individual knowing subjects may interpret the text, but they are not autonomous. On the contrary, individual readers are always involved in some kind of communicative interaction with regard to Scripture. Right interpretation depends on one's interacting with the Spirit through his internal witness in one's conscience and through his corporate witness in the catholic tradition of the church.[184] *The canonical-linguistic exegete-theologian, then, is not a subject handling an object but a speaker-actor caught up with others in search of theodramatic understanding.* The goal of canonical-linguistic theology is to become an apprentice to the script, adept at canonical practices, trained to see, feel and act in biblically patterned ways. Being biblical is a matter of cultivating

---

183. Assuming, that is, that one reads the biblical text in its proper canonical and redemptive-historical (which is to say, theodramatic) contexts, which in turn is another way of saying: if one reads the biblical text in faith.

184. Not even Martin Luther's appeal to conscience and to the grammar of the biblical text counts as a falsification of this point. As his disciple Martin Chemnitz makes clear, individual interpreters would do well to adhere to the Rule of Faith – catholic, not Roman, tradition – as a means of reading the apostolic tradition rightly (*Examination of the Council of Trent*, tr. Fred Kramer [St Louis: Concordia, 1971], Part 1, pp. 244–246, 256–257).

Christian wisdom: of learning to make judgments about how to speak and act in ways that best continue the theodrama in new situations. In the final analysis, therefore, Scripture enjoys not merely epistemic but *sapiential* primacy: it norms and nurtures Christian wisdom.

A future for doctrine sub specie theodramatis: *the fruit of systematics*

Doctrine as theodramatic direction: performance knowledge of God
The best dramas do more than display stories: they draw us into their action. Scripture is the church's theodramatic script: a polyphonic discourse that not only displays the theodrama but is caught up, and catches us up, in the action. Scripture is a 'Spirited' (inspired) script that not only records but aids and abets the main action: presenting Christ. The ultimate purpose of doctrine, similarly, is to facilitate our participation in the ongoing evangelical action: to equip us to be *doers* of the word, *imitators* of the disciples and apostles and, at the limit, to help us create an ecclesially embodied argument for the truth of Jesus Christ.[185]

If theology is faith seeking theodramatic understanding, then doctrine is both its fruit and catalyst. Doctrine is direction for the church's fitting participation in the ongoing drama of redemption as normatively specified in Scripture. First, doctrine helps us to identify the main *dramatis personae* (the triune God; the human creature) and to understand the basic theodramatic plot (creation, fall, redemption). Second, doctrine helps disciples faithfully to follow (act out) their script in new situations. Christian belief, thought and action must be 'fitting' not only with the canonical text but also with the contemporary cultural context. Doctrine serves the church today by helping us to interpret our current situation *sub specie theodramatis*.[186] In short, doctrine directs the church faithfully to embody the way, the truth and life defined by the history of Jesus Christ in fresh, contextually appropriate ways – in a word, to *triangulate*.

---

185. McGrath notes in passing the tie between theory (doctrine) and theatre: the purpose of theatrical presentation was to involve the beholder in the action, to draw the community into the world of the play and the play of the world (*Theory*, p. 8).

186. In this chapter, I am primarily concerned with what one might call doctrine *ad intra*; that is, on the derivation of doctrine from revelation and Scripture. Stephen Williams's chapter focuses on the relation of doctrine to Christian living (*ad extra*) and thus offers a complementary perspective.

Doctrine and theodramatic truth: triangulating scriptural beliefs, church practices and reality

Theology – understanding God, the world and ourselves in the light of the person and work of Jesus Christ – involves triangulating Christ, canon and the catholic tradition in and for cultural contexts. The canon is Spirited discourse about Christ; what God was and is doing in Christ is the subject matter of the canon; the catholic tradition is the church's Spirited reception of the biblical word about Christ spread across time and place. It is the Spirit's speaking the Son in and through the Scriptures that is at every point – canonical form, Christological matter, church tradition – decisive.

Doctrine gives direction for fitting the church's participation in the theodrama. Well and good. It is vitally important to acknowledge, however, that the directive theory of doctrine and theodramatic conception of theology outlined in these pages does more than say how Christians should behave. What of doctrinal truth? More to the point: where, and what, *is* truth if theology is faith seeking theodramatic understanding? A critic at this point would be well within his or her rights to enquire, 'Where's the metaphysical beef?'[187] How do Christian language, belief and practice relate to the real?

In terms of the older subject–object dichotomy, metaphysics pertains to the objective reality (content) that theories and doctrines (conceptual schemes) strive to grasp and represent. One of the more influential metaphysical theories throughout the history of theology has been that which thinks the content of reality in terms of 'being'. On this ancient and early-modern view, metaphysical categories such as 'substance', 'essence', 'nature', 'form' and 'matter' were considered omnicompetent, applicable to everything from atoms and Adam to the Alpha and Omega. In terms of the present chapter, however, the truth of the gospel – that to which theology corresponds – is not something we theoretically describe so much as something in which we actively participate. Theological truth is theodramatic: a matter of the words and ways of the free triune God and of God's communicative interaction with human creatures in the world. What, then, is the role of metaphysics in systematic theology?

As I have argued throughout this chapter, scheme–content dualism is the problem to which theodramatic triangulation is the solution, and that applies here too. Rowan Williams suggests that metaphysics concerns the ultimate convictions about reality to which our most important practices

---

187. It was my friend Philip Clayton who pressed this question home to me, though not exactly in these words.

commit us.[188] The most important practices for Christians are those that allow us to participate rightly in the theodrama: not only in liturgical celebrations but everyday witnessing and worshipping practices such as presenting our bodies as a service to God, giving and forgiving, eating and drinking, and doing everything to the glory of God.[189] Embedded in these theodramatic practices are implicit metaphysical beliefs.

A 'practice' is 'a dense cluster of ideas and activities that are related to a specific social goal and shared by a social group over time'.[190] A recent book produced by the Center for Catholic and Evangelical Theology has for its central claim 'that knowing the triune God is inseparable from participating in a particular community and its practices – a participation which is the work of God's Holy Spirit'.[191] Significantly, the authors go on to say that 'it is the concrete context of ecclesial practice that constitutes the framework of reflection *within which* agreements and disagreements over various methodological strategies . . . are contained'.[192] The way we live demonstrates what we really believe about the real: 'by their practices shall ye know them'. This notion of practice helps to heal the ugly ditch between thinking and doing that characterizes much modern

---

188. Williams says that metaphysics is the discourse about 'what constitutes [these commitments] as more than arbitrarily willed options', in 'Between Politics and Metaphysics: Reflections in the Wake of Gillian Rose', *Modern Theology* 11 [1995], p. 6). Cf. Charles Taylor's comment that excellence in philosophy consists in 'our being able to articulate the reality presupposed by our practices perspicuously' ('Overcoming Epistemology', in Baynes, Bohman and McCarthy, *After Philosophy*, p. 481).

189. In *The Drama of Doctrine* I argue not only that theodramatic practices have to do with fitting participation in the missions of the Son and Spirit (e.g. edifying the church) but also that they are normed by 'canonical practices' such as praying, truth-telling and figural interpretation (e.g. interpreting our own histories and universal history in the light of the history of Jesus Christ).

190. Dorothy C. Bass, 'Introduction', to Bass and Miroslav Volf, eds., *Practicing Theology: Beliefs and Practices in the Christian Life* (Grand Rapids: Eerdmans, 2002), pp. 2–3.

191. James J. Buckley and David S. Yeago, 'Introduction' to *Knowing the Triune God: The Work of the Spirit in the Practices of the Church* (Grand Rapids: Eerdmans, 2001), p. 1.

192. Ibid., p. 4. This manifesto seems to assign epistemic primacy, not to the Spirit speaking in the Scriptures but to the Spirit working in the church. Though their emphasis on knowledge embedded in practice is welcome, it is important to accord epistemic primacy to canonical, not community, practices.

systematic theology.[193] Doctrine directs disciples not to play-act (that way hypocrisy, delusion and despair lie) but to live according to the word of God. It is this word, and not some conceptual scheme, that truly cuts reality at its joints, 'piercing to the division of soul and spirit, of joints and marrow' (Heb. 4:12).

Practices such as praying, praising, calling for repentance and preaching the kingdom of God all imply that reality – God, the world and ourselves – is the way the theodrama goes. Excellence in theology consists in our being able to articulate the logic of the theodrama and the reality presupposed by the church's theodramatic practices. The raising of Lazarus is a key scene in the theodrama that further identifies Jesus and anticipates the drama's climax. After declaring, 'I am the resurrection and the life' (John 11:25) Jesus asks Martha, 'Do you believe this?' (11:26). Clearly, doing theology involves believing theodramatic propositions. But this is not all theology is. Earlier I mentioned belief-practices: simply shorthand for the notion that faith without works is dead. Miroslav Volf speaks of the 'as-so' structure of theodramatic correspondence: 'as God has received us in Christ, so we too are to receive our fellow human beings'.[194] What makes a practice Christian is the implied conviction about the history of Jesus Christ to which it ultimately commits us and to which it strives to correspond.

In sum, theodrama triangulates the Spirit's speaking in Scripture, the belief-practices of the church, and the world made new in Jesus Christ. Webster expresses this when he says that dogmatics 'aims at the conceptual clarification of the Christian gospel which is set forth in holy scripture and confessed in the life and practices of the church'.[195] Yet the Word of God, reality and practice are *already* coordinated in the theodrama and its authoritative script (Triangulation 1). The Bible is not some hermetic universe of its own but the result of previous communicative interaction. Thanks to the Spirit's vivifying presence in the church, however, these canonical practices invite continuing communicative covenantal interaction (Triangulation 2).

The truth of doctrine is thus a matter of theodramatic correspondence between God's understanding and ours, between our words and deeds and God's words and deeds. To speak, think and act truly requires speaking and thinking and acting that is according to the Scriptures and in accord with the

---

193. The ditch is also too often a fault-line between the so-called 'theoretical' and the so-called 'practical' disciplines in a theological seminary.

194. Volf, 'Theology for a Way of Life', in Bass and Volf, *Practicing Theology*, p. 250.

195. John Webster, 'The Self-Organizing Power of the Gospel of Christ: Episcopacy and Community Formation', *International Journal of Systematic Theology* 3 [2001], p. 70.

gospel. Two-dimensional pictures of schemes and contents or subjects and objects fall short of true theological understanding. Theodramatic truth is a matter of 'fittingness', and fittingness (theodramatic correspondence) is a three-dimensional affair.[196] Theodramatic fittingness is the result of triangulating Scripture, church and world (cultural context). On what precisely do these three coordinates get a fix? The knowledge of God. God is the 'doable knowable' and to know God is to know what to say and do to glorify him in any given situation or context. Theodramatic triangulation yields theodramatic understanding: in a word, *sapientia* – Christ, the wisdom of God.

Conclusion. Towards a theodramatic systematics: three theses

The best systematic theologies are cathedrals not only of the intellect but of the imagination inasmuch as the latter, thanks to its ability to view all things *sub specie theodramatis*, enables us to triangulate the cognitive, affective and volitional aspects of discipleship. Though it requires imagination rightly to participate in theodrama, the notion of theodrama itself is neither a convenient fiction nor even a model, but rather a fairly literal description of what the gospel presupposes and implies: God's communicative and self-communicative covenantal interaction with and on behalf of humanity. Now that we have specified theology's subject matter and method, it only remains to return to our original question about the nature and function of theological systems.

Theological systems may be 'hard' or 'soft'. A hard system is one that works with a single set of comprehensive categories or a fully developed conceptual scheme (e.g. Thomism, process theology). A kinder, softer version of systematicity requires coherence and consistency, but not necessarily that these be expressed in terms of a single conceptual scheme. For example, Colin Gunton states that 'The intrasystematic relations with which Irenaeus is concerned are chiefly those of the economy of divine action.'[197] We can reframe Irenaeus' system in terms of the present chapter by observing that his economy is precisely what I have described as a theodramatic unity – the unity of plot and of *dramatis personae* – that binds creation and redemption,

---

196. I offer something like a triangulation of the truth behind, of and in front of the biblical text in my 'Lost in Interpretation? Truth, Scripture, and Hermeneutics', *Journal of the Evangelical Theological Society* 48 (2005), pp. 89–114.

197. Gunton, '"A Rose by Any Other Name?" From "Christian Doctrine" to "Systematic Theology"', *International Journal of Theology* 1 (1999), p. 9.

the history of Israel to the history of Jesus Christ. Irenaeus' system depends on a unity of theodramatic rather than of conceptual relations.

In the final analysis, theology is systematic on two different levels: first, with regard to its method (a process of theodramatic triangulation); second, with regard to its product (a set of doctrinal directions). The principle that holds the various doctrines of a system together – the principle of their coherence – is not that of a conceptual scheme but of a theodrama, but it *is* a form of coherence. As we have seen, the understanding that is the fruit of theology is a matter of beliefs and practices. Gunton is right to say that systems are ultimately 'designs for living'.[198]

When we view systematic theology not in terms of the subject–object dichotomy but in terms of theodramatic triangulation, we see that it is a means of forming good – say, evangelically correct – judgment. A theodramatic systematics encourages 'designs for seeing, thinking and judging' through a cultivation of canonic sense and catholic sensibility. The aim is to convey not merely biblical information but to inculcate in disciples biblical habits of speaking, experiencing, thinking and acting that display theodramatic fittingness. Calvin knew this long ago: 'we cannot say that God is known where there is no religion or piety' (*Institutes* 1.2.1) or, to use the terms of the present essay, where there is no performance knowledge. If I have a system, then, it is limited to what Brian Gerrish calls the evangelical habit: whether in eating or drinking, living or dying, to see, think, judge and act all things in relation to the Word and Spirit of the gospel.[199] I conclude with three theses that expand on systematics as a theodramatic habit.

1. *The norming norm of theodramatic systematics is Scripture, the Spirit's polyphonic and multiperspectival speaking, a rich and imaginative resource for cultivating canonic sense.* This thesis responds to the first challenge mentioned above; namely, that systematic theology is *modern*, and hence reductionistic. It responds by recognizing that there is more to the Spirit speaking in and through Scripture than propositional revelation. Theodramatic systematics resists the temptation to reduce the many authorial voices and the many literary forms of Scripture to a single set of concepts. Let me be clear: while I affirm theodrama as a unified macroperspective, I also affirm a plurality of canonical microperspectives that bring different aspects of the theodrama into the foreground.[200]

---

198. Ibid., p. 11.
199. Gerrish, 'Tradition in the Modern World', p. 19.
200. On the role of perspectives in theology, see Clark, *To Know and Love God*, ch. 4, esp. pp. 138–140.

How many microperspectives are there in Scripture? In one sense, each authorial voice represents a distinct point of view. Luke's answer as to why Jesus is the Christ is neither Matthew's nor Mark's. On another level, we could say that the various literary genres of Scripture afford different perspectives on the action. Finally, we can identify three overarching agent-perspectives. We can relate the action from God's point of view, from humanity's point of view and from the point of view of what Scripture calls the 'powers and principalities'.

Mary Potter Engel explains and defends Calvin's 'system' by arguing precisely this multiperspectival point. What consistency there is in Calvin's *Institutes* is not a function of a single theme or even of a single framework, but is rather due 'to the employment of shifting perspectives'.[201] Engel illustrates her thesis with the doctrine of anthropology and argues that Calvin saw that a correct description of human existence required different perspectives. Sometimes Calvin speaks of salvation from the divine 'eternal perspective' where election comes to the fore; at other times he speaks from the human 'temporal perspective' where responsibility is paramount. The key to understanding Calvin, Engel suggests, is knowing when each perspective is contextually relevant.

The doctrine of atonement affords another example. From the divine agent-perspective favoured by Anselm, God is at work making satisfaction through the cross. From the human agent-perspective favoured by Abelard, the moral example of Christ's obedient suffering comes into focus. From the 'powers and principalities' agent-perspective, the cross is the site of a dualistic struggle whereby Christ vanquishes Satan, as some of the Fathers thought. Significantly, each of these atonement theories can enlist certain biblical metaphors and texts in support. Systematic theology may triangulate these perspectives, but it will resist the temptation to reduce the many to any one at the expense of the others. It is better to preserve the plurality and to view it as a way of enriching our understanding of the theodramatic action.[202]

2. *Theodramatic systematics is enriched by the polyphonic and multiperspectival scripted-yet-spirited performances that comprise church tradition, a rich resource for cultivating catholic sensibility.* This thesis responds to the second objection to systematics we considered above ('Systematic theology is *Western*, and hence imperialistic')

---

201. Mary Potter Engel, *John Calvin's Perspectival Anthropology* (Chico, Calif.: Scholars Press, 1988), p. xv, n. 12.

202. For a treatment of how to move from the multiple biblical metaphors to the doctrine of the atonement, see my 'The Atonement in Postmodernity: Of Guilt, Goats, and Gifts', in Frank James and Charles Hill, eds., *The Glory of the Atonement* (Downers Grove: IVP, 2004), pp. 367–404.

and extends the point I have just made about Scripture to tradition. Just as it takes four Gospels to tell the story of Jesus Christ, so it takes many interpretative communities and traditions fully to understand the Gospels (and the rest of Scripture). The church comes to a fuller understanding of its authoritative script to see what other local churches have made of it. In short, a Christologically centred and canonically bounded polyphonic tradition that includes Western and non-Western, ancient and contemporary voices best corresponds to the nature of the Scriptures themselves.[203]

Some theologians may at this point go away sorrowful, for it may seem that I am telling them to sell or give away the riches (e.g. *confessional* schemes) they possess (Matt. 19:21–22). Such is not my intent. It is not a matter of disowning confessional theology but of bringing it into conversation with the other confessional traditions that make up the catholic (whole) church. Doing theology in an era of world Christianity obliges us in the West to recognize that catholicity, a mark of the true church, may also be a mark of true doctrine. And attending to the church's understanding of her script across cultures and down through the centuries gives rise to an enlarged understanding, as Andrew Walls observes: 'It is a delightful paradox that the more Christ is translated into the various thought forms and life systems which form our various national identities, the richer all of us will be in our common Christian identity.'[204]

No one performance tradition, then, has a monopoly on understanding the theodramatic script. What this insight calls for is a dialogical systematics – a catholic conversation that employs diverse confessional and conceptual schemes better to fathom the one faith and the one gospel. Here it may perhaps help to see different theological systems – the theologies of Augustine, Calvin, Barth as well as McGrath, Grenz and Bloesch – as themselves voices in the ongoing theodrama.[205] And with regard to confessional

---

203. See my 'One Rule to Rule Them All?'
204. *The Missionary Movement in Christian History: Studies in the Transmission of Faith* (Maryknoll: Orbis, 1996), p. 54.
205. This is not to condone an anything-goes systematic theological relativism! Clearly, the voices of contemporary theologians are non-canonical in the sense that they are not inspired authors or witnesses to the theodrama. Consequently, the voices of post-canonical theologians must be measured (triangulated) against the canon and the catholic tradition. Some voices have more wisdom to offer than others; certain other voices may have to be excluded altogether from the conversation – the heretic you will always have with you! On the question of criteria for discerning heresy, see my *Drama of Doctrine*, pp. 421–426.

theologies (e.g. Reformed, Lutheran, Anabaptist etc.), we can perhaps view these systems not as necessarily conflictual but as complementary. After all, it takes many systems (nervous, digestive, reproductive, cardiovascular etc.) working together to maintain the health (*salus*) of the body.

3. *Theodramatics systematics is sapiential, a form of practical wisdom that seeks to embody the mind of Christ in new situations.* This final thesis responds to the third contemporary challenge we considered above: 'Systematic theology is *wissenschaftlich*, and hence impractical'. Theology is faith seeking theodramatic understanding, and understanding is best demonstrated not by those who can rightly parse Greek verbs (important as that may be) or by those who can defend past theological formulas but by those who can participate in the ongoing drama of redemption by speaking and doing the gospel truth in new cultural situations.

To be sure, the Spirit speaking in the Scriptures remains the authoritative script: the normative specification of Christian wisdom, a sapiential criterion. At the same time, deliberating about how to act well in particular situations demands what Aristotle calls *phronesis* (practical reason). In turn, *phronesis* – deciding what to say and do so as to correspond to God's making all things new in Christ – is a matter of triangulating the church's authoritative script, the church's earlier performances and the church's new cultural context.

The imagination – that cognitive faculty by which we discern meaningful patterns and meaningful wholes – is a vital aid in making judgments about particular situations in the context of the whole theodrama (*sub specie theodramatis*). Biblical interpretation actually requires imagination and *phronesis* on three distinct levels: first, to discern what the human author was saying; second, to discern what God was/is saying by means of the human discourse.[206] Finally, we need to discern how our saying and acting in the present situation contributes to the through-line of the evangelical action and to the 'superobjective' of the theodramatic plot.

The end of theology is not mere knowledge but understanding: a sense of where one is in the theodrama and a sense of how to continue on faithfully. To achieve theodramatic correspondence – truth – in theology, one needs to know where one is and where to go next; in a word, one needs to triangulate. Triangulation is the process by which the church lets the Spirit speaking in the Scriptures and the Spirit-guided tradition direct its present speech and action. Theodramatic systematics is a method for forming persons with good

206. Nicholas Wolterstorff, 'A Response to Trevor Hart', in Bartholomew, Greene and Möller, *Renewing Biblical Interpretation*, pp. 336–337.

judgment, what John Henry Newman called the 'illative sense'.[207] The present chapter works a Reformed variation on Newman, arguing that good theo-dramatic judgment proceeds from Word and Spirit or, in terms of the present essay, from Spirit-led canonic and catholic triangulation.[208]

If systematic theology is to prove itself useful to the church in the future, it must make good on the promise implied by its definition: it must help people of faith to *get* understanding. The way forward is clear: theology must focus not on producing theoretical systems of knowledge but on cultivating disciples who learn and embody practical wisdom. And the best way to do that is to approach the Bible not as a knowing subject, but as one who walks the way of Jesus Christ with others, triangulating our position by attending to the Spirit speaking in the Scriptures, to the church's great performances of the past, and to the church's situation today.[209]

© Kevin J. Vanhoozer, 2006

---

207. See his *An Essay in Aid of a Grammar of Assent* (New York: Doubleday, 1955).

208. See John S. McClure, 'In Pursuit of Good Theological Judgement: Newman and the Preacher as Theologian', in Michael Welker and Cynthia A. Jarvis, eds., *Loving God with our Minds: The Pastor as Theologian* (Grand Rapids: Eerdmans, 2004), pp. 202–219.

209. My thanks to Hans Madueme, Dan Treier, Adonis Vidu, Prem Williams, Stephen Williams and the members of the Center for Theological Understanding dinner-discussion group for their helpful comments on an earlier draft of this chapter.

I dedicate this chapter to the memory of Stan Grenz, fellow triangulator and sometime dialogue partner. The disagreements I may have with his proposals do not hinder me from recognizing and respecting Stan as a brother in Christ who sought creatively and constructively to rethink evangelical theological method in order to lead it out of what he perceived to be its bondage to modernity.

5. THE ATONEMENT AS PENAL SUBSTITUTION

A. T. B. McGowan

Introduction

The doctrine of the atonement is part of the unfinished business of Christian theology. The Councils and resulting creeds of the early church established the doctrines of the Trinity and the Person of Christ in such a way that Catholic, Protestant, Orthodox and most other Christian churches, agree on these matters, with relatively minor differences. The atonement, however, is a matter upon which Protestants cannot even agree among themselves. There has been, however, what we might call a central strand of Protestant theology in respect of the atonement; namely, the doctrine of penal substitution. Certainly, within the evangelical tradition, this has been the main position held. Nevertheless, many today, even evangelicals, reject this view of the atonement and have sought to put other theories in its place. In this chapter I shall re-examine the doctrine of the atonement and attempt to highlight some areas for further discussion.

Anthropology

Part of the problem for the church is that, in developing any theory of the atonement, an anthropology is assumed and it is notoriously difficult to get agreement on the range of issues which comprise a Christian anthropology. It is simply not possible to devise a theory of the atonement without first establishing the nature of the human condition, in order to determine, among other things, why the atonement was necessary and what it was intended to accomplish. We might express the problem in this way: what is the nature of human sin, how is that sin transmitted and how does Christ undo that situation and deal with sin?

Clearly, any theory of the atonement depends upon a theory of human sin. If, on the one hand, we hold to the doctrine of total depravity, with its corresponding commitment to a view of original sin, then that will have implications for how we understand the atonement, since the doctrines of total depravity and original sin pose a specific problem to which the atonement forms part of the answer. If, on the other hand, we hold to a post-Enlightenment view of humanity, in which sin plays little part, then our understanding of the atonement will of necessity be different, since the perceived problem is different. It is also the case that our view of the transmission of sin has implications for our doctrine of the atonement. For example, if we hold that Adam's sin was imputed to humanity and if we hold that it was therefore necessary for Christ's righteousness to be similarly imputed, then we shall devise a particular theory of the atonement.

It can easily be seen, then, that alternative theories of the atonement have developed because of alternative anthropologies. Had the Fathers reached an agreed position on sin and its transmission and on Christ's response to this, we might well have had agreement on the atonement but it was not to be. Origen, with his concept of hereditary pollution, came near to a doctrine of original sin, but his speculative Neoplatonism led him to positions that the church ultimately rejected. The doctrine of original sin did not really develop until Tertullian and that mostly in the Latin west. Even the more basic question as to the origin of souls was disputed between east and west. Greek theology, in so far as it had considered the subject, took a 'creationist' position; that is, each soul is created separately. Tertullian, on the other hand, took a 'traducianist' position; that is, souls result from procreation. Thus Tertullian, while never actually asserting it, paved the way for the doctrine of innate sin. Cyprian, Ambrose and Hilary, in that order, developed this more fully. It was only in response to Pelagius that the entire corruption of both the nature and the will was asserted, and hence prior to Augustine some form of synergism was accepted. Pelagius taught that each person, including Adam, is born in a perfectly free or neutral situation; that is, human beings are neither holy nor inherently evil, but have complete freedom to choose between good and evil. There is no imputation of anyone's sin to anyone else, and the widespread evil evident in the world is due to habit, custom and bad example. In response to this,

Augustine taught the total depravity of human beings. As part of the structure
of his response, Augustine also taught a clear view as to the transmission of sin.

Theories of atonement

These various developing understandings of anthropology had their counter-
parts in various theories of atonement. In the era of the Apostolic Fathers,
however, there was little in the way of systematic statement. They spoke in
scriptural language about the death of Christ, without speculating a possible
framework in which to comprehend this language. In the Epistle to Diognetus,
we have sin as deserving punishment and Christ as the ransom for sin, but no
further. In Marcion, the ransom is paid by the God of the New Testament to
the God of the Old Testament. This was rejected as heresy but other writers,
like Origen, argued that the ransom was paid to Satan. L.W. Grensted argues
that the notion of ransom to the devil 'remained the customary and orthodox
statement of the doctrine of the Atonement for nearly a thousand years'.[1]
Ultimately, this too was rejected by the church.

Tertullian coined the theological vocabulary that was destined to become the
future 'grammar' of the doctrine of atonement. His intensely legal mind formulated a system centring on 'satisfaction' and 'merit'. Augustine added little
but changed this anthropological emphasis to a more Christological one.
Gregory the Great draws these threads together, speaking of Christ as
Redeemer and Mediator; that is, the angry God being propitiated by a sacrifice
which, in the nature of things, had to be both God and man.[2] Irenaeus was the
first to relate the atonement to the justice of God, although not in the language
of Tertullian. He also stressed the theory of recapitulation; that is, sanctification
by living reversal. This is not the same as the active obedience of Christ to the
law in his role as the Second (or last) Adam, but it is closely parallel.

In Athanasius' *De Incarnatione* we have the first systematic statement of
the nature of the atonement.[3] He taught that Christ endured the wrath of

---

1. *A Short History of the Doctrine of the Atonement* (London: Manchester University Press,
   1920), p. 56.
2. See R. Seeberg, *Text-book of the History of Doctrines* (Grand Rapids: Baker, 1958),
   vol. 2, pp. 19ff.
3. Athanasius, *De Incarnatione*, in P. Schaff and H. Wace, eds., *A Select Library of Nicene
   and Post-Nicene Fathers of the Christian Church.* Vol. 4: *St Athanasius: Select Works and
   Letters*, 2nd series (Grand Rapids: Eerdmans, 1980), pp. 31–67.

God as a penalty on our behalf, although he maintained that this sacrifice was made to the honour or veracity of God and not to his justice. Anselm was the first to speak of the logical necessity of the atonement, it previously having been generally viewed as an act of God's will, which originated out of a choice from a number of possible alternatives, not excluding the possibility of forgiveness without atonement. He follows Athanasius in holding that the atonement is made to the honour of God and indeed specifically rejects penal interpretations.[4] Anselm believed that punishment and satisfaction were logical alternatives; that is, if satisfaction were not made to the divine honour then mankind must be eternally punished.[5] The Reformers argued that these were not opposites but rather complementary; that is, Christ received from the Father the punishment due to sinners, while making satisfaction.

Another view of the atonement received classic expression in the work of Abelard; that is, the moral influence or exemplarist theory. The death of Christ at Calvary becomes not an element in a juridical transaction but rather a great example of self-sacrifice, designed to highlight God's love and to bring humanity to the place of repentance and obedience. Aquinas presented a synthesis of Anselmic and Abelardian theories, but the Reformers returned to an exposition of the former, while rejecting Anselm's concept of the logical necessity of atonement. The Reformers, especially Calvin, placed great emphasis on Christ as 'victim' or 'lamb for the slaughter'. At the same time, however, Luther envisioned Christ as 'victor' defeating the powers of evil, a view later spelled out in more detail by Gustaf Aulén[6] and recently reappropriated in an important work by Hans Boersma.[7]

Federal theology and the atonement

The Reformers' emphasis on (and modification of) Anselm was further honed by those who followed in the Reformed tradition, within the context of what became known as 'federal theology', as represented by such documents as the *Westminster Confession of Faith*. This view comprises a certain position in respect

---

4. Anselm, *Cur Deus Homo* (London: Religious Tract Society, n.d.), Book 2, §18, part 2.
5. Ibid., Book I, §13.
6. Gustaf Aulén, *Christus Victor* (London: Macmillan, 1934).
7. Hans Boersma, *Violence, Hospitality, and the Cross* (Grand Rapids: Baker, 2004).

of the nature and transmission of sin, with a corresponding position regarding the nature of Christ's sacrifice and the transmission of his righteousness. Here we can see clearly the implications of an anthropology for the doctrine of the atonement.

In expounding the federal view, we must first distinguish between the Augustinian view of sin and the federal view of sin. It is best explained by saying that Augustine held to the 'natural headship' of Adam, whereas the federal theologians held to the 'federal headship' of Adam. The Augustinian theory is that God imputes the sin (singular, being only the first sin) of Adam to his posterity,

> in virtue of that organic unity of mankind by which the whole race at the time of Adam's transgression existed, not individually, but seminally, in him as its head . . . In Adam's free act, the will of the race revolted from God and the nature of the race corrupted itself. The nature which we now possess is the same nature that corrupted itself in Adam.[8]

For the Augustinian, it is morally reprehensible to suggest guilt without direct involvement in the sin, and hence it is taught that we are not guilty because of Adam's sin but because of our own. As G. P. Fisher writes:

> The fundamental idea of the Augustinian theory is that of a participation on the part of the descendants of Adam in his first sin; in consequence of which they are born both guilty and morally depraved. The fundamental idea of the federal theory is that of a vicarious representation on the part of Adam, in virtue of a covenant between God and him, whereby the legal responsibility for his first sinful act is entailed upon all his descendants; participation being excluded, but the propriety of his appointment to this vicarious office being founded on our relation to him as the common father of men.[9]

When we come to Anselm we see an important development. Like Augustine he saw Adam as the natural head of a generic type, but was more definite about imputation, by arguing that humanity after the fall is polluted by sin and, as such, guilty. Both the guilt and the pollution are passed on from

----

8. A. H. Strong, *Systematic Theology* (Philadelphia: American Baptist Publication Society, 1907), vol. 2, p. 619.

9. 'The Augustinian and the Federal Theories of Original Sin Compared', *New Englander* (July 1868), pp. 469–516.

parent to child. The criticism normally raised against this view is that it implies that the sins of our parents and other ancestors are imputed to us. As Louis Berkhof noted:

> This is undoubtedly a weak point in the system of Anselm, since all the following sins are committed by the same nature, though individualised, and because it does not answer the question, why only the first sin of Adam is imputed to his posterity, and not his later sins.[10]

The Reformers developed the covenant idea as a more exact way of speaking about the relationship between Adam's sin and our depravity. Those who followed them in the Reformed tradition developed the 'federal' view, but the seeds of it were already there in Calvin.[11] Between Calvin and the end of the seventeenth century, the federal system was elaborated in all its complexity.[12]

Federal theology (or covenant theology) teaches that the key to understanding God's dealings with humanity is the 'covenant' concept. The argument is that in Genesis 2:16, 17 God made a 'covenant of works' with Adam whereby life was promised to him on condition of perfect obedience, particularly to the command of God not to eat of the tree of the knowledge of good and evil. In this covenant Adam was not envisaged merely as a private individual, but as the representative head of all humanity or, to put it another way, the 'federal head' of the race. Hence we were all 'in Adam' when the covenant was made, not merely generically but federally. This being the case, when Adam broke the covenant, the judgement fell upon all those who had been representatively involved; namely, all humanity. Thus original sin comes to each person by the 'imputation' of Adam's sin.

Humanity being in the fallen state, God promises a 'covenant of grace' (so the federal theologians understood the *protoevangelion* of Gen. 3:15) which he duly instigated with Abraham (Gen. 12 and 15) who was promised life for himself and his descendants not on the condition of perfect obedience but by

---

10. Louis Berkhof, *The History of Christian Doctrines* (London: Banner of Truth, 1937), p. 143.

11. See Peter A. Lillback, *The Binding of God: Calvin's Role in the Development of Covenant Theology* (Grand Rapids: Baker, 2001).

12. D. A. Weir, *The Origins of the Federal Theology in Sixteenth-Century Reformation Thought* (Oxford: Clarendon, 1990); Charles S. McCoy and J. Wayne Baker, *Fountainhead of Federalism: Heinrich Bullinger and the Covenantal Tradition* (Louisville: Westminster John Knox, 1991).

grace. God could not merely ignore his own righteousness and justice, however, and so in order to forgive sinners there had to be a satisfaction made. This was to be in the form of a sacrifice as 'typified' by the ceremonial law. In what then did this consist? God elected some certain individuals out of the mass of fallen humanity and made a covenant with them in Christ their federal head, promising them eternal life on condition that Christ fulfilled the requirements of the covenant. This involved, on the one hand, a life of perfect obedience, succeeding where Adam had failed (his active obedience) and, on the other hand, death on the cross, offering himself as a penal substitutionary sacrifice to atone for the sins of the elect (his passive obedience).

It is this penal substitutionary view of the atonement that became the dominant view in Reformed theology and to which we must now turn.

Penal substitution

In 1974, the *Tyndale Bulletin* published J. I. Packer's Tyndale Biblical Theology Lecture, which had been delivered in July 1973 and was entitled 'What Did the Cross Achieve? The Logic of Penal Substitution'.[13] In the interim years, that published article has been recognized as something of a classic statement of the nature of the atonement.

Over thirty years later, it is useful to reflect on that lecture and on the changes that have taken place in attitudes towards this doctrine since then. In order to do this, I shall first review Packer's original lecture, highlighting its main argument. Second, I shall consider the range of views today concerning penal substitution. Third, I shall review a recent essay on the atonement by J. I. Packer, in order to see if there have been any changes in, or developments of, his view since the 1970s.

The logic of penal substitution
J. I. Packer began his 1973 lecture by identifying his purpose; namely, 'to focus and explicate a belief which, by and large, is a distinguishing mark of the word-wide [*sic*] evangelical fraternity: namely, the belief that Christ's death on the cross had the character of *penal substitutio*'.[14] In the light of what we shall see later, it is striking that, only in the early 1970s, Packer was able to identify penal

---

13. *Tyndale Bulletin* 25 (1974), pp. 3–45.
14. Ibid., p. 3. The 'word-wide' evangelical fraternity is an interesting typographical error!

substitution as a 'distinguishing feature' of evangelicalism. This was no periph-
eral issue where a range of views might legitimately be expected but one that
lay at the heart of what it meant to be an evangelical. It is also interesting to
note Packer's analysis of the history of the doctrine, indicating that the main
proponents of penal substitution were the magisterial Reformers and that the
main opposition came from Socinus and other Unitarian theologians. It is also
illuminating to note that the arguments used against penal substitution by
Socinus included the charges that it was 'irrational, incoherent, immoral and
impossible'.[15] These same criticisms of the doctrine, as we shall see, are used
today by some who lay claim to being evangelical. The theological landscape,
then, has changed quite dramatically since 1973.

Penal substitution, as defined by Packer, is the belief that Christ, on our
behalf, underwent 'vicarious punishment (*poena*) to meet the claims on us of
God's holy law and wrath (*i.e.* his punitive justice)'.[16] It must be noted,
however, that Packer is not prepared to defend every exposition of penal substitution, or at least every method of stating and defending it. Indeed, he is
quite critical of what he calls 'methodological rationalism'[17] and names
Turretin, A. A. Hodge and Berkhof as having fallen into this trap.[18] He writes:

> Their stance was defensive rather than declaratory, analytical and apologetic rather
> than doxological and kerygmatic. They made the word of the cross sound more like a
> conundrum than a confession of faith – more like a puzzle, we might say, than a
> gospel. What was happening? Just this: that in trying to beat Socinian rationalism at
> its own game, Reformed theologians were conceding the Socinian assumption that
> every aspect of God's work of reconciliation will be exhaustively explicable in terms
> of a natural theology of divine government, drawn from the world of contemporary
> legal and political thought. Thus, in their zeal to show themselves rational, they
> became rationalistic.[19]

In response to these writers, Packer says that we should not be afraid to
speak of 'mystery' and to have unsolved problems in our theology.[20] This is
simply a recognition that we are creatures and that we cannot exhaustively

---

15. Ibid., p. 4.
16. Ibid.
17. Ibid., p. 5.
18. Ibid., pp. 4, 5.
19. Ibid., p. 5.
20. Ibid., pp. 7, 8.

know the mind of God. He takes this further by noting the inherent problem of using human language to express divine realities,[21] except by means of 'parables, analogies, metaphors and images'.[22] To drive this point home, he argues that the traditional method of Christian theology is to take biblical models and to build our doctrinal systems on the basis of these models, which then act as 'controls'. He illustrates this with reference to scientific method:

> As models in physics are hypotheses formed under the suggestive control of empirical evidence to correlate and predict phenomena, so Christian theological models are explanatory constructs formed to help us know, understand and deal with God, the ultimate reality.[23]

The final strand of what he calls his 'methodological preliminaries'[24] is to indicate his doctrine of Scripture, what he calls, 'the mainstream Christian belief in biblical inspiration'.[25] He is quite clear that knowledge and understanding of the meaning of the cross can only come from one source. He writes, 'By what means is knowledge of the mystery of the cross given us? I reply: through the didactic thought-models given in the Bible, which in truth are instructions from God.'[26] This affirmation is identical to that of another significant Reformed writer on the atonement, John Murray, who says:

> There is only one source from which we can derive a proper conception of Christ's atoning work. That source is the Bible. There is only one norm by which our interpretations and formulations are to be tested. That norm is the Bible. The temptation ever lurks near us to prove unfaithful to this one and only criterion.[27]

Packer then moves into the first main theme of his paper and deals with the concept of 'substitution'.[28] He argues that substitution means taking the place of another and includes the concept of vicarious representation, which some

---

21. Ibid., pp. 8–11.
22. Ibid., p. 10.
23. Ibid., p. 12.
24. Ibid., p. 16.
25. Ibid., p. 13.
26. Ibid.
27. John Murray, *Redemption Accomplished and Applied* (London: Banner of Truth, 1961), p. 76.
28. Packer, 'What Did the Cross Achieve?', pp. 16–25.

had seen as an alternative.[29] He is quite clear that this concept of substitution is soundly based on Scripture, not least in Paul's statement in Romans 5:8 that 'Christ died for us', taken together with Paul's other statement in Galatians 3:13 that 'Christ redeemed us from the curse of the law, having become a curse for us'.[30] Packer notes that this idea of substitution was almost wholly rejected by British theologians of the time but that Barth and Pannenberg affirmed it.[31] In defending his argument for substitution, Packer notes that, in the history of the church, there have been essentially three ways of viewing the atonement. First, to say that it has effect entirely upon human beings, for example, as an example of self-sacrificial love which we ought to follow; second, to argue that the atonement is directed primarily at 'hostile spiritual forces'; or third, to say that the atonement includes both of these concepts but is primarily directed at God on our behalf. Packer argues for the third of these positions.

He then moves on to argue the case for adding the word 'penal' to that of 'substitution', in order to clarify the nature and intent of the substitution. He says that to add this word,

> is to anchor the model of substitution (not exclusively but regulatively) within the world of moral law, guilty conscience, and retributive justice. Thus is forged a conceptual instrument for conveying the thought that God remits our sins and accepts our persons into favour not because of any amends we have attempted, but because the penalty which was our due was diverted on to Christ.[32]

Rather than re-presenting traditional constructs of penal substitution, Packer devises his own and that for several reasons. First, he wishes to avoid ways of presenting the subject which are unhelpful, both those he calls 'devotionally evocative without always being theologically rigorous'[33] and those rationalistic constructs mentioned above which are essentially responses to Socinus on his own terms. Second, he wishes to highlight penal substitution's character as both dramatic and kerygmatic. Third, he wants to avoid the charge that penal substitution is impersonal and abstract. He is keen to demonstrate that, seen properly, it is truly moral, personal and relational.[34]

---

29. Particularly P. T. Forsyth, ibid., pp. 22, 23.
30. Ibid., p. 17.
31. Ibid., p. 19.
32. Ibid., p. 25.
33. Ibid.
34. Ibid., pp. 25–29.

There follows an extensive analysis of various scriptural passages which indicate that Christ bore the wrath of God on our behalf, under five themes: 'substitution and retribution; substitution and solidarity; substitution and mystery; substitution and salvation; substitution and divine love'.[35] Packer's conclusion is that penal substitution is 'the heart of the matter'.[36] Or, as he puts it earlier in his argument:

> This analysis, if correct, shows what job the word 'penal' does in our model. It is there, not to prompt theoretical puzzlement about the transferring of guilt, but to articulate the insight of believers who, as they look at Calvary in the light of the New Testament, are constrained to say, 'Jesus was bearing the judgement I deserved (and deserve), the penalty for my sins, the punishment due to me' – 'he loved me, and gave himself for me' (Gal. 2:20). How it was possible for him to bear their penalty they do not claim to know, and no more than they know how it was possible for him to be made man; but that he bore it is the certainty on which all their hopes rest.[37]

In my view, Packer's understanding of this doctrine is soundly based on Scripture and remains a definitive statement of the teaching of Scripture.

Recent views on penal substitution
When Packer wrote his lecture, the boundary lines, as he saw it, were clear. On the one hand, there were those who rejected the notion of penal substitution, largely those adhering to traditional liberal theology, represented by scholars like Vincent Taylor and F. W. Camfield, but also including some who were evangelical in other aspects of their theology but who denied some aspect of penal substitution, like P. T. Forsyth. On the other hand, there were those who supported penal substitution, identified as the worldwide community of evangelicals.

Today, the situation is much more complex. In order to demonstrate this complexity, I want to indicate some of those who today reject penal substitution, noting that this group now includes some who would claim to be evangelical.

The remnants of old liberal theology
The annual meeting of the Society for the Study of Theology, which took place in Newcastle in April 2003, had as its theme 'The Cross'. Many different

---

35. Ibid., pp. 29–43.
36. Ibid., p. 45.
37. Ibid., p. 31.

aspects of the atonement were dealt with but it was notable that no-one argued in favour of the traditional exposition of penal substitution, which can surely lay legitimate claim to being regarded as part of the mainstream tradition of atonement theology. For example, Peter Selby's presidential address focused on themes of social justice, and Mary Grey argued for an ecological under-standing of the implications of Christian theology. Like the others, Clive Marsh and Rita Nakashima Brock were fairly dismissive of traditional views of atonement, not least because of their feminist or womanist perspectives. Even Kathryn Tanner, who sought to argue for an incarnational understand-ing of the atonement, rejected notions of penal substitution, although she then struggled to explain what precisely it was that the death of Christ con-tributed to salvation, as over against that which had already been accomplished in the incarnation.

Most interesting, however, was the apparent consensus that the Bible did contain a doctrine of penal substitution but that we know better today and ought to dismiss it in favour of other models. These other models may be ones we create ourselves, since we are not bound by the biblical models. In other words, the issue with this group remains the authority of Scripture. Are we free to abandon models central to Scripture, just because they are inconsistent with the cultural consensus of the early twenty-first century? Many of these theo-logians would appear to answer 'yes'.

Radical theology, especially feminist theology

These scholars, however, were relatively mild in their critique of traditional views of the atonement compared to Daphne Hampson, whose position is much more radical and thoroughgoing than those just mentioned.[38] Having herself abandoned Christianity, she argues strongly that it is immoral, not least because of the way it has treated women. On the particular matter of sacrifice, she dismisses any notion of the Father punishing the Son as 'pernicious', since it involves a religious symbolism which can be used to justify violence against children by fathers. She appears to quote approvingly Rita Nakashima Brock's dismissal of penal substitution as cosmic 'child abuse'.[39]

What I want to note, however, is that for her also the key issue is revelation. At various points in her argument, she is quite dismissive of 'Christian feminists', viewing them as largely inconsistent and having not worked through the impli-cations of their theology. For example, she writes, 'Why anyone who calls herself

---

38. Daphne Hampson, *After Christianity* (London: SCM, 2002).

39. Ibid., pp. 151, 152.

(or himself) a feminist, who believes in human equality, should wish to hold to a patriarchal myth such as Christianity must remain a matter for bafflement.'[40] She continues to regard herself as a theist, however, since she believes that there is a dimension to reality, which she calls God. This reality, however, is not a personal being who is 'outside' or 'beyond' history as we know it.

On the person and work of Christ, Hampson struggles to identify any meaning that would be compatible with post-Enlightenment thought. She insists that the key problem in Christianity is its claim to be unique and to be historical in the sense of rooted in a specific, revelatory space-time event. She notes:

> What it is never necessary to do, given the religious position which I espouse, is to measure what one would say against some benchmark in history. For I am denying that there has been any particular revelation in history with which one should compare what one wishes to think.[41]

And again,

> The problem with Christianity is that Christians hold that there has been a revelation in history, so that the past becomes a necessary point of reference. That is heteronomous. It is not how we think today. We need to take responsibility for our ethical stance and, equally, for our spirituality.[42]

She is also dismissive of liberal scholars, who try to retain Christianity by demythologizing this concept of history:

> In response I must insist that if Christianity is called a 'historical' religion simply in the sense that Christians are part of a continuous history which reaches back to Jesus of Nazareth . . . as though being a Christian consisted in nothing more than siting oneself within a certain tradition, something essential has been lost. The decisive point about Christianity has always been (and surely always must be) that Christians believe there to have been a revelation in Christ. That in different ages Christians have spoken in different terms of the uniqueness which is the implication of such a revelation is certainly the case. But Christianity is not just 'historical' in the sense that historically it had its origin in the life, death and teaching of one particular man.

---

40. Ibid., p. 50.
41. Ibid., p. 57.
42. Ibid., p. 83.

Being Christian cannot be held to mean no more than being part of a particular community, like being English.[43]

She is also highly critical of all supposedly Christian scholarship that seeks to retain commitment to Christianity while rejecting its traditional Christological claims:

> I think, then, that one must round on the suggestion that what is rightly to be called a Christology could fail to make any claim to there having been a uniqueness. In the first place that is not congruent with what Christians have always believed. From the earliest days Christians have not simply proclaimed Jesus' message, but a *kerygma*, a message, about Jesus. To repeat what I said earlier: either the Christ event is shattering, or it is nothing. If it is nothing – that is to say, Jesus was just a rather fine human being and that is the end of the matter – then one can take or leave him as one will. No one who is Christian could possibly assent to such a proposition! Christianity is a religion for which people have died as martyrs – not inconsistently if it is true.[44]

This is a fascinating point. She is saying that liberal theologians and Christian feminists who seek to retain the language and liturgy of Christianity, while rejecting its content, are essentially being inconsistent and perhaps even dishonest! Her rejection of a traditional view of the atonement, then, is part and parcel of her rejection of Christianity as a whole and more specifically her rejection of the uniqueness of Jesus Christ as the God-man.

The neo-orthodox

If liberal theologians reject penal substitution because they have rejected the authority of Scripture, and radicals like Daphne Hampson reject penal substitution because they have rejected Christianity, this third group reject penal substitution because they believe it to be inconsistent with an orthodox doctrine of God.

Barth argues strongly in favour of using the word 'substitution' in respect of our redemption. It is, however, important to note two things. First, that the word translated as 'substitution' (*Stellvertretung*) incorporates the ideas of both substitution and representation.[45] Second, that when Barth uses the word substitution,

---

43. Ibid., p. 42.

44. Ibid., p. 43.

45. See Karl Barth, *Church Dogmatics*, English tr. edited by G. W. Bromiley and T. F. Torrance (Edinburgh: T. & T. Clark, 1936–69), IV/1, pp. vii–viii.

it is given a sense more radical than is normally the case in English, because Barth envisages it as a total displacement of sinful man by the incarnate, crucified and risen Son; and also more comprehensive, because it is related to the whole life and work of Jesus Christ, including His heavenly intercession.[46]

What is also clear, however, is that Barth and those who have followed in his footsteps reject the concept of 'penal' substitution, preferring instead to argue for an incarnational understanding of redemption. That is to say, he argues that the very act of the Word becoming flesh involved reconciliation. God, in the person of the Son, takes to himself a (fallen) human nature and thus, in the very person of Christ, God and humanity are reconciled. Effectively the judgment of God is taken upon God himself.[47] Salvation is no longer to be seen in the forensic terms of the courtroom, whereby Christ, by a substitutionary action, obtains a benefit that is then passed on to others. Rather, salvation is to be found in the very being of Christ, and therefore union with Christ becomes the key doctrine. Once we are united to Christ we share in his reconciled humanity and so receive all of the blessings God delights to pour out upon us. This obviates the need for penal substitution and the subsequent conferral of the benefits of Christ's death upon sinners.[48] In an important article, Trevor Hart spells out the implications of this for justification.[49] He critiques both traditional Protestant and traditional Roman Catholic views as teaching the notion of 'benefits' being obtained, rather than viewing justification Christologically.

If asked to identify an alternative model for understanding the atonement, most in this group would offer support for John McLeod Campbell, who rejected the *Westminster Confession of Faith's* penal substitutionary view of the atonement with its accompanying commitment to particular redemption, and developed his theory of 'Vicarious Repentance'. In this view, the incarnation and not the atonement is the key event and the love of God to all humanity is the key motif. As Ian Hamilton notes, 'The atonement is made not by Christ

---

46. Ibid.

47. Ibid., pp. 211–283.

48. This is appropriately the great theme of the Festschrift for James B. Torrance: Trevor Hart and Daniel Thimell eds., *Christ in our Place: The Humanity of God in Christ for the Reconciliation of the World* (Exeter: Paternoster, 1989).

49. Trevor Hart, 'Humankind in Christ and Christ in Humankind: Salvation as Participation in our Substitute in the Theology of John Calvin', *Scottish Journal of Theology* 42 (1989), pp. 67–74. See also 'Justification: Barth, Trent, and Küng', *Scottish Journal of Theology* 34.6 (1981), pp. 517–529.

suffering vicariously the wrath of God for sinners, but by Christ's perfect confession and repentance of sin . . .'[50]

Barth's Christological methodology and his incarnational understanding of atonement do not themselves, however, take us to the heart of his problem with respect to penal substitution. The key problem lies in the doctrine of God. The problem might be expressed in this way: 'How could it possibly be that the Father should punish the Son? Would this not involve an inner-trinitarian breach, which is surely unthinkable?'

Let me illustrate this by referring to a sermon I heard recently, preached by an evangelical minister. In the course of his sermon he noted the words of Jesus from the cross, 'My God, my God, why have you forsaken me?' He immediately said that, of course, Jesus was not *truly* abandoned, he only *felt* abandoned. I wanted to say, 'No, he truly was abandoned.' In other words, I wanted to argue that in some mysterious way, there takes place a breach within the inner councils of the Trinity at that moment on the cross because the divine Son who has taken to himself a human nature, becomes sin and is bearing the wrath of God for sin.

In pressing for the reality of the Father's punishing of the Son, however, one important qualification has to be made. Even in the midst of that great transaction on the cross, the Father never ceased to love the Son and to be well pleased with him. This was a point Calvin stressed:

> Yet we do not suggest that God was ever inimical or angry toward him. How could he be angry toward his beloved Son, 'in whom his heart reposed' [cf. Matt. 3:17]? How could Christ by his intercession appease the Father toward others, if he were himself hateful to God? This is what we are saying: he bore the weight of divine severity, since he was 'stricken and afflicted' [cf. Isa. 53:5] by God's hand, and experienced all the signs of a wrathful and avenging God.[51]

In other words, the Father was not hostile to the Son in and of himself, even though Christ 'bore the weight of divine severity'. This is essentially the same point made by George Smeaton, when he wrote that Christ

> endured divine wrath; that is, the divine desertion, as the Mediator between God and man, subjecting Himself to all that had devolved upon humanity as the curse of sin.

---

50. 'John McLeod Campbell', in S. B. Ferguson and D. F. Wright, eds., *New Dictionary of Theology* (Leicester: IVP, 1988), p. 126.

51. John Calvin, *Institutes* 2.16.11.

His substitution was not, indeed, identity. He could therefore be the object of the divine wrath in our place, while still the beloved Son and the sinless man. He was made sin while sinlessly perfect and accepted: He was made a curse while yet the faultless servant: He was the object of true punishment, and of all that goes to constitute true wrath, as He stood in our place to bear what was due to us for sin, while in Himself the Son of His love (Col.i.13), and the approved and accepted second Adam, and never more the object of His approval than when he offered Himself for others (John x.17). We draw the distinction between the personal and the official.[52]

Let me say that I fully understand the difficulty that attaches to this subject of the Son bearing the wrath of the Father, and I fully respect the theological complexity involved in maintaining penal substitution in the light of the need for a careful delineating of the relationship between the Father and the Son. In my view, this is the strongest theological argument to be faced by any doctrine of penal substitution.

There is, however, an alternative view of Barth; namely, that he can be viewed as a significant defender of penal substitution, albeit in a redefined manner. Bruce McCormack of Princeton University, in an article in a volume on the atonement, published as a recent Festschrift for Roger Nicole, outlines a way of reinstating penal substitution and defending it against its detractors by using Karl Barth's ontology![53] Essentially, his argument is that the opponents of penal substitution have been successful in their arguments because, in most of the Reformed tradition, the doctrine of penal substitution has been defined in ways that demonstrate an inadequate Christology and an inadequate doctrine of the Trinity. Once these problems are solved, however, a doctrine of penal substitution can be developed that is not subject to the normal criticisms levelled against it.

McCormack writes:

The subject who delivers Jesus Christ up to death is not the Father alone. For the Trinitarian axiom *opera trinitatis ad extra sunt indivisa* means that if one does it, they all

---

52. George Smeaton, *The Apostles' Doctrine of the Atonement* (Edinburgh: Banner of Truth, 1991), p. 314.

53. Bruce L. McCormack, 'The Ontological Presuppositions of Barth's Doctrine of the Atonement', in Charles E. Hill and Frank A. James III, eds., *The Glory of the Atonement: Biblical, Historical and Practical Perspectives* (Downers Grove: IVP, 2004), pp. 346–366.

do it. So it is the triune God (Father, Son and Holy Spirit) who gives himself over to this experience. And that also means, then, that the Father is not doing something to someone other than himself. The triune God pours his wrath out upon himself in and through the human nature that he has made his own in his second mode of his being – that is the ontological significance of penal substitution. The triune God takes this human experience into his own life; he 'drinks it to the dregs.' And in doing so, he vanquishes its power over us. That, I would submit, is the meaning of penal substitution when seen against the background of a well-ordered Christology and a well-ordered doctrine of the Trinity.[54]

What we have to decide, of course, is whether this reconstruction of the doctrine of penal substitution saves the doctrine from its detractors, or empties it of some of the significance accorded to it in the Scriptures.

Revisionist evangelicals

I must now draw attention to the fact that a number of those who would normally be regarded as mainstream evangelicals and who hold to evangelical views on most subjects, as identified, for example, by such documents as the Basis of Faith of the Evangelical Alliance, have now departed from a belief in penal substitution.

One interesting feature of this group is that they come to the same conclusion as the above-noted liberal theologians, but for very different reasons. The liberals say that penal substitution is taught in Scripture, but we are not bound by that. These evangelicals either say that the Bible does not teach penal substitution, or they say that penal substitution is only one model among many and therefore ought not to be the controlling interpretative theme in our theology of atonement.

Let me give three examples of this group.

1. *Green and Baker*. The evangelical credentials of Joel Green and Mark Baker are not in doubt, yet in a recent volume, *Recovering the Scandal of the Cross*,[55] they deny the notion of penal substitution. Many have hailed this book as an important contribution and, indeed, it has received strong commendations from various well-known evangelicals.

The core argument put forward by Green and Baker is that what we have in the New Testament is a range of models for understanding the atonement.

---

54. Ibid., p. 364.

55. Joel B. Green and Mark D. Baker, *Recovering the Scandal of the Cross: Atonement in New Testament and Contemporary Contexts* (Carlisle: Paternoster, 2000).

In this respect their argument is similar to that of Colin Gunton.[56] They go further, however, in arguing that the writers of the New Testament were not presenting models for all time but looking for models that would be understood by the specific communities to whom they were speaking. This means that we today must be developing models that speak to our own communities and societies, seeing the biblical models as examples rather than as solid and final parameters for our doctrine. Their desire to see new models developed, however, is coupled with a specific rejection of the model of penal substitution. As they say in their conclusion:

> We believe that the popular fascination with and commitment to penal substitutionary atonement has had ill effects in the life of the church in the United States and has little to offer the global church and mission by way of understanding or embodying the message of Jesus Christ.[57]

2. *St John's versus Oak Hill.* A second example of evangelicals rejecting penal substitution is represented by the dispute between two Anglican colleges traditionally regarded as evangelical: St John's Nottingham and Oak Hill College, London. This began with the publication in 1995 of the papers from a symposium on the atonement, which had taken place at St John's.[58] Some of the contributors (John Goldingay and Stephen Travis) rejected the connection between atonement and punishment, whereas others (Christina Baxter and Tom Smail) reinterpreted the words 'penal substitution' and used them in a different way.

The response came in the form of the published papers from another symposium; namely, the Fourth Oak Hill College Annual School of Theology.[59] Here we have an unequivocal defence of penal substitution, with an extensive analysis of biblical texts by David Peterson and theological articles by Garry Williams and others. Clearly this debate highlights a major fault line within evangelical theology, not least in mainstream denominations.

3. *Steve Chalke.* The third example is perhaps the most striking because, although over the years some evangelical theologians have rejected the notion

---

56. Colin E. Gunton, *The Actuality of Atonement: A Study of Metaphor, Rationality and the Christian Tradition* (Edinburgh: T. & T. Clark, 1988).

57. Green and Baker, *Recovering the Scandal of the Cross*, pp. 220–221.

58. John Goldingay, ed., *Atonement Today* (London: SPCK, 1995).

59. David Peterson, ed., *Where Wrath and Mercy Meet: Proclaiming the Atonement Today* (Carlisle: Paternoster, 2001).

of penal substitution, it has largely remained the standard view among popular evangelical writers. This recently changed when Steve Chalke, of Oasis Trust, argued against penal substitution.[60] His objection to penal substitution, and to some other evangelical beliefs, is on the basis of a general principle concerning God's love. For example, on the question of God telling his people Israel to engage in battle against their enemies, as recorded in the Old Testament, he says that this was not true to God's character and implies that the people of Israel either misunderstood or misrepresented God. He writes:

> Yahweh's association with vengeance and violence wasn't so much an expression of who he was but the result of his determination to be involved with his world. His unwillingness to distance himself from the people of Israel and their actions meant that at times he was implicated in the excessive acts of war that we see in some of the books of the Old Testament. From the very beginning, Yahweh's dealings with Israel were motivated by his desire to demonstrate his love. But to a people saturated in a worldview that saw him as power, this was always going to be a slow uphill struggle.[61]

His determination to vindicate God from anything that early twenty-first-century people might find unpalatable includes the following statement: 'The Bible . . . never makes assertions about his anger, power or judgement independently of his love.'[62] He does not attempt to justify this statement exegetically.

He explains his core working principle in this same section of the book when he writes, 'The fact is, however else God may have revealed himself, and in whatever way he interacts with the world he has created, everything is to be tempered, interpreted, understood and seen through the one, primary lens of God's love.'[63] He does not seek to justify this statement beyond arguing that the statement 'God is Love' is paradigmatic.

He further subverts the traditional evangelical view by denying the doctrine of original sin. He writes:

> To see humanity as inherently evil and steeped in *original sin* instead of inherently made in God's image and so bathed in *original goodness*, however hidden it may have become, is a serious mistake. It is this grave error that has dogged the Church in the

---

60. Steve Chalke and Alan Mann, *The Lost Message of Jesus* (Grand Rapids: Zondervan, 2003).
61. Ibid., p. 49.
62. Ibid., p. 63.
63. Ibid.

West for centuries. In the fourth century Augustine developed his influential theology that the material world and everything in it was inherently evil and corrupt. This 'fallenness' he said, was like a virus, and in humans was passed on through the act of sexual intercourse and conception. So from the seeds of Augustine's thinking, the doctrine of original sin was born. However, the Eastern Church instead followed the teaching of Irenaeus, who believed that all people were God's-image bearers and though flawed were, as he put it, like flowers in bud – slowly coaxed into full bloom by God's love.[64]

In the course of developing his argument he makes some quite dramatic claims. He argues that Jesus came to 'declare war on' the temple and that 'In effect, he was announcing that it was redundant, irrelevant and obsolete.'[65] This is not argued in the context of Christ's once-for-all sacrifice making unnecessary the sacrificial system established in the Old Testament, but as part of Jesus' ministry during his life.

He also says that 'when it comes to the God of the Bible there is only one kind of sin in the world – forgiven sin'.[66] This is said in the context of the parable of the prodigal son, but no theological rationale is given for the continued existence of unforgiven sin, nor for the continued existence of those who reject Christ.

In opposition to the view that someone is either a Christian or not a Christian, having either been born again or not born again, he quotes approvingly from C. S. Lewis who believed that no such clear divide existed.[67] In driving this point home, he notes that Jesus only used the expression 'you must be born again' twice, in one conversation with Nicodemus, and then goes on to say, 'And yet it has become the basis for one of the most confused, misused and abused, misunderstood and despised ideas in the history of the Church.'[68] He writes:

The truth is that when Jesus spoke to Nicodemus (a sincere, questioning and spiritually seeking Pharisee), he was not using the term 'born again' in the same sense we have come to do. Jesus was simply saying that entering into God's Kingdom or shalom is about seeing the world differently and adopting his new agenda. It is about

---

64. Ibid., p. 67.
65. Ibid., p. 105.
66. Ibid., p. 109.
67. Ibid., p. 141.
68. Ibid., p. 147.

dropping the crushing, life-draining, religious dogma and discovering the freedom that God loves you as you are and that his Kingdom is available to you.[69]

Just in case we have not yet grasped the point, he says, 'for John, being born-again wasn't the crisis experience we have made it'.[70]

With this background, then, it is no surprise that when he comes to deal with the atonement, he also rejects the traditional evangelical position. He writes:

> John's Gospel famously declares, 'God loved the people of this world so much that he gave his only Son' (John 3:16). How then, have we come to believe that at the cross this God of love suddenly decides to vent his anger and wrath on his own Son?
>
> The fact is that the cross isn't a form of cosmic child abuse – a vengeful Father, punishing his Son for an offence he has not even committed. Understandably, both people inside and outside of the Church have found this twisted version of events morally dubious and a huge barrier to faith. Deeper than that, however, is that such a concept stands in total contradiction to the statement 'God is love'. If the cross is a personal act of violence perpetrated by God towards humankind but borne by his Son, then it makes a mockery of Jesus' own teaching to love your enemies and to refuse to repay evil with evil.
>
> The truth is, the cross is a symbol of love. It is a demonstration of just how far God as Father and Jesus as his Son are prepared to go to prove that love.[71]

The rejection of penal substitution is clear. What is not so clear is the meaning of the cross in this new theological perspective. To say that it is a symbol of love is fine, but what does that mean? Is this the moral influence theory revisited? Or some other view where the love of God is used to deny or undermine anything that the Scriptures say about sin, judgment, death and hell? Above all, the question must be asked, 'What is the connection between the "Christ event" (for Chalke is rightly insistent that cross and resurrection must not be separated) and our salvation?'

Penal substitution reaffirmed

In the light of this increasing consensus against penal substitution, then, including many evangelicals, can we maintain penal substitution in 2004 as Packer did in his lecture published in 1974? It is clear that Packer himself

---

69. Ibid., p. 148.
70. Ibid., p. 149.
71. Ibid., pp. 182–183.

believes so. Some thirty years after his original article was published, he contributed an essay to the Festschrift for Roger Nicole.[72] This essay is not specifically on the issue of penal substitution but it is clear from the article that his view on that subject remains unchanged.

Having restated his commitment to penal substitution, however, he does make three 'caveats against undue narrowness'. In the first place he argues that 'we must not isolate the atonement from God's larger plan and strategy for his world'.[73] His concern here is to ensure that everything is seen in the light of God's eternal purpose. The death and resurrection of Christ is a 'decisive step', but only one step towards the achieving of God's overall plan for humanity and the consummation of all things.

In the second place he says that 'we must not define atonement in single-category terms'.[74] In making this point he is not following those who say that there are many models, none of which controls the others. He states quite clearly that 'penal substitution (Christ bearing in our place the curse, that is, the retribution that hung over us) is Paul's final and fundamental category for understanding the cross'.[75] He does, however, go on to say, having outlined a number of models and metaphors of atonement, that

> each of these conceptual categories, items already in the technical language of the apostolic age, covers its own distinct area of thought and meaning – its own semantic field, as we say nowadays – and the full range and glory of the atonement only appears when each is delineated in its own terms.[76]

Perhaps most striking of all is Packer's third caveat, where he places significant emphasis on union with Christ, a theme that was not central to his argument in the earlier paper. He writes:

> we must not treat the atonement as if its direct benefits to believers are the whole of our salvation, for they are not. Benefits that the atonement brings us directly are forgiveness and justification, that is, full cancellation of our demerit and present acceptance of our sinful persons into the covenant fellowship of our holy God;

---

72. 'The Atonement in the Life of the Christian', in Hill and James, *Glory of the Atonement*, pp. 409–425.
73. Ibid., p. 415.
74. Ibid., p. 416.
75. Ibid.
76. Ibid.

permanent peace with this God and adoption into his family, establishing us as his heirs . . . But the taproot of our entire salvation, and the true NT frame for cataloguing its ingredients, is our union with Christ himself by the Holy Spirit.[77]

Set the atonement in the light of God's overall purpose and plan; make use of every model and metaphor of atonement, albeit under the controlling model of penal substitution; and give proper emphasis to union with Christ. It seems to me, that these are significant and valuable caveats, which might well help to reassure some of those who have problems with penal substitution.

The extent of the atonement

Having considered penal substitution as the main Reformed perspective on the nature of the atonement, we must now note that another significant area of debate in Reformed theology concerns the extent of the atonement. As we have seen, the system of federal theology includes the conviction that the atonement is particular (or limited). That is to say, Christ's death was for and on behalf of the elect. He did not die for all humanity, although most Reformed theologians would agree that his death was sufficient for all and that it had a certain universal reference, although not in the sense of purchasing salvation for all humanity.

Quite apart from those in the Arminian tradition who naturally reject this teaching, there are many others within the Reformed tradition who challenge it and argue that it is a deviation from authentic Calvinism. The Calvin versus Calvinism debate which has been going on since the 1970s bears witness to this disagreement. Perhaps the most important disagreement within the tradition, however, is between traditional Calvinists and those who take an Amyraldian position. This debate is most hotly contested because, in so many other respects and on so many doctrinal issues, the combatants are in agreement.

The decision one makes in Calvinist versus Amyraldian debate depends upon one's view of the order of the decrees of God. Historically, there have been two main positions held within the Reformed community, supralapsarianism and infralapsarianism.

Supralapsarianism is the view that places election and reprobation at the head of the order of decrees (in all that follows, the 'order of decrees' is taken to mean 'logical' and not 'temporal' order). Thus it is taught that the election

---

77. Ibid., pp. 416–417.

of some human beings and some angels to eternal life with God preceded the permissive decree of the fall and even the decree of creation. Charles Hodge summarizes this well when he writes:

> According to this view, God in order to manifest his grace and justice selected from creatable men (ie. from men to be created) a certain number to be vessels of mercy and certain others to be vessels of wrath. In the order of thought, election and reprobation precede the purpose to create and to permit the fall. Creation is in order to redemption. God creates some to be saved, and others to be lost.[78]

Karl Barth lists 'Beza, Bucanus, Gomarus, Maccovius, Heidanus and Burmann' as the best-known exponents.[79] More recently, supralapsarianism has been advocated by a number of scholars, not least Robert Reymond.[80]

Infralapsarianism is the position held by those who 'conceive that the principle of particularism, in the sense of discrimination, belongs in the sphere of God's soteriological, not in that of his cosmical creation'.[81] In other words, infralapsarianism teaches the order of decrees as being creation, permission for the fall and election to life, hence seeing election as being from the mass of fallen humanity. Both the Synod of Dort and the Westminster Assembly, while not being specific, show clear bias towards this position. It is also generally held to be the orthodox view,[82] although attempts to have either position officially condemned have failed.[83]

Amyraldianism (or Hypothetical Universalism) claims to hold together both the universal reference of the atonement and also its particular application. On the surface this looks as if it might draw various biblical threads together. Those who hold this position would agree with the infralapsarians that the decree permitting the fall must be prior to the decree of election but, between these two is placed the work of Christ rendering salvation possible for all human beings. Hence there is posited a universal possibility but an elected actuality.

---

78. C. Hodge, *Systematic Theology* (New York: Scribners, 1874), p. 316.

79. This was recognized by Barth in his analysis of the problem: *Church Dogmatics* II/2, p. 127.

80. Robert L. Reymond, *A New Systematic Theology of the Christian Faith* (Nashville: Nelson, 1998), pp. 488–502.

81. B. B. Warfield, *The Plan of Salvation* (Grand Rapids: Eerdmans, 1942), p. 88.

82. Barth, *Church Dogmatics* II/2, p. 129.

83. See D. Jellema, 'Supralapsarianism', in J. D. Douglas, ed., *The New International Dictionary of the Christian Church* (Exeter: Paternoster, 1974).

This view has recently been advocated strongly by Alan C. Clifford, who is persuaded that this is the view held by Calvin himself, although most Calvinists remain unconvinced.[84]

The problem that opponents raise concerns the justice of God. It is usually expressed in the following way. If Christ died for all human beings, as is claimed by this system, why will all human beings not be saved? Does this mean that the death of Christ creates a potential for salvation rather than actually saving sinners, as in the Arminian scheme? To put it another way, did Christ's death remove my sins, or did it make it possible for them to be removed? Surely, if Christ's death paid the penalty for the sins of those who will not be saved, then a 'double penalty' is being extracted. In other words, those who are not saved will pay the penalty for their own sins by enduring eternal punishment, but if Christ has already paid the penalty, then this is clearly unjust. Thus, it is argued, if we are to view Christ's death as being penal and substitutionary, then we must limit the extent of this atonement to those whose sins will be eternally forgiven, and all are agreed that this means the elect. Warfield puts it this way, 'The things we have to choose between are an atonement of high value, or an atonement of wide extension. The two cannot go together.'[85]

Conclusion

Given that the remit of this book is to identify areas where certain evangelical positions might need to be reaffirmed, others to be reconstructed and still others to be rejected, having outlived their usefulness, there are several points I ought to make.

Penal substitution

It seems to me that Packer's argument in favour of penal substitution, both in its biblical foundations and in its theological development, is fundamentally sound. It must therefore be a matter of some concern that many evangelicals seem to be abandoning a belief in penal substitution in favour of other ways of expressing their understanding of the atonement. At the same time, it must be recognized that there are some complex theological issues at stake in this

---

84. Alan C. Clifford, *Atonement and Justification* (Oxford: Oxford University Press, 1990); *Calvinus: Authentic Calvinism, A Clarification* (Norwich: Charenton Reformed, 1996); *Amyraut Affirmed* (Norwich: Charenton Reformed, 2004).

85. Warfield, *Plan of Salvation*, p. 95.

debate and so we must be willing to do the hard theological work of rethinking such issues as how to solve the apparent inner-trinitarian conflict required by a doctrine of penal substitution. We must also be prepared to listen to those, like Bruce McCormack, who seek to maintain penal substitution but yet challenge the traditional formulations of the doctrine.

Extent of the atonement

It seems to me that there is much study still to be undertaken in relation to the extent of the atonement and the decrees of God. There has been a tendency to dismiss these matters as debates from a previous century, which are either settled or not capable of being settled. Even the most significant popular book on the subject of the cross, by John R. W. Stott, does not deal with the extent of the atonement.[86] There is scope for considerable work here. In carrying out this work it is important to continue to engage with Arminian scholars, since historically they too are a product of the Calvinist tradition. The reinvigorated Amyraldian position must also be tackled and their arguments must be faced seriously and carefully. Many pamphlets have been written, but few full-scale studies have been undertaken.

Christus Victor

I noted earlier that there has been a significant recent effort by Hans Boersma to reappropriate the notion of Christ as victor. He does this in a volume that seeks to reinterpret the way in which Reformed theologians deal with the themes of justice, punishment and violence. Some of his work is very persuasive, while sections of it seem, at first reading, to depart from or to undermine aspects of the Reformed doctrine of the atonement. Nevertheless, it is certainly one of the most important books to appear for some time and is worthy of further study and response. For too long the Christus Victor theme has been seen as an alternative to a penal substitutionary view of the atonement, rather than as a complementary view that can strengthen the core theory and also deal with some of the difficulties and 'hard edges' of the doctrine.

Ecumenical dialogue

Finally, I believe that there is need for these further studies to take place in the context of the church and of ecumenical dialogue, rather than simply in the Academy. The doctrine of the atonement is fundamental to our understanding of the Christian faith and we must not be content with a situation where

---

86. J. R. W. Stott, *The Cross of Christ* (Leicester: IVP, 1986).

the church remains divided on this matter. Every effort must be made to reach a unified conclusion, albeit firmly based on the teaching of Scripture. Our objective must be to achieve for the atonement what has already been achieved for other doctrines; namely, the near-universal agreement of the church. This may seem unrealistic but, like Jesus' prayer in John 17 that the church would be one, remains the goal for the theologians of the church.

6. THE RELATIONSHIP BETWEEN BIBLICAL THEOLOGY AND SYSTEMATIC THEOLOGY

Richard C. Gamble

Defining 'theology'

The first two sections will define theology within the context of God's self-revelation in Scripture. Those sections will make it possible to answer the question of the relationship between biblical theology and systematic theology.

General definition

The first step is to define theology in a general fashion. A simple yet accurate definition of theology could be, 'knowledge concerning God'.[1] That one sentence definition affirms many truths. It acknowledges that there is a God and that God can be known. It also recognizes that human beings are able to know 'things' or 'stuff', even 'things' about God. However, is it legitimate to make these assumptions concerning both God and humanity?

If theology is defined as 'knowledge concerning God', then there would be sufficient justification for this definition – only if we grant that God exists and that he has revealed himself to humanity.[2] Therefore, a more precise definition

---

1. Geerhardus Vos, *Biblical Theology* (Grand Rapids: Eerdmans, 1966), p. 4.
2. Many modern theologians do not grant this proposition. Their views will not be presented or debated.

of theology must necessarily be a more complex one. A better definition of theology would be something like, 'The study of God to the extent that he has revealed himself to humanity.' From this foundational definition, we can begin to develop the study of 'theology'.

The Bible, creation, and a better definition

The last phrase in the definition, 'to the extent that he has revealed himself to humanity', presents a number of problems.[3] Knowing the complexity of those

---

3. Stated technically, that problem is what philosophers call the 'subject–object problem'. We know that God has revealed himself to humanity in his creation and in his Bible. When one turns to the creation account, the reader immediately notices that 'theology', as an object of study, is quite different from any other area of human investigation or research. Theology as a discipline is different because God has not only revealed himself to humanity, but has actually created humanity.

To understand the first part of the definition, the 'study' of God, we have to agree on what it is for a person to 'study' something. Usually, it means to break the object into component parts and then to put all of them back together and understand them as a whole.

Such 'study' implies that there are different 'parts' to human knowledge. Starting from the beginning, for any human knowledge to occur there must be the one called the 'thinking subject', and the object of investigation. E.g. Adam and Eve (human thinking subjects) while in the garden could have investigated a tree. They could have examined the tree from every angle. Adam could have pushed on the tree to see if it would fall over, and compared the strength of this particular tree with others.

Today, the method of examination of a tree would be similar. However, today, photographs could be taken of the tree. Perhaps the tree could be sawed down to count and study its growth rings etc.

Obviously, the 'study of God' is not like the study of a tree! Theology as a discipline is unique. This normal type of human subject–object investigation relationship does not 'work'; for God is not like a tree. God, as the Creator, cannot be tasted, pushed or examined. All things in the created world stand in distinction from God. This is an absolute distinction. In theology, the relationship between the subject (humanity) and the object (God) can even be reversed!

Furthermore, in theology the supposed object of investigation (God), is far from being passive like the tree. God is in fact the first One active on the field, by the work of creation itself. Man (the subject) was created and defined by God (the object)! To make the situation more complicated, Genesis tells us that the subject (humanity)

problems, the additional pieces of the puzzle of human knowing in general (the subject–object problem) facilitate the creation of a better definition. Theology is more precisely defined as 'the appropriation by the regenerated mind of that supernatural/natural information by which God has made himself the object of human knowledge'. This better definition also needs to be understood in its various parts. The regenerated human mind needs to understand God's 'supernatural' communication. This information is found in God's holy Word.

Exegesis and hermeneutics

The method one uses to examine the Bible is usually termed 'exegesis', and exegesis and exegetical theology are based upon insights from the study of

---

could have no knowledge of the object (God) were it not for the fact that the object (God) graciously granted access to knowledge of himself. Thus, human study of theology will be different in many ways from other areas of human investigation.

The situation for the human study of God becomes more complex with the introduction of a limiting concept, termed 'sin'. Sin's entrance into the world will force a further refinement of a definition of theology. Sin produced a new subject–object relationship. The human subjects (Adam and Eve), because of their rebellion against God, no longer trust God (the object). That is why they hid from him immediately after their sin. Also, because of sin, the object of investigation (God) is in a different relationship with the subjects.

Paul commented on the situation in Rom. 1:18. After the fall, human beings retain some knowledge of God. However, because of their sin, humanity now needs a 'supernatural revelation' or a new self-disclosure from God about God. This supernatural revelation is required for humans (the subject) to understand any absolutely true and adequate information of divine things (the object-God). Yet, even more is required.

Besides the new revelation, there is need for a new relationship. The object (God) is 'angry' with the subject and the subject distrusts this Great Object. To create the new relationship, God had to be the active person. He alone has the ability to change the estrangement. That change arrives via conversion.

When human regeneration from sin comes by the gracious act of God, a new type of individual, or 'knowing subject', is created. Now, through examination of the deposit of truth found in the Scripture, the regenerated mind (subject) can obtain vast degrees of previously unknown knowledge concerning God (object). This newly obtained knowledge (because of regeneration) does not mean that there has been a transformation in God's divine acts, words and being; rather, the subject (humanity) has been changed.

Canonics.[4] From the historical work of Canonics, the exegete also uses what is generally termed the 'historical-grammatical' analysis of the received biblical text.[5]

When exegesis is combined with the Bible interpreter's own world-view, his or her unquestioned presuppositions concerning the whole body of Scripture, this process develops into what is termed 'hermeneutics'.[6] A proper hermeneutic will always acknowledge God as the revealer of himself and as the ultimate author of the Scriptures. Thus, the tools that the regenerated person will use to understand God's self-revelation are called exegesis and hermeneutics. Using those tools, the Bible speaks of its own supernatural characteristics. It would be helpful now to investigate those characteristics.

Characteristics of scriptural revelation

The Bible is a divine book, not just a human book. This section will investigate its human character.

Revelation is historically progressive
Scriptural revelation is grounded in history, and is structured in a historically progressive fashion.[7] Later biblical books follow from and are grounded upon

---

4. From Canonics, the Bible student knows the time of the writing, the place where it was written, the author of the material, and the first audience.

5. That is, she investigates the grammar of the text, she translates it into her own language, and studies the meaning of the original text within its literary-cultural context. For further literature on exegesis, see W. VanGemeren, *The Progress of Redemption: The Story of Salvation from Creation to the New Jerusalem* (Grand Rapids: Zondervan, 1988), pp. 27–37.

6. For more information on hermeneutics, see J. I. Packer, 'Biblical Authority, Hermeneutics, and Inerrancy', in E. Geehan, ed., *Jerusalem and Athens* (Nutley, N. J.: P. & R., 1971), pp. 141ff. See also George W. Knight III, 'The Scriptures Were Written for our Instruction', *Journal of the Evangelical Theological Society* 39.1 (1996). Richard Pratt, *He Gave Us Stories* (Brentwood: Wolgemuth & Hyatt, 1990), p. 1, defines hermeneutics as simply 'the study of all that goes into interpreting the Bible'.

7. Edmund P. Clowney, *Preaching and Biblical Theology* (Grand Rapids: Eerdmans, 1961), p. 15, 'This revelation was not given at one time, nor in the form of a theological dictionary. It was given progressively, for the process of revelation accompanies the

the earlier books. With the Bible, the regenerated mind must know that the truths of Scripture come to him or her in the form of 'historically growing' truth. The Bible is God's truth and each Old Testament book has both a historical past and a future. In that sense, none of the Old Testament books has a 'static' truth.

Therefore, since the Bible is not just a human book, but is supernatural information given in a historically progressive fashion, it would be helpful to see some of the Bible's claims concerning itself.

God's Word makes certain claims within itself concerning itself. It claims that for salvation, all human beings need a divine word from God and is, from the human angle, necessary. It also claims to be an authoritative word from God.[8] Therefore, the Bible is both necessary and authoritative for humanity. Given the fact that it is both authoritative concerning God's self-revelation, as well as necessary, it would be natural to assume that all humans who read this word from God would rejoice in it as if it were a great treasure. Sadly, that is not always the case.

The redemptive process

There is a connection between God's supernatural biblical revelation and other divine acts. This unified system of revelation and historical act could be called the 'redemptive process'.[9]

The whole of God's redemptive process has at least two parts or characteristics: 'objective' and 'subjective'. In both stages, the supernatural element is present.

---

process of redemption.' Clowney adds, p. 17, 'The most fruitful understanding of biblical theology is that which recognizes both the historical, the progressive character of revelation and the unity of the divine counsel which it declares.'

8. C. Van Til, *A Christian Theory of Knowledge* (Nutley, N. J.: P. & R., 1969), p. 15, 'As self explanatory, God naturally speaks with absolute authority. It is Christ as God who speaks in the Bible. Therefore, the Bible does not appeal to human reason as ultimate in order to justify what it says. It comes to the human being with absolute authority.'

9. To understand the redemptive process properly, we must first appreciate that revelation is not an isolated act of God, existing without connection to all the other divine acts of a supernatural character. We must not separate scriptural revelation from this comprehensive historical background of the total redemptive work of God. If we make that unwarranted separation, then we fail to appreciate Scripture's historic and progressive nature. Given that there is this redemptive process, to understand it better we should know its characteristics.

There is what can be termed an 'objective' part, which are the facts of Scripture.[10] However, God uses these objective events (facts) and also applies them to individuals. With that application, they then become 'subjective'.

In other words, the fact (objective) that Israel was liberated from slavery in Egypt, for example, or that Christ was raised from the dead, becomes something different from the fact (objective) that at one time John F. Kennedy, president of the United States, was assassinated. Each of the three events is a 'fact'. However, the objective facts that happened in history, and are recorded in the Bible, are of the most profound and important character. No other human 'facts' are applicable to all of humanity, in all cultures, for all of time. And it is when the facts of the Bible, specifically the fact of Christ's resurrection, grips the heart of an individual that the 'objective' fact of special revelation moves into a 'subjective' meaning. Thus, the 'objective' and the 'subjective' characteristics of God's special revelation are clearly seen within the process of his work in human history.[11]

Concerning the thousands of biblical 'facts', some must be singled out as 'special' objective facts. Within all of these facts, some carry with them a heightened meaning. There is no disputing the truth that the redemptive work of God carries with it a heightened interest from the human perspective.

There are also redemptive acts. God has accomplished wonderful redemptive acts that reveal vast principles of truth. Some of the greatest supernatural deeds are observed in Israel's liberation from bondage in Egypt and the crucifixion and resurrection of Jesus Christ. In these cases, the special history, or the events themselves, form a part of God's special revelation. These miraculous 'interferences' by God in history have a revealing character, a revelatory nature, and oftentimes furnish the great joints and ligaments by which the whole framework of sacred history is held together and through which its structure is determined.

These redemptive acts, since they are recorded in a written book, are therefore verbal and never consist only of an 'act' by itself. Redemptive acts never

---

10. The objective character or stage of redemption is the simple biblical events. In other words, it is the objective *fact* that Israel was liberated from bondage at a certain time and locatable place. It could be some other fact from Scripture; that David was Israel's king, or perhaps the fact that Jesus of Nazareth was born in time and space. These are all examples of this 'objective' character of God's revelation. This characteristic of God's revelation is not subjective and individual in its nature, but objectively addresses all of humanity.

11. G. Vos, 'The Idea of Biblical Theology', in R. B. Gaffin, Jr, ed., *Redemptive History and Biblical Interpretation* (Phillipsburg: P. & R., 1980), p. 8.

occur separated from God's verbal communication of truth. God's word (the text) and God's act (the event) always accompany each other and are never contradictory.[12] There is a similarity between text and event in the sacraments.[13]

There is therefore an intimate relationship between the text or words of the Bible, the mental images that form in the mind of the regenerated reader, and the subjective appropriation of that text in the believer's heart. While this may appear to be a complicated correlation, the Scriptures speak clearly to the nature of this relationship. This relationship could be called 'contemporary'.

Special revelation's 'practical' or 'contemporary' character
While asserting that God's revelation is 'practical', that does not mean that it is 'simple'. Actually, there is also a very complex epistemological aspect to it.[14] The first part of that epistemological aspect is commonly called God's 'accommodation' in special revelation.

---

12. The words that describe the event take hermeneutical priority over the event itself. Also, the words of the Bible do not 'become' the word of God by the 'event' of God speaking to the heart concerning that word. That last view would be termed 'Barthian'.

13. Whether speaking of baptism or of the Lord's Supper, both of these sacraments are meaningful when the 'act' of using water or eating bread and wine is accompanied with a mental understanding of the significance of those 'acts'. And that sacramental 'significance' (the mental understanding) can only be communicated by using words. The issue of the relationship between God's redemptive acts in time and space and God's written word must be understood. 'Events' that are recorded in God's Word can be considered 'revelatory'. The event, the fact, of Christ's resurrection from the dead is clearly revelatory. Yet those 'events' are found within the pages of the sacred text. Thus, the 'interpretation' or 'meaning' of the event can never be devoid of the written word. Unfortunately, John H. Sailhamer, in his *Introduction to Old Testament Theology*, (Grand Rapids: Zondervan, 1995) p. 68, demonstrates a fundamental confusion either in his own thoughts on this topic or, more likely, in his interpretation of G. Vos. He said, 'For Vos, special revelation may go far beyond the scope of the text of Scripture. The category of *salvation history*, which he had apparently inherited from earlier theologians, allowed him to see revelation in events quite apart from the text. At the same time his deep roots in Protestant orthodoxy kept him from severing completely his ties to the biblical text as revelation.' Sailhamer is mistaken in his analysis of Vos here.

14. By 'epistemological aspect' I mean that the nature of God's special revelation itself is integral to human knowing.

The word 'accommodation', relative to the Bible, simply means that God's revelation to humanity at that time was connected to the geographical, historical and social conceptions of the nation of Israel and the first century.[15]

Stated differently, God spoke to his people in a way that they could understand. The fact that God 'accommodated' his revelation indicates something of his nature. He wants to communicate to us.

One of the means or tools that God used to communicate in a special way is called a 'covenant'. God's supernatural revelation, in its form and content, has this covenantal character. The 'covenant' is the God-chosen form of God's progressive self-communication to his people.[16]

God gave the first 'special revelation' to Adam while he was in the garden. After the fall, as God continued to reveal himself in human history, it was often times in the context of a covenant. This was particularly the case with God's special revelation to Noah, with Father Abraham, and with David.

Thus, God's revelation is 'accommodated'; presented in a way that is clear and comprehensible. Yet, there is more information relative to the epistemological aspects of special revelation.

The historic-organic nature of special revelation

The word 'organic' oftentimes brings to mind certain fruits and vegetables. Thinking along agricultural lines, the kind of seed that farmers plant is very important to them. It is only out of a perfect seed that a perfect stem, then flower, or fruit, is produced. This agricultural image is analogous to what we observe in the Scriptures.[17]

The historically progressive nature of the Scriptures tells us that the 'gospel of Paradise' that was revealed to Adam and Eve was such a beautiful seed in

---

15. It was adjusted by him to Israel's capacity for knowledge at that time. Biblical revelation occurred in history, and was given in a way that was comprehensible to its historic audience. God's revelation is also scientific, and was couched in a way that was comprehensible to the scientific perceptions of the audience at that time and place.

16. By the word 'covenant' I mean simply that God enters into specific relationships with his people – relationships based upon promises given by God and agreed to by his people.

17. From the beginning to the climax of Scripture, revealed truth has been kept, like a perfect seed, in close contact with the soil of the wants and needs (sometimes even the emergencies!) of that living generation into which it had been planted.

which the 'gospel of Paul' was present in potential 'form'. Likewise, we can speak of the 'gospel' of Abraham, of Moses, of David, of Isaiah and Jeremiah as all expansions of this original message of salvation.[18]

This notion of progressive divine revelation is inherent in the Old Testament's own theological method. Within the Old Testament, later writers depended upon and expanded the work of the earlier ones. For example, the prophet Zechariah referred to the 'earlier' prophets (Zech. 1:4; 7:7, 12) – and there are other examples.[19]

Certainly, the New Testament writers used the Old Testament in the same manner that the inspired Old Testament writers used God's earlier inspired writings. With the possible exception of the book of Philemon, to exclude Old Testament references and allusions would gut the content of the New Testament. On the other hand, without the New Testament, the Old would be incomplete. That is one of the reasons why Reformed theologians say that Christ is the goal of the Old Testament. That Christ was the goal of the Old Testament is demonstrated in the divine institutions themselves.[20]

Old Testament revelation was, in a sense, a prelude to his arrival. This nature of the relationship was most dramatically portrayed in Malachi's statements concerning the coming of the Messiah. The great Messiah's future arrival would be with reference to the past coming of the great prophet Elijah (Mal. 4:5–6).

To express the idea in other words, the Old Testament has a thematic Christological centre; yet, all of the events themselves are still both factual and

---

18. Each presentation, each unfolding, points forward to the next stage of historic growth and development, and therefore brings the gospel idea one step nearer to its full flowering in the person and work of Jesus Christ.

19. Haggai indirectly referred to Jeremiah's prophecy concerning what God would do with Zerubbabel. Jeremiah looked backwards to the old covenants and looked forward to a new covenant. Isaiah looked backwards to the old exodus and looked forward to a new Exodus. Both Jeremiah and Ezekiel looked back at the great King David, and looked forward to a new King.

20. As Old Testament special revelation progressed historically, God established the office of the priest, who functioned culturally to draw the people of God into his presence. He also gave his people prophets, who spoke God's word and laboured to protect the theocracy. God established the theocracy itself, and the Davidic kingship that went with it. These institutions, the priestly, the prophetic and the theocracy (kingship), all helped the people of God to see the necessity and nature of the coming Messiah.

meaningful.[21] Therefore, the theologian must carefully handle the Hebrew Bible, and not try to make it say more than it should bear, given its place in God's history.[22]

Furthermore, there are various 'epochs' or 'periods' of God's special revelation. There are times of 'quickened' special revelation; that is, when God gave his revelation within very concentrated historical eras. These 'quickened' epochs oftentimes focus around particular individuals.[23] These historical epochs, like special revelation itself, are progressive in their character. The latter receives content from the former and goes on to expand the former.

Connected to 'epochs' of special revelation is the notion of connections between present and future 'epochs' or 'worlds'. God's method of self-revelation has been to create within the living organism or life of the past-present world yet another world. This other world centres upon a future redemption. These two spheres or worlds always live together, the 'secular' (past-present) world or sphere, and the 'divine' (future) world. Neither of the two can exist (at this point of human history) independently from the other, and each draws benefits from the other. Returning to agricultural imagery, it is as if God's supernatural revelation (divine history – which focuses upon redemption) was a seed planted in the gardener's prepared soil (secular history – or the present world) and in that soil the divine word grows and flourishes.

Genre

Within these various revelatory epochs, within redemptive history itself, there are also clear literary distinctions between the biblical texts. As a written document, these distinctions in the Bible are generally termed literary

---

21. Old Testament special revelation is itself meaningful. These two notions, the Christological centre and meaningfulness within its own historic context, must control Old Testament exegesis. While it is not fully developed, the Old Testament is still the Word of God!

22. Analysis of the creation account can be used to demonstrate a 'forced' interpretation; i.e. inserting later teaching into earlier. At creation, God said, 'Let us make man in our image' (Gen. 1:26). Should this particular passage, where God said 'Let us', be taken as a proof text for the doctrine of the Trinity? Because of later special revelation, we know that God is in fact Triune. Yet, the best exegesis of this passage will not force it to go beyond the meaning anchored in its own historical context, a context that was controlled by God.

23. Examples of these 'epochs' revolve around the patriarch Abraham, the law-giver Moses, David the great king, and Jesus Christ, King of Kings.

'genres'.[24] As a general rule, it can be said that over time differentiation in biblical genre increases rather than decreases.

In Scripture, the character, the personalities and even the sociological/historical backgrounds of the various biblical authors are not hidden, which also relates to literary genre.[25]

Because they were different persons living at different historical periods and writing in different languages, Bible students must not be surprised to observe differences in their writing styles; although both wrote under divine inspiration.

The scope of the distinctions among the biblical authors is perhaps most beautifully perceived in the writings of the apostle Paul.[26] In Paul's writings especially, the theologian can readily observe different ways in which Paul presented God's truth. Sometimes God's communication of truth through Paul came *via* the use of logic or rhetorical structures. At other places, he was more simply didactic. Even still, Paul was quite capable of being intensely emotive and doxological.

God intended to give full expression to all of the various ways in which his beautiful truth could be presented. He thus chose men like Moses and Paul from their mother's wombs, moulded their characters and their life experiences, plus gave them such training that the truth revealed through them necessarily bore the impress of God's own mind. There was no collision of thought or purpose here between a sovereign God on the one hand and humanity on the other, because the human author's (the biblical writer's) character and time frame, as well as his gifts and his training, were all subsumed under a comprehensive divine plan.

Furthermore, these differences of biblical literary genre, of human character and author, are important even when there is not a great difference of time

---

24. In the Old Testament, there are what scholar's term 'legal' genres. There are furthermore 'prophetic' genres, as well as historical-narrative genres, and wisdom and poetic genres. In the New Testament, besides those observed in the Old Testament, there are literary forms or genres called 'the Gospels'. They are different in character from the epistles, and both are differentiated from what is known as the genre of apocalypse.

25. E.g. Moses, who was raised in the house of Pharaoh, was a very different type of person, and lived in a historically different world from Luke the physician.

26. God's truth itself can be presented in different ways. Some means of communication are at times more effective than others. Since God is perfect, his special revelation is also perfect. Thus, whatever information he chooses to reveal will be expressed in the perfect form for that information.

between when the biblical writers put pen and ink together.[27] It is simply because God meant it to be so.[28] This analysis leads to a formal presentation of biblical theology.

Biblical theology and systematic theology

Foundation and definition of biblical theology
The discipline of biblical theology developed from the foundation of the organic-historic nature of Scripture,[29] that Christ is its ultimate goal, that there are 'epochs' of special revelation and that it was written by men who used literary 'genres'.[30] In other words, biblical theology is a hermeneutic that is founded upon the organic, historic development of the Bible. Furthermore, it is the study of the form and content of supernatural revelation in its historical unfolding, with the events of the historical unfolding considered as parts and products of a divine work. In biblical theology, the historical background and circumstances of the text are valued as an element of God's revealing activity. 'Biblical theology', said the discipline's founder Geerhardus Vos, 'is the exhibition of the organic progress of supernatural revelation in its historic continuity and multiformity.'[31]

---

27. E.g., although the Gospel of John was written at a similar time as the Synoptic Gospels, because of the author's gifts and character it is in a sense a fuller and wider self-revelation of Christ.

28. If John was written quite a bit later than the Synoptics, which is certainly possible and an opinion held by many scholars, then it would be easy to attribute the differences in the Johannine corpus to the added years of theological reflection.

29. A short bibliography on biblical theology can be found in Clowney, *Preaching and Biblical Theology* (pp. 122–124). A very helpful article on biblical theology is by James T. Dennison, 'What Is Biblical Theology? Reflections on the Inaugural Address of Geerhardus Vos', *Kerux* 2.1 (1987), pp. 33–41.

30. O. P. Robertson, 'The Outlook for Biblical Theology', in David Wells and Clark Pinnock, eds., *Toward a Theology for the Future* (Carol Stream: Creation House, 1971). James A Walther, 'The Significance of Methodology for Biblical Theology', *Perspective* 10 (1969), pp. 217–233.

31. Vos, 'The Idea of Biblical Theology', *Redemptive History*, pp. 6–11; idem, *Biblical Theology*, p. 5. Born in 1862, Vos came to the United States in 1881 and studied at Grand Rapids and then Princeton. He received his doctorate from the University of Strasbourg in 1888. Turning down Kuyper's offer to teach at the new Free

Stated differently, when believers exegete the Bible in its historical and organic continuity, they are doing 'biblical theology'. Biblical theology gives the exegete tremendous information concerning God, and thus about theology. Geerhardus Vos 'made redemptive revelatory acts of God his central concern. He focused on the form and content of divine revelation', says Richard Pratt, 'unique to each era'. Furthermore, Vos 'affirmed that redemptive history was the Bible's "own revelatory structure" and the "main stem of revelation"'.[32] Biblical theology is therefore more than a simple narrative of historical events. It is tracing God's finger through the history of revelation.[33]

The relatively recent rise of the discipline of biblical theology is one of the most important developments in the field of systematic theology. Biblical theology as a separate discipline has tried to keep its theologizing based upon grammatical-historical exegesis. That means theology is within the historical, linguistic and social structure of Scripture.[34] Thus, biblical theology is intimately bound to solid biblical exegesis. The biblical text is comprehended within its proper historic and literary framework. As hinted at earlier, without biblical theology, competent exegesis is impossible.

Definition of 'theology'

The formal definition of theology (as mentioned above) was, 'the appropriation by the regenerated mind of that supernatural/natural information by which God has made himself the object of human knowledge'. This 'appropriation' by the regenerated mind, this acquisition of 'theology', by its very nature transforms the student. The first and most important duty of every theologian is to let the image of God's self-revelation in the Scriptures reflect itself as fully and as clearly as possible in his or her own mind and life.

University in Amsterdam, he choose to begin his career at Calvin Theological Seminary in the autumn of 1888, where he taught for five years, including the subjects of Bible and Systematic Theology. He then moved to Princeton, where he stayed until retirement.

32. Pratt, *He Gave Us Stories* (Brentwood, Tenn.: Wolgemuth & Hyatt, 1990), p. 80.

33. Clowney, *Preaching and Biblical Theology*, pp. 17–18, 175, 'It is not precisely even a history of revelation, for its theological concern carries it beyond any merely historical study of the course of revelation . . . Abraham Kuyper prefers to speak of *historia revelationis* rather than biblical theology, but he would include in dogmatic theology the tracing of the development of each doctrine through the history of revelation.'

34. Pratt, *He Gave Us Stories*, p. 79, 'From its inception Biblical Theology was committed to reading Old Testament narrative with a historical orientation.'

Also, if one grants that Pratt's analysis of the nature of biblical theology is even partly correct, and it is the Bible's own 'revelatory structure', there should then be no formal opposition between biblical theology and the nature and method of a 'systematic' theology.[35] To determine if that is in fact the case, the next section will investigate how theology should be structured.

The task of systematic theology

If the task of systematic theology is to present the whole teaching of the Scriptures in a manner that is comprehensible,[36] then there at first appears to be only two general approaches to attain that goal. One option would be simply to read through the Bible many times. That would in one sense accomplish the goal, but that would not be 'systematic' theology. If the route of cover-to-cover reading is not taken, then some type of an organizational grid must be used to 'summarize' the contents of the Scriptures.

However, within the Reformed community, many agree that there is a need to redefine the way in which systematic theology is organized; that is, there needs to be a new 'grid'.[37] Some suggestions would entirely restructure the discipline of systematic theology.[38] For example, it has been boldly proposed that

---

35. Clowney, *Preaching and Biblical Theology*, pp. 15–16, 'Biblical theology formulates the character and content of the progress of revelation in these periods, observing the expanding horizons from age to age.'

36. Other definitions are possible.

37. The call for change is well expressed by J. Frame, 'Reflections on *Sola Scriptura*', *Westminster Theological Journal* 59 (1997), p. 277, 'There have been Reformed theologians (Berkouwer is the example that comes most readily to mind) who construct their theological writings as dialogue with past and contemporary theological texts. In these theologies, Scripture plays an important role, to be sure; but the exegesis is often somewhat sketchy and often seems like an addendum to the pages of historical analysis. Murray avoided that model of theology very self-consciously.'

38. To understand the necessity to redefine, we should start with a working definition of systematic theology. B. B. Warfield, 'Task and Method of Theology', *Studies in Theology* (Grand Rapids: Baker Book House, 1981), p. 91, defined systematic theology as 'That department or section of theological science which is concerned with setting forth systematically, that is to say, as a concatenated whole, what is known concerning God.' Compare his definition with John Murray's: 'To set forth in orderly and coherent manner the truth respecting God and his relations to men and the world,' 'Systematic Theology', *Westminster Theological Journal* 25.2 (1963), p. 133. These two definitions are still different from a third, submitted by David

the term 'systematic theology' be discontinued in favour of the term 'biblical theology'.[39] In addition, many missiologists have been less certain or daring in their proposals, but still express a lack of confidence in the typical structural forms of systematic theology.[40] Others, too, push the boundaries of systematic theology in new directions, challenging the very nature of theology itself.[41] From these broader discussions, we can focus attention on the narrower problem of biblical and systematic theology.

Biblical and systematic theology

The exact relationship between systematic theology and biblical theology has not been decisively determined. Several careful scholars have noted difficulties with this increasingly scrutinized relationship, and have suggested some solutions to the apparent problems.[42]

Over forty years ago, one of the earliest positions suggested that there should be no problem in the relationship.[43] It was thought that the two disciplines

---

Wells, 'the sustained effort to know the character, will and acts of the Triune God as He has disclosed and interpreted these for his people in Scripture, to formulate these in a systematic way in order that we might know him, learn to think our thoughts after him, live our lives in his world on his terms, and by thought and action project his truth into our own time and culture,' 'The Theologian's Craft', *Doing Theology in Today's World: Essays in Honor of Kenneth S. Kantzer* (Grand Rapids: Zondervan, 1991), p. 172.

39. R. B. Gaffin, Jr, 'Systematic Theology and Biblical Theology', *Westminster Theological Journal* 38.3 (1976), p. 298, 'To use [instead of 'systematic theology'] "biblical theology" to designate the comprehensive statement of what scripture teaches (dogmatics), always insuring that its topical divisions remain sufficiently broad and flexible to accommodate the results of the redemptive-historically regulated exegesis on which it is based.'

40. Those missiologists have problematically asserted that missiology needs to be systematic theology's 'gadfly'. See H. Conn, 'The Missionary Task of Theology: A Love/Hate Relationship?', *Westminster Theological Journal* 45.1 (1983), pp. 1–21.

41. J. Frame, *The Doctrine of the Knowledge of God* (Phillipsburg: P. & R., 1987), p. 206, n. 31, '*all* theology is application'.

42. Gaffin, 'Systematic Theology and Biblical Theology', pp. 281–299. He later outlined the history and nature of biblical theology in his introduction to G. Vos's *Shorter Writings*, ed. Richard B. Gaffin, Jr (Phillipsburg: P. & R., 1980), pp. xvi–xxiii.

43. Clowney, *Preaching and Biblical Theology*, pp. 15–16, 'There is, then, no opposition between biblical theology and systematic or dogmatic theology, though the two are

should be complementary.[44] Later writers suggest that biblical theology is 'normative' for theology, and should therefore set the agenda for systematic theology.[45] Others take what could be seen as a more modest view of biblical theology, simply articulating that a 'redemptive-historical framework is what gives us the substance, as well as the form, of what is authoritative'.[46]

These mature suggestions must be considered carefully because they carry with them important implications. If biblical theology is to be, in some sense, 'normative' for structuring systematic theology, then earlier systematic theologies, which did not incorporate the perspectives of biblical theology, would be qualitatively inferior.[47] This would suggest a major recasting of most systematic *loci* or topics.[48]

---

distinct. Systematic theology must draw from the results of biblical theology, and biblical theology must be aware of the broad perspectives of systematics. The two approaches differ in the development of material.'

44. Ibid., p. 16, 'The development of systematics is strictly thematic or topical. It seeks to summarize the total teaching of Scripture under certain "loci" – of God, man, salvation, the church, the "last things." The development of biblical theology is redemptive-historical. The divisions of biblical theology are the historical periods of redemption, marked by creation, the fall, the flood, the call of Abraham, the exodus, and the coming of Christ. Within these periods, or within further subdivisions of them, a systematic method is used . . . No doubt there is room for flexibility of organization. A scholar may write an "Old Testament Theology" in which the organization is topical and systematic rather than historical, but which justifies its title by tracing the development of each of the doctrines through the history of revelation before Christ. Such a treatment would bring biblical theology close to the form of systematics.'

45. R. B. Gaffin, Jr, 'Review Article: A New Paradigm in Theology?', *Westminster Theological Journal* 56 (1994), p. 390. Here he writes, 'The redemptive-historical substance of Scripture serves to define what theology ought to be.'

46. D. Wells, 'On Being Framed', *Westminster Theological Journal* 59 (1997), p. 299.

47. This appears to be Wells's criticism of some contemporary (not just past) theological work: 'Systematic theologians make a great mistake if they allow their systematic interests to carry them away too far from the kind of framework for understanding which Geerhardus Vos provided for us so well. In Professor Frame's case, then, exactly how this history enters into his theologizing remains obscure to me,' ibid.

48. Gaffin, 'Systematic Theology and Biblical Theology', *Westminster Theological Journal* 38.3 (1976), p. 299, 'requires recasting not only eschatology but also all the other *loci*

While the claims carry heavy responsibility, good arguments can be made for using biblical theology as a controlling model in systematic theology. The proposal that biblical theology should direct the method of systematic theology follows a pattern hinted at by the Scottish-American theologian John Murray. Murray's argument could be stated in this fashion: biblical exegesis is foundational to systematic theology, and, as noted above, all responsible biblical exegesis must be biblico-theological.[49] Therefore, biblical theology should direct the method of, or is foundational to, systematic theology. In other words, just as exegesis is indispensable to systematic theology, so is biblical theology indispensable to systematic theology.[50]

Addressing the need for a new methodological 'grid' for systematic theology, a better way to 'summarize' the contents of Scripture, biblical theology's grid, is the progressive historical unfolding of God's special revelation. It is a grid that is admittedly a human work, and therefore flawed and capable of improvement. Yet, this organizational grid is not imported from extra-biblical sources. The biblical theologian seeks to present the material of the text couched in its own historic, social and theological framework. The biblical theologian's failure comes from his lack of historical research and depth of study – not in forcing the text into a mould that is foreign to the text itself. 'A

---

as traditionally conceived, especially Christology, soteriology, both accomplished and applied, and Ecclesiology'.

49. Gaffin, 'Systematic Theology and Biblical Theology', p. 291, cites Murray ('Systematic Theology: Second Article', *Westminster Theological Journal* 26.1 [1963], p. 44) with approval: 'the exegesis with which it [systematic theology] is so intimately concerned should be regulated by the principle of biblical theology'. Eight years later Gaffin continued his thesis: 'Redemptive history . . . is the dominant concern of Scripture,' 'A New Paradigm in Theology?', *Westminster Theological Journal* 56 (1994), p. 383. Sinclair Ferguson, 'The Whole Counsel of God: Fifty Years of Theological Studies', *Westminster Theological Journal* 50 (1988), p. 261, comments, 'Murray reasoned that true biblical theology is not inimical to properly conceived systematics. Indeed, the reverse is the case. Systematics should be fed by biblical theology.'

50. Gaffin, 'Systematic Theology and Biblical Theology', p. 295, 'The indispensability of biblical theology to systematic theology is the indispensability of exegesis to systematic theology, no more and no less.' This is very similar to Murray's earlier assertion that 'biblical theology is indispensable to systematic theology', as cited by Gaffin, p. 291. Gaffin had already cited Warfield, which would further support his statement that biblical theology 'is the basis and source of Systematics', p. 286.

redemptive-historical approach is not imposed on Scripture,' says Pratt; 'it comes from the Bible itself'.[51]

While there is much value in this approach to God's Word, there is still at least one unresolved question and two arguments that can be made against biblical theology as a controlling motif for systematic theology.

The question concerns the inseparability of biblical theology and systematic theology. If biblical theology is indispensable to systematic theology, it is then argued by some that it is difficult or impossible to detect a separation between systematic theology and New Testament (as fulfilment of Old Testament) biblical theology.[52] Given the supposed impossibility of the separation, the question of how biblical theology relates to systematic theology is apparently removed. 'Theology' simply becomes a comprehensive statement of what Scripture teaches within wide topical divisions based upon redemptive-historical exegesis.[53] Biblical theology and systematic theology are thus not different, because this definition of 'theology' actually fits the nature of biblical theology precisely. Biblical theology thus swallows up or envelops systematic theology. It is therefore argued that biblical theology is and should be considered the natural, proper, and even exclusive, structural framework for systematic theology. This question continues to be a matter of debate among proponents of this school of thought, as well as its detractors.[54]

Objections to biblical theology

A basic argument made against biblical theology is that it unwisely mixes the relationship between the text of Scripture and the events narrated by the text of Scripture. 'The Biblical theology of Gerhardus Vos', argues one evangelical Old Testament scholar, 'is a classical evangelical work that exhibits clearly

---

51. Pratt, *He Gave Us Stories*, p. 80.

52. Gaffin, 'Systematic Theology and Biblical Theology', p. 298.

53. Ibid., p. 298, 'The comprehensive statement of what Scripture teaches (dogmatics) always insuring that its topical division remain sufficiently broad and flexible to accommodate the results of the redemptive-historical exegesis on which it is based.'

54. Richard Pratt, *He Gave Us Stories*, p. 79. Pratt rightly recognizes that proponents of this school 'assumed that this redemptive-historical orientation was central to the Bible itself'. He also notes their criticism of traditional systematic theology: 'Traditional systematic theology [according to biblical theology] derived its categories from Aristotelian philosophy, but the dynamic historical orientation of Biblical Theology was thought to be the heartbeat of Biblical texts themselves.'

the kind of mixture of text and event that characterizes many recent evangelical salvation-history approaches to the Old Testament.'[55] Yet, even more critical judgments are made. 'Those oriented toward "biblical theology" . . . find their authority not so much in Scripture itself', charges Frame, 'as in the events that Scripture describes.'[56] Both of these criticisms are harsh and, if true, should serve as clear warnings.

Another criticism is that biblical theology can 'eclipse other aspects of biblical truth, such as God's eternal (and therefore supra-historical) nature, his law, his wisdom, and his involvement in the believer's subjectivity'.[57] Certainly, *any* theological method that would necessarily eclipse parts of God's truth should be rejected!

However, it does not appear that biblical theology necessarily finds its authority in 'events', or that it eclipses 'aspects' of biblical truth.[58] On the other hand, a careful use of biblical theology should 'eclipse' unwarranted theological speculation.

In addition, as a relatively young theological field, biblical theology has been criticized for its very definition. Geerhardus Vos discussed the content of the 'special revelation' given by God in the days of Adam and Eve. He asserted that there was 'biblical theology' in the Garden of Eden. Yet, because Adam and Eve did not have a Bible to read, it has been argued that it was improper to say that there was 'biblical' theology at that time![59] Another critique levelled

---

55. Sailhamer, *Introduction to Old Testament Theology*, p. 67.

56. J. Frame, *The Doctrine of God* (Phillipsburg, P. & R., 2002), p. 197. It appears that in Frame's analysis there is actually a direct connection between heretical liberation theologians and biblical theologians. Both groups, Frame wrongly accuses, find their 'source of ethical certainty in the historical situation'. Such a yoking, creating a guilt by association, is quite uncharitable.

57. Ibid., p. 8.

58. Sadly, that biblical theology eclipses 'aspects' of biblical truth was offered with no corroborating evidence from the writings of any practitioner of biblical theology. Frame, simply citing his former colleague R. B. Gaffin, Jr, says, 'we should not allow this emphasis to eclipse'. It would be uncharitable to say that Frame accuses Gaffin of such an error. However, if Gaffin's theologizing does not eclipse 'God's eternal nature, his law, his wisdom, etc.', then Frame has simply succeeded in warning theologians not to do what, in fact, no-one does.

59. Sailhamer, *Introduction to Old Testament Theology*, p. 68, 'Can Vos' use of the word *Biblical* be related to the sense of the word Biblical as it is used of the Bible itself as Scripture? Does he think Adam and Eve had a Bible? Surely not . . . When he

against biblical theology is that it wrongly mixes the 'text' of Scripture and the 'event' narrated in Scripture.[60]

It is claimed that Vos saw two different 'forms' of divine revelation, revelation in the biblical text and revelation in certain historical events.[61] Such a differentiation in 'revelation' is considered by some to be irresponsible at best and dangerous at its worst.

Also, Vos supposedly equated the fixed world of the biblical narrative with his own historically different and constantly changing present world.[62] his approach apparently lacked maturity or, as it has been pejoratively expressed, had a 'naïveté' that should be rejected.[63] Whether this criticism can properly

---

speaks of Biblical theology in the days of Adam and Eve, Vos shows that he has not made a distinction between any kind of a special revelation in history or the human heart and God's revelation of his will in the inspired Scriptures.' Such comments, while interesting, appear to demonstrate a theological naivety, but not on Professor Vos's part.

60. Sailhamer, *Introduction to Old Testament Theology*, pp. 67–68, 'his [Vos's] salvation-historical approach has blurred the distinction between the Bible as a record of revelation and the Bible as that revelation itself'.

61. Ibid., pp. 68–70, 'Thus both forms [text and event] of revelation found their way into Vos' Biblical theology but for two quite different reasons. The one form of Biblical theology he called "Biblical" because it focused on the revelation of God referred to [*res gestae*] in the Bible. The other form of Biblical theology was "biblical" because it focused on the revelation of God that is the Bible itself [text].'

62. Ibid., p. 69. Geerhardus Vos's, as well as 'many recent evangelical approaches', says Sailhamer, 'can only be described as a curious lack of awareness of the way in which texts and events have meaning – for lack of a better term, text naïveté . . . To appreciate the naïveté of Vos's approach . . . the narrative world of Scripture has merged with the real world of historicism . . . Vos is naïve, in my judgment, in simply identifying *the world of the narrative* with whatever we may come to know and understand about the historical events. The *narrative* world is a fixed reality. It is a function of the narration in the text. The real world is ever changing and ever increasing.'

63. Ibid., p. 70, 'When one identifies, or equates, the real world and the narrative world as one and the same, the narrative world no longer remains constant. That is the unfortunate consequence of Vos' naïveté. The task of Biblical theology is to allow the fixed reality of the narrative world to shape and inform our understanding of the real world, not the other way around.'

be laid at Vos's feet is a question that could be debated.[64] Nevertheless, all theologians must guard against the mistake of simply equating the two worlds. Connected to a supposed lack of maturity is the charge of 'one-sidedness' or lack of concern for the insights of systematic theology.

According to some, the hermeneutic of biblical theology itself can obscure a principle of systematic theology called the 'analogy of faith'.[65] The 'analogy of faith' is simply a comparison of all relevant biblical passages on any one theme. It is charged that Old Testament biblical theology refuses to permit later (particularly New Testament) passages to elucidate the earlier.[66] If it is a tenet of biblical theology not to let a later document unpack an earlier document's meaning, then this is a valid criticism. However, while this principle may be employed by some evangelical scholars, a strong case could be made that this is not a tenet of biblical theology.[67] A more general charge is that biblical theology has failed to appreciate insights from systematic theology.[68] As a discipline, biblical theology has supposedly not always recognized the importance

---

64. Sailhamer's criticism of Vos has so far not seemed convincing. Rather, Vos speaks in a similar manner to H. Witsius, *The Economy of the Covenant* (Escondido, Calif.: Den Dulk, 1990), vol. 2, pp. 188–189. There Witsius says, 'Such is the inexhaustible copiousness of the holy scriptures, that not only the words are significative of things, but even the things, which are first signified by the words, do likewise represent other things, which they were appointed to prefigure long before they happened.'

65. R. Reymond, *A New Systematic Theology of the Christian Faith* (Nashville: Thomas Nelson, 1998), p. 535, 'It is possible to address the issue of the Old Testament saints' understanding of redemption so one-sidedly from the "biblical-theological" perspective that one permits the hermeneutic of that discipline to overpower the "analogy of faith" principle of systematic theology, and as a result neither the teaching of the Old Testament itself nor what the New Testament writers expressly report or imply that the Old Testament meant and that the Old Testament saints knew about the suffering Messiah and his resurrection from the dead is given its due.'

66. For more on this issue, see the debate between Reymond and Kaiser in ibid., pp. 50ff.

67. See Walter C. Kaiser, *Toward an Exegetical Theology* (Grand Rapids: Baker, 1981), p. 137.

68. Pratt, *He Gave Us Stories*, p. 81, 'Biblical interpreters have felt free to ignore systematic theology more and more. It is common to find Biblical Theologians overlooking the relevance of systematic theological questions for the interpretation of Old Testament stories.' This is, according to Pratt, a 'dangerous tendency'.

of the human mind's need to structure information systematically. It also supposedly fails to appreciate the importance of the church's creeds and historical theology.

Thus, biblical theology has been charged with various lacks and weaknesses. Some of those charges are stronger than others. Nevertheless, while biblical theology must stay on its guard to avoid pitfalls, there is much strength to this method of organizing the Bible's material.

Conclusion

Biblical theology may harbour unquestioned and even unwarranted epistemological presuppositions. To demonstrate those possible presuppositions, it is necessary to examine how the theologian's culture has influenced his theological method and exegesis.[69]

Reformed theologians agree upon the inerrancy of Scripture and that exegesis is foundational to systematic theology. They also concur that the best exegetical method would be the 'grammatical-historical'. With such fundamental agreements, one would expect more unity as they reflect on structure and theological method, but that unity is clearly missing.

Cultural context in theology

It appears that the cause or the 'roots' of the disunity may to some extent be found in differing biblical exegesis or hermeneutics. Some theologians have perhaps not sufficiently realized that there is a cultural influence upon all biblical exegesis. It is perhaps easier to demonstrate this influence by referring to historical examples.

Examples from the history of exegesis
The history of biblical exegesis demonstrates how the issues of the times of the commentator, or his 'cultural context', influences his exegesis and appear on the pages of his commentary.[70]

---

69. For a general analysis of culture and its relationship to theology, see Michael Warren, *Seeing Through the Media: A Religious View of Communication and Cultural Analysis* (Philadelphia: Trinity Press International, 1997). See also John Bennett and Melvin Tumin, *Social Life* (New York: Alfred Knopf, 1948).
70. 'The issues of the times of the commentator' is my working definition of the word 'culture'. See L. Newbigin's, *Foolishness to the Greeks: The Gospel and Western Culture*

The Reformation era provides good illustrations of this principle. Any time that the great German leader Martin Luther had an opportunity in his biblical commentaries to lambaste the pope of Rome, he would joyously seize that opportunity, even if there was only the slightest possible relationship between the text and the papacy! Today, a commentator may in fact analyse Roman Catholic theology or the particular actions or decrees of a pope, but unlike Luther, present North American Protestant commentators are not usually 'looking' for such opportunities.[71]

At about the same time as Luther, though different in some respects, cultural concerns also influenced John Calvin in both his theological method and his exegesis. As an example, in Geneva, as in all the other cities of Switzerland, one had to dress within the stipulated attire of his social class; so that on the street it would be easy to tell the difference between the mayor and a stable hand.[72]

Calvin, in his biblical commentaries and theological writings, insisted that such social class distinctions were given by God and should always be maintained. They were simply unquestioned. Yet today, especially in the United States, few would be in favour of legislation enforcing class distinction in dress. We do not 'see' it in the text of Scripture.

The two examples from Luther and Calvin could be multiplied, and the relationship between culture and exegesis could be traced into the twenty-first

---

(Grand Rapids: Eerdmans, 1986), p. 3, who has a good definition. See also Anthony C. Thistelton, *The Two Horizons: New Testament Hermeneutics and Philosophical Description* (Grand Rapids: Eerdmans, 1980), pp. 85–114.

71. There are many other vivid examples in his commentaries. One concerns his attitude towards women. In late medieval society, women were not treated with the dignity they deserved. Those cultural presuppositions were clearly part of Luther's exegesis, who argued in his Genesis commentary that women could not be created in the image of God. Certainly, their broad hips and intellectual inability makes that clear to anyone, he argued. Today, no biblical scholar would 'see' that in the text! Our contemporary cultural lenses, through which we view Scripture, are different. Ulrich Zwingli was also influenced by his own intellectual culture. Primarily in response to the theological debates raging in the late medieval period and into his own time, it was very important to Zwingli to hold on to the *simplicity (simplicitas)* of God. Yet, his dogged holding to that teaching negatively influenced his view of divine providence, which was later rejected by Calvin and the rest of the Reformed tradition.

72. For more information on Calvin, see R. C. Gamble, *The Whole Counsel of God*, vol. 3 (Phillipsburg: P. & R.) (forthcoming).

century.[73] No matter how diligent a biblical commentator or theologian, the presuppositions of his or her culture have, to some degree or other, influenced the way in which that exegete has understood the Scriptures.[74] This concept was well articulated by Herman Bavinck: 'Not only mankind, but also every individual, finds, as he grows to full consciousness, a view of the world already prepared for him, to the formation of which he has not consciously contributed.'[75] With these beginning examples in mind, primarily from exegesis, it will soon become apparent that the theologian's 'culture' has profound influence on his overall theological method.

Since culture influences biblical exegesis, as observable in the exegetical methods of the great Reformers, it is not difficult to take the next step and notice how its influence goes as deep as the very method of theology.[76] The next step would include observing in what ways, and to what extent, sixteenth-century (and earlier) culture impacted reformational theological method.

The theological method used at the time of the Reformation is sometimes called the 'classical method' of structuring systematic theology. At that time, it was termed the 'common places' or the *loci communes*. This *loci communes* method of structuring systematic theology, observable in textbooks from the early Middle Ages to that of Louis Berkhof, organized the Bible into 'topics' and provided the *way* by which those topics were investigated.[77]

---

73. For the sixteenth-century context, see R. C. Gamble, 'Calvin on Discipline and Freedom of Conscience: Observed within the Sixteenth Century Context', in H. Selderhuis, ed., *Ordenlich und fruchtbar*. Festschrift für W. Van't Spyker (Kampen: Kok, 1997), pp. 141ff.

74. R. Lints, *The Fabric of Theology* (Grand Rapids: Eerdmans, 1993), p. 10, 'Although culture does not determine one's theological vision (or lack thereof), it does influence that vision, and evangelicals are risking much by failing to take this influence seriously.' Later, on p. 105, he continues, 'As both a product and a producer of humankind, culture is never neutral with respect to the Creator.' For a broader picture, see also Claude Welch, *Protestant Thought in the Nineteenth Century*. Vol. 1: *1799–1870* (New Haven: Yale University Press, 1972).

75. H. Bavinck, *The Philosophy of Revelation* (Grand Rapids: Eerdmans, 1953), p. 84, n. 2.

76. See R. C. Gamble, '*Brevitas et Facilitas*: Toward an Understanding of Calvin's Hermeneutic', *Westminster Theological Journal* 47 (1985), pp. 1–17; 'Exposition and Method in Calvin', *Westminster Theological Journal* 49 (1987), pp. 153–165; 'Calvin as Theologian and Exegete: Is There Anything New?', *Calvin Theological Journal* 23 (1988), pp. 178–194.

77. A standard set of questions was established by Aristotle and those questions

This structural method was not 'neutral' relative to culture. History clearly demonstrates that the *loci* method was more than a simple topical presentation of doctrine.[78] Discussion of theological method, and how the philosophy of Aristotle, the inventor of the *loci* method, was to be combined with theology, are found in ancient texts.[79] The discussion did not end then;[80] it continued in extensive sixteenth-century treatises by the prince of humanist scholars, Desiderius Erasmus, by Luther's successor, Philip Melanchthon,[81] and by the Reformed theologians Peter Martyr Vermigli[82] and Martin Bucer.[83] Debate on the role of the *loci communes* raged through theological texts in the seventeenth century, and has continued even to today.[84]

---

continued through the Scholastic period. They would be, 'Whether the thing is? What is the thing? What are its parts? What are its species?' etc.

78. In the development of theological method, medieval logic recognized distinctions relative to certainty. There was what is termed 'absolute necessity', 'possibility' and 'relative necessity'. Late medieval new logic was born of the recovery of Aristotle's *Organon*. After that discovery came the rise of what is termed 'humanism'. Humanist logicians challenged Aristotelian logic by identifying dialectic with the 'art of persuasion' as part of an intellectual case for likelihood over certainty. For more information on this development, see Gamble, *Whole Counsel of God*.

79. H. Conn also addressed this issue in 'Contextual Theologies', *Westminster Theological Journal* 52.1 (1990), pp. 55–56, where he cited examples from the ancient church.

80. T. H. L. Parker, *John Calvin: A Biography* (Philadelphia: Westminster Press, 1975), p. 73, 'This view of the commentator's task was not peculiar to Calvin, but had been imported into Biblical work by Melanchthon from secular sources, and in fact went back to Aristotle by way of Cicero.'

81. Specifically, see Philip Melanchthon, *Erotematum Dialectices*, '*De Methodo*' (Lib. I); *Mel. Opera* 13; pp. 574ff. An English translation of this text can be found in Gamble, *Whole Counsel of God*.

82. *Peter Martyr Vermigli Early Writings* (Kirksville, MO: Thomas Jefferson University Press, 1994), vol. 1, pp. 88–89. Peter Martyr had a 'practical theology'! 'Like the moral rectitude of Erasmus or the *fructus pietatis* of Bucer, Martyr's pursuit of practical theology used the distinction in a loosely deductive manner . . . In his choice of method and selection of matter for debate Martyr shows the shape of his own early stage of Reformed theology.'

83. See '*Loci Communes* and the Rhetorical and Dialectical Traditions', in J. C. McClelland, ed., *Peter Martyr Vermigli and Italian Reform* (Waterloo, Ont.: Wilfred Laurier University Press, 1980), pp. 17–28.

84. See the discussions in Amandus Polanus, *Syntagma Theologiae Christianae* (1617) and

Therefore, theologians must be more careful than merely to assert that 'the [*loci* method] simply calls for a topical presentation of doctrine, and it is difficult to see why the biblical materials preclude such an approach'.[85] If the *loci* method were only a topical presentation of doctrine, then this assertion is possibly correct. However, on two points it could be challenged. The first is that while the *loci* approach may not be precluded by the biblical material, in fact the biblical material itself may suggest a better approach. Second, if the *loci* approach is used, how a theologian organizes or arranges his 'topics' is subjective – and based upon theological presuppositions.

It has been demonstrated that even the finest Christian exegesis and theology of the past has been influenced by its cultural context. From this demonstration, it would be difficult for any theologian to assert that he has been liberated from his own 'culture's' mark on exegesis and theological method. This reality forces any contemporary church leader to ask how present-day culture influences the way God's special revelation is presented to his people.

For example, in an age known as postmodern, the very use of logic has come under assault. There are questions being asked by our society that assail some of the basic pillars of Western culture.[86] The manner in which pastors should respond to the philosophical attacks, and, more importantly, to the honest questioning of someone like a college sophomore, is an issue not often raised in the church.[87] Can church leaders speak theologically to those who

---

Franciscus Gomarus, *Disputationes Theologicae* (1644). There was also debate on the systematic theology textbook used at Princeton Seminary before Charles Hodge's; namely, Francis Turretin (1623–87). Turretin's contemporary who taught in Amsterdam, Gisbert Voetius, in his *Disputationum Theologicarum Pars Prima* [disp. 1 and 2] (1648), went so far as to accept Thomas Aquinas's view of theology openly as a science that mirrors or is based upon the 'perfect science' of God's self-knowledge.

85. R. B. Gaffin, Jr, 'A New Paradigm . . .', *Westminster Theological Journal* 56 (1994), p. 380.

86. See J. I. Packer, 'Is Systematic Theology a Mirage? An Introductory Discussion', in J. D. Woodbridge and T. E. McComiskey (eds.), *Doing Theology in Today's World* (Grand Rapids: Zondervan, 1991), p. 21, for a history of the development. See also Lints, *Fabric of Theology*, pp. 193–234.

87. E.g. in W. Grudem's *Systematic Theology: An Introduction to Biblical Doctrine* (Grand Rapids: Zondervan, 1994), there is little or no discussion of culture, and the term is not in the index. It also set off from Gordon Lewis and Bruce Demarest, *Integrative Theology* (Grand Rapids: Zondervan, 1987), who assert that the task of systematic theology is to present doctrine in its transcultural significance (see vol. 1, p. 9).

fundamentally, yet honestly, disagree with them on such basic issues as the self-evident nature of the law of non-contradiction?[88]

More narrowly, consider how modern Western society has dealt with some of the basic issues of theology. Theologians assert that all theology is stated in human language, and that all correct theology is true. Yet, our own culture (including some contemporary theology) has very definite views of the nature of language, truth and logic; views that bring into question whether the word 'true' can even be meaningful for theology.[89] How often have pastors/theologians heard the retort 'Christianity may be true for you, but it is not true for me'? Given postmodernism's cultural assault on truth and language, our responsibility as theologians must be to present the truths of the Bible in a way that is both understandable to contemporary Christians, while also being able to withstand the scrutiny of present-day society. Furthermore, we must not only withstand illegitimate philosophical/cultural assaults, but we must also somehow rise above them and defeat the critiques.[90]

The culture and time period in which theology is written has affected and continues to shape the way in which biblical exegesis and theological method are done in every age. There is a great burden placed upon those who want to present the truths of God's Word to contemporary society, and unfortunately, there are ways in which theologians may operate with unquestioned philosophical/cultural presuppositions.[91] Thus, can a pastor or theologian ever break free of the shackles of his own culture? Must men always compose 'black/white American male' theologies? Do we have nothing more to offer

---

88. Briefly, the law of non-contradiction is that proposition A cannot mean non-A at the same time. Posing this question alone is not meant to avoid other equally difficult issues of the role of religious values inherent in the use of logic and the interpretation of current culture. The role of the rational human mind as well as criteria for truth and falsity are dealt with in Gamble, *Whole Counsel of God*.

89. Wells, 'The Theologian's Craft', pp. 185 ff., laments 'how troublesome and difficult it is to set text and interpreter, objective and subjective, in right relationship'.

90. It was Conn's assertion, 'Contextual Theologies', p. 59, that Western theologians have not sufficiently been critical of their culture. Those cultural influences have created the improper 'confusion of the Bible as norm with theology as a neutral search for the rationally ideal, the "heavenly principles." True theology is seen as *sui generis*, the liberating search of the mind for essence, core, unhindered by any kind of historical, geographical, or social qualifier. Theological pursuits are freed to become the Platonic search for abstract, rational principles.'

91. Those presuppositions are demonstrated in Gamble, *Whole Counsel of God*.

the church, or must this fact of human life leave the theologian in deep despair? The answer to the question is a resounding 'yes and no'.

It is a defensible thesis that the Bible itself provides a model for exegesis, and can supply a model for theological arrangement that comes from within its own pages.[92] The believer must not necessarily turn to the earlier teachings of the pagan philosopher Aristotle, or more current modern or postmodern philosophies for theological method (systematic theology).[93] As Christians, we are better able to formulate the way we look at and examine the doctrines of God's special revelation than are those who are outside Christ.[94]

However, each of us thinks in what is called his or her 'mother' tongue. We may know other languages and be able to speak in them, but a normal person cannot think in two languages at one time. Furthermore, the culture of a child's home, the following educational experiences and all other life events influence the nature and character of that person's theological thought and writing.

Because of these powerful influences on each person, theology must be structured in a way that attempts to stand above those cultural experiences, while recognizing the inherent limitations of any one author.[95] The need to communicate theologically to different types of persons, who live in different

92. The thesis is developed in ibid.

93. The issue stems from Gaffin's assertion that 'orthodox Protestant dogmatics, by allying itself . . . with Aristotelian . . . patterns of thought' fell into trouble. See his 'Systematic Theology and Biblical Theology', pp. 292–293. If the *loci* method is an 'Aristotelian pattern of thought', as can easily and clearly be demonstrated, and Aristotelian thought patterns get theologians into trouble, then do theologians not have an obligation to continue to explore patterns that are perhaps more biblical?

94. Recognizing legitimate differences in the Reformed theological tradition, I do not think that F. Turretin's theological method was an improvement over Calvin's. Turretin's analysis of the nature of theological knowledge was dependent upon at least two philosophical foundations, Aristotle and the Medieval Scholastics. If one compares Thomas Aquinas's *Summa* and Francis Turretin's *Institutio* 1.6.1–3 on the nature of theological knowledge, very few or no significant differences will be found.

95. As R. H. Bremmer, *Herman Bavinck als Dogmaticus* (1961), p. 331, said, even this great Reformed theologian found in 'the great systems of Plato, Augustine and Thomas the answer to the questions which modern times and modern thought have posed to the dogmatician', as cited by C. Van Til, 'Bavinck the Theologian', reprinted from the *Westminster Theological Journal* 24.1 (1961), p. 2.

cultures, has in some senses driven the search for a different theological model.[96]

In conclusion, the relationship between biblical theology and systematic theology should continue to develop so that the strengths of biblical theology inform the development of a 'biblical' 'system' of theology.

© Richard C. Gamble, 2006

---

96. Van Til was correct when he said, 'Fundamental to every present-day discussion of various theological questions is the problem of method,' ibid., p. 3.

7. OLD COVENANT, NEW COVENANT

Henri Blocher

The Sacred Scriptures of the Christian church give a maximum privilege of visibility to the theme of covenant (testament, *diathēkē*) as they set forth their structure in the twin titles of the old and new *diathēkai*. These, titles, to be sure, were attributed to the Hebrew and Greek collections by the ancient church, but with adequate warrant in the Scriptures themselves (2 Cor. 3:6, 14; Heb. 8:6–7, 13). Any theology that wishes to be biblical must invest time and energy in the study of covenant, and of the way the qualifications 'old' and 'new' apply to the realities the word denotes.

Reformed theology was not slow in picking up the importance of the theme. Already in 1525, Zwingli brought it to the fore, in his controversy with the first Anabaptists. In Calvin, we find the seeds of the later developed 'federal' theology, which has established itself, to this day, as the main form of orthodox Reformed doctrine. Divergences within the fold, hotly debated at times, have shown that the matter is not so simple, and calls for tactful treatment. In the British Isles, emphases on either law or grace, in the accounts of God's covenants, were the object of intense dispute;[1] there was no agreement

---

1. A. T. B. McGowan has recently recalled the controversy between the leading figures James Hadow and Thomas Boston, 'In Defence of "Headship Theology"', in Jamie A. Grant and Alistair I. Wilson, eds., *The God of Covenant: Biblical, Theological and*

on the precise relationship of the Sinaitic covenant to the covenant of works;[2] in the Netherlands, but with radiating influence beyond the borders (especially in England), Cocceius and his school contrasted old and new so sharply that their theses may appear to foreshadow some dispensationalist propositions – if the Dutch Reformed churches avoided schism and were able to settle for a compromise peace, they owed it, at least in part, to the magisterial biblical work of Herman Witsius, which drew a moderate line and is still worth pondering today.[3] One cannot deny that the measure of differences between the two regimes BC and AD has bearings on the dissent that separates Baptists and paedobaptists within the theologically Reformed family.

The study of this topic is most relevant to present-day concerns. After decades of frozen opposition between covenant theologians and dispensationalists (though Lewis Sperry Chafer, the most prominent dispensationalist dogmatician in his generation, was an ordained Presbyterian minister), avenues of dialogue have been opened.[4] On the Reformed side, Vern Poythress's *Understanding Dispensationalists*[5] was a milestone and implied a more sensitive perception of the differences between the divine economies (M. G. Kline's

---

Contemporary Perspectives (Leicester: Apollos, 2005), pp. 178–199, esp. 183–185, and pointed to essential similarities with the debate between John Murray and Meredith G. Kline in the twentieth century.

2. John Von Rohr, *The Covenant of Grace in Puritan Thought*, American Academy of Religion Studies in Religion 45 (Atlanta: Scholars Press, 1986), p. 50.

3. Herman Witsius, *The Economy of the Covenants between God and Man Comprehending a Complete Body of Divinity*, tr. William Crookshank, new edn, 2 vols. (London: Begg, 1837). The Latin original was published in 1685 (Leeuwarden) and a second edition in 1694 (Utrecht); the English translation was first published in London (Dilly) in 1763. It was warmly recommended by representative divines, including the learned Baptist minister and writer John Gill (vol. 1, p. iii). How deeply edifying are Witsius's introductory words 'It is . . . with a kind of sacred awe I undertake this work; praying God, that, laying aside every prejudice, I may demean myself a tractable disciple of the Holy Scriptures, and with modesty impart to my brethren, what I think I have learned from them: if happily this my poor performance may serve to lessen the number of disputes, and help to clear up the truth; than which nothing should be accounted more valuable' (vol. 1, p. 20 [Book 1, ch. 1, §1]; compare his gentle and humble reply to harsh, even abusive, critics, vol. 2, pp. 233–234 [Book 4, ch. 6, §74] and p. 347 [Book 4, ch. 12, §43]).

4. See the special issue of the *Grace Theological Journal* 10 (1989), pp. 125–182.

5. Grand Rapids: Academie/Zondervan, 1987.

new emphasis on these differences may have helped as a preparation). On the dispensationalist side, a new appreciation of the continuity of God's dealings in redemptive history has gained much ground.[6] While Karl Barth's monumental contribution again attracts much attention among evangelicals, one remembers that his doctrine of the covenant is an area of conflict with traditional federal theology: as he rejects emphatically any 'covenant of works' (there is only one covenant, of grace, in Jesus Christ, which is the inner foundation of creation itself) and assigns Israel and the church symmetrical places. Exploration of hermeneutics, whether referring to canon or intertextuality or community-reception and so on, often take the form of an examination of New Testament use of Old Testament texts or themes.[7] The relationship of economies is also a burning issue in debates aroused by the new perspective(s) on Paul.[8] And, of course, it is decisive for the theology of Israel, for any confrontation with schemes that enjoy a distinct favour in the *oikoumenē*, with the critique of 'supersessionism' and the affirmation of two parallel covenants, and therefore ways of salvation, in this our age.[9]

This brief chapter will not aim to comment on the gamut of issues just mentioned. It will revisit the doctrine of the covenant and its economies, spot the weaknesses of dominant forms and suggest a revised one: a form that should

---

6. Robert L. Saucy, *The Case for Progressive Dispensationalism: The Interface between Dispensational and Non-Dispensational Theology* (Grand Rapids: Zondervan, 1993).

7. At this present stage, I can witness that, in the PhD Program of Wheaton College Graduate School of Biblical and Theological Studies, a majority of dissertation topics actually fall into that field of study.

8. I hinted at the fact in my 'Justification of the Ungodly (*Sola Fide*): Theological Reflections', in D. A. Carson, Peter T. O'Brien and Mark A. Seifrid, eds., *Justification and Variegated Nomism*. Vol. 2: *The Paradoxes of Paul*, Wissenschaftliche Untersuchungen zum Neuen Testament 2.181 (Tübingen: Mohr Siebeck; Grand Rapids: Baker Academic, 2004), pp. 499–500; and D. A. Carson himself offers a forceful elaboration in his chapter 'Mystery and Fulfilment: Toward a More Comprehensive Paradigm of Paul's Understanding of the Old and the New', in ibid., pp. 393–436.

9. Eckhard Schnabel's major study 'Die Gemeinde des Neuen Bundes in Kontinuität und Diskontinuität zur Gemeinde des Alten Bundes', in Gerhard Maier, ed., *Israel in Geschichte und Gegenwart. Beiträge zur Geschichte Israels und zum jüdisch-christlichen Dialog* (Wuppertal: Theologische Verlagsgemeinschaft; Basel: Brockhaus/Brunnen, 1996), pp. 147–213, has been prompted, at least in part, by statements of such a theology, especially by Erich Zenger and Rolf Rendtorff in the journal *Kirche und Israel*.

give more space to discontinuity without jeopardizing overall and essential unity. It will draw the boldness to do so from elements found in respected 'doctors' of the Reformed tradition ([Credo] Baptists and paedobaptists).

Pointing to weaknesses in current forms of covenant theology

Covenant theology has been the target of all kinds of criticisms. To dispel possible misunderstandings, one may start with criticisms that are *not* to be received. The recognition of the unity of God's purpose of redemption, unfolding from Abel (probably even Adam and Eve) to us, is a strength, not a weakness! When liberals (1) sacrifice the harmony of identical inspiration, throughout the whole Bible, on the altar of a 'scientific' handling of the various books, (2) adopt as an 'assured result' (and almost as an axiom) that there is a wide gap (another *garstige breite Graben*!) between the intrinsic, proper, meaning of Old Testament texts and their use by New Testament writers, (3) *de facto* hold Rabbinic Judaism to be the legitimate heir of Moses and the Prophets – they forsake the way primitive Christianity defined itself in the first generations. For the original Christian faith, 'conversion to Christ removes the veil to enable the reader to see what is actually *there*'.[10] Barthian strictures on the doctrine of the 'covenant of works', and, more generally, charges of legalism, should not intimidate us. More will be said below on the issue; suffice it to respond at this stage that legalism – when the notion is clarified – may be a temptation but is by no means necessarily entailed.[11]

Barth's refusal of a prior covenant proceeds from the great reversal of order, Christ really the first Adam, reconciliation theologically prior to creation, which he champions and which squares so uneasily with the presentation of Scripture.[12] Anabaptist and dispensationalist downgrading of the Old

---

10. Carson, 'Mystery and Fulfilment', p. 411 (emphasis his; he describes Paul's position, 'as far as Paul is concerned'); cf. p. 435: Paul 'wants to show that when the Old Testament Scriptures are *rightly* interpreted, they agree with this thesis. *Not* to see this point is to remain unconverted.'

11. See the fine article by Donald MacLeod, 'Federal Theology – An Oppressive Legalism?', *Banner of Truth* 125 (February 1974), pp. 21–28.

12. And so strikingly with Calvin's concern not to blur the distinction and order: *Institutes of the Christian Religion* 1.6.1 and 10.1: though he is led to mention redemption as he expounds the doctrine of general revelation and creation, he almost apologizes for doing so, and stresses that redemption will be dealt with later.

Testament and denial that Old Testament believers were regenerate cannot be sustained: New Testament believers are sharing in the blessing of Abraham, their father, and Abraham's case is not to be interpreted as an isolated exception, since the same experience of justification by faith was enjoyed by David (and since Ps. 32 was given as a prayer to the people, logically by those also who truly sang and prayed after the pattern of the words). H. Witsius's refutation of statements of Cocceius's that appear to deprive Old Testament believers of regeneration, of the abiding presence of the Spirit, and of remission of sins worthy of the name, is a splendid piece of work.[13] Covenant theology borrows its structure from the sketches already offered in Scripture, especially Galatians 3 – 4, Romans 11 (or 5 and 9 – 11), Hebrews 8 – 10 and 11 – 12 . . .

'The biggest defect of penetration is not the failure to reach its goal but going beyond it' (François, duc de La Rochefoucauld).[14] Many feel that covenant theology overdoes its advantage regarding unity and continuity. A New Testament scholar like George R. Beasley-Murray, who cannot pass for a Reformed theologian, protests, with covenant theology in view:

> Allowing for all elements of continuity between the old and the new covenant, old and new revelation, old and new people, to put them under a common denominator is to identify the unidentifiable – life and death, flesh and Spirit, old creation and new creation, life of this age and the life of the age to come. This attempt to reduce to uniformity the old and new covenants and their respective sacraments belongs to an unrealistic mode of exegesis . . .[15]

A similar complaint, though in more moderate terms, comes from the pen of the (neo-evangelical) Reformed Baptist, Paul King Jewett: covenant theologians 'have so far pressed the unity of the covenant as to suppress the diversity of its administration. They have, to be specific, Christianized the Old Testament and Judaized the New.'[16] On the same side, James Orr

---

13. *Economy*, vol. 2, pp. 325–362 (Book 4, ch. 12).

14. *Sentences et Maximes de morale* n° 377 ('Le plus grand défaut de la pénétration n'est pas de n'aller point jusqu'au but, c'est de le passer').

15. *Baptism in the New Testament*, 2nd edn (Exeter: Paternoster, 1972), p. 338.

16. *Infant Baptism and the Covenant of Grace: An Appraisal of the Argument That Infants Were Once Circumcised, So They Should Now Be Baptized* (Grand Rapids: Eerdmans, 1978), p. 91, quoted by David Kingdon, *Children of Abraham: A Reformed Baptist View of Baptism, the Covenant, and Children* (Worthing: Henry E. Walter/Carey, 1973), p. 42

himself! He could write that covenant theology 'failed to seize the true idea of development and by an artificial system of typology, and allegorizing interpretation, sought to read back practically the whole of the New Testament into the Old'.[17] Covenant theology, in the versions that have been dominant in tradition, tends to flatten, to level down, the diversity between the old and the new.

The rhetoric of Calvin, and of many who follow him in this respect, reflects an all-consuming zeal in the affirmation of unity and the tendency to minimize differences. He uses the strongest possible language: the covenant made with the fathers of old 'was so similar to ours, in its substance and truth, that one can say it was identical with it';[18] the apostle (Paul) 'makes the people of Israel equal and on a par with us in the grace of the covenant, and also in the significance of sacraments'.[19] Witsius, in his exact manner, maintains the identity of substance and draws original arguments from John 5:39 and Hebrews 4:2.[20] The diversity (that is not denied) is consistently defined as a diversity of 'administration' or 'manner of dispensing'.[21] Those elements that are sometimes given the very name 'old covenant' in Scripture, and are now obsolete,

---

(with another reference, since Kingdon is quoting from mimeographed lecture notes). He has in view the defence of infant baptism based on the analogy of, and continuity with, circumcision.

17. *The Progress of Dogma*, Elliot Lectures (London: Hodder & Stoughton, 1901), p. 303, as quoted by Charles C. Ryrie, *Dispensationalism Today* (Chicago: Moody, 1965), p. 19.

18. *Institutes* 2.10.2, from Calvin's French: 'en sa substance et vérité est si semblable à la nostre, qu'on peut la dire une mesme avec icelle'; Latin: 'substantia et re ipsa nihil a nostro differt, ut unum prorsus atque idem sit'.

19. Ibid., 2.10.5, 'fait le peuple d'Israël pareil et égual à nous en la grâce de l'alliance, mais aussi en la signification des sacrements'; 'non foederis tantum gratia pares nobis facit Israelitas, sed etiam sacramentorum significatione'.

20. *Economy*, vol. 1, pp. 259–273 (Book 3, ch. 2); p. 260 (§3) on John 5:39, p. 269 (§33) on Heb. 4:2.

21. Calvin, *Institutes* 2.10.2, 'Seulement elle diffère en l'ordre d'être dispensée'; 'Administratio tamen variat': 11.1, differences 'appartienent toutes, et se doyvent référer à la manière diverse que Dieu a tenue en dispensant sa doctrine, plustost qu'à la substance': 'ad modum administrationis potius quam ad substantiam pertineant'. Witsius, vol. 1, p. 275 (Book 3, ch. 3, §3): 'The difference of the testaments consists in the different manner of dispensing and proposing the same saving grace, and in some adjuncts and circumstances.'

are called mere 'accidents' or 'accessories'.[22] The choice of words is quite revealing, and the very category of 'administration' may be too vague and abstract to bear the weight of a serious account of differences.

A symptom? Some prominent representatives betray a degree of impatience and are able only grudgingly to accept the language of Scripture. Pierre Ch. Marcel warns, 'One must vigorously denounce the most sorry habit of designating the Old Testament under the words *old covenant.* It generates unfortunate confusions'[23] (despite 2 Cor. 3:14). As he faces the biblical use of 'new covenant', he explains it (away) in a threefold manner: (1) it is new by contrast with the Pharisaic *mis*understanding of the Mosaic covenant; (2) it is new in form of administration (the law is changed, the covenant continues); (3) it is new by virtue of God's freedom: 'this event of the free grace of God, of his free covenant, is at every moment something entirely *"new"*'.[24] And, yet, Marcel was no Barthian . . . Calvin's strategy does not make itself so vulnerable, but it is still remarkable. His chapter (*Institutes* 2.11) offers a fairly comprehensive summary of the differences between the Testaments (as announced in his title); but how does he handle them? He takes each item separately (*divide et impera*) and argues for a minimal interpretation in each case: there is a transfer of name; things are said by way of comparison (*per comparationem*); degrees only differ, in clarity and enjoyment. Had he discerned that the differences have ties that bind them to one another, constitute a web or system (as the author to the Hebrews intimates, 7:12ff., 9:9ff. etc.), he would have felt the cumulative weight of their significance; they imply a greater discontinuity, a change of 'level' in the transition from the older to the new regime.

A telling illustration of the tendency to ignore the change of level is the way Calvin can speak in the same breath of the church in Geneva in his own time and of the church in Jerusalem in Hezekiah's time. The word 'church' is, of course, a legitimate translation of Hebrew *qāhāl* (*ekklēsia* in the LXX and Acts

---

22. Calvin, *Institutes* 2.11.4: 'accidens ou accessoires du Vieil Testament': 'foederis duntaxat accidentia erant, vel certe accessiones ac annexa, et (ut vulgus loquitur) accessoria'. For Witsius's 'adjuncts', see preceding note.

23. 'Le Baptême, sacrement de l'alliance de grâce', special issue of *La Revue Réformée* 2–3 (October 1950), p. 56, n. 11: 'Il faut dénoncer vigoureusement la très fâcheuse habitude de désigner l'Ancien Testament par le terme d'*ancienne alliance.* Cela conduit à de regrettables confusions.'

24. Ibid., pp. 54–56 (p. 56: 'cet événement de la libre grâce de Dieu, de son alliance libre, est à chaque instant quelque chose de tout à fait *"nouveau"*').

7:38), but Calvin's use seems to neglect any change of status and of the church's relationship to the 'body politic'. As he had done in Israel, God 'has placed his covenant in France, in Italy, in Germany and other countries'.[25] It may be significant that Witsius devotes a most detailed analysis to the fate of ceremonies but only touches on the changes linked with the political constitution of Israel.[26] That 'nation' cannot apply in the same way to the New Testament church (1 Pet. 2:9) and to Israel (in Exod. 19:6) hardly seems to be considered. Not seldom, the analogy of ordinary citizenship, which one acquires either through natural descent or through naturalization, is pressed into literal service for membership in the church.[27] Several covenant theologians argue that requirements for membership in the old covenant were essentially the same as under the new, from the fact that law-breakers, especially in religious matters, were to be disciplined under the Old Testament: 'The supposition that a man could be a Jew without professing, at least, his belief in these promises and prophecies, without acting *as a disciple*, is a contradiction.'[28] But, as Kingdon replies, no-one has been able to show 'that a confession of personal faith was necessary to ensure the enjoyment of the temporal blessings of the covenant'; '[t]he delinquent was cut off as a breaker of the law of the theocracy, not as an unbeliever in the New Testament sense'.[29] Nowhere

---

25. *Institutes* 4.2.11: 'il a mis une fois son alliance en France, en Italie, en Alemagne et autres païs': 'foedus suum in Gallia, Italia, Germania, Hispania, Anglia deposuerit'.

26. *Economy*, vol. 2, p. 411 (Book 4, ch. 15, §19) mentions, as a benefit of the New Testament, 'immunity from the forensic or judicial laws of the Israelites'. This brevity contrasts with the several chapters devoted to types and ch. 13, 'Of the real defects of the Old Testament', pp. 362–377.

27. P. Marcel, p. 93: 'Ainsi, l'Etat donne sa nationalité aux nouveaux-nés.' Similarly, Hodge, quoted by Kingdon (after Jewett, *Infant Baptism*), p. 47.

28. P. Marcel, p. 71 (italics mine): 'Supposer qu'un homme pût être Juif, sans professer au moins sa croyance en ces promesses et en ces prophéties, sans faire acte de disciple, c'est une contradiction.' Similarly, Herbert S. Bird, as quoted by Kingdon, *Children of Abraham*, pp. 42–43. Edmund P. Clowney, *The Doctrine of the Church*, International Library of Philosophy and Theology/Biblical and Theological Studies (Philadelphia: P. & R., 1969), pp. 15–16, in very carefully guarded language, comes close to this position; he stresses that in Israel's case, just as in the New Testament church, 'God's covenant with his people is neither individualistic nor ethnic in the modern sense.'

29. Kingdon, *Children of Abraham*, p. 43. He also argues from Deut. 23:1 (Hebrew 2) that a mere physical defect prevented participation in the *qāhāl*.

in Scripture do we find the suggestion that personal unbelief, such as the most hostile of Pharisees demonstrated in the Gospels, should have entailed the loss of Israelite citizenship (in contrast with spiritual life and eternal destiny), whereas the *ekklēsia* of Jesus Christ marks itself off, within the earthly nation, by the commitment of faith of men and women (Acts 8:12), through saving demarcation from their kin (*apo tēs geneas tautēs*, Acts 2:40) and being added to a community (*epi to auto*, v. 47) commonly called a 'sect' (Acts 24:14).

The lack of distinction between church and nation leads to a strong affirmation of the mixed character of (visible) church membership. With Calvin (and Augustine), many have quoted the parable of the tares to buttress this affirmation. However, as Klaas Runia has well perceived, this use collides head on with Jesus' own explanation: 'The field is the *world*', not the visible church (Matt. 13:38).[30] It is an important theme in prophecies of the messianic age that the unfortunate mixture that was characteristic of the old regime will cease to be: all Zion's sons will be intimately taught of God (Isa. 54:13; cf. John 6:45); there will only be righteous persons among the people (Isa. 60:21); under new covenant conditions, everyone in the covenant community will personally know the Lord (Jer. 31:34). The burden of John the Baptist's message is that the great sifting, the separation of grain and chaff on the Lord's threshing-floor, is now starting! The end of the mixed situation is also represented by the cutting off of the unbelieving branches in the Romans 11 olive tree (and, I would argue, of the Vine in John 15) – a cutting off that had not taken place in the Old Testament. The church of Christ, which, in some respects at least, is another 'nation' (Matt. 21:43, represented by 'other tenants' in v. 41),[31] is the believing part, the Israel of God (Gal. 6:15), no longer mixed, the remnant made visible (Rom. 11:5ff.). The discourse of continuity tends to mask this basic scheme.[32]

---

30. *Reformation Today* (Edinburgh: Banner of Truth, 1968), pp. 113–116.
31. Eckhard Schnabel, 'Die Gemeinde . . .', p. 182, underlines this verse (with 8:11–12) and writes: 'das heißt einem neuen Volk anstelle des alttestamentlichen Israel'. He goes on, p. 183, and highlights a change in identity: 'eines neuen Zugehörigkeitskriteriums: das neue Volk ist ein Volk, wo man nicht automatisch durch das Recht der Geburt Mitglied wird, sondern ein Volk, das Frucht bringt'.
32. Clowney, *Doctrine of the Church*, p. 23, both affirms 'the remnant is the elect nation' and argues that '[i]ndividual sonship is not in contrast to the family of God', 'the principle which operated in the Old Testament operates also in the New: not all are Israel which are of Israel'. He appeals to 1 John 2:19 and 1 Cor. 10:1–12 to establish the mixed character of the New Testament church; but John does not acknowledge

Closely related is the issue of the two sides of the covenant. It has been a thorn in the flesh of many covenant theologians. Leaving aside the mono-pleuric/dipleuric polarity (although it is not foreign to that debate), the deli-cate question has been, Who, exactly, belongs to the covenant? Louis Berkhof's account, a model of candour, reveals a degree of embarrassment.[33] 'The great majority' of Reformed theologians, he writes, maintain that God 'entered into covenant relationship with the elect or the elect sinner in Christ' – and this, 'in spite of all the practical difficulties involved'; they did so 'in the light of Scripture': 'Reformed theologians found abundant evidence that fun-damentally the covenant of grace is a covenant established with those who are in Christ.'[34] Yet, at the same time, they wished to include the children of believers, among whom there are a number of non-elect, after the promise 'You and your seed'.[35] W. Brakel cut the Gordian knot and 'virtually' excluded all the non-elect, but he was the exception.[36] T. Blake, still bolder, distin-guished 'between an external and an internal covenant'.[37] Most tried to soften the difference and spoke of sides or aspects, of essence and administration, of the covenant 'as legal relationship' and 'as a communion of life' (with G. Vos).[38] H. Bavinck wrote of unregenerate and unconverted persons that they are *in foedere* (in) but not *de foedere* (of);[39] it is a titillating detail that P. Marcel just switches the prepositions: will these children *of* the covenant enter *into* the covenant?[40]

---

any right of citizenship to the 'false brethren' in the visible church: they never were 'of us' (*ex hēmōn*) – deceptive appearances involving some element of objective untruth are not equivalent to legitimate, though merely external, status in the visible institution; Paul's warnings are directed to those standing, lest they fall, and imply no mixture of elect and non-elect in the congregation.

33. *Systematic Theology*, 3rd edn (Grand Rapids: Eerdmans, 1946), pp. 273–289.

34. Ibid., pp. 273, 274. So Witsius in his definition, vol. 1, p. 137 (Book 2, ch. 1, §5).

35. Bible quotations in this chapter are from the NASB.

36. Ibid., p. 274.

37. Ibid., p. 284.

38. Ibid., pp. 286–287.

39. Ibid., pp. 288–289.

40. 'Le Baptême', p. 83: 'Tous les enfants *de* l'alliance entreront-ils *dans* l'alliance et la confirmeront-ils?' Marcel can also write, e.g. p. 80, that God considers the children *in* the covenant ('and therefore in his Kingdom and in his Church') and that the question left is whether he will make them 'living members of the covenant' ('membres vivants de l'alliance').

A further ambiguity attaches to the promise of the covenant (signified and sealed in circumcision and baptism). Some speak out quite clearly. For Auguste Lecerf, the promise is essentially conditional, 'if you believe', and therefore general, indeterminate and universal in character: the offer of grace.[41] A discriminating exegesis ascribes this understanding to Calvin;[42] it was also Klaas Schilder's.[43] But P. Marcel passionately claims that God 'works out the necessary conditions for the promise being efficacious. The covenant is more than a simple offer of salvation, more indeed than an offer of salvation to which belief in the Gospel would be joined.'[44] Berkouwer emphatically refuses the idea of a merely conditional promise.[45] And yet, they cannot affirm a universal election and salvation of the children. Berkouwer renounces rational transparency. One solution offered turns around the idea of probability: Berkhof adds, 'a reasonable expectation that the external legal relationship will carry with it the glorious reality of a life in intimate communion with the covenant God';[46]

---

41. 'La Doctrine de l'Eglise dans Calvin', in *Etudes calvinistes* (Neuchâtel: Delachaux & Niestlé, 1949), p. 59: 'la promesse . . . aura nécessairement un caractère général, indéterminé, universel'.

42. In his commentary on Gen. 17:7 (Latin in 1554), Calvin interprets the *promissio* as offer (as Luther had done), and he even uses 'to confer' for this offer that does not imply that the person externally in covenant will actually enjoy the spiritual reality of divine grace: he distinguishes between the 'promissio' which 'generaliter accipitur pro externo verbo, quo Deus suam gratiam tam reprobis quam electis conferebat', in which 'negari non potest oblatam fuisse omnibus aeternam salutem', and the one 'ad efficacem vocationem quam intus obsignat per spiritum suum' (*Ioannis Calvini opera quae supersunt omnia*, ed. G. Baum, E. Cunitz and E. Reuss, 59 vols. [Brunswick: Schwetschke, 1863–1900], vol. 23, col. 238); in the French version (1564) between the promise 'prise . . . en général, pour la parole extérieure par laquelle Dieu conférait sa grâce tant aux réprouvés qu'aux élus', of which 'l'on ne saurait nier que le salut éternel n'ait été offert en elle', and the one involved in 'la vocation qu'il scelle par son Esprit dans les coeurs'.

43. According to Gerrit C. Berkouwer, *The Sacraments*, tr. Hugo Bekker (Grand Rapids: Eerdmans, 1969), p. 186, n. 43.

44. 'Le Baptême', p. 82: 'il réalise les conditions nécessaires pour que la promesse puisse être efficace. L'alliance est plus qu'une simple offre de salut, plus encore que l'offre du salut à laquelle s'ajouterait la promesse de croire à l'Evangile' (the last clause is unclear; the meaning seems to require that the 'promesse' last mentioned be the human response to the Gospel offer – hence my translation).

45. *Sacraments*, p. 186.

46. *Systematic Theology*, p. 287.

Marcel follows Cullmann: subsequent faith is probable, though it is not guaranteed.[47]

Having recourse to probability is hardly satisfactory. The wording of the promise never hints at such. Hermeneutical rigour enjoins that a clean decision be made between the two logical possibilities: either the promise is unconditional, therefore absolute, backed by the very sovereignty of grace, and there should be no exception (that is to say, no breach of promise on God's part), or it is conditional, and, as such, it is entirely devoid of statistical implications. One may also ask how the affirmation of high probability harmonizes, not only with modern experience, but with so many biblical statements about stiff-necked Israel, so prone to idolatry, and to Calvin's estimate that there were very few true believers in Israel![48] For the promise refers to a thousand generations . . .

Even more serious: in order to hold together the propositions he has brought forward, P. Marcel is led to statements strange to Calvinistic ears. Beyond mere offer, 'God restores in the children of the covenant the freedom of choice, so that, when presented the two alternatives of life and death, they may decide freely and voluntarily either for the one or for the other';[49] this possibility (only a possibility) is 'already the work of the special grace of God'.[50] *Arminius redivivus!* That special resistible grace that restores free will is precisely what Arminians had devised![51] Kingdon thinks he has found a similar *lapsus* in Charles Hodge himself![52]

---

47. 'Le Baptême', p. 84. Other Reformed theologians have offered thoughts more or less similar; for Geerhardus Vos, 'The Doctrine of Covenant in Reformed Theology', in Richard B. Gaffin, Jr, ed., *Redemptive History and Biblical Interpretation: The Shorter Writings of Geerhardus Vos* (Phillipsburg: P. & R., 1980), pp. 263–264, while the 'hidden judgment must be left to God', all children born of believers are sanctified 'normally', and he lists many authorities (including Witsius) for the view they 'generally' possess the Spirit from early childhood.

48. *Institutes* 22.11.8: 'paucissimos ac paene nullos dicemus'.

49. 'Le Baptême', p. 82: 'Dieu restaure chez les enfants de l'alliance la liberté du choix, si bien que, mis en présence de l'alternative de la vie et de la mort, ils puissent se prononcer voontairement et librement soit pour l'une, soit pour l'autre.'

50. Ibid., p. 80, n. 50.

51. Ibid., p. 82, n. 53, Marcel asks, 'How?'; and answers, 'by inner regeneration' ('par régénération intérieure') – but then the possibility of the rejection of the gospel and unbelief, which he also stresses, pp. 82–83, defies all rational consistency. One may also note that Marcel affirms that the covenant child has a right to forgiveness (p. 173): how can a non-elect child have such a right in a Reformed reading of Scripture?

52. Kingdon, *Children of Abraham*, p. 65, with n. 30 on p. 67.

Excessive concern for continuity may blunt the edge of Pauline antitheses. As already mentioned, P. Marcel wishes to think that grace, for Paul, is not opposed to God's law, but to a false construal of that law in Judaism.[53] More cautiously, O. Palmer Robertson also suggests, 'It is the legalistic misapprehension of the Sinaitic law-covenant that is in the mind of the apostle.'[54] Even Thomas McComiskey (whose endeavour, in general, may be compared to that of the present chapter) tries to soften the meaning of Leviticus 18:5, which Paul quotes in his antitheses of the two righteousnesses (Rom. 10:5; Gal. 3:12).[55] The limitations of this treatment precludes our entering the exegetical arena,[56] but I feel that attempts at softening disregard the force of scriptural language, its repetition, and parallels in terms of covenants contrasted (Gal. 4; 2 Cor. 3; Heb. 8 etc.), not to speak of faith and works, letter and Spirit. (One additional motive may have been to avoid too close a similarity between the Mosaic covenant and the 'covenant of works', understood as offering a way of deserving eternal life, the final reward of good works; on this point, more will be said below.)

Discerning the complexity of biblical data

Before any attempt to remedy the weaknesses just exposed, a glance at the scriptural data may be helpful, with some effort at ordering and understanding.

---

53. 'Le Baptême', p. 55: 'Voilà la clé qui permet de comprendre sous quel angle Paul adresse ses critiques à la "loi", non pas celle de l'alliance, mais celle du judaïsme légaliste pré-chrétien en particulier qui abusait de la circoncision.'

54. *The Christ of the Covenants* (Grand Rapids: Baker, 1980), p. 181. His caution is seen in the statement on p. 182, 'It may be acknowledged that something in the form of law-administration lent itself to an easy misapprehension of its proper purpose in man's redemption.' I shall not come very far from this thought, below.

55. *The Covenants of Promise: A Theology of the Old Testament Covenants* (Grand Rapids: Baker, 1985), pp. 121–124. Though he rightly maintains (esp. against D. P. Fuller) the adversative meaning of *de* in Rom. 10:6, he suggests that 'life' means in Lev. 18 not 'the giving of the inheritance but the maintenance of the inheritance', temporal, it seems, and 'we may not read into Paul's usage of the verse the concept of eternal life'.

56. See, in *Justification and Variegated Nomism*, vol. 2, the contributions of Douglas J. Moo, 'Israel and the Law in Romans 5–11: Interaction with the New Perspective', pp. 185–216, esp. 214–216 on Rom. 9:31 – 10:6, and Moisés Silva, 'Faith Versus Works of Law in Galatians', pp. 217–248, esp. 241–244 on Gal. 3:12.

The first theme one meets and impression one receives is that of fulfilment: the New Testament ushers in the things that had been hoped and prepared in previous generations; it is the economy of the last days, the *plērōma tōn kairōn*. There is no need to substantiate such a summary here. The scheme suggests continuity with a mild contrast: that of expectation and realization, inchoative and full-blown forms (flower and fruit!), meagre tokens and overflowing abundance.

A second theme, however, soon adds louder colours. Antitheses rather sharp seem to interpret 'old' and 'new' as embodying conflicting principles: not under law, but under grace, not of the letter, that kills; not of the servant girl, but of the free woman; not of works, but of faith (which has just now come, Gal. 3:23); the former commandment abrogated as being weak and useless (Heb. 7:18); Moses, on one hand, who brought the law, and Jesus Christ, in whom are grace and truth. One imagines two regimes in succession with two mutually exclusive formulas.

A closer look, however, discovers a much more complex state of affairs. Before Christ, one must reckon not only with the law, but also with the promise. 'The aim of Paul's exegesis of the Old Testament', Gerhard Ebeling perceived, 'is precisely this: sharply to distinguish and sort out what is entangled, in a misleading way, in the Old Testament: the line that starts with Abraham and the line that starts with Moses, the *epangelia* and the *nomos*, the *pistis* and the *erga*.'[57] The New Testament blessing of pure grace, of justification by faith (not works), is the blessing Abraham enjoyed – and it is ours as we prove to be his true children, sharing in his relationship with God (Gal. 3:7–9, 14; Rom. 4:1–5; cf. John 8:56). Instead of two towering figures, three: Abraham, Moses, Jesus.

It is not, furthermore, a mere matter of chronological succession. Paul insists that the law, which came 430 years after the Abrahamic promise, did not cancel the latter (Gal. 3:17ff). This is why David also could enjoy 'our' justification by faith (Rom. 4:6–8), and Hebrews 11 implies that all the Old Testament believers reach the goal (*teleiōthōsin*, v. 40) with us. So, in Moses', David's and Isaiah's times a twofold regime obtained, determined by the

---

57. 'Erwägungen zur Lehre vom Gesetz', in *Wort und Glaube* (1960), p. 276, as quoted (my tr.) by Eberhard Jüngel, 'Das Gesetz zwischen Adam und Christus: Eine theologische Studie zu Röm 5,12–21', *Zeitschrift für Theologie und Kirche* 60 (1963), p. 47, n. 23: 'Der Skopus des Paulinischen Exegese des Alten Testaments ist gerade der, scharf zu unterscheiden und auseinanderzuhalten, was im Alten Testament in verwirrender Weise ineinander verschränkt ist: die Linie von Abraham her und die Linie von Moses her, die *epangelia* und den *nomos*, die *pistis* und die *erga*.' Jüngel observes that *both* are bound to the divine identity.

promise and by the law. This dual character is confirmed by a somewhat para-
doxical Pauline fact: Paul draws from Moses' own words not only the formula
of justification by works, Leviticus 18:5 (Gal. 3:12; Rom. 10:5), but also the
formula of the other way, justification by faith, Deuteronomy 9:4 and 30:12–14
(Rom. 10:6–8; the quotation plays the same role as Hab. 2:4 in Gal. 3:11).
Complexity!

Just as the line of promise–faith–grace runs down into Moses' ministry, the
line of law is found before him. It can be discerned in Abraham's life. Against
the preachers of circumcision, Paul had argued that the promise had priority,
since the law (to which circumcision logically belongs) had been given only 430
years later; but we may guess that his adversaries triumphantly retorted that
circumcision had not been given by Moses but to Abraham! So Paul refined
his argument (still basically the same) in Romans 4: he argues that the promise
(justification by faith) has priority, since circumcision was given two chapters
later (Gen. 17; Rom. 4:9–12). Circumcision represents an element of 'law' (in
Paul's sense) with Abraham. In this, he was following our Lord himself, who
tied circumcision, in its theological essence, to the law of Moses (John 7:22).[58]
It is no surprise, therefore, if Hagar represents the covenant of Sinaitic law,
whose heirs and children, in Paul's time, are identified as the authorities of
Israel according to the flesh (Gal. 4:21–31). Both lines must be recognized
already at the Abrahamic stage.

There are indications that they can be recognized even further back.
Hebrews 11 starts our great genealogy of faith not with Abraham, but with
Abel; we may affirm a continuity of the line of grace since the dawn of human
history – Christian tradition was not misguided when it understood Genesis
3:15 as the *Protevangel*. Conversely, the legal principle 'he who does these things
shall live in (probably instrumental) them', is no more recent: Romans 2 highlights the functional equivalence of the law written in the hearts of all people
from creation with the law (of Moses), which only Israel possessed. Later, he
explains that the law of Moses was added to amplify what was established on
the basis of Adam's headship (Rom. 5:20, as I have argued elsewhere). Both
lines, it seems, start 'in the beginning'.

Sketching a revised model for covenant theology

Main propositions may follow the order of diachronic (biblical) history.

---

58. Witsius did not miss the point, vol. 1, p. 282 (Book 3, ch. 3, §15).

The relationship of humankind with God is first determined by the Eden Charter, the creational covenant, made 'in Adam'. God sovereignly grants human beings the free enjoyment of the goods of creation and the constant renewal of life, both physical and spiritual (represented by the fruit of the Tree of Life); continuation in this benefit of grace is offered on condition of obedience; that is, ratification of dependence (represented by humans abstaining from the fruit of the Tree of Knowledge of Good and Evil). Disobedience entails condemnation and death as a retribution. These clauses remain in force throughout human history, for all those who are born of Adam and are 'in Adam'.

The great majority of Reformed theologians have spoken of a 'covenant of works'.[59] A. T. B. McGowan follows John Murray in rejecting the concept of covenant for what he prefers to call the 'Adamic Administration'.[60] I have argued elsewhere in favour of the use of 'covenant', in agreement with a traditional reading of Hosea 6:7;[61] parallels between the Eden story and material relating to the Promised Land and the sanctuary could be added, as confirmatory arguments. Yet I fully share not only McGowan's interest in 'headship' but also his emphasis on *grace*, in the sense of prevenient, undeserved favour as the main characteristic of the foundational arrangement God provided for his image-creatures. In this respect, the name 'of works' is unfortunate, and bound to arouse misunderstanding. With Robertson, I prefer to speak of the covenant of creation.[62]

The underlying issue, a significant one, is whether that covenant had a probationary character. Reformed tradition, almost unanimous, has affirmed the same. Witsius, for instance, teaches that the human creature, 'even in the state of innocence', had no right to life: 'He was only in a state of acquiring a right, which would at length be actually acquired, when he could say, I have fulfilled the conditions of the covenant, I have constantly and perfectly done what was commanded; now I claim and expect that Thou, my God, wilt grant the promised happiness.'[63]

---

59. McGowan, 'In Defence', p. 182, quotes David Poole: the phrase was introduced by Dudley Fenner in 1585 (Geneva). (In McGowan's text, a misprint changes the date to 1565.)

60. Ibid., pp. 185 ff.

61. Mainly in my *In the Beginning: The Opening Chapters of Genesis*, tr. David Preston (Leicester: IVP, 1984); more or less implicitly in *Original Sin: Illuminating the Riddle* (Leicester: Apollos, 1997).

62. *Christ of the Covenants*, pp. 67–87.

63. *Economy*, vol. 1, p. 47 (Book 1, ch. 3, §25).

He insists that '[t]he promises, therefore, of the covenant contain greater things than this communion and fruition of God, of whatsoever kind it be, which Adam already enjoyed whilst still in the state of trial'.[64] G. Vos argues that man's salvation being to reflect the blessedness of God, '[t]herefore, he must not immediately and prematurely possess the highest enjoyment, but be led up to it along a rational way'.[65] Inasmuch as this scheme suggests that life is not first given (at least in its higher quality and fullness) but earned as a reward for works, the name 'covenant of works' is rather fitting, and it does not differ so much from legalism in the eyes of many (with the achievement of one's 'own' righteousness, Phil. 3:9).

I still fail to see any hint pointing in that direction, when I read the opening chapters of Genesis, and I draw comfort from a similar observation on Berkouwer's part.[66] Nowhere does the text allude to a higher good to be gained after a time. G. Vos advances:

> It appears from Gen. 3:22 that man previous to his probation had not eaten of it [the fruit of the Tree of Life], while yet nothing is recorded concerning any prohibition which seems to point to the understanding that the use of the tree was reserved for the future, quite in agreement with the eschatological significance attributed to it later.[67]

This is far from convincing. Genesis 3:22 may suggest that man had not eaten of the fruit before only on the supposition that one bite, once, would have secured life for ever; but the text says nothing of the sort; if the fruit (of life) represents the daily, life-renewing, communication from God, 3:22 stresses that it is no longer available to sinners (even in the eschatological use of the symbol, Rev. 22:2, with fruit borne every month, it is a matter of constant supply – and, of course, it fits the nature of food!). The idea that Adam and Eve refrained from eating does not fit the narrative: the Tree of Life, in the midst of the Garden, epitomizes the central goodness of God's generous gift, to be freely enjoyed ('eating you shall eat', 2:16), and the Woman said: 'We eat' (3:2). The extraordinary twist in Vos's comments is that they give the impression that the forbidden fruit was the fruit of life! Only if the state of innocence lasted only a few instants could one wonder whether Adam and

---

64. Ibid., p. 56 (Book 1, ch. 4, §20).

65. 'Doctrine of Covenant', p. 245.

66. *Man: The Image of God* (Grand Rapids: Eerdmans, 1962), p. 345.

67. *Biblical Theology: Old and New Testaments* (Grand Rapids: Eerdmans, 1948), p. 38.

Eve had actually eaten, but Witsius refutes this groundless opinion of some rabbis.[68]

Witsius himself, who never tires of seeking a biblical warrant for his propositions, offers another argument:

> That man was not yet arrived at the utmost pitch of happiness, but to expect a still greater good after his course of obedience was over. This was hinted by the prohibition of the most delightful tree, whose fruit, as any other, was greatly to be desired; and this argued some degree of imperfection in that state, in which man was forbid the enjoyment of some good.[69]

Ascribing imperfection to the Garden of Delight and the *tôb mĕ'ōd* completion of God's work (Gen. 1:31) is rather daring. But a more precise objection would be that the goodness of the forbidden tree (3:6), in the dramatic sequence of the narrative, is a *deceptive appearance* (just as the suggestion that man and woman lacked something, of which they were deprived by a niggardly God, is the *serpent's lie*). As the outcome showed, the banning from that tree was a protection, an expression of the goodness of God. Witsius, who did not study the meaning of the phrase 'knowing good and evil', with its idiomatic flavour and in its various Old Testament occurrences, missed the significance of the tree and its fruit.[70] If it is properly understood as the divine prerogative of determining good and evil, autonomy in the strongest sense,[71] it is no good for any human being. Playing at God, pretended independence, means self-destruction for a creature, suicide for the image-creature.

---

68. *Economy*, vol. 1, pp. 100–101 (Book 1, ch. 7, §§20–21).

69. Ibid., p. 45 (Book 2, ch. 3, §21).

70. Ibid., pp. 88–89 (Book 2, ch. 6, §§16ff.), a woefully inadequate explanation, through the weaknesses in method indicated above (p. 112, ch. 8, §7, he suggests that the Serpent perverted the meaning of the name). Analogous criticisms apply to G. Vos's treatment, *Biblical Theology*, pp. 39–43.

71. McGowan, 'In Defence', p. 192, offers a clear summary of this view; on pp. 193ff., he combines it with D. Bonhoeffer's proposition (in his *Ethics*, ed. Eberhard Bethge, tr. N. Horton Smith [London: SCM, 1955]), so understood as to converge with C. Van Til's (p. 195); I am slightly less optimistic about Bonhoeffer's meaning: the forbidden knowledge, for him, is not only false autonomy, but (I feel) also moral deliberation per se, trying to apply set rules and principles – his aversion to moral deliberation has Lutheran and Barthian roots.

How were the brightest luminaries in the Reformed tradition misled on the issue? It reminds us all of our fallibility. Three factors may have played a part. The natural (seductive) wish of human reason to explain how evil arose generates hypotheses of some weakness, imperfection, an imperceptible crack in the original state. A measure of Platonism and the correlative deval-uation of the bodily and earthly makes it hard to imagine that Eden was intended to be the final stage in God's purpose.[72] Too literal a reading of the narrative focuses on the tree (or fruit) itself, and it looks so irrational that a simple act of eating should have cast the whole of humankind into unspeak-able tragedy that the trial or test hypothesis is invented to inject some ration-ality into the story; but if one reads Genesis 2 – 3 in a way attuned to its literary genre, the fruit is identified as the symbol of independence, claimed vis-à-vis God, making oneself into a god – and the dreadful consequence is understood.

Obviously, questions of the type 'What would have happened had human-kind remained obedient?' swim in the dangerous waters of unreality, whether another stage is affirmed or denied: before the foundation of the world, God had decreed both the fall and our redemption in Christ! But it is more sober not to imagine what the text does not say.

If unwarranted speculations of a 'probationary' character are left aside, all ambiguity is swept away: the benefits of the Eden covenant are purely gratu-itous; the condition (unfailing ratification of one's image-creature dependence on God) is nothing else than continuation in that grace.[73]

It must be noted, however, that the legal principle 'He who does these things shall live in them' and 'He who does not shall die' is strictly in force. This is no legalism! Life is no reward given after works have been done, it is first a gift of grace. Yet, it is responsibility. The creational covenant establishes the regime of human responsibility *coram Deo* (before God).

The clarification of the character of the creational covenant and dismissal of the probationary hypothesis disposes of an unfortunate refinement of Witsius's: his claim that the covenant was not only violated by man but abrogated by God.[74]

---

72. This motif is definitely present in Witsius; e.g. vol. 1, pp. 56, 60 (Book 1, ch. 4, §20, 'a more spiritual state' was in view; ch. 5, §3).

73. Ibid., p. 31 (Book 1, ch. 2, §8) speaks of 'salvation', though not of 'redemption', in this respect. With salvation as, generally, the gift of well-being (a meaning of Greek *sōtēria*), this would be acceptable. I fear, however, that he uses the word more strongly, in close combination with the 'probationary' theory.

74. *Economy*, vol. 1, pp. 131–132 (Book 1, ch. 9, §§18–19).

His proposition, though not entirely unambiguous,[75] focuses on the divine declaration that eternal life can no longer be attained by works (Gal. 3:21; Rom. 8:3).
Apart from the fact that this is rather the application of the Eden clauses than
their abrogation ('You shall die'), Witsius's meaning depends on his idea of
eternal life, as distinct from the life Adam enjoyed and was offered as a future
reward for obedience – and this we may leave aside. Probably, the difficulty is
linked, somehow, with the awkward suggestion that 'Adam ceased to be a federal
head when the covenant was once broken'.[76] On the contrary, the implication of
the apostle's word is that the covenant remains the frame of reference for all
those who are born of Adam, and his headship the basis on which their sins are
imputed: 'in Adam all die' (1 Cor. 15:22).

When sin is in the world, *all the new arrangements made by God express his gracious redemptive purpose and, in the last analysis, are subordinate to the covenant of grace
in Jesus Christ.*

This covenant is concluded in Jesus Christ, its Mediator, as the New Adam,
with all who are 'in him' (under him and united with him, their Head). It
involves the justification of whoever believes in him, by virtue of his substitution, as the Head of his own, which is why Jesus spoke of 'the new covenant
in My blood'(Luke 22:20). There has never been any share in life and access to
fellowship with God apart from incorporation into this covenant; this was true
of believers (who received life and walked with God) in ancient dispensations,
Abel, Noah, Abraham, David – all who constituted the remnant according to
the election of grace.

There is no need to elaborate, since practically all who stand in the tradition
of Reformed theology so confess. Some diversity of opinion could obtain on
the precise role of Abraham: Pierre Marcel, for instance, so emphasizes Genesis
15:1–18 and talks of 'the covenant concluded with Abraham' that Abraham
appears as *the* partner, in the name of humankind.[77] The patriarch's stature as
the 'father' of believers does not appear to warrant such a 'headship' role; the
presence of redeemed believers before his time and the symmetry in the two-
creations, two-Adams, scheme lead to a preference for reference to Christ.[78]

---

75. Ibid., vol. 2, p. 409 (Book 4, ch. 15, §17) he writes, 'the covenant of works, which in
    regard to all believers, is abrogated, by the introduction of the covenant of grace'. If
    the abrogation is only for believers, I heartily subscribe to it!
76. Ibid., vol. 1, p. 124 (Book 1, ch. 8, §35).
77. 'Le Baptême', pp. 48–49; but he does discern the covenant of grace in Gen. 3:15
    (p. 48).
78. Berkhof, *Systematic Theology*, p. 273, offers the following summary: 'Reformed

Since the covenant of grace is founded on a precise historical event (the cross of Calvary), since it is concluded in Jesus Christ the incarnate Son, believers in previous ages could share in its benefits only proleptically. Abel, Abraham, David were able only to taste the 'good things' (Heb. 9:11) Christ was going to secure *in* advance. As Robertson observes, 'Only in anticipation of the finished work of Christ could an act of heart-renewal be performed under the provisions of the old covenant.'[79] Calvin, following Augustine, affirms that all the regenerate, from the beginning of the world, belong to the New Testament.[80]

The value and validity of temporal sequence in Scripture, before/after, precludes an abstract symmetry in the application of the benefits of the cross BC and AD. Theologians who tend to eternalize (or detemporalize) the sacrifice of Christ,[81] easily imagine its effects to be the same in anterior and posterior times, but biblical writers think differently: they represent sins that God had forgiven under the Old Testament, but which had not been objectively done away with by the sacrifice of goats and bulls, as 'stored' somewhere and waiting for the true atonement to be made: [82] Hebrews 9:15, Romans 3:25 (*paresis*, God had left them unpunished, in an apparent denial of his justice). With such a sense of

---

theologians are not unanimous in answering this question. Some simply say that God made the covenant with the sinner, but this suggests no limitation whatsoever, and therefore does not satisfy. Others assert that He established it with Abraham and his seed, that is his natural, but especially his spiritual, descendants; or, put in a more general form, with believers and their seed. The great majority of them, however, maintain that He entered into covenant relationship with the elect or the elect sinner in Christ.' Berkhof, pp. 282–283, presents Christ as the Mediator of the covenant (*mesitēs, engyos*).

79. *Christ of the Covenants*, p. 292; he relies on Calvin, whom he quotes (from his commentary of *Jeremiah's Lamentations*): 'The power, then, to penetrate into the heart was not inherent in the law, but it was a benefit transferred to the law from the gospel.'

80. *Institutes* 2.11.10: 'tous les fidèles qui ont esté régénérez de Dieu dès le commencement du monde, et ont suyvi sa volonté en foy et en charité, appartienent au nouveau Testament': 'pertinere ab initio mundi ad novum testamentum filios promissionis, regeneratos a Deo, qui fide per dilectionem operante, obedierunt mandatis'.

81. They often rely on a mistaken exegesis of Rev. 13:8: they bind 'from the foundation of the world' to the verbal form 'slain', whereas it should be bound to 'written', as the parallel passage 17:8 shows (and the regular use of Scripture confirms).

82. Storing up until judgment is a metaphor used in Hos. 13:12 (Deut. 32:34; Job 14:17; Rom. 2:5); it points to the objective character of guilt, which requires punishment as a debt requires payment.

successive time, the proleptic character of the experience of grace before the coming of Christ called for a concrete marking. Enjoyment in advance could not be full and free, as full and free as it is in the Christian era.

Reformed theologians generally recognized this inferiority. Calvin insisted on the lack of clarity (only sparks in Abraham's time) and subsequent increase in light and knowledge.[83] Witsius insisted on the burden of rites and the bondage to the elements of the world (a phrase that impressed him, as it should);[84] and on the scantier dispensation of the Spirit and of his gifts.[85] Abraham Kuyper brought forward a most interesting scheme, which gives precise contours to the 'not yet' of the Old Testament. It centres on the idea that the elect and regenerate are only constituted a *body* by the fulfilment of Christ's mission in the flesh, and that it was the condition of the promised 'baptism in the Holy Spirit'. He wrote:

> This special union of the elect did not exist among Israel, nor could it exist during their time. There was a union of love, but not a spiritual and vital fellowship that sprang from the root of life. This spiritual union of the elect was made possible only by the incarnation of the Son of God.[86]
>
> Formerly isolation, every man for himself; now organic union of all the members under the one Head: this is the difference between the days before and after Pentecost. The essential fact of Pentecost consisted in this, that on that day the Holy Spirit entered for the first time into the organic body of the Church, and individuals came to drink, not each by himself, but all together in organic union.[87]

This entails a new inwardness: the Holy Spirit works on Christians 'from *within*'.[88]

---

83. *Institutes* 2.10.20 and 11.10.

84. *Economy*, vol. 2, pp. 364–365 (like a veil), 366ff. (Book 4, ch. 13, §§6–7, 10ff.); cf. pp. 410–411 (ch. 15, §§18–19).

85. Ibid., pp. 371–372 (Book 4, ch. 13, §22); cf. pp. 388 (ch. 14, §21, 'a more plentiful unction of the Spirit' in the New Testament), p. 404 (ch. 15, §2, 'A more abundant and delightful measure of the Spirit').

86. *The Work of the Holy Spirit*, tr. Henri De Vries (Grand Rapids: Eerdmans, 1956, repr. of 1900 Funk and Wagnalls edition), p. 120 (original Dutch published as a book in 1888, after instalments in *De Heraut*).

87. Ibid., p. 124 (and this is what the Bible calls baptizing with the Spirit).

88. Ibid., p. 573: 'In fact, His [the Holy Spirit's] work in the souls of men is as old as the generation of the elect, and originates in Paradise. But to the saints under the old

Though Kuyper's explanation of the reasons for such an arrangement are not always clear and convincing, one may be grateful for a deep insight in the difference between the old and the new economies. It achieves a better balance of continuity and discontinuity. In this light, one understands that the covenant of grace, although it was open in advance to Abel, Seth, Noah and so on, should be called the *new* covenant. It really dates from the days of Jesus Christ: its ground then became actual, and so fully operational.

Before the coming of Jesus Christ, God's action did not limit itself to allowing his elect to connect themselves, in advance, with the covenant of grace; he also made temporary arrangements to regulate his relationships with them, and to prepare the coming of his Son. These may be called 'the covenants' (Rom. 9:4).

The covenantal arrangements, of necessity, involve complexity – a basic duality: they are subservient to the already of the anticipatory enjoyment of new covenant goods, among the elect and believers; but they must show the not yet of a merely preparatory dispensation – lest anyone forget that the fulfilment, the decisive work of salvation, was still future. Lack of appreciation of this complexity has (mis)led scholars into overly continuous or overly discontinuous readings of the evidence.

Arrangements that openly refer to the future can safely highlight the 'already' element. The danger would be, when the availability of free justification and heart-renewal (circumcision) is proclaimed, that people imagine that they have reached the goal, that God's word of grace in their present is his final word; if the theme is coupled with an explicit stress on the blessing, deliverance, king and kingdom, still to come, the danger (in principle) is averted.

This is, typically, the regime of promise. Abraham gazed upon the day of Christ, a future that contrasted with the conditions of his present, and it is revealed that he already received the blessing of that day – 'he believed in the LORD; and He reckoned it to him as righteousness' (Gen. 15:6, 'as' added by the translators).

Conversely, arrangements that refer primarily to their own times must bear the obvious 'not yet' mark. They must appear different from the covenant of grace fully

---

covenant this operation came from *without*; while now, being freed from the fetters of Israel, the body of the Church itself becomes the bearer of the Holy Spirit, who descends upon it, dwells within it, and thus works upon its members from *within*.'
On the differences between economies with respect to the work of the Spirit, see further the brilliant synthesis by Sylvain Romerowski, *L'Oeuvre L'Oeuvre du Saint-Esprit dans l'histoire du salut*, coll. Théologie biblique (Cléon-d'Andran: Excelsis, and Nogent-sur-Marne: Editions de l'Institut Biblique, 2005).

established – precisely, to cause the people to look ahead, to expect from God new gifts and rules in the future.

This is, typically, the regime of the law. Moses had to define how Israel was to live and to worship, in the desert and in the land. The body of the Mosaic *tôrâ* does not look like the New Testament teachings and guidelines! The dissimilarity was required to ward off any confusion, any illusion that God had fulfilled his purpose at Sinai and given his people the true 'rest' (*sabbatismos*, Heb. 4:9) with the ensuing conquest of Canaan. Moses, although he had been allowed to behold the revelation of grace and truth (Exod. 34:6), should not be mistaken for the One who brings grace and truth to us (John 1:17). Hence the name *old covenant*, which is not devoid of inferior connotations (Heb. 8:7, 13); hence, Paul's antitheses.

Jüngel expressed a perception not far removed from this sketch when he suggested that the promise is, in the past, the *Zuvor* of the gospel, whereas the law is to be considered as the *Vorher* of the same.[89] Both *Zuvor* and *Vorher* convey the idea of 'coming before' (dictionaries may give the equivalent for both), but *Zuvor* seems to intimate a movement towards the future, and *Vorher* a fixed point in the past from which the distance is measured. James W. Leitch offers the following translation of Jüngel's key passage:

> Since the promise has its future in the gospel and has its own time because of this future, I call the mode in which the promise belongs to the past as compared with the gospel the *anticipation* of the gospel (*das Zuvor des Evangeliums*). Because the law has its end in the gospel and is made past because of this end, I call the mode in which the law belongs to the past as compared with the gospel *the antecedent* of the gospel (*das Vorher des Evangeliums*).[90]

'Anticipation' evokes a qualitative kinship, which 'antecedent' does not.

Complexity still characterizes the arrangements made with Abraham (no pure promise) and Moses (no mere law). A legal appendage is added to the promise to regulate Abraham's life before God (and that of his house and descendants): with sacrifices, and circumcision (John 7:22, as quoted above). In Moses' *tôrâ*,

---

89. 'Das Gesetz', p. 45; a further refinement, p. 46, is that the promise is the *Vorher* of the law.

90. In his translation of Jürgen Moltmann, *Theology of Hope: On the Ground and the Implications of a Christian Eschatology* (New York: Harper & Row, 1967), p. 153, n. 2, translating Moltmann's quotation from Jüngel. I was led to Jüngel's article by this footnote.

especially in its 'second' reading (Deuteronomy), the promise is also present: far from being cancelled or forgotten, it is the basis for the Exodus deliverance and, next, for the conquest of Israel's inheritance, as sworn to Abraham (Deut. 7:8); it is renewed with the suggestion that a new Moses is to come (Deut. 18:15, 18); it gives rise to statements, as we saw, where Paul finds a formulation of the righteousness of faith, as opposed to works (Deut. 9:4 and 30:11ff., explained in Rom. 10:6ff.).

The duality is so significant that Paul can speak of *two covenants* in Abraham's case, represented by Sarah and Hagar. Charles Hodge himself was able, at least once, to give a remarkable account of this arrangement – he was opposing the 'fallacy' of the Roman Catholic argument, which 'lies in the false assumption, that the external Israel was the true Church', but also realized the opinion is not found among Roman Catholics only: he was 'sorry to say [it] is the argument of some Protestants, and even of some Presbyterians'.[91] Hodge draws clear lines:

It is to be remembered that there were two covenants made with Abraham. By the one, his natural descendants through Isaac were constituted a commonwealth, an external, visible community. By the other, his spiritual descendants were constituted a Church. The parties of the former covenant were God and the nation; to the other, God and his true people. The promises of the national covenant were national blessings; the promises of the spiritual covenant (*i.e.* of the covenant of grace) were spiritual blessings, reconciliation, holiness, and eternal life. The conditions of the one covenant were circumcision and obedience to the law; the condition of the latter was, is, and ever has been, faith in the Messiah as the seed of the woman, the Son of God, and the Saviour of the world. There cannot be a greater mistake than to confound the national covenant with the covenant of grace, and the commonwealth founded on the one with the Church founded on the other.

When Christ came 'the commonwealth' was abolished, and there was nothing put in its place. The Church remained.[92]

This perspective, which espouses the language of Scripture, provides a solution to the problem Ishmael poses for many versions of covenant theology.

---

91. 'Visibility of the Church (art.VI)', *Biblical Repertory and Princeton Review* 25.4 (October 1853), p. 683. I was led to this article by the quotation made in G. S. Harrison, 'The Covenant, Baptism and Children', *Tyndale House Bulletin* 9 (October 1961), pp. 10–11.

92. Ibid., p. 684.

Genesis 17 reports that Abraham circumcised Ishmael, in clear obedience to God's word (vv. 23ff.), while he had been told that God would not establish his covenant with Hagar's son (vv. 18–21, esp. 21): how can one reconcile the fact with the proposition that circumcision sealed the promises of the covenant of grace to the one circumcised? The usual rationale for circumcising the non-elect among the children born 'according to the flesh' is based upon our ignorance of God's secret election: all children must be presumed to be among the elect, or, at least, must be offered the grace of the covenant; but this does not apply to Ishmael! If we distinguish the temporary external covenant from the covenant of grace itself, an adequate solution emerges: the administration of circumcision belonged to the former, which included Ishmael and Abraham's slaves (Gen. 17:27). This does not deprive circumcision of its spiritual significance: the external 'Hagar' covenant was appended to the covenant of grace and subservient to it; it was also typical, and, so, signified heart renewal and called for heart renewal.[93]

As noted by David Kingdon,[94] Calvin, as he deals with Genesis 17:7 in relationship with Romans 9:8, also acknowledges the key covenant-duality – though his wording has proved misleading to many. He maintains that the covenant was made with all natural descendants but immediately introduces, to solve the difficulties that arise, 'distinct degrees of adoption'.[95] For all he claims membership in the 'church' (contrary to Hodge's choice), the titles 'sons of God' and 'heirs of eternal life', and can say that God 'conferred' his grace to them.[96] But this is meant only of the lower degree of adoption: an outward one, in which the external word only offers the benefits of grace – and this to no avail in the case of the non-elect.[97] Those in whom faith does

---

93. The consideration of Ishmael's case (and of the sons of Keturah) was marshalled by Jewett, *Infant Baptism*, pp. 99–101. Oral tradition, as I received it, tells that it was decisive for young Jewett when a doctoral student at Westminster Theological Seminary: he found in it the way to loosen the grip of John Murray's arguments.

94. *Children of Abraham*, p. 47.

95. *Commentary on Genesis*, *Calvini Opera*, 23.237: 'cum filiis Abrahae, qui naturaliter ex eo gignendi erant', 'ceux qui devaient être naturellement engendrés de lui': 'distinctos adoptionis gradus', 'des degrés d'adoption déterminés et distincts'.

96. Ibid., 237: 'omnes Israelitas domesticos fuisse ecclesiae et Dei filios, et vitae aeternae haeredes': 238: 'Deus suam gratiam tam reprobis quam electis conferebat', 'Dieu conférait sa grâce tant aux réprouvés qu'aux élus'.

97. Ibid., 238: grace (as already quoted above, n. 41) that is said to be conferred is 'externo verbo', 'in ea non potest *oblatam* fuisse omnibus aeternam salutem'; it is a

not meet the promise are not counted as sons of God 'in God's secret sanctuary'; Calvin even labels them spurious children.[98] This offsets the rhetorical effect of giving the most glorious titles to all – it shows some awareness of the duality Hodge has stressed. Furthermore, Calvin realizes that this regime was changed by Christ's first advent, and the 'natural sons were disinherited';[99] logically, this could mean the end of the external, lower, degree of adoption (Hodge's external commonwealth), though Calvin did not openly draw the consequence.[100]

Hodge may have borrowed the phrase 'national covenant' from Witsius! Our learned Dutch divine did not develop the duality scheme from the time of Abraham, but carefully distinguished the Sinai 'agreement' from the, or a, covenant of grace: it was 'a consequent both of the covenant of grace and of works; but was formally neither the one nor the other': 'What was it then? It was a *national covenant* between God and Israel.'[101] He delineates the relationship to the covenant of grace:

> As the covenant of grace, under which the ancients were, is not to be confounded with, so neither is it to be separated from, the Sinaitic covenant: neither are we to think that believers were without all these things, which were not promised by the Sinaitic covenant, and which the typical covenant, because of its weakness and

---

matter 'de oblata *extrinsecus* gratia', not 'de ea quam efficaciter *soli* electi percipiunt': 'la parole extérieure', 'l'on ne saurait nier que le salut éternel n'ait été *offert* en elle', 'la grâce qui est *offerte extérieurement*', not 'celle que les *seuls* élus reçoivent avec efficacité' (my italics, of course).

98. Ibid., 238: 'in arcani Dei sacrario non alii censentur Dei filii quam in quibus fide rata est promissio', 'quant au sanctuaire de Dieu qui nous est caché, ne sont réputés enfants de Dieu que ceux pour lesquels la promesse est ratifiée': 'ideo fidei et infidelitatis nota veros filios a spuriis discernimus', 'la foi et l'infidélité sont les droites marques par lesquelles nous distinguons les vrais enfants d'avec les bâtards'.

99. Ibid., 239: 'exhaeredatis naturalibus filiis': strangely enough, the French version says the opposite, contrary to the flow of thought, so certainly by mistake and oversight (at least in the edition I used, with the spelling and even wording modernized, ed. André Malet [Geneva: Labor & Fides, 1961], here p. 261, 'les enfants selon la nature étant à la fin héritiers'.).

100. Neither did he draw any implication for Ishmael's case (he jumps over the difficulty).

101. *Economy*, vol. 2, pp. 190–191 (Book 4, ch. 4, §54).

unprofitableness, could not bestow; as they were likewise partakers of the Abrahamic covenant, which was a pure covenant of grace: and hence were derived the spiritual and saving benefits of the Israelites.[102]

Witsius chooses to ignore the duality at Abraham's stage ('pure covenant of grace')[103] but offers a fine account of the data concerning Moses'. The model this chapter has been sketching is not devoid of Reformed genealogical claims.

The 'not yet' character of arrangements made before Christ is chiefly marked in two ways: showing difference in 'principle' and in 'level'. This is most manifest where the 'not yet' is most conspicuous, the Mosaic covenant.

Ultimately, there can be only two 'principles' of justification or salvation: either a person can be saved (declared 'righteous' at God's judgment seat) because that person has perfectly obeyed the law, practised inward and outward righteousness, lived in love (essentially equivalent descriptions), or because a legitimate Substitute has fulfilled all that is required on her or his behalf. The covenant of grace, eternal and new covenant, is characterized by the latter principle; this is the reason why it is 'in the blood of Christ'. Hence, the only way for covenant arrangements to differentiate themselves with regard to principle from the covenant of grace is to incorporate a measure of the other principle: 'the man who obeys them will live by them' (Lev. 18:5). Since the same arrangements are subordinate to the covenant of grace, whose benefits believers already taste proleptically, a complex structure ensues, which is liable to misunderstanding.

Why the fire and thunder at Sinai? Witsius discerns that the awful signs and threatenings were given 'to display the nature of the law, which by

---

102. Ibid., 337 (ch. 12, §26).

103. Before Abraham, however, Witsius detects the duality at Noah's stage. Of the Noachic covenant, he writes, 'it was not formally and precisely the covenant of grace', yet it presupposed it and it was 'therefore an appendage of the covenant of grace with regard to the earthly promise' (vol. 2, pp. 242–243, Book 4, ch. 7, §§18–19). In favour of continuity in the series of 'arrangements' before Christ (and, therefore, of the recognition of a constitutional duality, I suggest), one can mention the exegetical contributions in the symposium Grant and Wilson, *The God of Covenant*, especially those from David L. Baker, 'Covenant: An Old Testament Study' (e.g. p. 25: 'the Mosaic covenant is a confirmation and elaboration of that made with Abraham, not something new or different': cf. p. 31) and James Hely Hutchinson, 'A New Covenant Slogan in the Old Testament' (e.g. p. 102).

demanding perfect obedience, and ... without any mixture of Gospel grace, leads to despair, and is to them "the ministry of death and condemnation," 2 Cor. iii.7,9'.[104] In the same passage, Witsius refers to the contrast made by Hebrews 12:18, 22 between the frightening, almost unbearable, presentation of the law (at Mount Sinai) and the welcoming presentation of the gospel to which we have come, which leads us to Mount Zion. This amounts, Witsius argues, to 'a repetition of the doctrine concerning the law of the covenant of works',[105] with even more terrible comminations.[106] Despite McGowan's criticism of such a proposition[107] (set in the context, it is true, of Kline's overall interpretation, not Witsius's nor mine), the idea does suit the biblical data Witsius adduces,[108] to which one can add Romans 2 and the essential equivalence of the law given Israel and the law written, from creation, in every heart. It is not so surprising if 'the carnal Israelites, not adverting to God's purpose or intention, as they ought, mistook the true meaning of that covenant, embraced it as a covenant of works, and by it sought for righteousness'.[109]

For such was not God's intention. The repetition of the principle of legal responsibility, which, in Eden, was the formula of life enduring in fellowship with God and, after sin, becomes that of inescapable condemnation, is only one element in the complexity of the Sinaitic arrangement. Witsius's words, again, encapsulate its function:

> The Israelites were ... thus put in mind of the covenant of works, in order to convince them of their sin and misery, to drive them out of themselves, to show them the necessity of a satisfaction, and to compel them to Christ. And so their being thus brought to a remembrance of the covenant of works tended to promote the covenant of grace.[110]

This logic corresponds to Paul's argument in Galatians 3 and Romans 1 – 4, and already to the mysterious necessity that the 'power [or resources, *yad*] of

---

104. Ibid., vol. 2, p. 174 (Book 4, ch. 4, §12).
105. Ibid., vol. 2, p. 187 (§47); cf. 188 (§48): 'a repetition of the covenant of works'.
106. Ibid.
107. 'In Defence of "Headship Theology"', pp. 186ff.
108. *Economy*, Lev. 18:5; Ezek. 20:11, 13; Rom. 10:5; Deut. 27:26; Gal. 3:10, 12; Deut. 29:4 [Heb. 3]; 2 Cor. 3:7, 9; Heb. 12:18–22.
109. Ibid., vol. 2, p. 189 (§52).
110. Ibid., p. 188 (§49); already, using the term 'law', vol. 2, p. 185 (§41).

the holy people be utterly broken' (Dan. 12:7), and cut off every human hope (Isa. 6:11–13). It spells out the 'not yet' in order to lead to Christ, and leads to Christ through the *pedagogy of failure* (see Gal. 3:24).

The complexity also included 'the repetition of some things belonging to the covenant of grace'.[111] Apart from the character of anticipation already dealt with, how was the 'not yet' apparent in elements that witnessed of divine (redemptive) grace? Since, in those elements, there was identity of principle, differentiation obtained through *a change of 'level'*. The level of the operations of the covenant of grace is, emphatically, inward and spiritual (scriptural proof is abundant; there is no need to rehearse it here). In the 'not yet' institutions, the principle of free grace is being displayed on the level of outward being, the 'flesh', as the word is used in the epistle to the Hebrews (7:16; 9:10,13; probably implicit in 10:20).

The great variety of *types*, which Witsius exploited with dazzling ingenuity,[112] with a possible centre in the sacrificial system, both expressed the 'not yet' (Israelites were to discern the inefficacy of the blood of bulls and goats for inward cleansing) and led to Christ, the spiritual antitype. It led to Christ through the *pedagogy of images*.

The Old Testament believer, within the complexity of the temporary covenants God made with his people, was first taught to despair of self, *coram Deo*, by the repetition of the principle of responsibility; second, thus and then to trust in God's mercy and future work of deliverance, as promised in prophecies and represented in typical institutions or events. Thus was he able to be *proëlpikōs en tō Christō* (Eph. 1:12). The typical institutions, especially, involved an external 'commonwealth' (to use Hodge's word), which was discontinued when the fullness of times arrived. Such a model, a revised covenant theology, appears to avoid the tensions that plague current forms, and to fit the biblical evidence better – it is able quite closely to espouse preliminary syntheses found in the Scriptures themselves (Gal. 4; Heb. 9, as already suggested).[113] It may

---

111. Ibid., p. 188 (§50).

112. Ibid., p. 196 (ch. 6, §8), he urges caution, but no abstinence – 'measure in all things': obviously, his measure is not the one accepted in present-day scholarship.

113. It is not possible here to unfold an exegesis of 2 Cor. 3:7–18, but let me indicate that I hold the duality structure of the Old Testament to be the key of Paul's midrash on Exod. 34: Moses already anticipates the freedom of the new covenant when he turns to the Lord – he enjoys a transforming fellowship with God *in the Spirit*, probably represented for Paul by the cloud-pillar – but his ministry in

contribute to the refinement and strengthening of Reformed theology – *semper reformanda.*

© Henri Blocher, 2006

---

relationship to the people is affected by the 'veil', the symbol of the 'not yet'. *We* enjoy Moses' spiritual privilege all the time.

8. UNION WITH CHRIST: SOME BIBLICAL AND THEOLOGICAL REFLECTIONS

Richard B. Gaffin, Jr

The doctrine of union with Christ has been given incisive and masterful expression by John Calvin at the beginning of Book 3 of his *Institutes of the Christian Religion* as well as in many places elsewhere throughout his commentaries and shorter writings. Subsequently, as a fair generalization, Reformed theology has certainly continued to have an appreciation of this doctrine, but at times has lost sight of its centrality and its full biblical dimensions. For instance, particularly within North American Presbyterianism from the nineteenth century to the present there has been a persisting tendency to view union with Christ as largely or even exclusively legal or representative in nature.

Against this background of relative neglect or narrowed understanding, among more recent efforts to rehabilitate this doctrine is John Murray's. His contribution lies in the way he highlighted and developed it, especially as he elaborated biblical teaching on it. This chapter, then, is a brief exercise, with an eye to his treatment and Calvin's, in pointing up the prominence and some of the implications in Scripture of union with Christ.[1]

---

1. The sketch that follows makes use of John Murray's chapter on union with Christ in his *Redemption Accomplished and Applied* (Grand Rapids: Eerdmans, 1955) and my student class notes from his 1960 lectures. Murray (1898–1975) taught systematic theology at Westminster Theological Seminary in Philadelphia from 1930 until he

Union with Christ

The expression 'union with Christ' does not occur in the Bible. But it fairly describes the central reality in the salvation revealed there, from its eternal design to its eschatological consummation. Human beings were created in God's image to live in fellowship, or covenant, with God, trusting his promises and obeying his commands, being loved and loving. Sin, however, destroyed this fellowship bond, this union, by rendering humanity guilty and corrupt, and so, alienated from God and deserving of death. In response to human sin, God, as Saviour, undertakes to restore and perfect the life and communion lost. This saving purpose, intimated already in Genesis 3:14–15, unfolds toward its fulfilment primarily in God's ongoing dealings with Israel as his covenant people, a bond expressed variously but perhaps most evocatively in the description of God himself as 'the portion' of his people (Pss. 73:26; 119:57; Jer. 10:16). Reciprocally, they are 'the LORD's portion' (Deut. 32:9).[2]

The climactic realization of this covenantal bond between the triune God and the church is union with Christ, specifically, the exalted Christ. This union finds its most prominent New Testament expression in the phrase 'in Christ' or 'in the Lord', with slight variations, occurring frequently and almost exclusively in Paul's letters (elsewhere, e.g., John 14:20; 15:4–7; 1 John 2:28). Scholarly debate about its meaning focuses on the Greek preposition (*en*) and ranges from a purely instrumental understanding to a local or atmospheric sense, and even the notion of an actual physical union between Christ and believers.

In fact, Paul's usage is varied, its scope best gauged by the contrast between Adam and Christ, as second/last Adam (Rom. 5:12–19; 1 Cor. 15:20–23; cf. vv. 45, 47). What each does is determinative, respectively, for those 'in him', as their representative. For those 'in Christ' this union or solidarity is all-encompassing, extending from eternity to eternity. They are united to Christ not only in their present possession of salvation but also in its past, once-for-all, accomplishment (e.g. Rom. 6:3–7; 8:1; Gal. 2:20; Eph. 2:5–6; Col. 3:1–4), in

---

retired in 1965. This chapter, slightly modified, is a lecture, 'John Murray on Union with Christ', the first annual John Murray Lecture at Highland Theological College, Scotland, 1 October 2004.

2. Noteworthy here is Isa. 53:12, with its anticipatory messianic reference and the final accomplishment of God's saving purposes in Christ: 'I will allot him a portion with the great / the many' (Bible quotations in this chapter are from the ESV).

their election 'before the creation of the world' (Eph. 1:4, 9), and in their still future glorification (Rom. 8:17; 1 Cor. 15:22).

Focusing now particularly on present union, in the actual appropriation or application of salvation, such union is what John Murray has in view in his chapter on it in *Redemption Accomplished and Applied*, and he dealt with it similarly in his class lecturing. Presupposing its continuing representative character, he treats it in terms of four other interrelated aspects, designated 'mystical', 'spiritual', 'vital' and 'indissoluble'.

Both 'mystical', the standard classical designation, and 'spiritual' are subject to misunderstanding. In view is not a mysticism of ecstatic experience at odds with or indifferent to reasoned understanding. Rather, union with Christ is a mystery in the New Testament sense of what has been hidden with God in his eternal purposes but now, finally, has been revealed in Christ, particularly in his death and resurrection, and is appropriated by faith (Rom. 16:25–26; Col. 1:26–27; 2:2). Certainly, in its full dimensions this mystery is beyond the believer's comprehension. Involved here, as much as in anything pertaining to salvation and the gospel, is the hallmark of all true theological understanding, that knowledge of Christ's love 'that surpasses knowledge', the knowledge of what is beyond all human knowing (Eph. 3:18–19; cf. 1 Cor. 2:9).

Ephesians 5:32 highlights the intimacy of this union ('a profound mystery') by comparing it to the relationship between husband and wife. Elsewhere in the New Testament other relational analogies picture this union: the foundation-cornerstone together with the other stones of a building (Eph. 2:19–22; 1 Pet. 2:5), a vine and its branches (John 15:1–7), the head and the other members of the human body (1 Cor. 12:12ff.), the genetic tie between Adam and his posterity (Rom. 5:12–19). But the climactic comparison is to the ontological union, the unique eternal oneness in being, between Father, Son and Spirit (John 17:20–23). Similarity is not identity, but especially this inner-trinitarian analogy shows that the highest kind of union that exists for an image-bearing creature is the union of the believer with the exalted Christ. 'But the greatest mystery of creaturely relations is the union of the people of God with Christ. And the mystery of it is attested by nothing more than this that it is compared to the union between the Father and the Son in the unity of the Godhead.'[3]

Mystical union is what it is because it is spiritual. This is so not in an immaterial, idealistic sense, but because of the activity and indwelling of the Holy Spirit. This circumscribes the mystery and protects against confusing it with

---

3. Murray, *Redemption Accomplished and Applied*, p. 209.

other kinds of union. As spiritual, that is, effected by the Holy Spirit, it is neither ontological, like that between the persons of the Trinity, nor hypostatic or unipersonal, like that between Christ's two natures, nor psychosomatic, like that between body and soul in human personality, nor somatic, like that between husband and wife; nor is it merely intellectual and moral, a unity in understanding, affections, purpose.

Spiritual union stems from the relationship between Christ and the Holy Spirit, given with his glorification and lying behind that union. Because of his resurrection and ascension, the incarnate Christ, 'the last Adam', has been so transformed by the Spirit and is now in such complete possession of the Spirit that he has become 'life-giving Spirit' and, as a result, 'the Lord [Christ] is the Spirit' (1 Cor. 15:45; 2 Cor. 3:17).[4]

In view in these statements of Paul is a functional equation, a oneness in the activity of giving resurrection life and eschatological freedom, so that in the life of the church and within believers, Christ and the Spirit are inseparable (cf. John 14:18). So, for instance, in the sequence in Romans 8:9–10, 'you ... in the Spirit' (9a), 'the Spirit ... in you' (9b), by implication 'you ... of Christ', equivalent to the much more frequent 'in Christ' (9d) and 'Christ ... in you' (10a) are not four separate realties but are all facets, in its fullness, of a single union. And in Ephesians 3:16–17, to have 'his Spirit in your inner being' is for 'Christ ... [to] dwell in your hearts'. As 'Spiritual',[5] then, mystical union has a reciprocal character. Not only are believers 'in Christ'; he is 'in them' (John 14:20; 17:23, 26), and for them: 'Christ in you' is 'the hope of glory' (Col. 1:27).

Accordingly, such union is also inherently vital. Christ indwelling by the Spirit is the very life of the believer: 'I no longer live, but Christ lives in me' (Gal. 2:20); 'your life is now hidden with Christ in God' (Col. 3:3). Finally, it is indissoluble, rooted as it is in the unconditional and immutable decree of divine election 'in [Christ] before the creation of the world' (Eph. 1:4). The salvation eternally purposed for believers 'in Christ' is infallibly certain of reaching its eschatological consummation in their resurrection-glorification 'in Christ.'

To summarize, according to Scripture, as Murray puts it, 'union with Christ is in itself a very broad and embracive subject'; it is the 'central truth of soter-

---

4. See my *Resurrection and Redemption: A Study in Paul's Soteriology* (Phillipsburg: P. & R., 1987), pp. 78–97; and '"Life-Giving Spirit": Probing the Center of Paul's Pneumatology', *Journal of the Evangelical Theological Society* 41.4 (December 1998), pp. 573–589, as well as the literature cited.

5. There is some value in capitalizing the adjective to keep clear that the work of the Holy Spirit, not some immaterial and merely internalized state of affairs, is in view.

iology, . . . not only in the application of salvation, but also in its eternal origin and its historical accomplishment'.[6] Accordingly, it promotes needed clarity in discussing union to make certain categorical distinctions, prompted by the biblical materials themselves. There is the *predestinarian* 'in Christ' (Eph. 1:4), the *redemptive-historical* 'in Christ', the union involved in the once-for-all accomplishment of salvation, and the *existential*, or perhaps better, *applicatory* 'in Christ', union in the actual possession or application of salvation.[7]

In making such distinctions it is important to keep in mind that they refer to different aspects of the same union, not different unions. At the same time, it is no less important to maintain each of them and to do so without equivocating on them, either by denying any one of them or blurring the distinction between them.

The *ordo salutis*

While, as we have noted, Murray recognizes that the scope of 'in Christ' is all-inclusive, he discusses union within his overall treatment of the application of redemption. In fact, only such applicatory or existential union is 'spiritual', 'mystical' and 'vital'. Those terms do not properly describe either predestinarian or redemptive-historical union, which may be designated 'representative' and involves our being reckoned 'in Christ', our being contemplated as united with him.

But now, in this regard, a problem emerges in Murray's treatment. He tells us, with sound biblical instinct, that union with Christ is not simply one step in the application of redemption. It is not just one link in the *ordo salutis* (order of salvation) he seeks to establish from Scripture. Rather, he says, it underlies every step in that *ordo*. But putting it that way gives rise to asking how, more exactly, union relates to the other elements in the application of redemption. Pointedly, where is the inception of this union to be placed or located in the *ordo salutis*? How is the event of the sinner being initially united to Christ to be sequenced with other acts, like justification and sanctification, in the *ordo* being presented?

Murray does not address this question, nor, as far as I can see, does what he says enable us to surmise what his answer would be. As an indication of this

---

6. *Redemption Accomplished and Applied*, p. 201; class notes.

7. See the parallel discussion of S. B. Ferguson, *The Holy Spirit* (Leicester: IVP, 1996), pp. 106–111, who distinguishes these three 'moments' of union as 'the eternal, the incarnational and the existential'.

uncertainty, in *Redemption Accomplished and Applied* (1955) the chapter on union is towards the end, just before the chapter on glorification and following chapters, in order, on effectual calling, regeneration, faith and repentance, justification, adoption, sanctification and perseverance. Five years later, however, in his classroom lectures, reflecting better biblical insight, union is treated at the beginning, between calling and regeneration. This ambiguity, present as well in treatments of the *ordo salutis by* others, prompts some further reflections on union with Christ and the *ordo salutis*. Here I shall first consider some pertinent material in Calvin and then, more briefly, from the Westminster Standards, followed by some conclusions.

Preliminary to doing that, however, a clarifying comment about the expression *ordo salutis* is advisable, perhaps even mandatory. As it has been employed, it can have two distinct senses, one more general, the other more elaborated. The latter, more detailed sense is the usual, more common usage. It has in view the logical and/or causal, or even temporal 'order' or sequence of various discrete saving acts and benefits, as these are unfolded within the actual life of the individual sinner.[8] However, the expression *ordo salutis* may also be used, without having yet settled on a particular 'order' or even that there is one in the sense just indicated. It may refer, more generally, simply to the ongoing application of salvation, in distinction from its once-for-all accomplishment, from what we may call, following Herman Ridderbos in coining a Latin counterpart, *historia salutis* (history of salvation).[9]

One must be alert to confusing or otherwise equivocating on these two senses of *ordo salutis*. Briefly here, while the sequential steps involved in the *ordo salutis* in the usual, technical sense may be debated at this or that point, the integrity of the gospel itself stands or falls with the *ordo salutis* broadly understood, equivalent to the application of salvation and distinct from its accomplishment. The distinction between redemption accomplished and applied is irreducible. Accordingly, the question of application, of the *ordo salutis* in the

---

8. If the secondary sources are correct, the first occurrence of *ordo salutis* is in this sense, in the eighteenth century within emerging pietism, from where it is taken over and eventually becomes widely current in both Lutheran and Reformed orthodoxy.

9. I have not found this distinction (*historia salutis – ordo salutis*) earlier than in his essay 'The Redemptive-Historical Character of Paul's Preaching', in *When the Time Had Fully Come* (Grand Rapids: Eerdmans, 1957), pp. 48, 49. It occurs repeatedly in his *Paul: An Outline of His Theology* (English tr.; Grand Rapids: Eerdmans, 1975), e.g. pp. 14, 45, 63, 91, 177 (n. 53), 205–206, 211, 214ff., 221–222, 268, 365, 378, 404.

more general sense, is unavoidable. Neither concern, with *historia salutis* or *ordo salutis*, may be allowed to diminish or eclipse the other.

The crucial question of the *ordo salutis*, then, is this, as it may be put variously: How does the 'then and there' of Christ's transition from being under God's wrath for sinners to being restored to his favour under conditions of (eschatological) life relate to the 'here and now' of the individual sinner's transition from wrath to grace? How do Christ's death and resurrection, then and there, benefit sinners, here and now? What are those benefits and what is the pattern (the *ordo*) in which they are communicated to sinners?

Calvin

I turn now to Calvin and do so for two closely related reasons.[10] In a most instructive and edifying way, unparalleled in the Reformed tradition, at least as far as I have seen, he shows the absolute necessity of *ordo salutis* / applicatory concerns. At the same time, he has led the way in pointing us toward an *ordo salutis* faithful to the *historia salutis*, toward an appropriation of salvation that honors the redemptive-historical structure and substance of Scripture, in particular, the *ordo salutis* we find in Paul.

Book 3 of his *Institutes of the Christian Religion* is entitled 'The Way in Which We Receive the Grace of Christ: What Benefits Come to Us from It, and What Effects Follow'. As this title plainly shows, Calvin understands himself to be concerned throughout Book 3 with the application of salvation ('the grace of Christ'), its 'benefits' and consequent 'effects', in their irreducible plurality and diversity as he will go on to show. All told, his concern is 'the way',[11] in which 'we' (believers) 'receive' this grace, in which this salvation is appropriated by 'us'. With this concern restated in the opening words of 3.1.1, the next sentence reads, 'First, we must understand that as long as Christ remains outside of us, and we are separated from him, all that he has suffered and done for the salvation of the human race remains useless and of no value to us.'

In my opinion, on the matter before us it would be difficult to find more important words written than these. Incisively and in a fundamental way, they

---

10. What follows here incorporates material from R. B. Gaffin, Jr, 'Biblical Theology and the Westminster Standards', *Westminster Theological Journal* 65 (2003), pp. 169–179.

11. The original Latin is not *ordo*, but *modus*: 'mode', 'manner', 'method'. All the citations from Calvin that follow here are from *Institutes* 3.1.1, tr. F. L. Battles, Library of Christian Classics 20 (Philadelphia: Westminster, 1960), vol. 1, pp. 537–538.

address both the necessity and nature of application, the basic concerns of the *ordo salutis*. So far as necessity is concerned, to put it somewhat provocatively and anachronistically with an eye to some current debates,[12] Calvin is saying something like, 'the redemptive-historical Christ, the Christ of redemptive history, as often conceived, is not enough'. In fact, that Christ, a *Christus*, who is only *extra nos*, 'outside us', is, in his own words, 'useless and of no value to us'! Certainly, this Christ, his death and resurrection, including his ascension and Pentecost, as the culmination of redemptive history, are the heart-core of the gospel. They are, as Paul says, 'of first importance' (1 Cor. 15:3). He and other New Testament writers make that abundantly clear. The controlling centrality of Christ's work is not at issue here.

But to punctuate the gospel, particularly its proclamation, with a full stop after Christ's death, resurrection and ascension, allowing for his future return, does not do the gospel full justice, as 'the power of God for the salvation *of everyone who believes*' and as that gospel involves the revelation of the righteousness of God 'from faith to faith' (Rom. 1:16–17). In fact, as Calvin intimates, that sort of parsing of the gospel misses an integral component, something absolutely essential. Or, as subsequent Reformed theology affirmed with aphoristic pointedness: 'Without application, redemption is not redemption.'[13]

The second sentence of Book 3 of the *Institutes*, quoted earlier, not only highlights the necessity of *ordo salutis* concerns but also their essence. The pivotal, absolutely crucial, consideration, the heart of the matter, put negatively as Calvin does here, is that Christ not remain 'outside us' (*extra nos*), that we not be 'separated from him' (*ab eo*). Or, expressed positively, as he presently does, that 'we grow into one body [*in unum*] with him'. Here Calvin has in view the union that exists between Christ and the believer, referred to repeatedly and in a variety of ways throughout Book 3 and elsewhere in his writings. This union he sees to be central and most decisive in the application of redemption.

It is essential to be clear about this union, about its nature and scope. Expressed in terms of the categorical distinctions, the need for which we noted earlier, the union of which Calvin speaks here is neither 'predestinarian' nor 'redemptive-historical'. Those aspects are surely not being denied, but they are in the background. Rather, in view is the union of application and

---

12. I have in mind some not always lucid ongoing discussions about 'redemptive-historical' preaching.

13. 'Dempta applicatione, redemptio non est redemptio'; quoted in H. Bavinck, *Gereformeerde Dogmatiek* (Kampen: Kok, 1976), vol. 3, p. 520.

actual appropriation, or as he immediately specifies, as it is 'obtained by faith' (*fide*), that is, union as it does not exist apart from or prior to faith but is given with faith, in fact is inseparable from faith. This is union that is 'spiritual' or 'mystical', as it has been categorized subsequently by Murray and others before him.

This mention of faith, and the key role accorded to it, immediately prompts Calvin to touch on what would become a central question in subsequent discussions about the *ordo salutis*, namely the origin of faith, giving rise eventually in Reformed theology to the doctrine of regeneration in a narrower sense. We observe 'that not all indiscriminately embrace that communion with Christ which is offered through the gospel'. Why is that? Not because of some differentiating factor on our side. The answer is not to be found by looking into ourselves or contemplating the mystery of human freedom and willing. Rather, consistent with his uniform teaching elsewhere about the total inability of the will due to sin, we must 'climb higher' and there consider 'the secret energy of the Spirit'. Faith, then, is Spirit-worked, sovereignly and efficaciously. The union Calvin has in view, then, is union forged by the Spirit's working faith in us, a faith that 'puts on' Christ (citing Gal. 3:27), that embraces Christ as he is offered to faith in the gospel. Faith is the bond of that union seen from our side. 'To sum up, the Holy Spirit is the bond by which Christ effectually unites us to himself.'

This, in a nutshell, is Calvin's *ordo salutis*: union with Christ by faith, Spirit-worked faith; being and continuing to be united with Christ by faith, faith that, through the power of the Spirit, 'embraces Christ, freely offered to us in the gospel'.[14] This *ordo* is as simple as it is profound and comprehensive, because in matters of application it keeps the focus squarely on *Christ*, specifically on Christ as crucified and resurrected, on Christ who is what he now is, as he has suffered and is now glorified. This is an *ordo* that does not lose sight of any of the various 'benefits' and 'effects' of salvation; nor does it blur the differences between them. However, it recognizes, as Calvin goes on to show, that, in all of their multiplicity, these benefits have their place only within union with *this* Christ, Christ presently exalted, only as they are its specific outworkings, the inseparable as well as mutually irreducible manifestations of this union. Here is an *ordo*, I take it, that captures, better than other proposals, the essence of 'the great eschatological *ordo salutis*'[15] taught in the New Testament, particularly the *ordo* taught by the apostle Paul.

---

14. The language of the Westminster Shorter Catechism, answer 31.

15. Adapting the language of Ridderbos, *Paul*, p. 200.

Post-Reformation developments

Developments beyond Calvin in subsequent, post-Reformation theology represent something of a shading of his outlook. Certainly, we must be on guard against overstating any differences here, and in the area of application important advances took place in developing specific doctrines of grace, most notably the doctrine of regeneration as it was formulated in Reformed theology in the aftermath of the emergence of Arminianism. But it does seem fair to observe that a prevailing tendency down to the present has been to be preoccupied with the various benefits of Christ's work and their interrelations, logical, causal and sometimes even temporal, *ordo salutis* in this sense. So that while Christ himself is certainly there, the danger is that, in matters of application, he fades, more or less, into the background. In effect, in some instances more than others, the focus has been, we may say, on *ordo* at the expense of *salutis*. Preoccupation with various acts of application in their logical/causal and even temporal sequence and interconnections has been such that salvation itself, in its wholeness, becomes eclipsed. In concentrating on the various benefits of Christ's work or on one particular benefit, like justification, he, in his person and work, recedes into the background.

What particularly needs to be noted in this development is that where to position union with Christ in the *ordo salutis* is and remains a conundrum. In fact, the better the biblical doctrine is understood, as in the work of Murray and Reformed theology generally, the more apparent it becomes that such union, mystical and spiritual, is an all-encompassing reality that resists being correlated as one benefit among others, like a single link in a chain.[16]

How do the Westminster Standards fit within this assessment of post-Reformation developments? I pose that question here not so much for their widespread normative role as subordinate standards in Presbyterian and Reformed churches since the seventeenth century but for their historical significance. Perhaps better than any other documents, they provide us with a

---

16. If I understand correctly, Lutheran theology, characteristically, sees no problem here, since union is regularly put after justification, as just one among others of its attendant benefits and is viewed variously as an 'effect' or 'fruit' or 'result' of justification; so, e. g., J. T. Mueller, *Christian Dogmatics* (St. Louis: Concordia, 1934), pp. 320, 381; F. Pieper, *Christian Dogmatics* (St. Louis: Concordia, 1951, 1953), vol. 2, pp. 410, 434, n. 65; vol. 3, p. 8, n. 9, p. 398; and H. Schmid, *The Doctrinal Theology of the Evangelical Lutheran Church*, 3rd edn (Minneapolis: Augsburg, 1961), pp. 481ff., 407–409, and the table of contents, p. 11.

window on what has proven to be the settled consensus down to the present of Reformed thinking on the matters they address.

Two observations are in order. First, in distinction from positions no doubt held by a number of the framers, the Standards themselves do not spell out a particular *ordo salutis* of causally concatenated acts or works of God in applying salvation. Within the bounds of what these standards do teach, an explicitly articulated *ordo salutis* is left an open question. Some semblance of an *ordo* might seem to be implied at points in the Confession (e.g. 3:6; 8:1) or by the sequence of pertinent chapters, and of questions and answers in the Catechisms. But a comparison of the three documents also reveals differences. The Standards do not provide a uniform sequence.

Second, such indications as the Standards do contain point to an outlook close to Calvin's. That can be seen most easily from two essentially parallel sections in the Larger and Shorter Catechisms. I make no claim for an exhaustive survey of the Standards here, although I hope not to have overlooked anything important or counter-indicative to the following observations.

At Question and Answer 58 the Larger Catechism begins to take up 'the application' of 'the benefits which Christ hath procured'. The questions immediately following (59–64) deal primarily with the visible/invisible church distinction and the 'special privileges' of those in the visible church. Question 65 then asks about the 'special benefits' of the invisible church (the elect) with this answer: 'The members of the invisible church by Christ enjoy union and communion with him in grace and glory.' This answer, in turn, structures the basic flow all the way through question and answer 90: union with Christ (66–68); communion in grace with Christ (69–81); communion in glory with Christ (82–90). Within the scope of the application of redemption to the elect, then, union and communion with Christ are seen as most basic, encompassing all other benefits.

Answer 66 speaks of this union as being 'joined to Christ', specifying it as effected 'spiritually and mystically, yet really and inseparably', and the next two answers, considering this union as the intended result of effectual calling, describe it as being 'draw[n] ... to Jesus Christ' (67) and as 'truly com[ing] to Jesus Christ' (68). Answer 69, then, in addressing 'the communion in grace which the members of the invisible church have with Christ', speaks of 'their justification, adoption, sanctification, and whatever else, in this life, *manifests their union with him*' (my emphasis).

Answer 69 is the most explicit assertion in the Westminster Standards relating union with Christ to *ordo salutis* issues as usually discussed. And, most notably, that union is not put in series with the other benefits mentioned, like one link in a chain. Rather, those other benefits 'manifest' being united with Christ. Those multiple benefits are in view as functions or aspects of union.

Shorter Catechism 29–32 is to the same effect, though less clearly. Answer 29 brings into view 'the effectual application' of redemption. Answer 30 is properly read as expressing that the essence of application, taking place in effectual calling, is the Spirit's 'working faith in us, and thereby uniting us to Christ', and answer 31 reinforces that this union ('to embrace Jesus Christ') is the goal of effectual calling.

Question and Answer 32 enumerate the present benefits of redemption applied, but are silent about union with Christ. This omission is somewhat surprising and certainly unlike its parallel in Larger Catechism 69. In light of the latter, as well as the immediate context of Question and Answer 32, an alternative and perhaps preferable wording, better expressing the framers actual intention, might be:

> Question 32: 'What benefits do they that are *united to Christ* [instead of: 'effectually called'] partake of in this life?
> Answer: 'They that are *united to Christ* do in this life partake of justification, adoption, and sanctification, and the several benefits which . . .'

Larger Catechism 69 and Shorter Catechism 32 also differ in perspective. In the former, as noted, justification, adoption, sanctification and whatever other blessings, all 'manifest' union with Christ. In the latter these other 'several benefits' are said to 'either accompany or flow from' justification, adoption and sanctification. Both perspectives are true, but that of the Larger Catechism is surely more basic and controlling.

We may conclude, then, that in the Westminster Standards the heart of the application of salvation, underlying all further consideration of *ordo salutis* questions, is being united to Christ by Sprit-worked faith. This union provides for multiple other confluent benefits, without any one benefit either being confused with or existing separately from the others. This is essentially Calvin's *ordo salutis*, though not as clearly expressed as it could be.

Strengths in Calvin's approach

Calvin's approach to *ordo salutis* issues, an approach, as just noted, provided for as well in the Westminster Standards, has multiple strengths. Here I can highlight just two that emerge as he deals with the application of redemption in Book 3 of the *Institutes*. Both have a bearing on an increasingly contentious issue at present, the doctrine of justification and its biblically faithful maintenance today.

First, the basic flow of Book 3 is noteworthy. Chapter 1, as already noted, introduces union with Christ by Spirit-created faith. Chapter 2 further treats faith, its 'definition' and 'properties'. Chapters 3–10 take up 'regeneration by faith' and the Christian life, 'regeneration' being used here in a broader sense, equivalent to sanctification in subsequent theology. Chapters 11–18 then focus on justification by faith, followed by chapters on Christian freedom, prayer, election and the final resurrection.

What is noteworthy here is how Calvin orders his discussion in Book 3. He first discusses the change that takes place *within* the sinner, our ongoing inner renewal and personal transformation, *before* discussing the definitive change effected in the sinner's legal status, our forensic standing *coram Deo*. He addresses the removal of the corrupting slavery of sin before considering the abolition of the guilt it incurs. All told, he treats sanctification, and that at some length, before justification. Such an approach contrasts conspicuously with subsequent Reformed and Lutheran theology, where justification always precedes sanctification. Exceptions to this generalization, if any, are rare, as far as I can see.

Why does Calvin proceed as he does? More importantly, what enables him to take this approach, without compromising or minimizing the Reformation doctrine of justification, but rather, in doing so, to provide one of the classic discussions of that doctrine? One can only admire what Calvin has achieved in structuring the first 18 chapters of Book 3 as he has. Here is a notable moment in the history of doctrine, a truly impressive 'theological coup'.

The constantly echoing charge from Rome at that time, and ever since, is that the Protestant doctrine of justification, of a graciously imputed righteousness received by faith alone, ministers spiritual slothfulness and indifference to holy living. Subsequent Reformed and Lutheran theology has responded to this charge by asserting, more or less adequately, that faith as the alone instrument of justification is never alone in the person justified but is a working, obedient faith, in the sense that it is 'ever accompanied with all other saving graces' (Westminster Confession, 11.2). But post-Reformation orthodoxy has also stressed the priority of justification to sanctification, especially against what is, in effect, Rome's reversal in basing and suspending justification on an ongoing process of sanctification.

Calvin's approach is different. He counters Rome's charge, masterfully and, in my opinion, much more effectively, by dwelling at great length (133 pages!) on the nature of faith, particularly its inherent disposition and concern for holiness, distinct from the issue of justification and before beginning to discuss justification. He concerns himself extensively with sanctification and faith in its sanctified expressions, largely bypassing justification and without having yet said virtually anything about the role of faith in justification. He has taken this approach, he says, in a transitional passage right at the beginning of chapter 11, the first on justification, because 'It was more to the point to understand first how little devoid of good works is the faith, through which alone we obtain free righteousness by the mercy of God.' Calvin destroys Rome's charge by showing that faith, in its Protestant understanding, entails a disposition to holiness without particular reference to justification, a concern for godliness that is not to be understood only as a consequence of justification.

Calvin proceeds as he does, and is free to do so, because for him the relative *ordo* or priority of justification and sanctification is indifferent theologically. Rather, what has controlling soteriological importance is the priority to both of union with Christ by faith. This bond is such that it provides both justification and sanctification, 'a double grace', as he frequently speaks of it, as each is distinct and essential. Because of this union, both, being reckoned righteous and being renewed in righteousness, are given without confusion, yet also without separation. To illustrate, Calvin uses a metaphor that seems hard to improve on (*Institutes* 3.11.6): Christ, our righteousness, is the Sun, justification, its light, sanctification, its heat. The Sun is at once the source of both, so that light and heat are inseparable. But only light illumines and only heat warms, not the reverse. Both are always present, without the one becoming the other.

Or, as he puts it elsewhere, Christ 'cannot be divided into pieces' (*Institutes* 3.16.1). We must not, he says on more than one occasion, 'rend Christ asunder', by envisioning a justification without sanctification.[17] There is no partial union with Christ, no sharing in only some of his benefits. If believers do not have the whole Christ, they have no Christ. Unless they share in all of his benefits they share in none of them. Justification and sanctification are inseparable not

---

17. E.g. those who 'shamefully rend Christ asunder' when 'they imagine that gratuitous righteousness is given by him, apart from newness of life' (*Commentaries on the Epistle of Paul the Apostle to the Romans*, tr. J. Owen [Grand Rapids: Eerdmans, 1948], p. 217). My thanks to Mark A. Garcia for pointing me to this and other places in Calvin where this expression occurs; in general on the place of union with Christ in Calvin's soteriology, see his 'Life in Christ: The Function of Union with Christ in the *Unio – Duplex Gratia* Structure of Calvin's Soteriology with Special Reference to the Relationship of Justification and Sanctification in Sixteenth-Century Context' (unpublished PhD dissertation, University of Edinburgh, 2004).

just because God has decided that, subsequent to forgiving sinners and extrinsic to that forgiveness, he will also renew them. Rather, the two are inseparable because of who Christ is and the nature of our union with him. Calvin calls justification 'the main hinge on which religion turns' (*Institutes* 3.11.1). But as 3.1.1 makes clear, it is that for him only as that hinge is firmly anchored, and religion pivots, within the believer's union with Christ.

Second and finally, some comment on the imputation of Christ's righteousness, particularly on the relation between union and imputation. I make two related observations, looking in different, in fact opposite, directions.

1. Prominent in Protestant, especially Lutheran, development of the doctrine of justification is the notion of Christ's imputed righteousness as an 'alien' righteousness. The righteousness that justifies is apart from us; it is not our own, of our own doing, but Christ's. At issue here is the concern, not only understandable but necessary, not to confuse Christ's righteousness, as the sole ground for justification, with anything, any change or transformation, that takes place within the sinner. The concern here, again, is not to obscure that justifying righteousness is perfect and complete, in what Christ has done, once for all, in his finished work, apart from anything the believer does or is done in the believer. In this sense, to speak of 'alien righteousness' is surely defensible, even helpful.

At the same time, however, we should recognize a definite liability that attaches to this expression. 'Alien' can suggest what is detached, at a distance. It can easily leave the impression of an isolated imputative act, remote from the believer and without a clear relationship to Christ and the other aspects of salvation. In this regard, I have the impression that some Reformed thinking on justification, past and present, at least practically or popularly, centres on a line, focused on the individual sinner, that moves from my eternal election to its realization and documentation in history by my faith, produced by regeneration, faith that then receives justification. With this view Christ and his work are surely essential but recede into the background, along with other aspects of salvation.

A different tone is heard in Calvin. In expressing himself on justification, including imputation, he always, explicitly or implicitly, relates it to union with Christ. Perhaps his most pointed and remarkable statement on imputation in this regard is the following:

> Therefore, that joining together of Head and members, that indwelling of Christ in our heart in short, that *mystical union* are accorded by us the highest degree of importance, so that Christ, having been made ours, makes us sharers with him in the gifts with which he has been endowed. *We do not, therefore, contemplate him outside ourselves*

from afar in order that his righteousness may be imputed to us but because we put on Christ and are
engrafted into his body in short, because he deigns to make us one with him. For this reason, we
glory that we have *fellowship of righteousness* with him.[18]

Here there is no mingling of Christ's righteousness with some presumed
righteousness of our own that supplements his. But, at the same time, that
righteousness, *as imputed,* is, in an absolutely crucial sense, anything but 'alien'.
Here imputation, realized in union with Christ, results in a 'fellowship of righteousness'. It is an imputed righteousness, which does not, indeed cannot, exist
apart from that union. Why? Because it is not an abstract entity but *his* righteousness that is imputed to me, reckoned as mine.

2. While there is no imputation without union or antecedent to union,
neither is there union without imputation. There are those, in the past and
presently, who, grasped by some understanding of union, conclude that union
excludes any notion of imputation or at least renders it unnecessary. As it has
been put recently, union 'makes imputation redundant'.[19]

I am unable here to enter in any detail into the reasoning that comes to
such a conclusion, only to say that it is troubling and, I judge, more disturbing to a biblically sound doctrine of justification than the view that ignores
or obscures union in maintaining imputation. Why more disturbing? Because,
as far as I can see, it leaves us unclear about what is absolutely essential to our
justification; namely, its ground or basis. Specifically, what is left unclear or
perhaps even being denied is Christ's own righteousness as the exclusive
ground, on which, solely, our hope of acquittal before the bar of God's
justice rests.

If it is excluded or deemed unnecessary that in justification Christ's righteousness, his finished righteousness, is imputed to sinners, then the ground of
their justification must lie elsewhere. If I understand correctly, what is being
proposed with this dismissal of imputation is that the ground is either the
union itself; that is, the fact of the relationship, the existence of the uniting
bond, itself. Or, alternatively, that ground is righteousness being produced in
me, as it flows from that union.

Suffice it to say here, the basis of my justification is not a relationship, no
matter how real and intimate. Nor is the basis a righteousness that results in

---

18. *Institutes* 3.11.10 (my emphasis).

19. R. Lusk, 'A Response to "The Biblical Plan of Salvation"', in E. C. Beisner, ed., *The
Auburn Avenue Theology, Pros and Cons: Debating the Federal Vision* (Fort Lauderdale:
Knox Theological Seminary, 2004), p. 142.

me from that union, no matter how otherwise important such Spirit-worked righteousness is, no matter how integral to the salvation received in Christ. Rather, that basis is Christ's own righteousness, established and completed in his obedience culminating in his death, which, in union with him, is imputed to me. Just as it is *his*, as distinct from any righteousness I might manifest, it is reckoned as *mine*.

Conclusion

Such compelling words as those of Calvin quoted above, with the balance they maintain, could only have been written, I dare say, by someone with the *ordo salutis* intimated in *Institutes* 3.1.1, someone who has also incisively anticipated subsequent insights, like those of John Murray, into the redemptive-historical substance of Scripture and the gospel, particularly the soteriology of the apostle Paul.

Calvin's words are no less timely today, when, perhaps as never before, the notion of imputed righteousness is either misunderstood or rejected. Only as we maintain imputation as a facet of what Calvin calls our 'fellowship of righteousness' with Christ, as an integral aspect of our union with Christ crucified and exalted, will we do so in a fashion that is fully cogent biblically. As added value, doing that will provide a much more effective response to the persisting misunderstanding of Roman Catholics and others that the Reformation doctrine of justification renders sanctification unnecessary. And it will also help those who would be heirs of the Reformation to keep clear to themselves something they have not always or uniformly appreciated; namely, how integral sanctification is, no less than justification, to the salvation accomplished and applied in Christ, involving as sanctification does the pursuit of that holiness, without which 'no-one will see the Lord' (Heb. 12:14).

In discussions about the *ordo salutis* no single passage has figured more prominently than Roman 8:29–30. What is noteworthy here is that, though the term is not explicit, sanctification is more ultimate than justification, strategically more ultimate we may say. For here the final goal of predestination, seen from the side of believers, is glorification (v. 30), in view, at least primarily, as being 'conformed to the image of his Son' (v. 29). That conformity, contemplated here in its full finality and perfection, is the culmination of the sanctification presently underway in the believer. Note in this regard especially 2 Corinthians 3:18: 'And we all, with unveiled face, beholding the glory of the Lord, are being transformed into the same image from one degree of glory to another'.

But this sanctification-glorification, this being conformed to Christ's glory-image, has an even more ultimate end: 'that he might be the firstborn among many brothers' (Rom. 8:29). That, too, is what is at stake in our union with Christ. The personally involved, intimately engaged stake he has in our sanctification, as well as our justification, is nothing less than his own ever-accruing glory in the midst of that brotherhood comprising those, as freely justified, who are also being conformed to his image. That, his all-surpassing glory being realized as he is the 'firstborn among many brothers', in union with them, that glory, as much as anything, ought to be our constant and controlling preoccupation in all matters that concern the *ordo salutis*.

9. JUSTIFICATION: THE ECUMENICAL, BIBLICAL AND THEOLOGICAL DIMENSIONS OF CURRENT DEBATES

Cornelis P. Venema

Perhaps at no time since the upheaval within the Western Christian Church that occurred in the sixteenth century has the doctrine of justification received the attention that it has garnered in recent decades. Though the respective views of justification within the Roman Catholic Church and Protestantism remained largely settled and widely divergent for several centuries, in recent decades the doctrine of justification has once more emerged as a focal point of discussion. The current debates regarding justification reflect a readiness to explore new perspectives that hold the promise for ecumenical convergence and even consensus. The importance of these contemporary discussions of justification can hardly be exaggerated. Not only does the subject of justification touch upon the central question of the nature of the gospel of Jesus Christ, but it also concerns a doctrinal issue that has been at the centre of the greatest disruption within the Christian church since the first century of the Christian era.

To sort out the contemporary state of theological discussion regarding justification is a daunting task. The literature on the subject is enormous and constantly growing. Furthermore, the subject of justification has tentacles that reach into virtually all other areas of Christian theology. The doctrine of justification can hardly be adequately understood without considering its connection with the doctrines of God, of sin, of Christ, of the church, and the like. Current debates on the subject of justification attest to this complex interrelationship between justification and other areas of Christian theology. Many of the debates regarding justification also require a measure of familiarity with the history of theology. Some recent proposals for a fresh understanding of justification appeal to a revisionist reading of the history of doctrine in the Reformation period, and argue that the traditional interpretation of the views of leading Reformers may be in error. For this reason, any contemporary consideration of the doctrine of justification demands a considerable measure of acquaintance with the history of theology since at least the sixteenth century. Other debates require some familiarity with the disciplines of exegesis and biblical theology. New approaches to an understanding of the apostle Paul's understanding of justification, for example, require an examination of the more recent history of Pauline studies. To sort through the thicket of these discussions demands a rare kind of interdisciplinary ability to cross the boundaries between exegesis, historical theology and constructive theology.

Due to the complexity of the subject, my aim in this chapter will have to be modest. Rather than attempting to sort out and resolve the various debates regarding justification, I shall be largely content to survey the state of recent discussion. To achieve my limited purpose, which is to summarize the state of contemporary theological discussion of justification, I shall begin with a short sketch of the classic form of the dispute regarding justification at the time of the Reformation. Here it will be my interest to provide a summary of the historic divergence between Protestantism and Roman Catholicism on the matter of justification. After sketching the classic dispute regarding justification, I shall consider two areas of special importance to contemporary discussion: the recent ecumenical discussions regarding justification, and the emergence of the so-called 'new perspective on Paul'. These are undoubtedly the two most significant developments with regard to the doctrine of justification in contemporary theological discussion. Then in the last section of this chapter, I shall offer a series of observations that identify key biblical and theological aspects of the doctrine of justification that continue to be disputed or require further exploration.

Historic Protestant and Catholic views

Before taking up the more recent debates on the subject of justification, I need to set the stage by summarizing the historic divergence between Protestant and Roman Catholic views. Though some recent studies have questioned traditional assumptions about the dispute over justification in the sixteenth century, any present-day reflection on justification must start from a clear understanding of the official consensus of these traditions regarding the doctrine of justification.[1] The proper setting for contemporary ecumenical discussion between Roman Catholics and Protestants is not the individual views of particular theologians, but the broad consensus of their church traditions. More important than the individual views of Protestant and Roman Catholic figures of this period are the ecclesiastical documents that set forth the official views of the churches. The following summary of the historic Protestant and Catholic views of justification, therefore, represents the broad consensus expressed in these traditional documents.

The nature of justification: forensic or transformative?

In the Protestant understanding of the gospel of Jesus Christ, justification is a benefit of Christ's saving work whose importance can hardly be overemphasized. The Lutheran tradition is well known for its insistence that justification is 'the article of the standing or the falling church' (*articulus stantis et cadentis ecclesiae*).[2] However, Calvin, who had the highest regard for Luther's rediscovery of

---

1. A striking example of a revisionist interpretation of Luther's view of justification is defended by the so-called 'Finnish' school. In the context of ecumenical dialogues with Eastern Orthodoxy, a number of Finnish Lutheran theologians have argued that Luther's understanding of justification was closer to the Eastern Orthodox doctrine of a 'deification' or a 'realistic' transformation of the believer than the forensic emphasis of Luther's successor, Melanchthon, whose view came to dominate traditional Lutheran confessional theology. For an introduction and evaluation of the Finnish interpretation, see Carl E. Braaten and Robert W. Jenson, eds., *Union with Christ: The New Finnish Interpretation of Luther* (Grand Rapids: Eerdmans, 1998); Carl R. Trueman, 'Is the Finnish Line a New Beginning? A Critical Assessment of the Reading of Luther Offered by the Helsinki Circle', *Westminster Theological Journal* 65.2 (autumn 2003), pp. 231–244; Paul Louis Metzger, 'Mystical Union with Christ: An Alternative to Blood Transfusions and Legal Fictions', *Westminster Theological Journal* 65.2 (autumn 2003), pp. 201–214; Mark A. Seifrid, 'Paul, Luther, and Justification in Gal. 2:15–21', *Westminster Theological Journal* 65.2 (autumn 2003), pp. 215–230; and Robert W. Jenson, 'Response to Seifrid, Trueman, and Metzger on Finnish Luther Research', *Westminster Theological Journal* 65.2 (autumn 2003), pp. 245–250.

2. Though this language is often attributed to Luther, it actually reflects the language of the *Smalcald Articles* (1537), an early Lutheran statement of faith that was later included among the Lutheran confessional documents with the *Formula of Concord* (1576). Article 2.1 states, 'On this article [Christ alone is our salvation] rests all that

the gospel of free justification, also insisted that this doctrine was 'the main hinge of the Christian religion'.[3] Because justification addresses the most basic religious question, namely, 'How do offending sinners find favour and acceptance with God?', it lies close to the heart of the saving message of the gospel.

The point of departure for the historic Protestant understanding of justification is the insistence that it is a *judicial or forensic declaration* by God, which pronounces God's acceptance of sinners for the sake of the work of Christ. Justification is *not a transformative process*, which makes sinful humans become righteous, but a free act of God's gracious judgment, which declares that believers are received into God's favour in spite of their inherent sinfulness. Justification is a legal declaration by God, which declares that the justified person is forgiven and regarded as righteous in the divine court or forum.[4] By

---

we teach and practice against the pope' (quoted from Theodore G. Tappert, ed., *The Book of Concord: The Confessions of the Evangelical Lutheran Church* [Philadelphia: Fortress, 1959], p. 292). Luther, however, used similar language in his *A Commentary on St. Paul's Epistles to the Galatians*, ed. P. S. Watson (Grand Rapids: Baker repr., 1979 [1891]), p. 143: '[justification is] the principal article of all Christian doctrine, which makes true Christians indeed'. References to the Lutheran confessions in the following will be to the translations in the volume edited by Tappert.

3. *Institutes* 3.11.1, ed. John T. McNeill (Philadelphia: Westminster, 1960). Calvin uses language similar to Luther's and the Lutheran tradition in a sermon on Luke 1:5–10: '[justification is] the principle of the whole doctrine of salvation and the foundation of all religion' (as cited by Francois Wendel, *Calvin* [London: Collins repr., 1963], p. 256). Though for Calvin justification was not the whole of the gospel – Calvin insisted that justified sinners were simultaneously sanctified by the grace of Christ's Spirit – it was no doubt the most pivotal feature of the good news of God's salvation in Christ.

4. Cf. the *Heidelberg Catechism*, a classic statement of the Reformed churches of the sixteenth century, which states that the primary benefit of faith in the Christian gospel is that believers are 'righteous in Christ before God' and therefore heirs of eternal life (Q. & A. [Question and Answer] 59). The question of justification answers how believers 'can stand before the tribunal of God' and be regarded as holy and innocent (Q. & A. 62). In the early seventeenth-century Westminster Larger Catechism, which provides an authoritative account of the teaching of the English-speaking Reformed churches, justification is defined as 'an act of God's free grace unto sinners, in which he pardoneth all their sins, accepteth and accounteth their persons righteous in his sight' (Q. & A. 70). Likewise, in the late sixteenth-century consensus statement of Lutherans, *The Formula of Concord*,

contrast, the traditional Roman Catholic view maintains that justification also includes a process of moral transformation equivalent to what, in evangelical parlance, is known as the work of sanctification. The historic dispute between Protestant and Roman Catholic can be focused, therefore, on the question 'Does justification declare someone to be righteous or acceptable to God, as the Reformers maintained?' Or, 'Does justification involve a process whereby someone is made to be righteous, as the Roman Catholic Church insists?' The Protestant view of justification emphasizes its *forensic* nature, and sharply distinguishes it from the work of regeneration and renewal by the working of the Holy Spirit. The Roman Catholic view virtually equates the whole process of salvation, which includes the forgiveness of sins as well as the process of moral and inward renewal in righteousness, with justification.

The basis of justification: imputed or infused righteousness

More decisive than the difference of views on the nature of justification is the divergence between Protestant and Roman Catholic views of the basis upon which believers are justified by God.[5] In the Protestant conception, justification is a gracious act, which is based wholly upon a righteousness that God grants or imputes (attributes) to believers. In the Roman Catholic teaching regarding justification, God justifies believers in part on the basis of their own righteousness. Because justification includes a process of moral renewal

---

justification is defined as God's act in Christ whereby he forgives the sins of his people and counts them righteous and acceptable to him: '[In justification] God forgives us our sins purely by his grace, without any preceding, present, or subsequent work, merit, or worthiness, and reckons to us the righteousness of Christ's obedience, on account of which righteousness we are accepted by God into grace and are regarded as righteous', Article 3 (Tappert, *Book of Concord*, p. 473). Unless otherwise indicated, quotations of the Reformed confessions are taken from the volume *Ecumenical Creeds and Reformed Confessions*, Classroom ed. (Orange City, Iowa: Mid-America Reformed Seminary, 1991).

5. While it may surprise some contemporary Protestants, even the Council of Trent, in its reply to the Reformation's doctrine of justification, acknowledged that justification includes a judicial declaration by God. For example, the Council of Trent defines justification in a way that includes God's act of declaring believers to be righteous: 'Not only are we *reputed* to be righteous, but we are *called* righteous, receiving justice within us' (*The Canons and Decrees of the Council of Trent*, Sixth Session, Decree on Justification, ch. 7; quoted from Philip Schaff, *The Creeds of Christendom* [Grand Rapids: Baker repr., 1985 (1931)], vol. 2, p. 95).

whereby believers are made righteous through the sacramental infusion of
grace, the righteousness that justifies believers is an 'inherent righteousness'
(*iustitia inhaerens*).[6] When God justifies believers, he does not do so solely upon
the basis of the merits of Christ, which are granted and imputed to believers
by grace, but partly upon the basis of the merits of believers.[7] The basis or
ground for justification includes those meritorious works of believers that are
the fruit of their cooperation with the grace of God communicated through
the sacraments (especially baptism, the Mass and Penance). Furthermore, the
justification of believers is, in the Catholic conception, maintained and
increased when believers perform good works by the grace of God. On the
other hand, if believers fail to persist in cooperation with God's grace and in
doing such good works, they risk the 'shipwreck' of faith and loss of their state
of grace before God. Thus, justification includes not only the initial introduction of believers into a state of grace, but also their continuation through personal holiness in this state of grace ('further justification').[8] The works of
believers, which are acknowledged to be prompted by the grace of God in
Christ, are an essential means whereby believers ultimately receive the fullness
of salvation in communion with God.[9]

---

6. See *Canons and Decrees of the Council of Trent*, Sixth Session, Decree on Justification,
   ch. 7: 'For, although no one can be just, but he to whom the merits of the Passion
   of our Lord Jesus Christ are communicated, yet is this done in the said justification
   of the impious, when by the merit of that same most holy Passion, *the charity of God
   is poured forth*, by the Holy Spirit, *in the hearts* of those that are justified, and is
   inherent therein [*atque ipsis inhaeret*]' (Schaff, *Creeds of Christendom*, vol. 2, pp. 95–96).
   Cf. *Catechism of the Catholic Church* (United States Catholic Conference; Liguori, Mo.:
   Liguori, 1994), par. 1992: 'Justification is conferred in Baptism, the sacrament of
   faith. It conforms us to the righteousness of God, who makes us inwardly just by
   the power of his mercy.'
7. For this reason, those who obey the commandments of God and of the church,
   'faith cooperating with good works, increase in that justice received through the
   grace of Christ and *are further justified*' (my emphasis; *Canons and Decrees of the Council
   of Trent*, Sixth Session, ch. 10; Schaff, *Creeds of Christendom*, vol. 2, p. 99).
8. *Canons and Decrees of the Council of Trent*, Sixth Session, chs. 10–16 (Schaff, *Creeds of
   Christendom*, vol. 2, pp. 99–110).
9. See *Canons and Decrees of the Council of Trent*, Sixth Session, ch. 16 (Schaff, *Creeds of
   Christendom*), vol. 2, p. 108, 'we must believe that nothing further is wanting to the
   justified, to prevent their being accounted to have, by those very works which have
   been done in God, fully satisfied the divine law according to the state of this

In their repudiation of this Roman Catholic understanding of the basis for the justification of believers, the Reformers insisted that the 'righteousness of God', which is revealed in the gospel (Rom. 1:17), is not a righteousness that demands obedience to the law, but a righteousness that is freely given to believers. The righteousness revealed in the gospel of Jesus Christ is a gift of a new status with God. By means of his suffering and cross, Christ suffered the curse of the law on behalf of his people (penal substitution). The righteousness of God that is demonstrated in the gospel, according to this reformational view, refers to the work of Christ in which he satisfies all of the claims of the law of God on behalf of his people.[10]

In order to preserve this difference between justification upon the basis of an imputed righteousness, the Reformers sharply distinguished between the law and the gospel. When distinguished from the gospel, the law of God refers

and to have truly merited eternal life'. Traditional Catholic theology distinguishes 'true merit' (*meritum de condigno*), which consists of those works performed by virtue of God's infused grace in the believer that justly deserve their reward; and 'half' or 'congruent merit' (*meritum de congruo*), which consists of those works performed by the believer's cooperation with the grace of God that receive a reward that is not strictly deserved. For a contemporary discussion of the subject of merit from a Roman Catholic perspective, see under 'Merit', *Sacramentum Mundi: An Encyclopedia of Theology*, ed. Karl Rahner (London: Search, 1969), vol. 4, pp. 11–14; and *Catechism of the Catholic Church*, paras. 2006–2011.

10. Cf. Louis Berkhof's definition of justification in his *Systematic Theology* (Grand Rapids: Eerdmans repr., 1939, 1941), p. 513: 'Justification is a judicial act of God, in which He declares, on the basis of the righteousness of Jesus Christ, that all the claims of the law are satisfied with respect to the sinner.' Traditional Reformed theology distinguished in this connection between the 'active' and 'passive' obedience of Christ. The purpose of this distinction was not to divide Christ's obedience into two chronological stages (the first being his earthly ministry, the second being his sacrificial death upon the cross) or even into two parts, but to distinguish two facets of the one obedience of Christ. Christ's active obedience refers to his life of conformity to the precepts of the law; Christ's passive obedience refers to his life of suffering under the penalty of the law, especially in his crucifixion (Rom. 5:12–21; Phil. 2:5ff.; Gal. 4:4). For traditional presentations of this distinction and its significance for justification, see Berkhof, *Systematic Theology*, pp. 379–382, 513ff.; Francis Turretin, *Institutes of Elenctic Theology* (Phillipsburg: P. & R., 1994), vol. 2, pp. 646–659; and James Buchanan, *The Doctrine of Justification* (Grand Rapids: Baker repr., 1955 (1867), pp. 314–338.

to the righteous requirements that God imposes upon human beings as his image bearers. Whether Jews, who received the law of God in written form through Moses, or Gentiles, who have the works of the law written upon their consciences, all human beings fail to live in perfect conformity to the law's demands (Rom. 2 – 3). By the standard of the perfect law of God, all human beings stand condemned and are worthy of death (Rom. 6:23). Though the law of God is good and holy, it can only require believers to do what they cannot do because of their sinfulness. The law, though it may promise life to those who perfectly do what it requires, can only actually condemn those who seek to be justified by its means. No-one can be justified by the works of the law because no-one actually does perfectly what the whole law requires. Only the righteousness of Christ can satisfy the requirements of God's law and thereby constitute the basis for the justification of believers.

Since the righteousness that is imputed to believers is not their own righteousness, but the righteousness of Christ, the Reformers also spoke of the justified person as *simul iustus et peccator*, 'at once just and a sinner'. This expression was a deliberately provocative one, since it called attention to the sharp difference between the Roman Catholic view that sinners are *made* righteous and the Reformation view that sinners are *declared* righteous in justification. By using this language, the Reformers intended to emphasize that what distinguishes the grace of free justification is that it involves the 'justification of the *ungodly*' (*iustificatio impii*; Rom. 4:5). Justification reveals the sheer grace of God who welcomes sinners in spite of their utter unworthiness. Full acceptance with God does not wait for the transformation of believers into righteous people. Full acceptance with God is found in Christ whose righteousness is perfectly adequate to the need of believers. Grace triumphs in the gospel of free justification, even in the face of continued human sinfulness and unworthiness.[11]

---

11. In the confessional statements of the churches of the Reformation, the justification of believers is clearly based upon the righteousness of God in Christ, which is freely granted and imputed to believers by grace alone. See the Heidelberg Catechism, Q. & A. 59: 'How are you righteous before God? A. Only by a true faith in Jesus Christ; that is, though my conscience accuse me that I have grievously sinned against all the commandments of God and kept none of them, and am still inclined to all evil, yet God, without any merit of mine, of mere grace, grants and imputes to me the perfect satisfaction, righteousness, and holiness of Christ, as if I had never had nor committed any sin, and myself had accomplished all the obedience which Christ has rendered for me; if only I accept such benefit with a believing heart.'

The reception of justification: by 'faith alone' or by 'faith formed by love'?

The Protestant insistence that believers are justified 'by faith alone' (*sola fide*) was a necessary corollary of its insistence that justification is a free gift of God's grace in Christ. If justification is a free gift, which is based upon the righteousness of Christ graciously granted and imputed to believers, it is most emphatically not by works. 'Grace alone', 'Christ alone' and 'faith alone' are corollary expressions in the Protestant conception. If we are saved by grace alone, then works must be excluded as a necessary precondition for our being accepted into favour with God. If we are saved by the person and work of Christ alone, then nothing believers do before God in obedience to the law could possibly compensate for anything lacking in him. According to the Reformers, this is precisely what the language of 'faith alone' maintains.

In the Roman Catholic view, faith also plays an indispensable role in the reception of the grace of justification. The first step in the process of justification is a believing assent to and cooperation with the grace of God, which is communicated through the sacrament of baptism. For this reason, the Council of Trent acknowledges that faith alone is the 'foundation' or 'beginning' (*initium*) of the process of justification.[12] Faith alone, however, does not justify in the full sense. Such faith, which is only an assent to the gospel promise, must become a 'faith formed by love' (*fides caritate formata*) as it receives the further sacramental infusion of justifying grace. Faith justifies only by virtue of its performance of good works, which are the fruit of the cooperation of the believer with the infused grace of God. Strictly speaking, the instrument of the believer's justification is the sacrament of baptism, not faith. However, through the grace that the sacrament communicates, believers are enabled to perform good works that merit further justification. Thus, in the same manner in which the Reformation view insisted upon faith alone as the way whereby the grace of free justification is received, the Roman Catholic view insisted upon faith plus works as the way whereby justification is maintained and increased.

In their understanding of faith as the exclusive instrument of justification, the Reformers argued that faith is peculiarly appropriate to the reception of free justification. This was not due merely to the fact that faith was a gift of God's grace in Christ (Eph. 2:6). All the various facets of the Christian believer's response to the gospel are the fruit of God's gracious initiative in

---

12. See *Decrees and Canons of the Council of Trent*, Sixth Session, ch. 8: 'faith is the beginning of human salvation, the foundation, and the root of all Justification' (Schaff, *Creeds of Christendom*, vol. 2, p. 97).

Christ. What distinguishes faith from other features of the believer's response to the gospel is its essentially self-effacing quality. Faith boasts not in itself or any other human achievement but in the grace of Christ alone. Faith answers to the free gift of justification in Christ, because it is principally the humble acknowledgment by believers that their only boast before God is in the work of Christ.

To express the unique suitability of faith to receive the gift of free justification, the Reformers used various expressions. Calvin, for example, spoke of faith as an 'empty vessel' in order to stress its character as a receptacle that brings nothing to God but receives all things from him.[13] Luther used the striking analogy of a ring that clasps a jewel; faith has no value of itself, but clasps the jewel that is Christ and his righteousness.[14] Calvin also remarked that, in a manner of speaking, faith is a 'passive thing', because it is the cessation of all working and striving to obtain favour with God.[15] What makes faith a suitable instrument for the reception of free justification is that it is marked by a readiness to acknowledge humbly that all honour in salvation belongs to God in Christ.[16]

Summary

As my summary indicates, the main lines of the historic divergence between Protestant and Roman Catholic views of justification are sharply drawn. In the

---

13. *Institutes* 3.11.7.

14. *Luther's Works*, ed. Jaroslav Pelikan and Helmut T. Lehmann, 55 vols. (St. Louis: Concordia; Philadelphia: Fortress, 1955–86), vol. 26, pp. 89, 134 (hereafter, *LW*).

15. *Institutes* 3.13.5.

16. To prove that faith alone, apart from works, is the exclusive instrument by which the grace of justification is received, the Reformers noted that this best accords with the language of Paul's epistles. In the writings of the apostle Paul, the justification of believers occurs 'through' faith and not 'on account of' faith. In particular, the apostle uses three related expressions in his epistles to describe the role of faith: first, in some passages, Paul uses the preposition 'through' with the genitive case to express the instrumental role of faith (e.g. Gal. 2:16); second, in other passages, the apostle uses the preposition 'out of' or 'by' with the genitive case to identify faith as the occasion, though not the cause or basis, for justification (e.g. Rom. 5:1); and third, Paul also speaks simply of justification 'by faith' in passages that use 'faith' in the dative case; this language expresses the idea of faith as the means or instrument whereby the righteousness of God is received (e.g. Rom. 3:28).

Protestant view, justification refers to a judicial act wherein God graciously forgives and accepts sinners on the basis of the righteousness of Christ alone. The principal promise of the gospel is that ungodly sinners may be assured of God's favour toward them in Christ, when they embrace this promise by faith alone. Though justification is inseparable from the renewal of the believer's life in sanctification, the free gift of justification is not based upon works, nor is it increased by them. Because this free justification is based solely upon the perfect righteousness of Christ imputed to believers, it produces an assurance of favour with God. In the Roman Catholic view, justification refers not only to the forgiveness of sins but also to the process whereby sinners are renewed in righteousness. The righteousness that justifies believers is not an imputed righteousness, but an infused and inherent righteousness. Only as believers cooperate with the grace of God and perform works in obedience to the law of God can their justification be maintained, increased and ultimately secured. Though it is possible for some to obtain a measure of the assurance of salvation, ordinarily such assurance is tempered by the awareness that justification requires the performance of good works that merit the reward of eternal life. On the critical questions of the nature, the basis and the means of justification, the historic differences between Protestant and Roman Catholic are stark and seemingly insuperable.

Justification: recent ecumenical discussion

Until recently, the Protestant and Roman Catholic views of justification were stable components of their respective traditions. Though some dissatisfaction with the traditional Protestant view of justification surfaced within the orbit of liberal Protestant scholarship in the aftermath of the Enlightenment, the principal features of the Protestant view in distinction from that of historic Catholicism remained relatively intact.[17] However, recent decades have witnessed a burst of new interest and deliberation about the doctrine of justification. Undoubtedly, the most prominent expression of this interest in the doctrine of justification is the one that has arisen within the context of an ecumenical desire to resolve the long-standing disagreement between Roman Catholic and Protestant understandings of the gospel. As I noted in

---

17. For a significant recent survey of the history of the doctrine of justification, see Alistair E. McGrath, *Iustitia Dei: A History of the Christian Doctrine of Justification*, 2nd edn (New York: Cambridge University Press, 1998).

my introduction, at no time since the Protestant Reformation of the sixteenth century has there been the kind of keen interest in a dialogue at the
highest level between representatives of these traditions on the subject of
justification.

Though these recent ecumenical discussions of justification have taken
place between a wide variety of church communions, my summary will only
feature two of its more important expressions, the discussions between representatives of the Lutheran and Roman Catholic churches, and between evangelicals and Roman Catholics.[18]

Lutherans and Catholics Together

Perhaps the most striking instance of ecumenical discussions of the doctrine
of justification is the sustained dialogue that has occurred in recent decades
between representatives of the Roman Catholic and the Lutheran churches.
Since the Lutheran churches represent the first branch of the Protestant
church, these discussions are of particular importance. The principal reason
for the separation between the Lutheran churches and the Roman Catholic
Church was the disagreement regarding justification. The remarkable feature
of the discussions in recent times between Lutherans and Roman Catholics is
not that such discussions are taking place at a level unsurpassed since the early
years of the sixteenth-century Reformation. What is most remarkable about
these discussions is that they have produced joint statements that purport to
demonstrate that such unity in an understanding of the gospel of free
justification may now be a reality.

During the course of the discussions between Roman Catholics and
Lutherans, a series of documents have been produced, which purport to show
that the old divisions of the past need no longer separate them. The earliest
indication of the course of these discussions was provided by the Helsinki
Assembly of the Lutheran World Federation in 1963. Even though this assembly spoke only for the Lutheran churches, it did draw the conclusion, based
upon a series of conferences with Catholic representatives, that there was

---

18. For an extensive summary of these ecumenical discussions and documents, which
    includes a thorough bibliography of primary and secondary sources, see Anthony
    N. S. Lane, *Justification by Faith in Catholic–Protestant Dialogue: An Evangelical Assessment*
    (Edinburgh: T. & T. Clark, 2002), pp. 87–126. Lane also treats high-level ecumenical
    discussions between Catholic and Anglican, and Catholic and Methodist,
    representatives. For our purposes, I shall only summarize the discussions between
    Catholics and Lutherans, and Catholics and North American evangelicals.

really no longer any substantial difference between Rome and the Lutheran churches on the doctrine of justification. Subsequently, three major declarations by Lutheran and Catholic representatives were issued that claimed to show a growing consensus on the meaning of the gospel.[19]

The first of these declarations is included in the document *Justification by Faith*, which was the seventh in a series of joint statements by representatives in the United States of the Roman Catholic Church and the Lutheran World Ministries, a branch of the Lutheran World Federation.[20] This document included a 'Common Statement' that begins and ends with the affirmation that '[o]ur entire hope of justification and salvation rests on Christ Jesus and on the gospel whereby the good news of God's merciful action in Christ is made known; we do not place our ultimate trust in anything other than God's promise and saving work in Christ'.[21] While admitting that this affirmation did not resolve all of the remaining differences between Roman Catholic and Lutheran views (including the Lutheran insistence that 'God accepts sinners as righteous for Christ's sake on the basis of faith alone'[22]), the authors of the joint statement maintained that these differences were not 'church-dividing' in nature.[23] In the opinion of participants in the discussions that produced this statement, a consensus on the essential teaching of the gospel was achieved, which was sufficient to overcome the most significant historical differences between their respective traditions.

Shortly after the appearance of this first statement in 1983, a Joint Ecumenical Commission on the Examination of the Sixteenth-Century Condemnations, which was composed of a number of Roman Catholic and Lutheran theologians, produced a second statement, *The Condemnations of the Reformation Era*.[24] The impetus for the formation of this Commission was a

---

19. For a survey and critical evaluation of these Lutheran–Catholic discussions, which is written from a confessionally Lutheran standpoint, see Robert D. Preus, *Justification and Rome: An Evaluation of Recent Dialogues* (St. Louis: Concordia, 1997).

20. H. George Anderson, T. Austin Murphy and Joseph A. Burgess, eds., *Justification by Faith: Lutherans and Catholics in Dialogue VII* (Minneapolis: Fortress, 1985). For a summary of the biblical discussions that form a background to this report, see John Reumann, *'Righteousness' in the New Testament* (Philadelphia: Fortress, 1982).

21. Anderson, Murphy and Burgess, *Justification by Faith*, 'Common Statement', par. 4, 157.

22. Ibid., par. 157.

23. Ibid., par. 4.

24. K. Lehmann and W. Pannenberg, eds., *The Condemnations of the Reformation Era: Do They Still Divide?* (Minneapolis: Fortress, 1990). A chapter by W. Pannenberg, 'Can

visit by the Pope to Germany in 1980. This papal visit stimulated interest
among Roman Catholic and Lutheran theologians in the question whether
justification was still a doctrine that divided them. As the name of this Joint
Commission suggests, its task was to examine the condemnations of the
Reformation period, particularly the Canons (with their anathemas) against
the Protestant view adopted at the Roman Catholic Council of Trent and the
condemnations in the Lutheran confessional documents. The principal
outcome of the work of the Commission was the sweeping conclusion that
the mutual condemnations of the Reformation era no longer apply to the
teaching of the contemporary Roman Catholic and Lutheran communions.[25]

Due in part to the divergence of opinion over this second statement, discussions between representatives of the Roman Catholic church and the
Lutheran World Federation continued. The outcome of these continued discussions was perhaps the most remarkable chapter in the yet-unfinished dialogue between the two communions: the issuing of a *Joint Declaration on the
Doctrine of Justification* in 1999.[26] This statement, which includes a supplemen-
tary 'Annex' that clarified some issues of continuing debate and an affirmation
of the *sola fide* formula by Rome, was signed by official representatives of the
Lutheran World Federation and the Roman Catholic Church on 31 October, a
date chosen because of its association with the beginning of the Protestant
Reformation in the sixteenth century. Two statements in this *Joint Declaration*
capture its tenor and emphases. In a section of the *Joint Declaration* entitled,
'The Common Understanding of Justification', the common teaching of the
two communions is summarized: 'Together we confess: By grace alone, in faith

---

the Mutual Condemnations Between Rome and the Reformation Churches be
Lifted?' (pp. 31–43), describes the process followed by the Joint Committee. The
original document was printed in German: K. Lehmann and W. Pannenberg, eds.,
*Lehrverurteilungen-kirchen-trennend? I: Rechtfertigung, Sakramente und Amt im Zeitalter der
Reformation und Heute* (Freiburg: Vandenhoeck & Ruprecht, 1986). It should be noted
that, though most of the participants in this project were Catholic and Lutheran, a
few Reformed theologians also took part.

25. For a summary of the various responses to this document, see Lane, *Justification by
Faith*, pp. 101ff.

26. An English translation of this declaration was issued by the Lutheran World
Federation and The Pontifical Council for Promoting Christian Unity (Grand
Rapids: Eerdmans, 2000). The original declaration was published in German:
Gemeinsame Erklärung zur Rechtfertigungslehre (Frankfurt am Main: Lembeck,
1999).

in Christ's saving work and not because of any merit on our part, we are accepted by God and receive the Holy Spirit, who renews our hearts while equipping and calling us to good works.'[27] In a final section of the declaration entitled, 'The Significance and Scope of the Consensus Reached', the two communions conclude that a fundamental consensus now exists on the nature of the gospel, despite some differences in formulation and theological expression:

> The understanding of the doctrine of justification set forth in this *Declaration* shows that a consensus in basic truths of the doctrine of justification exists between Lutherans and Catholics. In light of this consensus the remaining differences of language, theological elaboration, and emphasis in the understanding of justification described in [section 4] are acceptable. Therefore the Lutheran and the Catholic explications of justification are in their difference open to one another and do not destroy the consensus regarding the basic truths.[28]

In its exposition of this common understanding of justification, the *Joint Declaration* is organized into seven sections. Each section contains a statement of consensus, which is followed by a distinctly Lutheran and Catholic perspective. In this manner, the *Joint Declaration* acknowledges a measure of agreement between the two traditions, while admitting that significant areas of difference remain. The headings and content of each of these sections are as follows:[29]

4.1 *Human Powerlessness and Sin in Relation to Justification.* In this section, it is noted that Lutherans and Catholics 'confess together that all persons depend completely on the saving grace of God for their salvation'. Though it is also acknowledged that all persons are 'incapable of turning by themselves to God', the Roman Catholic perspective insists that persons are able to '"cooperate" in preparing for and accepting justification'. The Lutheran perspective rejects this idea of cooperation, even though the full personal involvement of believers is affirmed.

4.2 *Justification as Forgiveness of Sin and Making Righteous.* This section of the *Joint Declaration* addresses the pivotal issue of the nature of justification. Both Lutherans and Catholics affirm that when persons 'come by faith to share in Christ, God no longer imputes to them their sin and through the Holy Spirit effects in them an active

---

27. *Joint Declaration*, par. 15.

28. Ibid., par. 40. For a critical appraisal of the *Joint Declaration*, which is written from a confessionally Reformed standpoint, see W. Robert Godfrey, 'The Lutheran–Roman Catholic Joint Declaration', *Banner of Truth* 432 (January 2000), pp. 17–20.

29. *Joint Declaration*, paras. 19–39.

love'. These two aspects of salvation, the forgiveness of sins and the saving presence of God himself, are 'not to be separated'. The Lutheran perspective insists upon a clear distinction between God's forgiving love or favor, and the renewal of the Christian's life, lest the former come to depend or be based upon the latter. The Catholic perspective, on the other hand, maintains that 'God's forgiving love always brings with it a gift of new life, which in the Holy Spirit becomes effective in active love.'

4.3 *Justification by Faith and Through Grace.* This section declares that 'sinners are justified by faith in the saving action of God in Christ'. The faith by which sinners are justified is 'active in love', though 'whatever in the justified precedes or follows the free gift of faith is neither the basis of justification nor merits it'. In the Lutheran and Catholic perspectives on justification by faith and through grace, the Lutherans insist upon a distinction between justification and renewal whereas the Catholics include both 'forgiveness of sins and being made righteous by justifying grace, which makes us children of God'.

4.4. *The Justified as Sinner.* Both Lutherans and Catholics admit in this section that the 'justified also must ask God daily for forgiveness'. According to the Lutheran perspective, the justified person is simultaneously 'totally righteous' and 'totally sinner' (*simul iustus et peccator*). Though the 'enslaving power of sin is broken on the basis of the merit of Christ', believers always remain under the condemnation of the law and require the forgiveness of sins. In the Catholic perspective, 'the grace of Jesus Christ imparted in baptism takes away all that is sin "in the proper sense"'. Though there remains 'an inclination (concupiscence) that comes from sin and presses toward sin', this inclination is not sin 'in an authentic sense'.

4.5 *Law and Gospel.* Both Lutherans and Catholics maintain that persons are 'justified by faith in the gospel' apart from works required in the law, even though the law remains a proper standard for the conduct of the justified. In the Lutheran perspective, the law functions primarily in its 'theological use' as a means of accusing sinners and compelling them to seek God's mercy in Christ. In the Catholic perspective, believers are reminded by the law of their need to observe God's commandments. However, this does not remove the need for God's merciful promise of the grace of eternal life.

4.6. *Assurance of Salvation.* In this section of the *Joint Declaration,* it is commonly acknowledged that believers 'can build on the effective promise of God's grace in Word and Sacrament and so be sure of his grace'. In the Lutheran perspective, this emphasis upon the assurance of salvation is of particular importance. In the Catholic perspective, it is also noted that a believer 'may be concerned about his salvation when he looks upon his own weaknesses and shortcomings'.

4.7. *The Good Works of the Justified.* Both Lutherans and Catholics share the conviction that good works 'follow justification and are its fruits'. For the Lutherans, justification brings full acceptance with God as well as growth in its effects. For Catholics, good works 'made possible by grace and the working of the Holy Spirit' are 'meritorious', since 'a reward in heaven is promised to these works'. However, Catholics do not deny that these works remain 'gifts' and that justification 'always remains the unmerited gift of grace'.

I shall withhold judgment at this point whether these sections, which constitute the most important part of the *Joint Declaration*, articulate a genuine consensus on the doctrine of justification between Romans Catholics and Lutherans. Among both Roman Catholic and Lutheran critics, responses to the *Joint Declaration* have varied widely. As a symbol of contemporary interest in a resolution of the dispute between Protestant and Lutheran views of justification, however, the *Joint Declaration*'s importance can hardly be exaggerated.

Evangelicals and Catholics Together?
It is not only in the broader context of ecumenical discussions between Lutherans and Roman Catholics that the doctrine of justification has achieved a position of prominence. In addition to these remarkable statements of a new consensus on the doctrine of justification between Catholic and Lutheran representatives, similar discussions have taken place between other branches of the Reformation and the Roman Catholic Church. Among the more important of these are discussions that have taken place in North America between a number of prominent evangelical theologians and representatives of the Roman Catholic Church. Arising out of a desire to offer a unified witness in the public square, these discussions have sought to demonstrate that Roman Catholics and evangelicals, as 'co-belligerents' in combating the social and moral decay of modern American society, also share many fundamental articles of the Christian faith. This shared faith extends even to some, though not all, aspects of the disputed doctrine of justification.

Like the discussions between Lutherans and Roman Catholics, these discussions in North America between evangelicals and Roman Catholics have produced documents that aim to present a consensus on the doctrine of justification by their signatories. Two documents in particular, which were endorsed and signed by a number of representatives of both Catholic and evangelical persuasion, are of special importance.

The first of these was produced in 1994, and bore the revealing title 'Evangelicals and Catholics Together'.[30] Signed by a number of prominent

---

30. 'Evangelicals and Catholics Together: The Christian Mission in the Third Millennium', *First Things* 43 (May 1994), pp. 15–22. For other printings of this

306   ALWAYS REFORMING

representatives of the Catholic and evangelical communities in North
America, this declaration included a summary statement regarding the doctrine of justification:

> We affirm together that we are justified by grace, through faith, because of Christ.
> Living faith is active in love that is nothing less than the love of Christ, for we
> together say with Paul: 'I have been crucified with Christ; it is no longer I who live,
> but Christ who lives in me; and the life I now live in the flesh I live by faith in the Son
> of God, who loved me and gave himself for me' (Galatians 2).[31]

Because the burden of the declaration 'Evangelicals and Catholics
Together' was to demonstrate the substantial similarities of viewpoint
between evangelicals and Catholics, the remainder of the document says
nothing more about differences between them on the subject of justification.
The doctrine of justification is treated as a point of consensus, rather than a
point of disagreement. However, the brevity of the statement on justification
allows for a considerable difference of opinion among those who might find
it acceptable. Evangelical critics of the statement, for example, were able to
point out that it says nothing more than was said by the Catholic church at the
Council of Trent in the sixteenth century. The chief point of dispute, whether
justification is by grace *alone* through faith *alone* on account of the work of
Christ *alone*, is glossed by this statement. It is not surprising, therefore, that this
declaration was strongly criticized by theologians within the evangelical community.

Due to the perceived weaknesses of 'Evangelicals and Catholics Together',
a number of its signatories joined with other evangelicals to prepare a sequel
declaration. This declaration was published in 1997, and bore the title 'The
Gift of Salvation'.[32] Written in order to clarify some of the issues that the first

---

declaration, including discussion and responses by various authors, see Charles
Colson and Richard John Neuhaus, eds., *Evangelicals and Catholics Together: Toward a
Common Mission* (London: Hodder & Stoughton, 1996); T. P. Rausch, ed., *Catholics
and Evangelicals: Do They Share a Common Future?* (Downers Grove: IVP, 2000); R. C.
Sproul, *Faith Alone: The Evangelical Doctrine of Justification* (Grand Rapids: Baker, 1995);
and Norman L. Geisler and R. E. MacKenzie, *Roman Catholics and Evangelicals:
Agreements and Differences* (Grand Rapids: Baker, 1995).

31. Colson and Neuhaus, *Evangelicals and Catholics Together*, p. xviii.

32. Like its predecessor, this document was printed in several publications: Timothy
George, 'Evangelicals and Catholics Together: A New Initiative', *Christianity Today*, 8

statement raised – and to assuage the concern expressed within the evangelical community that some of its authors signed the earlier, ambiguous statement in 'Evangelicals and Catholics Together' – the authors of this declaration attempted to offer a more clearly evangelical statement on the doctrine of justification. Regarding justification, this statement affirmed that

> [j]ustification is not earned by any good works or merits of our own; it is entirely God's gift, conferred through the Father's sheer graciousness, out of the love that he bears us in his Son, who suffered on our behalf and rose from the dead for our justification. Jesus was 'put to death for our trespasses and raised for our justification' (Rom. 4:25). In justification God, on the basis of Christ's righteousness alone, declares us to be no longer his rebellious enemies but his forgiven friends. And by virtue of his declaration it is so. We understand that what we here affirm is in agreement with what the Reformation traditions have meant by justification by faith alone.[33]

The language of this statement is far clearer than that of the earlier 'Evangelicals and Catholics Together'. It affirms several traditional features of the Protestant view of justification, particularly that it is by grace alone, apart from works, and received through faith alone. However, despite the apparent consensus on key elements of the doctrine of justification, this statement also noted that there were areas of continued disagreement between Protestant and Catholic. These areas included

> the meaning of baptismal regeneration, the Eucharist, and sacramental grace; the historic uses of the language of justification as it relates to imputed and transformative righteousness; the normative status of justification in relation to all Christian doctrine; the assertion that while justification is by faith alone, the faith that receives salvation is never alone; diverse understandings of merit, reward, purgatory, and indulgences . . .[34]

December 1997, pp. 34–38; 'The Gift of Salvation', *First Things* 79 (January 1998), pp. 20–23; and R. C. Sproul, *Getting the Gospel Right: The Tie that Binds Evangelicals Together* (Grand Rapids: Baker, 1999), pp. 179–184. For critical assessments of this declaration, which are written from a classic Protestant perspective, see Sproul, *Getting the Gospel Right*, pp. 45–93; and Mark Seifrid, '"The Gift of Salvation": Its Failure to Address the Crux of Justification', *Journal of the Evangelical Theological Society* 42 (1999), pp. 679–688.

33. *Christianity Today*, 8 December 1997, p. 36.
34. Ibid., p. 38.

The admission of these areas of continued disagreement suggests that this second declaration, though offered to address criticisms of the earlier declaration, has not produced anything like a consensus within the evangelical community in North America. Not only are these declarations unofficial in character, and therefore without any ecclesiastical authority within the Catholic and evangelical communities; but they are also the subject of continued discussion and even considerable criticism within the evangelical community. In the context of this discussion, a third statement was drawn up by representative evangelical theologians, *The Gospel of Jesus Christ: An Evangelical Affirmation.*[35] As the title of this document indicates, it is intended to serve the evangelical community as a unifying testimony to the doctrine of justification in its Protestant understanding. Since the publication of this statement, discussion and controversy within the evangelical community in North America has ebbed.[36] Whether the doctrine of justification will be a further subject of discussion in the future between Catholic and evangelical representatives remains to be seen.

Summary

Though I shall not assess the extent to which these ecumenical discussions have achieved a genuine doctrinal consensus on the subject of justification until the closing section of this chapter, these discussions constitute one of the most important components of any contemporary theological restatement of the doctrine of justification. Not since the early period of the Reformation in the sixteenth century have there been the kinds of high-level discussions between representatives of the Protestant and Roman Catholic communions on the doctrine that was the occasion for the division between them. One of the most significant questions facing evangelical theology today, accordingly,

---

35. For printings of this declaration together with responses and critical evaluation, see Sproul, *Getting the Gospel Right*, pp. 95–195; *Christianity Today*, 14 June 1999, pp. 51–56; J. N. Akers et al., eds., *This We Believe: The Good News of Jesus Christ for the World* (Grand Rapids: Zondervan, 2000); and P. R. Hinlicky et al., 'An Ecumenical Symposium on "A Call to Evangelical Unity"', *Pro Ecclesia* 9 (2000), pp. 133–149.

36. Though there has been a waning of interest in these earlier discussions between evangelicals and Catholics, a recent symposium at Wheaton College, which was devoted to current debates regarding the justification and imputation, indicates that the subject of justification remains an important one for contemporary evangelicals. For a printed version of the papers presented, see Mark Husbands and Daniel J. Treier, eds., *Justification: What's at Stake in the Current Debates?* (Downers Grove: IVP, 2004).

is the question of the extent to which these discussions have brought about a greater unity of teaching on the nature of the gospel of justification than at any time since the sixteenth century.

The 'new perspective' on Paul[37]

Since the Reformation of the sixteenth century, Protestant New Testament scholarship was governed by the perspective on the apostle Paul that I summarized in the first part of this chapter. In the more recent history of New Testament scholarship, especially Pauline studies, however, this dominant perspective on Paul's understanding of justification has been seriously challenged.[38] As important as the recent ecumenical discussions of the doctrine of justification may be, the emergence in Pauline studies of what is known as 'the new perspective on Paul' is a development of similar importance.[39] This new

---

37. Some of the material in this section on the new perspective is a revision and abridgment of material that was originally published as part of a series of articles in *Outlook* (Grand Rapids: Reformed Fellowship, September 2002 to October 2004), and is used with permission.

38. A review of the history of biblical studies for at least the last century reveals a growing dissatisfaction with the traditional Protestant or 'Lutheran' understanding of Paul. For a sketch of this history, see Stephen Westerholm, *Perspectives Old and New on Paul: The 'Lutheran' Paul and His Critics* (Grand Rapids: Eerdmans, 2004), pp. 101–163.

39. For an introduction to the history and development of the new perspective, see Douglas Moo, 'Paul and the Law in the Last Ten Years', *Scottish Journal of Theology* 40 (1986), pp. 287–307; Frank Thielman, *Paul and the Law: A Contextual Approach* (Downers Grove: IVP, 1994), pp. 9–47; Thomas R. Schreiner, *The Law and Its Fulfillment: A Pauline Theology of Law* (Grand Rapids: Baker, 1993), pp. 13–31; Westerholm, *Perspectives Old and New on Paul*, pp. 101–149, 178–200; and Guy Prentiss Waters, *Justification and the New Perspectives on Paul* (Phillipsburg: P. & R., 2004), pp. 1–150. James D. G. Dunn first coined this language in a 1982 address, 'The New Perspective on Paul' (reprinted in *Jesus, Paul, and the Law: Studies in Mark and Galatians* [Louisville: Westminster John Knox, 1990], pp. 183–214). In a recent address, 'New Perspectives on Paul', N. T. Wright argues for a multiplicity of new perspective views: 'there are probably almost as many "New Perspective" positions as there are writers espousing it'. This article is available at http://home.hiwaay.net/~kbush/Wright_New _Perspectives.pdf.

perspective on Paul, which has become arguably the reigning point of view within contemporary biblical scholarship, openly challenges a number of the key features of the Reformation's understanding of justification, and even elements of the broader Western theological tradition. Due to the limitations of my survey of recent debates regarding justification, I shall summarize this perspective by considering the contributions of three of the principal authors who have played a formative role in its development: E. P. Sanders, James D. G. Dunn and N. T. Wright. In doing so, I shall be deliberately selective, ignoring some authors of considerable influence and presenting an overly tidy account of the emergence of this view.

E. P. Sanders: a new view of 'Second Temple Judaism'

Even though there are a number of forerunners who made significant contributions to the emergence of a new perspective on Paul,[40] the most influential and pivotal figure is undoubtedly E. P. Sanders. Sanders's 1977 volume *Paul and Palestinian Judaism* is now generally regarded as a classic presentation of the view of Second Temple Judaism that is formative for the new perspective. Sanders's stated purpose in his classic study was to compare the pattern of religion evident in Paul's writings with the pattern of religion in Jewish literature during the period between 200 BC and AD 200. By a 'pattern of religion' Sanders means the way a religion understands how a person 'gets in' and 'stays in' the community of God's people.[41] Traditional accounts of the differences between religions, particularly the differences between Judaism and Christianity, focused upon the distinctive essence or core beliefs of these religions. In doing so, Judaism was often simplistically described as a 'legalistic' religion, which emphasizes obedience to the law as the basis for inclusion among God's people, and Christianity was described as a 'gracious' religion, which emphasizes God's free initiative in calling his people into communion with himself.

---

40. One of these figures whose work is of special significance is W. D. Davies. Davies's study *Paul and Rabbinic Judaism: Some Rabbinic Elements in Pauline Theology*, 4th edn (Philadelphia: Fortress, 1980), anticipates some features of Sanders's work, especially the claim that Paul was thoroughly shaped by his background within the Rabbinic Judaism of the first century of the Christian era. Sanders acknowledges that Davies was, in this respect, a 'transitional figure' in New Testament studies. For Sanders's assessment of Davies's contribution, see his *Paul and Palestinian Judaism: A Comparison of Patterns of Religion* (London: SCM, 1977), pp. 7–12.

41. *Paul and Palestinian Judaism*, p. 17.

The first part of Sanders's study involves a comprehensive study of Jewish literature during the two centuries before and after the coming of Christ. Based upon this study, Sanders concludes that Judaism exhibits a pattern of religion best described as 'covenantal nomism'. Sanders defines covenantal nomism as follows:

> The 'pattern' or 'structure' of covenantal nomism is this: (1) God has chosen Israel and (2) given the law. The law implies both (3) God's promise to maintain the election and (4) the requirement to obey. (5) God rewards obedience and punishes transgression. (6) The law provides for means of atonement, and atonement results in (7) maintenance or re-establishment of the covenantal relationship. (8) All those who are maintained in the covenant by obedience, atonement and God's mercy belong to the group which will be saved. An important interpretation of the first and last points is that election and ultimately salvation are considered to be by God's mercy rather than human achievement.[42]

Contrary to the typical Protestant assumption that Palestinian Judaism was legalistic, Sanders appeals to evidence in Jewish writings of the Second Temple period to support the view that it was a religion of grace. In the literature of Judaism, God is represented as graciously electing Israel to be his people, and mercifully providing a means of atonement and opportunity for repentance in order to deal with their sins. So far as Israel's 'getting in' the covenant is concerned, this was not by human achievement but by God's gracious initiative. Obedience to the law was only required as a means of maintaining or 'staying in' the covenant.

One of the immediate problems that surfaces, as a result of Sanders's argument for a new view of Judaism, is what to do with the apostle Paul and his polemics against Judaism. If Judaism was not a legalistic religion, what are we to make of Paul's vigorous arguments against claims to find favour with God on the basis of works? Is Paul combating a kind of 'straw man' in his letters (especially in Romans and Galatians), when he combats a righteousness that is by the 'works of the law'? Sanders, both in his *Paul and Palestinian Judaism* and in a sequel, *Paul, the Law, and the Jewish People*,[43] answers this question by suggesting that Paul's view of the human plight was a by-product of his view of salvation. Paul started with Christ as the 'solution' to the human predicament, and then worked backward to explain the 'plight' to which his saving work

---

42. Ibid., p. 422.
43. Minneapolis: Fortress, 1983.

corresponds. Though Paul has traditionally been interpreted to teach that the problem of human sinfulness, which is made known and aggravated through the law's demand for perfect obedience, calls for a solution in Christ's person and work, we should recognize that his description of the problem of sin derives from his prior convictions about Christ. Paul, in effect, starts from the basic conviction that Christ is the only Saviour of Jews and Gentiles. On the basis of this conviction, he then develops a doctrine of the law and human sinfulness that corresponds to it.

According to Sanders, the great problem with Judaism, so far as the apostle Paul was concerned, was not that it was legalistic. Paul did not contest Palestinian Judaism's insistence upon zeal for the law. Nor did he object to Judaism on the basis of a conviction that no amount of effort to obey the law could ever make a person acceptable to God. His real (and only) objection to Judaism was that it denied the new reality of God's saving work through Christ. In words that have often been quoted, Sanders concludes, 'In short, *this is what Paul finds wrong in Judaism: it is not Christianity.*'[44]

James D. G. Dunn: a new view of the 'works of the law'

Among advocates of a new view of the teaching of the apostle Paul, James D. G. Dunn is a second figure of considerable prominence.[45] In a 1982 lecture, 'The New Perspective on Paul', Dunn acknowledged that Sanders's study *Paul and Palestinian Judaism* represented a 'new pattern' of understanding the apostle Paul. In this lecture, Dunn credited Sanders with breaking the stranglehold of the older Reformation view that had dominated Pauline

---

44. *Paul and Palestinian Judaism*, p. 552. Cf. Sanders's comment on p. 497: 'It is the Gentile question and the exclusivism of Paul's soteriology which dethrone the law, not a misunderstanding of it or a view predetermined by his background.'

45. Among the more important sources for an understanding of Dunn's view are the following: James D. G. Dunn, 'The New Perspective on Paul', in *Jesus, Paul and the Law: Studies in Mark and Galatians* (Louisville: Westminster John Knox, 1970), pp. 183–215; 'Paul and "Covenantal Nomism"', in *The Partings of the Ways Between Christianity and Judaism and their Significance for the Character of Christianity* (Philadelphia: Trinity Press International, 1991), pp. 117–139; 'Works of the Law and the Curse of the Law (Galatians 3.10–14)', *New Testament Studies* 31 (1985), pp. 523–542; *The Theology of Paul the Apostle* (Grand Rapids: Eerdmans, 1998), pp. 334–389; Word Biblical Commentary, vol. 38a: *Romans 1–8*, and vol. 38b: *Romans 9–16* (Dallas: Word, 1988); 'Yet Once More – "The Works of the Law": A Response', *Journal for the Study of the New Testament* 46 (1992), pp. 99–117.

studies for centuries.[46] The idea that there is a basic antithesis between Judaism, which supposedly taught a doctrine of salvation by meritorious works, and Paul, who taught a doctrine of salvation by faith apart from the works of the law, needs to be set aside once and for all. Judaism, as Sanders has convincingly demonstrated, was a religion of salvation that emphasized God's goodness and generosity toward his people, Israel. The law was given to Israel, not as a means for procuring favour with God, but as a means to confirm the covenant relationship previously established by grace. Dunn fully concurred with Sanders's argument that Judaism's pattern of religion was that of *covenantal nomism*.

In spite of Sanders's groundbreaking insight into the nature of Judaism, Dunn claims that he nonetheless failed to provide a coherent explanation of Paul's relation to Judaism. Though Sanders provided the occasion for a new perspective on Paul, his own interpretation of Paul's gospel fails to show how Paul's view of the law arises within the context of the Judaism of his day. If the problem with Judaism's understanding of the law was not legalism, which teaches that obedience to the law's requirements is the basis for inclusion among God's covenant people, what was wrong with its teaching? To what error is the apostle Paul responding, when he speaks of a justification that is not according to 'works of the law' but according to faith?

If we approach the apostle Paul from the perspective of the new view of Judaism, we shall discover, Dunn argues, that Paul was objecting to *Jewish exclusivism* and not legalism. The problem with the use of the law among the Judaizers whom Paul opposed was not their attempt to find favour with God on the basis of their obedience to the law, but their use of the 'works of the law' to exclude Gentiles from membership in the covenant community. The Judaizers were insisting upon certain 'works of the law' that served as 'boundary markers' for inclusion or exclusion from the number of God's people. The law functioned in their thinking and practice as a means of identifying who properly belongs to the community of faith. It was this *social* use of the law as a means of excluding Gentiles that receives Paul's rebuke, not an alleged appeal to the law as a means of self-justification. According to Dunn, Paul's real objection to the Judaizers' appeal to 'works of the law' is clearly disclosed in passages like Galatians 2:15–16 and Galatians 3:10–14. In these passages, Paul was not opposing an allegedly legalistic teaching that obedience to the law of God in general is the basis for finding favour with God. Rather, Paul was opposing the idea that the 'works of the law'; that is, those observances that

---

46. 'New Perspective on Paul', p. 184.

particularly distinguish Jews from Gentiles, are necessary badges of covenant membership. What Paul objects to are those 'works of the law' that served as ritual markers of identity to separate Jews from Gentiles.[47]

N. T. Wright: a new view of justification as an ecclesiological doctrine

The third 'new perspective' author that we consider, N. T. Wright, shares Dunn's conviction that Sanders's study of Second Temple Judaism requires a new perspective on Paul's doctrine of justification. He also agrees with Dunn that, when Paul speaks of the 'works of the law', he primarily refers to those 'boundary marker requirements' of the law that distinguished Jews from Gentiles. Wright's contribution to the formulation of a new perspective is the way he argues for a new view of justification as an ecclesiological, rather than a soteriological, doctrine.

Before considering directly Wright's view of justification, it should be noted that he regards this doctrine to be a subordinate theme in Paul's understanding of the gospel. Though it is often assumed that the gospel is a 'system of how people get saved', Wright insists that this seriously misrepresents the real meaning of the gospel.[48] The gospel does not answer the question of the guilty sinner 'How can I find favour with God?', but rather it answers the question 'Who is Lord?' One of the unfortunate features of the Reformation and much evangelical thinking is that it reduces the gospel to 'a message about "how one gets saved," in an individual and ahistorical sense'.[49] In this kind of thinking, the focus of attention, so far as the gospel is concerned, is upon 'something that in older theology would be called an *ordo salutis*, an order of salvation'.[50] The doctrine of justification, though an essential, albeit subordinate, theme in Paul's preaching, does not address the issue of how guilty sinners can find

---

47. Ibid., p. 200.

48. N. T. Wright, *What Saint Paul Really Said: Was Paul of Tarsus the Real Founder of Christianity?* (Grand Rapids: Eerdmans, 1997), p. 45. Wright is a prolific author and has produced a number of volumes that express his understanding of Paul's doctrine of justification. In addition to this popular presentation of his view, the following sources are of particular significance: *The Climax of the Covenant: Christ and the Law in Pauline Theology* (Minneapolis: Fortress, 1991); 'The Law in Romans 2', in *Paul and the Mosaic Law*, ed. James D. G. Dunn (Grand Rapids: Eerdmans, 1996), pp. 131–150; and *The Letter to the Romans*, vol. 10 of *The New Interpreter's Bible* (Nashville: Abingdon, 2002).

49. *What Saint Paul Really Said*, p. 60.

50. Ibid., pp. 40–41.

favour with God. When we view the gospel in terms of the lordship of Jesus Christ, the proper meaning and place of the doctrine of justification becomes apparent. Wright says:

> Let us be quite clear. 'The gospel' is the announcement of Jesus' lordship, which works with power to bring people into the family of Abraham, now redefined around Jesus Christ and characterized solely by faith in him. 'Justification' is the doctrine which insists that all those who have this faith belong as full members of this family, on this basis and no other.[51]

Students of the Reformation know that one of the key Pauline phrases for a proper understanding of justification is the phrase 'the righteousness of God' (Rom. 1:16–17; 3:21–26). Following Luther's 'rediscovery' that the righteousness of God is not so much the demand of God's law as the gift of his grace in Christ, the Reformers taught that we are justified by the free gift of God's righteousness in Christ. Following the lead of Sanders, Dunn and others, Wright insists that this Reformation view amounts to a profound misunderstanding of Paul's language of the 'righteousness of God'. Wright maintains that

> [f]or a reader of the Septuagint, the Greek version of the Jewish scriptures, 'the righteousness of God' would have one obvious meaning: God's own faithfulness to his promises . . . God has made promises; Israel can trust those promises. God's righteousness is thus cognate with his trustworthiness on the one hand, and Israel's salvation on the other.[52]

Though the Reformation view rightly emphasized that the 'righteousness of God' reflects a 'legal metaphor' taken from the law court, it misapplies this language by misunderstanding the way the Hebrews understood the functioning of righteousness in the judgment of the court.[53] In the Hebrew law court,

---

51. Ibid., p. 133.
52. Ibid., p. 96. For a similar treatment, see *Letter to the Romans*, pp. 398–408, and various places throughout.
53. Wright does not believe, however, that the idea of righteousness and the 'legal metaphor' it reflects is the most important theme of the book of Romans or Paul's other epistles. In a very telling observation at the close of his discussion of justification in *What Saint Paul Really Said*, p. 110, he remarks that 'Romans is often regarded as an exposition of judicial, or law-court, theology. But that is a mistake.

there are three parties: the judge, the plaintiff and the defendant. When the Judge pronounces a verdict in the court in favour of the plaintiff or the defendant, we may say that he has been 'vindicated against the accuser; in other words, acquitted'.[54] This is the only meaning that the term 'righteous' has, when it is applied to the person in whose favour the Judge acts: that person is, so far as the court's action is concerned, in the *status of being acquitted or righteous*. Even though Wright acknowledges, as the Reformation view also insisted, that the language of the 'righteousness of God' reflects a legal or forensic setting, he also insists that the vindication of someone in God's court *does not involve God's granting or imputing anything whatever to the person whom he vindicates.*

> If we use the language of the law court, it makes no sense whatever to say that the judge imputes, imparts, bequeaths, conveys or otherwise transfers his righteousness to either the plaintiff or the defendant. Righteousness is not an object, a substance or a gas which can be passed across the courtroom.[55]

Just as the Reformation misunderstood the language of the 'righteousness of God', so it also misunderstood, Wright maintains, the language of justification. In the popular mind, justification is taken to be the answer to the problem of sinners who try to find favour with God by doing good works. There is a sinful tendency in all of us to try to pull ourselves up by our own moral bootstraps, to seek to find favour with God on the basis of our achievements or efforts. Whether in the dress of Pelagianism, which teaches that sinners are saved on the basis of the performance of good works in obedience to the law, or semi-Pelagianism, which teaches that sinners are saved on the basis of God's grace plus our good works, there is an inescapable tendency to base human salvation upon self-effort. The doctrine of justification is the only antidote to all such Pelagian or semi-Pelagian views of salvation, because it

---

The law court forms a vital metaphor at a key stage of the argument. But at the heart of Romans we find a theology of love ... If we leave the notion of "righteousness" as a law-court metaphor only, as so many have done in the past, this gives the impression of a legal transaction, a cold piece of business, almost a trick of thought performed by a God who is logical and correct but hardly one we would want to worship.' This remark assumes the doubtful thesis that love and justice are not equally essential features of the gospel's revelation of God's character.

54. Ibid., p. 98.

55. Ibid.

teaches that salvation is an unmerited gift of God's grace in Christ to sinners who receive the gospel promise by faith alone. In Wright's estimation, this popular opinion regarding justification, whatever its merits, 'does not do justice to the richness and precision of Paul's doctrine, and indeed distorts it at various points'.[56]

According to Wright, Paul's doctrine of justification did not serve to answer the 'timeless' problem of how sinners can find acceptance with God, but to explain how you can tell who belongs to 'the community of the true people of God'. When the language of justification is interpreted in terms of its Old Testament and Jewish background, we shall recognize that it is covenantal language. Justification does not describe how someone gains entrance into the community of God's people but *who is a member of the community* now and in the future. In Paul's Jewish context, Wright maintains,

> 'justification by works' has nothing to do with individual Jews attempting a kind of proto-Pelagian pulling themselves up by their moral bootstraps, and everything to do with the definition of the true Israel in advance of the final eschatological showdown. Justification in this setting, then, is not a matter of *how someone enters the community of the true people of God*, but of *how you tell who belongs to that community*, not least in the period of time before the eschatological event itself, when the matter will become public knowledge.[57]

Because justification has to do with God's recognition of who belongs to the covenant community, it is not so much a matter of 'soteriology as about ecclesiology; not so much about salvation as about the church'.[58] However, now that Christ has come to realize the covenant promise of God to Abraham, faith in Christ is the *only badge* of membership in God's worldwide family, which is composed of Jews and Gentiles alike. 'Justification . . . is the doctrine which insists that all who share faith in Christ belong at the same table, no matter what their racial differences, as together they wait for the final creation.'[59]

---

56. Ibid., p. 113. Cf. *What Saint Paul Really Said*, p. 115: 'The discussions of justification in much of the history of the church, certainly since Augustine, got off on the wrong foot – at least in terms of understanding Paul – and they have stayed there ever since.'

57. Ibid., p. 119 (emphasis Wright's). Cf. 'The Law in Romans 2', pp. 139–143; and *Letter to the Romans*, pp. 482, 490, and various places throughout.

58. *What Saint Paul Really Said*, p. 119.

59. Ibid., p. 122.

One of the surprising and provocative implications of this understanding
of justification, according to Wright, is that it radically undermines the usual
polemics between Protestants and Catholics. Whereas many Protestants have
historically argued that justification is a church-dividing doctrine, precisely the
opposite is the case: Paul's doctrine of justification demands an inclusive view
of membership in the one family of God.

> Many Christians, both in the Reformation and in the counter-Reformation traditions,
> have done themselves and the church a great disservice by treating the doctrine of
> 'justification' as central to their debates, and by supposing that it describes that system
> by which people attain salvation. They have turned the doctrine into its opposite.
> Justification declares that all who believe in Jesus Christ belong at the same table, no
> matter what their cultural or racial differences.[60]

Protestants who insist upon a certain formulation of the doctrine of
justification as a precondition to church fellowship, accordingly, are guilty of
turning the doctrine on its head.[61]

Summary

My brief sketch of the contributions of three formative authors of the new
perspective indicates that each has provided a key element of its understanding of Paul's doctrine of justification. The occasion for the new perspective's
claim that we need to revise the older Protestant view of Paul is Sanders's historical study Second Temple Judaism. The older perspective on Paul was built
upon the conviction that Second Temple Judaism was a legalistic religion, and
that the influence of its legalism constituted the background to Paul's development of the doctrine of free justification. However, the monumental work
of E. P. Sanders, demonstrates that Judaism was a religion of grace. In
Sanders's terms, it was a form of 'covenantal nomism', which taught that one
entered the covenant community of Israel by grace and was maintained by
obedience to the law. If this revised portrait of Judaism is assumed as the background for Paul's articulation of the gospel in his writings, the proverbial rug

---

60. Ibid., pp. 158–159.
61. 'The Shape of Justification', http://www.angelfire.com/mi2/paulpage/Shape.html,
    p. 3. This article is Wright's response to Paul Barnett's critical evaluation of his
    understanding of justification. Barnett is an Anglican bishop from the diocese of
    Sydney in Australia. See 'Tom Wright and The New Perspective',
    http://www.anglicanmediasydney.asn.au/pwb/ntwright_perspective.html.

is pulled out from underneath the Reformation's assumption that Paul was opposing Jewish legalism.

Once the older assumptions regarding Judaism and Paul's polemics with the Judaizers are debunked, the question that arises is, 'What was the problem to which Paul's doctrine of justification was an answer?' Though writers of the new perspective offer various answers to this question, the predominant answer is that Paul's doctrine of justification addresses the particular problem of Gentile inclusion among the covenant people of God. As Dunn in particular argues, the problem Paul addresses, when he rejects justification on the basis of the 'works of the law', is the problem of the identity of the people of God. The 'works of the law', which Paul's opponents appealed to as the basis for their justification, were not any acts of obedience to the law of God. They were those acts that set the boundaries around the people of God, and that excluded the Gentiles from membership in the covenant. Paul's doctrine of justification, accordingly, is not his general answer to the universal predicament of sinners before God, but a particular answer to the problem of Jewish exclusivism in the first century of the Christian era.

Observations regarding current debates

I have spent the bulk of this chapter surveying the state of contemporary theological discussion of the doctrine of justification. My survey has focused upon two principal foci of current debate, the ecumenical dialogue between Protestants and Catholics and the emergence of a 'new perspective' on Paul. Due to the significance of these two subjects, I have had to neglect a number of other important, albeit subsidiary, features of contemporary discussions of the doctrine of justification. As I noted at the outset, the current debates over justification involve so many distinct methodological, historical, biblical and theological dimensions that is scarcely possible to do them justice in the compass of a single chapter.

Upon the basis of the discussions of justification in contemporary theology that we have considered, I would like to conclude with a series of brief observations regarding current debates, especially the two principal debates I have surveyed. These observations will suggest only issues that require particular attention, if contemporary evangelical theology is going to keep faith with its Protestant roots and yet do so in a manner that is responsive to the challenges of the present day. In the interests of systematic order, these observations will be distributed according to three categories: (i) observations regarding the ecumenical dialogue on justification; (ii) observations regarding the claims of the 'new perspective' on Paul; and (iii) observations regarding a contemporary evangelical restatement of the doctrine of justification.

Observations regarding the ecumenical dialogue on justification

1. In my introductory treatment of the historic Protestant and Roman Catholic views, I noted that the basis for any fruitful dialogue between Protestants and Roman Catholics on the subject of justification must be the official, confessional documents of these respective church traditions. One problematic feature of some contemporary ecumenical dialogues is the temptation to adopt a revisionist view of the history of doctrine, and to employ this revisionist view as the basis for claiming a convergence of viewpoint. For example, the so-called 'Finnish' school of Luther scholarship has argued, in the setting of ecumenical dialogue with Eastern Orthodoxy, that Luther's understanding of justification emphasized the realistic transformation of the justified person in a manner analogous to Orthodoxy's doctrine of salvation as 'theiosis' or 'deification'.[62] Some historians of doctrine also maintain that Luther's view of justification was not strictly forensic but a more realistic one, and suggest that Luther's colleague and successor, Melanchthon, pushed the Lutheran tradition to define justification in predominantly forensic categories.[63] Such revisionist readings of the history of doctrine do not further ecumenical dialogues as much as confuse them. The resolution of differences between the Protestant and Roman Catholic traditions on the doctrine of justification must acknowledge the priority of official, ecclesiastical formulations of doctrine, not the individual emphases or formulations of particular theologians.

2. If we measure the statements that these ecumenical discussions have produced by the standard of the historic differences between Protestant and Roman Catholic, it is difficult to find much evidence that a truly substantive consensus on the doctrine of justification has been achieved. Though representatives of the two traditions have maintained that a consensus is emerging, it is not clear that the principal points of contention regarding the nature, the basis and the reception of justification have been overcome.[64]

---

62. For sources on the Finnish school, see n. 1 above.

63. See, e.g., Otto Ritschl, *Orthodoxie und Synkretismus in der altprotestantischen Theologie, Dogmengeschichte des Protestantismus* 2.1 (Leipzig: Hinrichs, 1912), pp. 226–273.

64. Cf. Lane, *Justification by Faith*, pp. 223–231, who argues that progress has been made towards consensus between Protestants and Roman Catholics. However, he also acknowledges that the formulations of the Council of Trent remain incompatible with a Protestant view of justification. A brief perusal of the summary provided in

A close reading, for example, of the *Joint Declaration* of 2002 indicates that the two parties simply agreed to disagree on these matters, while dropping the mutual anathemas of the Reformation era. The substantive differences in doctrine between Protestant and Roman Catholic views, which I detailed in the opening section above, have not yet been resolved. Whether justification is a judicial declaration or a moral process of renewal; whether justification is based upon an imputed righteousness or an infused righteousness; whether justification is received instrumentally through faith alone or through faith formed through love, these traditional points of dispute remain largely unresolved. To put the matter in the starkest terms, the *sola*s of the Reformation have not been embraced by contemporary Roman Catholicism. Unless these *sola*s were to be abandoned by contemporary Protestants, the debate between Protestant and Roman Catholic teaching on justification will undoubtedly continue.

Observations regarding the 'new perspective' on Paul

3. The new perspective on Paul is only credible on the basis of the assumption that E. P. Sanders's study of Second Temple Judaism requires a revolution in our understanding of the apostle Paul. However, the profile of Second Temple Judaism in the new perspective does not truly undermine the Reformation view. 'Covenantal nomism', which is Sanders's term for the pattern of religion that marked Second Temple Judaism, corresponds rather closely to the kind of 'semi-Pelagian' teaching that the Reformers opposed in the sixteenth century. Despite the claims of new perspective authors, the Reformers never argued that the medieval Roman Catholic doctrine of justification was 'Pelagian' or, strictly speaking, graceless. What the Reformers opposed was the idea that works of any kind, even those prompted by grace, constitute a partial basis for a believer's acceptance with God. Studies of Second Temple Judaism, including those of Sanders, confirm that Paul was not only familiar with but could well have opposed views that were comparable to the medieval Roman Catholic conception of justification by grace and works. Nothing in the contemporary study of Second Temple Judaism requires the kind of radical revision of our understanding of Paul's doctrine of justification that the new perspective represents. If advocates of the new perspective were more sensitive to the theological nuances of the Reformation dispute about Paul's understanding of justification, they would not be able to

the *Catechism of the Catholic Church*, paras. 2017–2029, indicates that the Tridentine formulations remain the official teaching of the Roman Catholic Church.

make the kind of overreaching claims for the significance of Sanders's study of Second Temple Judaism that often characterize their writings.[65]

4. The new perspective contends that Paul's view of the law was shaped, not by his opposition to a form of legalism, but by his opposition to Jewish exclusivism. However, the new perspective fails to deal adequately with the radical contrast that Paul draws between any acts of obedience to all that law requires and the believing reception of the free gift of justification. When Paul appeals to the law to expose human sinfulness and inability to do what the law requires in order to be justified on that basis, he draws the kind of radical contrast between the law and the gospel that the Reformation perspective identified in its interpretation of Paul's doctrine of justification. Paul's handling of the universal problem of human sin and guilt (e.g. Rom. 1 – 3), which the law reveals and even aggravates, confirms the validity of the Reformation view. It is simply not possible to sustain the new perspective's claim that Paul's references to 'works' and 'works of the law' describe only those acts that conform to the boundary marker requirements of the law.[66]

5. The new perspective rejects the Reformation view that the language of 'justification' refers to the way God receives guilty sinners into his favour. Justification is not so much a soteriological theme, which describes how sinners may be received into God's favour, as it is an ecclesiological theme, which describes who belongs to God's covenant family as an heir of the promise to Abraham. This approach to the doctrine of justification is unnecessarily reductionistic. Though Paul's doctrine of justification undoubtedly has ecclesiological implications, including some of those emphasized by new perspective authors, its principal meaning relates to the soteriological issue of how sinners, who have disobeyed the law of God and stand under its condemnation, can become acceptable to God. For example, when Paul presents the doctrine of justification in the opening chapters of Romans, he begins with a lengthy indictment of Jews and Gentiles alike, all of whom are by nature under the wrath and judgment of God because of their unrighteousness. The setting for the Pauline theme of justification indicates that it is a soteriological theme before it is an ecclesiological one.

6. Just as the new perspective reduces the weight and narrows the meaning of Paul's language of 'justification', so it offers an unsatisfying account of the

---

65. For studies of Paul and Second Temple Judaism that raise questions regarding the claims of the new perspective, see D. A. Carson, ed., *Justification and Variegated Nomism*, 2 vols. (Grand Rapids: Baker, 2001, 2004).

66. See Schreiner, *Law and Its Fulfillment*, pp. 41–72.

'righteousness of God' that is revealed in the gospel. One of the more troubling features of the new perspective is its failure to offer a clear explanation of the connection between the justification of believers and Christ's work of atonement. In the Reformation perspective on Paul, there is a close and intimate connection between Christ's obedience, satisfaction and righteousness, and the benefit of free justification that derives from the union of believers with him. Christ's objective work on behalf of believers, his death for their sins and his resurrection for their justification (Rom. 4:25) constitutes the basis for the verdict that justification declares. However, in the new perspective, no comparable account is provided of the intimate conjunction between Christ's saving work and the believer's justification. The new perspective offers no satisfactory account of Paul's emphasis that believers are justified by the blood of Christ (Rom. 5:9) or through the redemption and propitiation he provided (Rom. 3:23).[67] Nor does the new perspective's explanation of the righteousness of God explain why Paul insists that, were righteousness to come through the law, Christ would have died in vain (Gal. 2:21). Justification is not only a soteriological theme. It is first and foremost a Christological theme. Any contemporary restatement of the doctrine of justification, therefore, will have to explain the intimate connections between the obedience, sacrifice and righteousness of Jesus Christ, and the justification of believers who are joined to him by faith.

Observations regarding a restatement of the evangelical doctrine of justification

7. Any restatement of the evangelical doctrine of justification will have to revisit the question of definition that was at the core of the historic dispute between Protestantism and Roman Catholicism. Was the Reformation correct when it argued that the biblical usage of the language of justification is thoroughly judicial or forensic in nature? Or does the justification of the ungodly include the idea of the 'transformation' of the believer through an inward renewal of the Holy Spirit, which in the language of historic Protestant soteriology is termed

---

67. Cf. Wright, *Climax of the Covenant*, pp. 150–153. Wright rejects the traditional treatment of Galatians 3:13 and other Pauline passages on the atonement. We should beware, he argues, the temptation to develop a general theology of atonement on the basis of Paul's argument in Galatians 3. Paul is not speaking of Christ's substitutionary endurance of a curse that hangs over all sinners, Jew and Gentile alike. Rather, Paul is describing how Christ represented the people of Israel when he suffered the curse of her 'exile' upon the cross.

'sanctification'? In my judgment, the case made by the principal authors of the Reformation for a strictly judicial or forensic sense of the language of justification remains unimpeached. Justification is the antonym of condemnation (Rom. 8:33–34), and it is almost always used in the Old and New Testaments to refer to a judicial pronouncement, which declares a person to be innocent and in favour with the court. The justification of the ungodly is an irreducibly religious and soteriological theme, and it has to do, as the Reformation so vigorously insisted, with the principal issue of where a believer stands before the tribunal of God.[68]

8. Despite the frequent criticisms of the traditional Protestant emphasis upon an imputed righteousness, the Protestant doctrine of justification stands or falls with the idea of imputation.[69] Any contemporary reformulation of the Protestant understanding of justification, therefore, requires that the idea of imputation be retained and articulated in a cogent manner.[70] In the evangel-

---

68. This illustrates the much larger theological framework within which evangelical theology must seek to articulate the doctrine of justification. What makes justification such a significant subject in the Scriptures (and not simply in Paul!) is that it builds upon a substructure, namely, a theology of God's holiness and righteousness, and an anthropology of human beings who, though created in God's image, have become culpably sinful and worthy of condemnation and death. The absence of an emphasis upon these larger theological and anthropological assumptions of the doctrine of justification make the contemporary challenges particularly great.

69. See Bruce L. McCormack, 'What's at Stake in Current Debates over Justification?', in Husbands and Treier, *Justification*, p. 83: 'At the heart of the Reformation understanding of justification lay the notion of a positive imputation of Christ's righteousness. That was the truly distinctive element in the Reformation understanding, and given the centrality of the doctrine for defining Protestantism, its abandonment can only mean the transformation of the Reformation into something qualitatively different.'

70. In recent evangelical discussion, a debate has arisen regarding the identification of the 'righteousness' that is imputed to the believer as the basis for his or her justification. Robert H. Gundry, 'The Nonimputation of Christ's Righteousness', in Husbands and Treier, *Justification*, pp. 17–45, has argued that 'faith' is what is imputed to believers for righteousness, not the 'righteousness' of Christ, as in the classic Protestant view. For critical evaluations of Gundry's view, which offer a defence of the more traditional Protestant view, see John Piper, *Counted Righteous in Christ: Should We Abandon the Imputation of Christ's Righteousness?* (Wheaton, Ill.:

ical and Protestant understanding of justification, the imputation of Christ's righteousness to believers is a necessary corollary of the themes of 'Christ alone' and 'faith alone'. In the classic reformational view of justification, we are said to be justified 'by faith alone' (*sola fide*), not because the faith that alone justifies is an alone faith (without works), but because it is the exclusive instrument to *receive* the free gift of righteousness that is from God. A gift can only be received. It cannot be earned. Faith, therefore, as a receiving instrument is just the response that answers to the granting and imputing of righteousness that justification requires. Similarly, to say that our justification is 'on account of Christ alone' (*solo Christo*) is equivalent to saying that it is on account of the righteousness of Christ that becomes ours through imputation. Even as imputation affirms what is expressed by the language of 'faith alone' and 'Christ alone', it also affirms what belongs to the biblical doctrines of Christ's substitutionary atonement and the believer's union with Christ. If Christ's life, death, and resurrection occurred by God's design *for* or *in the place of* his people, then it follows that all that he accomplished *counts as theirs*, so far as God is concerned. To say that God imputes the righteousness of Christ to believers is, accordingly, to acknowledge what is required by the doctrines of Christ's substitutionary atonement and the believer's union with Christ through faith.[71]

Crossway, 2002); and D. A. Carson, 'The Vindication of Imputation: On Fields of Discourse and Semantic Fields', in Husbands and Treier, *Justification*, pp. 46–80. Though I concur with the arguments of Piper and Carson, the discussion illustrates the importance of a renewed exegetical and theological attention to the idea of imputation in relation to justification.

71. See Carson, 'The Vindication of Imputation', pp. 46–80. Recent evangelical attempts to argue that the idea of 'union with Christ' constitutes an alternative to the judicial idea of imputation are, for this reason, fundamentally misguided. Imputation is the judicial act/pronouncement that answers to Christ's substitution for believers. To put it as simply as possible, Christ 'paid for' the sins of his people when he suffered the curse that sinners deserve. The 'verdict' of justification is that God reckons that to us, as though we had done what Christ did (or better: because 'we' did it in him!). For recent examples of the attempt to substitute union language for imputation language, see Don Garlington, 'Imputation or Union with Christ? A Response to John Piper', *Reformation & Revival* 12.4 (autumn 2003), pp. 45–113; and Michael F. Bird, 'Incorporated Righteousness: A Response to Recent Evangelical Discussion concerning the Imputation of Christ's Righteousness', *Journal of the Evangelical Theological Society* 47.2 (June 2004), pp. 253–276.

9. In John Calvin's magisterial treatment of justification in Book III of his *Institutes*, he notes that there are two particular themes that belong to the doctrine of free justification. The one theme is the singular honour of God whose grace and mercy in Jesus Christ are the sole basis for the justification and acceptance of believers. The gospel of free justification reveals the sheer graciousness of God's favour in Jesus Christ. Therefore, any ascription of merit to human works before God represents an ungrateful and irreligious dividing between God and sinners what belongs to God alone. The other theme is the assurance or confidence of God's favour, which rests securely upon the foundation of free justification. No contemporary formulation of the doctrine of justification may ignore these principal emphases of the historic Protestant view. If any part of the basis for the free acceptance of believers before God is made to rest upon their works or achievements, the Pauline insistence upon the radical nature of God's grace in Christ is imperilled. What distinguishes the Protestant view is that it insists upon the radical truth of the justification of *the ungodly*. Any attempt to ascribe merit to human works of obedience to the law of God can only transmute the doctrine of justification into a justification of *the godly*. Furthermore, unless the basis for the free justification of believers is found in Christ alone, the assurance of the forgiveness of sins and acceptance with God can only be undermined. Only the free justification of the ungodly upon the basis of the righteousness of Christ alone can provide a sure basis of confidence before God. Any contemporary formulation of the doctrine of justification must face the same questions that the Reformers faced; namely, are believers justified by grace alone on the basis of the work of Christ alone? And, can anything other than a ringing endorsement of free justification secure the believer's confidence of acceptance and forgiveness with God?[72]

10. The biblical doctrine of imputation is often charged with being a 'legal fiction'. God is said to regard sinners *as though they were righteous*, even though they remain sinners still. For the same reason that many object to the imputation of the guilt of Adam's sin to his posterity – the guilt is 'alien', not personal and real – imputation is often decried as a cold, legal transaction that leaves sinners in the same condition as before. Any contemporary restatement of the Protestant understanding of justification must address, accordingly, the *ordo salutis* question of the relation between justification and sanctification. Though justification and sanctification are to be distinguished, they may not be separated. Christ is given to believers for righteousness and sanctification (1 Cor.

---

72. See Henri Blocher, 'Justification of the Ungodly (Sola Fide)', in Carson, *Justification and Variegated Nomism*, vol. 2, pp. 495–496.

1:30). The classic Protestant view never taught a doctrine of 'cheap grace'. This view did insist, however, that the good works of believers are the fruit of a true and living faith. The complexion and tenor of the Christian life is fundamentally altered when good works are performed with a view to obtaining or preserving God's favour. Justification is a necessary prerequisite to sanctification, lest the obedience of the Christian devolve into the performance of a duty in the interest of currying favour with God. Because justification liberates believers from bondage to sin and guilt, it issues in a life of Spirit-born freedom in service to God and others. A contemporary restatement of the doctrine of justification requires that evangelical theology steer a steady course between the Scylla of legalism and the Charybdis of antinomianism.

© Cornelis P. Venema, 2006

10. THE DOCTRINE OF THE CHURCH IN THE TWENTY-FIRST CENTURY

Derek W. H. Thomas

Surviving postmodernity

In the 1559 edition of *The Institutes of the Christian Religion*, John Calvin begins the massive fourth section, '*The External Means or Aims by Which God Invites Us Into the Society of Christ and Holds Us Therein*', by citing Cyprian approvingly: 'those to whom [God] is Father the church may also be Mother'.[1] It is almost inconceivable that a Protestant could say such a thing today without extensive qualification! The fact that Book 4 of Calvin's *Institutes*, comprising in length over one-third of the entire book, is devoted to the doctrine of the church shows that for Calvin, at least, ecclesiology was considered of supreme importance. Given, too, that the first edition (1536) was subtitled *summa pietatis*, ecclesiology was, for Calvin, formative in the development of true godliness.

Evangelical and Reformed students attending seminary these days are likely to be puzzled by the discovery of ecclesiology as a major concern of biblical-theological as well as systematic study in the curriculum.[2] A growing number

---

1. John Calvin, *Institutes of the Christian Religion*, tr. Ford Lewis Battles, 2 vols., Library of Christian Classics, 20–21 (Philadelphia: Westminster, 1960), vol. 2, p. 1012 [4.1.1].

2. In contrast, perhaps, to Catholic students who might still expect to study at some length what Aquinas called 'that wonderful and sacred mystery'.

of such seminary students are, in the main, in their twenties, having little firsthand knowledge of the institutional church as might have been the case in previous generations. Denominational concerns occupy 'practical' courses, ensuring that future ministers are aware of the idiosyncrasies of particular rites and forms. These are largely concerned with 'how to' questions of the practitioners of technique and rarely uncover theological principle or biblical paradigms.

It is almost unimaginable that treatises such as the mid-nineteenth century *The Church of Christ*, by James Bannerman (2 vols. and over 900 pages!), would find a ready readership were it to be written today. Hans Küng's *The Church* (1976) continues to be cited as a twentieth-century treatment of reactionary response to conservative Catholicism, but more for its novelty than its content. It would be disturbing to enquire too deeply into the confidence with which today's seminary student could affirm the dogma 'I believe in the holy, catholic church' (*Credo in . . . sanctam ecclesiam catholicam*) of the Apostles' Creed, or the statement 'and in one, holy, catholic and apostolic church' (*et unam, sanctam, catholicam et apostolicam Ecclesiam*) of the Nicene Creed (AD 325). Still more doubt would ensue in seeking affirmation of the Cyprian formula *extra ecclesiam nulla salus* (outside the church there is no salvation), even if Puritan Confessions (like the Westminster Confession) added the qualifier ('ordinarily', 25.2).[3] In the mid-1970s G. C. Berkouwer wondered if such statements could be considered 'relevant' by modern students of ecclesiology.[4]

More recently, Donald G. Bloesch, writing from a position of self-confessedly 'evangelical neo-orthodoxy' reminded us that doubt over theological dogma (doctrine, rationalism) can be traced to the writings of Friedrich Schleiermacher (1768–1834), who argued that preaching is basically 'testimony . . . to one's own experience' and that theology is the collective amalgam of 'the soul's experience of spiritual life within the Christian Church'.[5] It is not at all insignificant that Schleiermacher's *On Religion: Speeches to its Cultured Despisers* of

---

3. It should be noted again that the qualification was not an attempt to lessen the importance of the church within the divine economy, but to suggest some hope with regard to the death of infants or the fate of those who are incapable of rationally understanding the gospel due to mental impairment. It was not an invitation to so-called 'anonymous Christianity'.

4. G. C. Berkouwer, *The Church* (Grand Rapids: Eerdmans, 1976), p. 7.

5. Donald G. Bloesch, *The Church: Sacraments, Worship, Ministry, Mission* (Downers Grove: IVP, 2002), p. 19, citing Friedrich Schleiermacher, *The Christian Faith*, ed. H. R. Mackintosh and J. S. Stewart (New York: Harper & Row, 1963), vol. 1, p. 5.

1799 should find itself republished in 1996.[6] In this work Schleiermacher attempted to salvage the church from its critics, arguing that despite being largely a 'Church Contemptible', the 'Church Militant' still brings folk into the 'Church Triumphant'. What emerges is a view of the church that is anthropocentric, a social gathering where religious sentiment is allowed freedom of expression, where one experience is as valid as any other, and the institution of the church is a convenient way of bringing some coherence into what otherwise would be hopelessly diversified and inchoate. The ecumenicity of our present age finds in this line of thought a ready formula for maintaining an institutionalized church where the various strands of religious feelings are allowed freedom of expression and affirmation.

Those who have rejected, and continue to reject, such subjectivism and anthropocentrism, have not always returned to a more theologically driven and biblically expressed formulation of what the church *is*. It is difficult for post-Enlightenment individualists to share the vision for a *churchly* consciousness; we tend to read the New Testament data, for example, as not giving us a coherent doctrine of the church – at least, not of an institutionalized church that can be defined as strictly as we define a denomination. Not without importance has been a century of suggestion that the church is essentially *charismatic* – in the sense that it is made up of a diversified group of individually and differently gifted men and women.[7] Paul does not address the ecclesiastical errors that trouble us today in the same way he does more doctrinal issues such as justification or sanctification. We tend therefore to individualize the New Testament data, undervaluing its metaphors of unity and coherence ('the people of God', 'the body of Christ', 'the bride of Christ', 'the flock of Christ', a 'building fitly framed together' etc.).

Then again, the shadow of the Reformation with its understandable fear of tyrannical control and pontifical authority has caused us to be fearful of structure and coherence. Within denominationalism, for example, debates as to the authority of presbyteries and general assemblies over local congregations still

---

6. Friedrich Schleiermacher, *On Religion: Speeches to its Cultured Despisers*, tr. and ed. Richard Crouter, Cambridge Texts in the History of Philosophy (Cambridge: Cambridge University Press, 1996).

7. Such a view stems from more than one source, and involves very different agendas, including the views of Emil Brunner in neo-orthodoxy, Hans Küng in reaction to Catholicism, and the modern charismatic phenomenon emphasizing the return of supposed New Testament apostolic gifts (tongues, prophecy, knowledge, healing etc.).

rage on without any sign of being extinguished. We still tend to view church as we experience it. Thus suburban corner-block churches tend to emphasize community and body-life issues. Conservative denominational churches stress doctrinal formulation as the point of coherence, but sometimes stress secondary issues to the point of fostering a lack of catholicity, resulting in the unchurching of those whose practice is different from theirs. Charismatic churches stress every-member gifting in ways that are not always in the interests of the body, but are expressions of self-fulfilment and narcissistic indulgence. It is almost impossible for some to imagine the church other than in its denominational and institutional dimension, a view that would be difficult for Christians in the New Testament era to recognize.

More particularly, in the Western world of today, Christianity is no longer the dominant cultural force; we live in a post-Christian pluralistic society. The antihistorical trend of recent decades (Foucault's thesis that histories do not offer explanations but bids for power, 'attempts to legitimize particular institutions or attitudes in the present') elicits responses of an antihistorical kind in the loss of consciousness in the communion of saints. The church of today has lost sight of its place within the historical tradition, leaving itself somewhat rootless. The 'worship wars' evidence an abandonment of traditional liturgy, leaving contemporary worship adrift from the past and from what previous generations regarded as essential in defining what true *corporate* worship is. In addition, the cult of youth, the introduction of modern musical genres for reasons of taste without reasoned argument for its propriety adds significantly to the rootlessness of the modern church.[8]

In reaction, and at first glance, certain movements have adopted a 'Back to the Bible' formula, not wishing to distance themselves entirely from the past, merely the cultural baggage of more recent history. But it has proven a simplistic, often thoughtless, response, ignoring received formulations of truth and practice that have no need of being fought all over again lest, this time around, we get the formula wrong (cf. the Socinians of the sixteenth century, rejecting even Trinity and incarnation on grounds of literalist hermeneutics and rejection of metaphysics in theology).

In reaction to the blatant consumerism and antihistorical emphasis of a market-driven ideology of church growth, some have found refuge in edgy

---

8. Carl Trueman's comment 'no one should make the mistake of seeing the move to contemporary praise songs and service styles as simply a straightforward, value-neutral repackaging or rebranding of a traditional product' seems apposite here, *The Wages of Spin* (Geanies: Mentor, 2005), p. 23.

formulations such as the 'Celtic Way' as an attempt to recover a lost past. But in doing so they have committed fallacies of their own, missing the emphasis of the Reformation on the Word as central to what the church is and does.[9]

Others, dismayed by what C. S. Lewis termed 'chronological snobbery',[10] have attempted to find their roots in a return to liturgical worship, sometimes showing little discernment of the traditions from which they now borrow. Within this reactionary group are others who have sought meaning in church government (emphasizing in one direction, 'elders', or in another, 'bishops'). Often the two go together, the rediscovery of the value and historical connectivity of liturgy (and as knee-jerk reaction to the free-for-all democratizing – and therefore 'lowest-common-denominator' nature of the modern church) suggesting the need for more authoritative leadership (priests and bishops rather than ruling and teaching elders), downplaying if not altogether denying 'the priesthood of all believers' so beloved of the Reformation.

Vatican II (1962–65) succeeded in redefining traditional ecclesiology where the World Council of Churches did not. Siren voices were raised at the time suggesting that little had changed (thus, interestingly, Cardinal Joseph Ratzinger, now Pope Benedict XVI). Others (Edward Schillebeeckx) insisted that everything had changed.[11] More recent history has tempered such claims to change and it remains to be seen how wedded the modern Catholic church is to its traditional and sacerdotal nature.

---

9. See Donald Meek, 'Modern Celtic Christianity', *Scottish Bulletin of Evangelical Theology* 10 (1992), pp. 6–31; and 'Modern Celtic Christianity', *Studia Imagologica: Amsterdam Studies on Cultural Identity* 8 (1996), pp. 143–157.

10. C. S. Lewis, *Surprised by Joy: The Shape of my Early Life* (London: Geoffrey Bles, 1955), p. 196; and 'Nothing is more characteristically juvenile than contempt for juvenility: . . . youth's characteristic chronological snobbery', C. S. Lewis, *An Experiment in Criticism* (Cambridge: Cambridge University Press, 1961), p. 73. Lewis borrows the phrase from his friend Owen Barfield, who defines it as 'the presumption, fueled by the modern conception of progress, that all thinking, all art, and all science of an earlier time are inherently inferior, indeed childlike or even imbecilic, compared to that of the present. Under the rule of chronological snobbery, the West has convinced itself that intellectually, humanity languished for countless generations in the most childish errors on all sorts of crucial subjects, until it was redeemed by some simple scientific dictum of the last century', *History in English Words* (Hudson, N. Y.; Lindisfarne Press, 1967), p. 164.

11. Edward Schillebeeckx, *The Church: The Human Story of God* (London: SCM; New York: Crossroad, 1990).

A seemingly potent reaction is now gripping the USA in the form of the 'Emergent Church' phenomenon,[12] a movement that thinks that changes in the culture signal that a new church is 'emerging'. Central to its philosophy is the idea that cultural accretions have eclipsed the gospel from the present generation. It appears to be a reaction to seeker-sensitive churches and what is felt to be a dilution of gospel priorities on the one hand and a distrust of the institutional church (and its confessionalism) on the other.[13] One of its leaders, Brian McLaren claims to uphold the ancient creedal forms (Nicene, Apostles'), but denies that truth must be articulated in propositional form. It is a movement that ransacks the Christian tradition, picking and choosing whatever seems appropriate to form a language that is meaningful to Christians, if not objectively true. Concern for propositional truthfulness is an artefact of the modern age. Christianity, according to this movement, must embrace a pluriform understanding. It is the child of our times.

Another 'reaction' to the Reformation formula (soteriology impacting ecclesiology) can be traced in the rise of the 'new Perspectives on Paul' (Krister Stendahl, E. P. Sanders, Heikki Räisänen, James D. G. Dunn, N. T. Wright) over the past half century. It has recently gained even more prominence and is likely to be with us for some time. It may even change forever the way systematic theology is done in more than one department. These 'perspectives' engage several disciplines (Judaism, intertestamental studies, New Testament theology, categories of justification/righteousness in soteriology, sacraments etc.), and occupy comments made elsewhere in this book, but important here is the way these views increasingly reshape traditional ecclesiology. Wright's contribution in particular is category-shifting: ecclesiology not soteriology becomes the paradigm of justification and thus the main emphasis of a book like Romans, for example. The 'distortion' of justification by the Reformers (which Alistair McGrath has also voiced) shifted the focus from Paul's concern

---

12. See Andy Crouch, 'The Emergent Mystique', *Christianity Today*, November 2004, pp. 36–41.

13. See Brian D. McLaren, *A Generous Orthodoxy* (Grand Rapids: Zondervan, 2004), 'The last thing I want is to get into nauseating arguments about why this or that form of theology (dispensational, covenant, charismatic, whatever) or methodology (cell church, megachurch, liturgical church, seeker church, blah, blah, blah) is right (meaning approaching or achieving timeless technical perfection).' Shock, obscurity, playfulness, and intrigue often communicate better than clarity has been McLaren's motto. See D. A. Carson's response in *Becoming Conversant with the Emerging Church* (Grand Rapids: Zondervan, 2005).

for ecclesiology (*Who* can be considered members of the covenant community?) to soteriology (*How* can we become members of the covenant community?). It is a view that seriously alters how we understand justification/
righteousness, downplaying the role of experience and conversion as prerequisites for a valid profession of faith and 'full' or 'communicant' church
membership (a major concern in traditional ecclesiology). Indeed, church
membership (attending to its outward forms and symbols, including sacraments) takes on the role of a confirming sign of inclusion. It is a view better
wedded to a 'parish' view of the church than a 'gathered' one, and it is unsur-
prising that its devotees have largely been of this persuasion.

The marks (*notae*) of the church

The Nicene (AD 325) and Niceno-Constantinopolitan Creed (AD 381) affirmed
four marks (*notae*) of the church: unity, holiness, catholicity and apostolicity.[14]
It is doubtful that the modern church would come up with these four either
individually or collectively as summarizing the essential marks of the church.
Unity is a fairly obvious qualification, even if it does sound Pickwickian and
can at best be affirmed (as Protestants do) only of the *invisible* church.[15]
Theologians regularly define it by employing language that suggests it is a
'complex' or 'mystical' entity. The continued fractioning of the visible church
has caused a retreat among some, and a reaffirmation among others, suggesting that unity is a chimera-like attribute true only of the status quo in defiance
of the rest of Christendom, or of some future, eschatological reality not yet
in existence (cf. Eph. 4:13–16).

Is this expression of unity too abstract to be of any significance in the day-
to-day existence of the church in the world? Even the Lausanne Covenant
(1974) acknowledged that 'organizational unity may take many forms' as
though conceding (justifying?) the fractured nature of the bride of Christ on
earth. Reverberations from *Evangelicals and Catholics Together: The Christian
Mission in the Third Millennium* (1994), co-authored by such notable theologians

---

14. In Greek, *eis mian, hagian, katholikēn kai apostolikēn ekklēsian*, and in Latin, *Et unam,
    sanctam, catholicam et apostolicam Ecclesiam.*
15. John Murray's equivocation over the visible/invisible nature of the church makes it
    even more difficult to affirm in any meaningful way. See 'The Church: Its Definition
    in terms of "Visible" and "Invisible" Invalid', in *Collected Writings of John Murray*,
    4 vols. (Edinburgh: Banner of Truth Trust, 1976), vol. 1, pp. 231–236.

as J. I. Packer, Chuck Colson, Bill Bright and Pat Robertson, continue, mainly because unity across soteriological and sacerdotal lines continues to be non-negotiable for most evangelical Christians.[16] Given recent developments in 'New Perspectives on Paul', calling into question what Jaroslav Pelikan called the 'tragic necessity' of the Reformation with its understanding of justification, unity among Protestant churches seems to be heading for greater strain. It remains to be seen whether, in the face of a displacement of forensic categories of justification, the shape of unity as a confession of ecclesiastical dogma can be sustained.[17]

Given the onslaughts of postmodernity and the increasing sign of evangelical accommodation,[18] it is understandable that Christians of all persuasions (and of little persuasion!) feel the need to embrace each other against the juggernaut of secularism. Christianity in the West is rapidly becoming a minority view, and ethical relativism, on the one hand (the need to unify across Christendom on such issues as abortion, euthanasia and homosexuality), and the rise of militant (proselytizing) Islam, on the other (the need to secure a response to what appears to be the alarming rate at which Islam has spread into Europe and the Far East), make *some* expression of unity all the more necessary.[19]

Holiness as a mark of the church seems self-evident, too, if the church is the physical embodiment of Christ (as diverse theologians, both Protestant and Catholic, have affirmed). Donatist (and Novationist) concerns over the

---

16. Cf. J. I. Packer and Thomas C. Oden, *One Faith: The Evangelical Consensus* (Downers Grove: IVP, 2004).

17. See John Armstrong, ed., *Roman Catholicism: Evangelical Protestants Analyze What Divides and Unites Us* (Chicago: Moody, 1994); Norman Geisler and Ralph E. MacKenzie, *Roman Catholics and Evangelicals: Agreements and Differences* (Grand Rapids: Baker, 1995); William Webster, *The Church of Rome at the Bar of History* (Edinburgh: Banner of Truth, 1995).

18. Our culture resembles the pagan pluralism of the early church, but, unlike the early church period, ours has understood Christianity and rejected it. See Millard J. Erickson, Paul Kjoss Helseth, Justin Taylor, eds., *Reclaiming the Center: Confronting Evangelical Accommodation in Postmodern Times* (Wheaton, Ill.: Crossway, 2004).

19. See Christine Mallouhi, *Waging Peace on Islam* (Downers Grove: IVP, 2002); Miriam Adeney, *Building Bridges with Muslim Women* (Downers Grove: IVP, 2002); Chawkat Moucarry, *The Prophet and the Messiah: An Arab Christian's Perspective on Islam and Christianity* (Downers Grove: IVP, 2002); Bassam Chedid, *Islam: What Every Christian Should Know* (Darlington: Evangelical Press, 2004).

purity of the church (who could or could not be allowed into the church who had fallen under Roman persecutions, together with the vexed issue of [re]-baptism of those 'improperly baptized') is a reflection of the church's holiness. At what point does the church's *un*holiness call into question its right to be considered a church? Denominationalism has concerned itself more with doctrinal than ethical aberration and the worldliness of the contemporary church – its unashamed adoption of marketplace business strategies as a model for 'doing church' and, in another area, its uncritical assumption of secular anthropology and therapeutic models seriously distorts its holiness. Many might legitimately complain that it is difficult to see the boundary between church and secular society.

The church is the covenant community of those who share in the redemptive renewal of a sin-spoiled creation, which began when Christ rose from the dead, but whose embryonic origins begin in the Old Testament and the formation of Israel (cf. Gal. 6:16). What is true individually of the people of God is also true collectively. Just as individual believers are a *new creation* in union with Christ, raised with him out of death to life, possessed and led by the life-giving Holy Spirit, so also is the church as a whole. The church's life springs from its union with Christ, crucified and risen. The church is Christ's *building*, growing into a 'holy temple in the Lord' (Eph. 2:1ff.);[20] his *body* now growing into a state of full edification (Eph. 4; Rom. 12; 1 Cor. 12; and Col. 1); and his *bride*, now being sanctified and cleansed in readiness for 'the marriage of the Lamb' (Rev. 19:7ff.; cf. Eph. 5:25ff.). Holiness is God's calling for God's people, both individually and collectively. Believers have failed (and *continue* to fail) to appreciate the corporate dimension of discipleship – that the church functions as the organism by which individual growth is encouraged, energized and achieved (hence the emphasis on the church as dispenser of the 'means of grace').

The corporate character of the church as a doctrinal and systematic category[21] is one of those concepts best approached through a careful biblical-theological and exegetical study of the various analogies employed by the New Testament – sheep in a flock, branches of a vine, friends of a bridegroom, stones in a temple, the new Israel. Many of the ethical exhortations of the New Testament are, in fact, given within a corporate dimension rather than an individualistic one (cf. Rom. 8:13; Phil. 2:12–13). For Paul, none seems more prom-

---

20. Bible quotations in this chapter are from the ESV.

21. See David VanDrunen, ed., *The Pattern of Sound Doctrine: Systematic Theology at the Westminster Seminaries. Essays in Honor of Robert B. Strimple* (Phillipsburg: P. & R., 2004).

inent than that of the church as the 'body of Christ', understood relationally rather than anatomically – suggesting the way believers are drawn into fellowship with each other, mutually sharing a common life and goal *because* they have been brought into relationship with Jesus Christ as their head (Col. 1:18).[22]

The affirmation of the church's catholicity (geographically across national and international boundaries as well as temporally across the centuries), first coined by Ignatius of Antioch,[23] protects the church against parochialism, sectarianism and an ever-present incipient racism and conceit of chronology. Just as the church faces the attraction of pluralism alluring a broader definition of the church with boundaries that are intentionally blurred, so, too, it faces the obscurantism of elitist groups unwilling to acknowledge the right of others to be the church of Jesus Christ. Central here especially are the concepts of 'heresy' and 'schism'. The kind of opinion expressed by Paul of Judaistic belief and practice in Galatia as 'another gospel' (Gal. 1:6; cf. 2 Cor. 11:4) requires a view that the church ceases to be the church in any meaningful sense when certain truths are denied. Postmodernity makes such identifications more difficult, as does 'anonymous Christianity' – the view that true Christians may be found in parts of the world where the gospel has never reached. Those with true notions will be saved by Jesus Christ even though they do not know it.

Cyprian's formula *extra ecclesiam nulla salus* sounds impossibly sacerdotal to modern ears and brings to mind Rousseau's quip 'anyone who dares to say, "Outside the Church there can be no salvation," should be banished from the State' (*Social Contract* 4.8). Modern Protestantism has so devalued the church that it is difficult to give a defence that does not appear hopelessly non-evangelical – defending outward forms and structures rather than a relationship with God by faith in Jesus Christ! Calvin's approval of this (as cited at the beginning of this chapter), affirming that God and the church are related to the Christian as 'Father' and 'Mother', in which he adds 'one may not put asunder what God has joined together' (*Institutes* 4.1.1), is equally unnerving to those whose view of the church is governed more by the individualism and subjectivism of our age than by a robust understanding of the role of the church in redemptive history. Some branches of the church continue to wrestle over Cyprian's avowal of rebaptism/rejection of heretic

---

22. See Sinclair Ferguson, *The Holy Spirit* (Downers Grove: IVP, 1996), pp. 192–193.

23. *Smyrna* 8.2, cited by C. C. Richardson, ed., *Early Christian Fathers* (Philadelphia: Westminster, 1953), p. 115. 'Where Jesus Christ is, there is the catholic church,' he wrote in AD 110.

baptism,[24] particularly, interestingly enough, of Roman Catholic baptism, and of related issues of the validity of ordination.[25]

Apostolicity links the church with the apostles of the New Testament, thus earthing the church historically (important to do in a postmodern culture) as well as establishing a line of continuity to the present. By affirming apostolicity, Protestants imply faithfulness to *apostolic doctrine* and *apostolic commission* rather than any genetic linkage to the apostles, especially Peter by way of succession of office (an issue Protestants assert with conviction as nothing but religious fantasy). 'Holding fast the traditions' (2 Thess. 2:15), with its noun *paradosis*, is a deeply significant concern of the New Testament (cf. 2 Thess. 3:6; 1 Cor. 11:23; 15:3; Col. 2:6), to such an extent that Paul was conscious of this normative canon *over and above* his own words and opinions (which themselves become normative and canonical through inspiration). Thus, writing to the Corinthians, he can say, 'To the married I give this charge (not I, but the Lord)' (1 Cor. 7:10), citing words of Jesus during his earthly ministry (Matt. 5:32). 'It is the exalted Lord', wrote Oscar Culmann, 'who now proclaims the Corinthians through the tradition that he had taught His disciples during His incarnation on earth.'[26] Apostolicity affirms that there exists a clearly definable *content* ('deed/act' *plus* interpretative word) to the Bible's message.

Continuity and anchorage are provided by one phrase, *credo . . . apostolicam Ecclesiam*, suggesting the 'given*ness*' of truth and the doctrine based upon it. Understanding of truth develops but not to the point where the church declares apostolic truth a falsehood. The church's greatest theologians have always engaged and interacted with unbelief and errant philosophies. In her best moments, she has plundered Philistinism and emerged with booty to

---

24. Strictly speaking, it is not *re*baptism, since the validity of the initial baptism is denied. See, e.g., the 'Minority Report: *Ad Hoc* Committee to Study the Validity of Certain Baptism', in *PCA Digest, Position Papers: 1973–1998*, at http://www.pcanet.org/history/pca/2-093.html.

25. See Pope Leo XIII's declaration (in 1896) on the invalidity of Anglican ordination in *Apostolicae Curae* and the declarations on it by the ARCIC (Anglican-Roman Catholic International Commission) I and II reports. Several complications have emerged in this dialogue, not least the problematic issue of papal infallibility that was pronounced upon *Apostolicae Curae* and the difficulty, therefore, of its withdrawal, and, more recently, the ordination of women by the Anglican communion making the issue less likely of any imminent resolution.

26. Oscar Cullmann, *The Early Church* (Canterbury: SCM, 1966), p. 68.

better defend and assert what is core belief: think of Augustine's use of Plato, Aquinas's employment of Aristotle, Calvin's engagement with Cicero or John Owen's interest in Maimonides. Today's church must do the same (and show increasing robustness in engaging postmodernity), but not in such a way as to blur the edges of received truth as understood through the disciplines of exegetical, hermeneutical, biblical-theological and systematic appraisal. This calls for seminaries to train ministers of the gospel to levels of expertise adequate to meet the onslaught of relativism that marks our age. It is to be feared that the democratization of the theological process (every blogger now demands the right to have centre stage and equal validity) destabilizes serious theological engagement. The church's affirmation of its 'tradition' becomes an engagement with last week's posting. Novelty rather than precision thus threatens to formulate opinion. Abraham Kuyper observed that it is an 'unhistoric' illusion to think that, Bible in hand, one could 'leap backward' across the centuries to study the Scriptures as though there had been no intervening 'history of interpretation, theological debate, and confessional formulation'.[27] Thus it is not so much 'No creed but the Bible' that threatens the church, as the viewpoint 'No creed is safe'. True, the Reformation cautioned against idolizing the past, including itself. The First Confession of Basel stated:

> Finally, we desire to submit this our confession to the judgment of the divine Biblical Scriptures. And should we be informed from the same Holy Scriptures of a better one, we have thereby expressed our readiness to be willing at any time to obey God and his holy Word with great thanksgiving.[28]

Preaching, sacraments

Two further necessary marks of the church have been identified: biblical preaching and the right use of the sacraments.[29] Thus Calvin says, 'Wherever

---

27. Abraham Kuyper, *Encyclopedia of Sacred Theology* (New York: Scribner's, 1898), p. 574.
28. Arthur C. Cochrane, *Reformed Confessions of the 16th Century* (Philadelphia: Westminster, 1966), p. 96. See also Jaroslav Pelikan and Valerie Hotchkiss, eds., *Creeds and Confessions of Faith in the Christian Tradition*, 4 vols. (New Haven: Yale University Press, 2003), vol. 2, pp. 272–279. Cf. Westminster Confession of Faith 1.10; 31.4.
29. Donald Bloesch, *The Church* (Downers Grove: IVP, 2002), p. 103.

we see the Word of God purely preached and heard, and the sacraments administered according to Christ's institution, there, it is not to be doubted, a church of God exists.'[30] The writings of Pope Benedict XVI (as the then Cardinal Joseph Ratzinger) in an official note released on 5 September 2000, warning that declaring Protestant churches as 'true churches' can cause 'ambiguities', is sure to play itself out on the stage of ecclesiology in coming years. It was a comment on the papal document *Dominus Iesus* ('On the Unicity and Salvific Universality of Jesus Christ and the Church'), published the same day, which declared that churches that do not have a 'valid Episcopate [bishops] and the genuine and integral substance of the Eucharistic mystery are not Churches in the proper sense'.

Defining the church's essence remains difficult and there is a growing sense in which systematic theology has not served us adequately. Increasingly, the church's *suffering* in its present pilgrim status is considered central. In an age where persecution remains a significant (though underappreciated issue), it is requisite for systematic theology to consider how to answer the questions raised by the persecuted. One way is to draw attention to the fact that the Scriptures seem to teach that suffering is always going to be a mark of the church. Jesus hints at it in the seminal passage at Caesarea Philippi when he announces that the church is built in enemy-occupied territory within sight of the gates of Hades (Matt. 16:13–19).

On the right administration of the sacraments several key issues have merged recently that require systematic consideration: Reformed churches continue to debate and disagree over the nature of the presence of Christ in the Supper, both sides often calling Calvin as chief defence witness; paedo-communion has re-emerged in some circles, partly as a result of the worship wars and a return by some to more historic ecclesiastical traditions, some of which have held different views as to the propriety of children (infants) partaking of the elements of the Supper, and partly due to re-emergence over the past half-century of the idea of covenant as the central unifying theme of Scripture (rather than, e.g., God, salvation or kingdom); the nature of the relationship between 'Israel' and 'church' necessitating a reappraisal of the distinctive 'newness' of the new covenant and where lines of discontinuity and continuity may lie; and surprisingly, the definition of the parties involved in the 'covenant of grace' (some alternatives being God [the Father] and Christ, God and the elect, or God and believers together with their children) as expressive of covenant inclusion or exclusion.

---

30. *Institutes* 4.1.9.

The debate over church offices continues apace. Systematic theology has perhaps focused too intently upon the historic discussions (mainly between Episcopalians and Presbyterians) over the understanding of the eldership. Thus, the writings of Thornwell, Dabney and Hodge (in the USA) and Witherow, Miller and others (in Britain) have been pitted against the seminal essays of the Anglican triumvirate, Hort, Lightfoot and Hatch. Both parties have claimed modest (and sometimes less than modest) victories. But the route from *presbyteros, episkopos, poimēn* and *prestos* to 'the preacher' (as a distinct, ordained office either distinct from *or* functionally but not essentially different from the 'ruling elder') remains a difficult one. Systematic theology attempted to find a way to assemble the New Testament data to confirm one or other polity, but the tendency to make the 'eldership' a shibboleth continues.[31]

Matthew 16:13–19 continues to occupy centre-stage in discussions ecclesiastical. Papal authority has been grounded on the identification of Peter as the rock (16:18, *petros*) upon which the church is built, and the keys of the kingdom that 'bind' and 'loose' as those that belong to the exercise and power of papal authority.[32] The passage is important for the doctrine of the church, and systematic theology (for understandable reasons) has been too preoccupied with opposing triumphalist claims by Roman Catholics as to the role of Peter and the papacy in the church's authority to notice how seminal the passage is in relationship to the overall design of redemption as announced in the *protoevangelium*, Genesis 3:15. The 'seed of woman' has been born and will systematically undo what the fall brought about, and what the architect of the fall (Satan) designed. Christ builds his church in enemy-occupied territory, but the 'gates of Hades' will *not* prevail. Christ will be victorious over Satan's schemes. Christus Victor! The church, far from being something of a *hiatus* or *parenthesis*, is central to redemption's unfolding story. From Genesis onwards, this is what redemption has had in view. Attempts to suggest that what is in view is not Peter 'the man' but Peter 'the Confessor' seem astonishingly naive, considering Paul's declaration in Ephesians that the church is built on the foundation of apostles and prophets (Eph. 2:20). The apostles did indeed have great power and authority at a time when the church was in its infancy.

Debate concerning continuation/cessation of apostolic gifts must take into

---

31. See Donald MacLeod, *Priorities for the Church: Rediscovering Leadership and Vision in the Church* (Fearn, Ross-shire: Christian Focus, 2003), pp. 43–56.

32. Interestingly, Pope Benedict XVI has written, 'if the church is founded on Peter, it is not founded on his person but on his faith'. Cited by Hans Küng, *Christianity: Essence, History, and Future* (New York: Continuum, 1996), p. 314.

consideration that the New Testament divides itself into apostolic and post-apostolic periods, the former being *foundational*. It is not difficult, then, to argue that certain phenomena associated with the former should not necessarily be manifest in the era of the latter. Systematic theology must take careful and nuanced exegetical care to reflect this redemptive-historical timeline that impacts the understanding of the nature of the church today in distinction to the nature of the church in the days of the apostles.

This gives rise to the continued debate on gifting that ranges through a variety of issues, including the nature of the church as *charismatic* (bestowed with gifts, though not necessarily apostolic sign gifts, especially *glossolalia*), the nature of the 'diaconal' ministry, what 'appointment' to office implies (Latin, *officium*, Greek, *cheirotoneō* and *kathistēmi*), and the vexed issue of the ordination of women to office, whether minister (teaching elder, priest) or positions of rule (ruling elder) or diaconate.

Attention must be given to the New Testament understanding of every-member ministry (Eph. 4:12).[33] Every member of the church is a priest and therefore ministers in the sanctuary, holding in trust gifts of service for the edifying of the one body of Christ.

On the issue of women's ordination to office, theological issues that deserve exploration and attention must include (1) that God reveals himself in his tri-unity in male terms, and the Son of God became incarnate as a male (not a female or androgynous being), (2) the rescuing of Galatians 3:28 from the quagmire of egalitarianism to its more obvious role in defending complimen-tarity – equality of *status* (cf. Gen. 1:26–27) rather than *function*, (3) a robust defence of the gifting of women for a multiplicity of roles and functions, all of which the church must recognize (and not muddy by concepts of ordin-ation), and (4) realize that sexuality implies a necessary distinction between male and female and that theological fudging in ecclesiology has implications for the home as much as it has for the church.[34]

---

33. 'To equip the saints for the work of the ministry . . .' The comma after 'saints' in some versions has been called 'the fatal comma', suggesting clericalism (it is the officially ordained that performs work of ministry rather than the saints themselves, aided and encouraged and informed by the officially set apart).

34. For varying viewpoints (in addition to others cited below), see S. B. Clark, *Man and Woman in Christ* (Ann Arbor: Servant, 1980); J. B. Hurley, *Man and Woman in Biblical Perspective* (Grand Rapids: Zondervan, 1981); G. W. Knight III, *The Role Relationship of Men and Women* (Chicago: Moody, 1977); B. and R. B. Clouse, eds., *Women in Ministry: Four Views* (Downers Grove: IVP, 1989); S. T. Foh, *Women and the Word of God*

Those who argue (1) that the New Testament does not forbid women to teach or exercise rule, or (2) that gifted women are an undeniable fact and we need to validate it (some women *can* teach and are *better* teachers/preachers than men are, and God would not thus order providence for these gifts to be wasted), or (3) that God orders things differently according to the extremities of the hour (this is a judgment of the male population rather than a wholesale selling out to secular feminism) must, by turns, address the core issue of hermeneutical considerations and the plain text of Scripture that limit the presbyterate as well as the diaconate (considered as office)[35] to males. This is no insignificant issue and systematic theology must address the implications for the true meaning of a text when cultural and temporal considerations can redefine what seems self-evident in the grammar. Such cultural accommodation spells the end of exegesis as previously understood – a commitment to *grammatico*-historical methodology replaced by cultural-chronological relativism. The issue of practising homosexuality and the ministry (let alone

---

(Grand Rapids: Baker, 1979); E. Storkey, *What's Right with Feminism* (London: SPCK, 1989); G. G. Hull, *Equal to Serve: Women and Men in the Church and Home* (London: Scripture Union, 1989).

35. Irrespective of issues of office and ordination, it is clear that women *function* as deacons in the New Testament (Matt. 8:15 [Mark 1:31; Luke 4:39]; 27:55 [Mark 15:4; cf. Luke 8:3]; Luke 10:40; John 12:2; Rom. 16:1). It is possible that Romans 16:1 refers to a deacon's wife, though the reading would be strained, but 1 Timothy 3:11 makes more sense as a reference to deacons' wives rather than deaconesses. Historical analysis of the New Testament reveals a growing move to ordination to office in the pastoral epistles and is confined to men, an issue embryonically anticipated in the selection of *men* (despite already existent evidence of women performing diaconal functions) to help alleviate the apostles from more mundane tasks in order that they might devote themselves to prayer and the ministry of the Word (Acts 6:3ff.). Despite the difficulty in attributing the term 'deacon' to this group, as they function more as deacons here than temporary elders, in this sense they seem to have been chosen with other issues in mind. They are chosen, however, to aid in the task of oversight and governance as directed by the elders of the church. It is for this reason that the *ordination* of deacons is limited to men. On the interpretation of 1 Tim. 3:11, see John Piper and Wayne Grudem, eds., *Recovering Biblical Manhood and Womanhood* (Wheaton, Ill.: Crossway, 1991); Wayne Grudem and Dennis Rainey, eds., *Pastoral Manhood and Womanhood* (Wheaton, Ill.: Crossway, 2002); Wayne Grudem, *Biblical Foundations for Manhood and Womanhood* (Wheaton, Ill.: Crossway, 2002).

homosexuality and the church generally) is an issue that belongs to the same hermeneutical problem – though it must be admitted that while there are some texts of Scripture that favour the gifting of women (if not ordination), the issue of practising homosexuality is devoid of any biblical support.

Worship wars and mother kirk

Cultural and historical theological dislocation is no more acutely observed than in what takes place on Sunday morning in gathered congregations of Christian worship. The advent of the 'worship wars' is testimony to much theological confusion, indifference and a penchant for the bizarre. Abandonment of distinctive theological categories in favour of more nuanced ('symphonic') theology has not been helpful. Biblical-theological categories have given rise to the idea that there is a definable template for corporate worship (high liturgy reflects Old Testament temple worship, informal worship reflects that which emerged in the early chapters of Acts, more structured ordered worship according to a basic formula is reflective of later New Testament teaching etc., but none is a full paradigm of what is desirable). Attempts to suggest that the New Testament does not recognize 'formal gathered worship' (all of life is worship and what is evidenced in the New Testament is more of a continuum than an informal/formal structure) seem doomed to failure upon recognition of such factors as ordination to office, discipline and the employment of the sacraments, to raise but three issues that distinguish the one from the other.[36] It seems to me that a study of the *Directory for the Public Worship of God* (1545) is in order, notwithstanding the nature of the document as an example of ecclesiastical compromise. At the heart of it lies an outworking of a regulative principle of worship, *nothing must be required as essential in public worship except that which is commanded by the Word of God*, as opposed to what is sometimes referred to as a Lutheran/Episcopalian principle, *anything is acceptable in public worship so long as Scripture does not explicitly forbid it* – the former given confessional status in the Westminster Confession of Faith in three of its chapters.[37]

---

36. My esteemed colleague John Frame has given a valiant defence of this view in
    Worship in Spirit and Truth: A Refreshing Study of the Principles and Practice of Biblical Worship (Phillipsburg: P. & R., 1996). See also Robert A. Morey, *Worship is All of Life* (Camp Hill, Pa.: Christian Publications, 1984).
37. Westminster Confession of Faith 1.6; 20.2; 21.1.

Criticisms of the Regulative Principle of Worship come from many different quarters. Some are knee-jerk cultural expressions of postmodernity. Others are thoughtful, if sometimes incoherent, attempts at continuing reformation: *semper reformanda reformata est.* Sometimes one suspects that a theological veneer is being given to baptize a particular practice. And sometimes there is no theological justification given at all. It is a disturbing fact that our culture can affect our manner and style of worship more drastically than we give credit. Marva Dawn has written extensively on this issue.[38] To that extent she has applied to worship what David Wells has trumpeted more generally: that culture affects us in deep and serious ways and we had better wake up to it or find ourselves at culture's mercy.[39] The call for the church to be truly counter-cultural (to borrow John Stott's phrase[40]), an 'alternative society' as Dawn has labelled it,[41] has never been more urgent than it is now, and nowhere is this seen more poignantly than at 11.00 a.m. on a Sunday morning. Public worship ought to be different from the routine of daily life, but in what way? It would be relatively easy to present a case for what some would regard as high-brow culture (I prefer Bach to the Back Street Boys) – and such a case needs to be done (and *can* be made) on grounds other than mere prejudice. But the point here is that what makes worship *different* is that its cultural ethos is determined by Scriptural commands and principles rather than personal or collective tastes and mores.

Several matters emerge from a consideration of a regulative principle of worship: (1) the corporate nature of the church as a disciplined, worshipping body is given theological status and affirmation. Any other view merely fosters ecclesiastical relativism, which may further the interests of church unity (though little evidence of this exists at present), but at an unacceptable price as to the church's identity and *notae*; (2) it gives a vehicle for defining the nature of the church's relationship to culture, suggesting on the one hand that there exists cultural variation both geographically as well as temporally, in addition

---

38. Marva Dawn, *Reaching Out without Dumbing Down: A Theology of Worship for the Turn-of-the-Century Culture* (Grand Rapids: Eerdmans, 1995); *A Royal Waste of Time: The Splendor of Worshipping God and Being Church for the World* (Grand Rapids: Eerdmans, 1999).

39. David Wells, *No Place for Truth: Or, Whatever Happened to Evangelical Theology?* (Grand Rapids: Eerdmans, 1993).

40. Stott gave this as a title to his study of the Sermon on the Mount, *Christian Counter-Culture: The Message of the Sermon on the Mount* (Leicester: IVP, 1978).

41. *Reaching Out without Dumbing Down*, p. 9.

to suggesting a pathway into the more difficult area of cultural evaluation and criticism. Only a commitment to a regulative principle can provide a means of expressing valid cultural differentiation without sacrificing essential theological commitment; (3) it fosters a truer understanding of the communion of the saints, identifying the worshipping community with the historic creedal formulations and liturgical boundary markers of the past; (4) it validates the central doctrine of the *sola Scriptura*, a commitment which ensures that ecclesiology is subject to this rubric as much as any other tenet of theology.[42]

Summary and conclusion

What can we say about the current state of theological understanding in matters ecclesiastical? It may be helpful to provide a summary of desiderata as prerequisites for any future consideration of the doctrine of the church.

1. *At the risk of sounding naive, future Reformed ecclesiology must return to the Bible.* It is par for the course of criticism to point out the error of church-growth strategies that employ marketplace principles in church planting, adopting a 'seeker-friendly' methodology in attracting today's unchurched into what is otherwise an alien environment. It can also be pointed out that we have reaped what we have sown – a consumer mentality in worship and Christian lifestyle that is barely distinguishable from the world. A church that is wedded to Jesus Christ necessarily produces cultural and methodological alienation: the Lord's people are strangers and pilgrims in an alien environment and the attraction of the church is as much its *difference* from the world as anything else. Only a return to the Scriptures and the disciplines of sound exegesis and doctrinal formulation can redress this imbalance. Only a return to the Bible can show us the distinctive nature of the church as well as its remarkable breadth. The tendency of triumphalism within Reformed denominations is a matter greatly to be regretted and a study of the Scriptures will surely enable us to distinguish the core and fundamental (the issues that are 'first importance' [1 Cor. 15:3]) from the secondary.

2. *Reformed ecclesiology must be wedded to a robust embrace of Reformed theology at its best and a re-evaluation of the discoveries of biblical theology.* As has been pointed out elsewhere in this volume, systematics has sometimes been divorced from the

---

42. For a fuller treatment of this issue, see my chapter 'The Regulative Principle: Responding to Recent Criticisms', in J. Ligon Duncan III, Phillip Ryken and Derek W. H. Thomas, eds., *Give Praise to God* (Phillipsburg: P. & R., 2003).

rigours of biblical exegesis and a sensitivity to the flow of redemptive history. Equally strong claims may be made of biblical theology, too, but it does not help us in the concerns that have occupied this volume merely to point out the speck in our brother's eye. Whether a *jus divinum* exists for ecclesiology will need to be proven from the data of Scripture, and the data often proves more difficult to line up than is often claimed. Rarely, for example, do the various biblical metaphors of the church's relationship to Jesus Christ (body of Christ, people of God, Israel of God etc.) play a part in systematic formulation of the varied ways in which the church can be viewed. The way churches identify, train and call ministers (teaching elders) for example is a long way removed from biblical testimony as to what occurred in the early church.

3. *A future Reformed ecclesiology must not abandon its commitment to Scripture and what it perceives as fundamental doctrine in the interests of ecumenicity.* Anyone who observed the secular media's coverage of the inauguration of Pope Benedict XVI will have witnessed the ideological gulf that separates their respective agendas. The West has lost its sense of value and truth and is incapable of discerning how doctrinal certainty and ethical principle can be reflective of a received tradition – be that scriptural or ecclesiastical pronouncement. On more than one issue (women and the priesthood, same-sex marriage, even birth-control) the Vatican's position was so resolute that discussion was unnecessary – to the immense consternation and puzzlement of the liberal media. Conservative Protestantism increasingly finds that its allies, particularly in ethical matters (e.g. abortion, stem-cell research, euthanasia), and increasingly in affirming the dignity and historic nature of its worship, are to be found in Catholicism and Eastern Orthodoxy. It is not insignificant that since the 1980s there has been a steady trickle of Reformed clergy who have moved in these directions, increasingly disaffected by the moral and confessional relativism of fellow Protestants. What, for example, our Protestant forefathers warned about the deviation of Catholicism from the truth, the Reformed churches of today are beginning to identify in the hermeneutical accommodation of contemporary evangelicalism. It is pointless to deny that the Reformed tradition is thoroughly infused with Augustinianism and for that reason is closer to Roman Catholicism than Eastern Orthodoxy. The latter shows increasing signs of disaffection with the Western church, particularly its openness to feminism and homosexuality, and it is likely to strain still further its membership of the World Council of Churches. The draw of Catholicism however remains a chimera, for the very reason that caused B. B. Warfield to speak of Augustinianism in terms of the triumph of the doctrine of grace over Augustine's doctrine of the church! The Roman church shows no signs of yielding on core issues such as justification by faith alone (surely still the *articulus stantis vel cadentis ecclesiae!*).

Whether the advent of the 'new perspective(s) on Paul' moves the Protestant church closer to Rome remains to be seen,[43] but the uncritical embracing of the Roman tradition in the interests of shielding the church from the increasingly unprincipled mores of contemporary evangelicalism would be a tragic mistake. It will be increasingly necessary for the Reformed ecclesiastical community to find ways of uniting on ethical principles without compromising essential biblical doctrine or forfeiting its right to criticize aberrant and ultimately damning doctrine.

4. *A future Reformed ecclesiology must be deeply committed to historic formulations of confessional Christianity.* 'Identity theft' is a modern problem not confined to the corporate world. The predilection of contemporary Christianity to be swayed by the latest best-seller is indicative of its loss of identity. Whatever the current fad for 'Celtic worship' means (and at best it means something noncerebral and Word-based, appealing to modern ideas of non-propositional communication, the historical validity of which is severely in question), it is not the way forward for Reformed ecclesiology. Postmodernity highlights the poverty of the church to provide an anchor for Christians in an ecclesiastical tradition competent to meet the range of philosophical and theological assaults – chiefly because it has met these before in other guises. The rootlessness of contemporary Christianity can only be resolved by affirming the communion of the saints through the ages. It is indicative of such rootlessness that *inclusive* psalm singing, for example, has been abandoned by evangelical churches and increasingly minimized in Reformed churches. It will be a tragic mistake to consider the adoption of contemporary worship's adoption of popular culture as value-neutral made in the interests of evangelism and communication.[44] One relatively simple remedy for the church is to discover its own tradition in the singing of the psalms – a liturgical practice that links the people of God with three thousand years of historical practice. Weekly singing of the psalms provides a sense of continuity in an age of instantism and throw-away consumerism that breeds scepticism and egocentricity. The church's abandonment of its sense of place within the historical tradition is to be lamented, and not a little of this is due to the fragmentation of the theological discipline. Biblical theologians rarely consult systematic theologians (or vice versa), and consequently the nuancing of theology results in fragmentation and lack of synthesis. Historical theology is too often considered the domain of the culturally elite, those who have not embraced the modern and

---

43. Guy Waters, *Justification and the New Perspectives on Paul* (Phillipsburg: P. & R., 2004).
44. See Trueman, *Wages of Spin*, pp. 23–24.

the new. But the advancement of theology without being rooted in the past is at best folly and at worst an act of intellectual excommunication. The fear of liturgy (though every church has a liturgy!) is to be lamented, and openness to liturgical variety without necessitating ecclesiastical fragmentation is something to be embraced.

5. *A future Reformed ecclesiology must take the initiative in fostering biblical spirituality.* Current confusion over the nature of biblical (Reformed!) spirituality is not without ecclesiastical ramifications. The fact that it is quite common for Reformed publishers to include a spectrum of authors and traditions in compilations on spirituality ranging from Brother Lawrence to Teresa of Avila to John Calvin is indicative of how minimal an influence Reformed ecclesiology has had in fostering the role of corporate worship and the 'means of grace' in the development of biblical piety. Spirituality has become the domain of the individual and parachurch movement, and this needs to be redressed. Reformed spirituality alone is adequate to meet the onslaught of secularism and consumerism. Only a robust theology rooted in justification by faith alone, and sanctification in terms of its twin components, mortification and vivification, nourished in the power of biblical expositional preaching, can provide the basis for the Christian Life lived *coram Deo* and *sub specie aeternitatis.*

6. *A future Reformed ecclesiology must adequately address the role and significance of the sacraments as signatory and sealing ordinances of the gospel.* Reformed ecclesiology suffers from the pendulum effect in its handling of the sacraments. On baptism, it is unlikely that the Reformed community will resolve the issue of modality this side of the second coming! *De facto* we must resign ourselves to disagreement and misunderstanding. It is, of course, a severe blow to unity, necessarily problematic for administration of church membership 'in good order'. However, a way of accommodation needs to be found in the interests of a greater good, and the refusal to allow the non-credo-baptized admittance to the Lord's Table is (while rare) to be regretted. On the other side, it remains doubtful how clearly paedobaptists understand the significance of their baptism, and the ability of some to reintroduce the liturgical formula 'This child is now regenerate' by stressing the 'objectivity' of baptism in inaugurating covenant inclusion is without doubt an issue that will only further divide the Reformed community, however dexterous the interpretation. It does not help the Reformed community when adroit attempts are made to interpret Paul's 'baptism into Christ' (Rom. 6:3; Gal. 3:27) without any reference to water baptism whatsoever. The Reformed churches must develop a working usage of baptismal language that rightly integrates water and Spirit baptism, sacramentology and soteriology. Continued debate over memorialist

and virtualist[45] understandings of the Supper has been befuddled by more heat than light,[46] as has the issue of the Supper's frequency of celebration. It might be pointed out again that Paul's 'for as often as you eat . . . and drink' (1 Cor. 11:26) signifies that weekly was not necessarily uppermost in his mind. The issue of paedocommunion has called for a reappraisal of the biblical data with respect to the Passover, as well as the role and function of the sacraments in the early church. It is an issue that has often been ignored, for example, that the Lord's Supper, while dominating ecclesiology in the past and present, is rarely mentioned in the pages of the New Testament. Had Paul not written a letter to Corinth we might have concluded that the early church had entirely misread Jesus' words in the upper room! This is not to downplay the import-ance of the Supper; but it does caution us to be circumspect and less strident in our accusations over issues of the Supper frequency. It is to be feared that too little has been made of the Supper by some. It is interesting to observe that memorialists who have tended to infrequency in its celebration have unwit-tingly heightened thereby its significance by its very occasionalism. Of greater return will be a renewed focus on the way the sacraments function as means of spiritual development (the language of the seventeenth century on 'improving our baptism' [Larger Catechism 167]).

7. *Reformed ecclesiology must find some meaningful way to express the church's unity in Jesus Christ.* Reformed theologians have long since conceded (perhaps *too* easily) that organizational unity is not what Jesus had in mind in his high priestly prayer 'that they might be one' (John 17:11, 21, 22, 23). It is undoubt-edly true that it would be difficult to find in the pages of the New Testament anything like denominationalism as we know it today. But this should not prej-udice the attempt to achieve such organizational unity. 'By schisms rent asunder' is not a meaningless aphorism. Nevertheless it will be a fruitless exer-cise to attempt resolution of what appears as necessary divisions – divisions caused by doctrinal considerations that effectively spell in reality a non-church; the withdrawal from what has become a scandalous fellowship [thus Jaroslav Pelikan's description of the Reformation as a 'tragic necessity']; church order (e.g. credo- and paedobaptism, or episcopacy and Presbyterian polity – these could not live in harmony with each other); and even cultural issues reflecting

---

45. From Calvin's use of the Latin *virtus* in describing the real presence of Christ in the Supper.

46. See Ligon Duncan's essay 'True Communion with Christ: Calvin, Westminster and Consensus on the Lord's Supper', in Ligon Duncan, ed., *The Westminster Confession into the Twenty-first Century*, vol. 3 (Fearn, Ross-shire: Mentor, 2005), pp. 429–476.

ethnicity (difficult as this is to maintain without appearing racist or defeatist, it is difficult to see how deeply engrained Black or West Indian churches can be integrated on a local level even though the attempt is a worthy one). There is no future if we concede to the notion that all divisions are by definition schismatic. What needs to be done? To begin with, a greater emphasis within the local church needs to be given of the way the unity of believers reflects the relations between God the Father, God the Son and God the Holy Spirit. Some effort in this direction has been made already. The World Fellowship of Reformed Churches (WFRC) formed in 1994, now known as World Reformed fellowship (WRF), is an attempt to bring together churches as well as parachurch organizations. On a more specifically ecclesial basis is the International Council of Reformed Churches (ICRC) – an attempt to unite various Reformed denominations by acknowledging common understanding on church planting, mission and theological education. It is an attempt to express the church's *international* dimension, something that denominations have understandably failed to do.

8. *Reformed ecclesiology must assert the corporate nature of the Christian life.* The late Edmund Clowney whose promotion of the church was legendary, regarded individualism as 'among contemporary challenges to scriptural church order, the first, and strongest'.[47] Nathan Hatch's description of [American] evangelicalism as a 'Democratic Movement'[48] is particularly telling, highlighting the 'club' mentality of the way Christians of today view the church. It is an extension of the idea of choice (something that Barth also addressed in a different context). It is interesting to note how the reinterpretation of the Supper rubric concerning 'discerning the body' (1 Cor. 11:29) is currently understood as a reference to the corporate nature of the church rather than the physical body of Christ on the cross. Whatever the merits of the exegesis, it cannot but aid in the promotion of dignifying the church as Christ's body, in union and communion with him.

These concerns are not exhaustive, nor could they ever be, but it is difficult to see how these issues would not play a significant role in future discussions on ecclesiology. The next generation of theologians will contribute significantly to the health and vitality of the church if they can help us in these areas and once again enable us to affirm with Calvin that

---

47. Edmund Clowney, 'Authority: The Church and the Bible', in John Armstrong, ed., *The Compromised Church* (Wheaton: Crossway, 1998), p. 42.

48. George Marsden, ed., *Evangelicalism and Modern America* (Grand Rapids: Eerdmans, 1986), pp. 71–82.

there is no other way to enter into life unless this mother conceive us in her womb, give us birth, nourish us at her breast, and lastly, unless she keep us under her care and guidance until, putting off mortal flesh, we become like angels. Our weakness does not allow us to be dismissed from her school until we have been pupils all our lives . . . away from her bosom one cannot hope for any forgiveness of sins or any salvation.[49]

© Derek W. H. Thomas, 2006

---

49. *Institutes* 4.1.4.

INDEX OF NAMES

Abelard 53, 179, 186
Adeney, M. 335
Akers, J. N. 308
Alter, R. 58
Ambrose 184
Anderson, H. G. 301
Anselm 22, 28, 47, 159–160, 179, 186, 187–188
Aquinas *see* Thomas Aquinas
Aristotle 181, 234–235, 238, 339
Arius 69
Arminius 62
Armstrong, J. 335
Athanasius 119, 121, 185, 186
Augustine 22, 26, 28, 30, 34, 114, 118, 119, 154, 180, 184–185, 187, 248, 260, 339, 347
Aulén, G. 186

Baker, D. L. 267
Baker, J. W. 188
Baker, M. 200–201
Bannerman, J. 329
Barfield, O. 332
Barnett, P. 318
Barth, K. 16, 21–22, 30, 54, 62, 64, 127, 134, 136, 147–148, 149, 150, 166, 167, 171, 180, 192, 196–198, 199, 207, 242, 243, 351
Bass, D. C. 175
Bauckham, R. 58
Bavinck, H. 64, 164, 168, 234, 249, 278
Baxter, C. 201

Baxter, R. 51
Beasley-Murray, G. R. 244
Beckwith, R. 102, 103, 113
Benedict XIII (Pope) *see* Ratzinger, J.
Bennett, J. 232
Berkhof, L. 122, 188, 190, 234, 249, 250, 259–260, 295
Berkouwer, G. C. 60, 62–66, 124, 250, 256, 329
Bhaskar, R. 139
Bird, H. S. 247
Bird, M. F. 325
Blake, T. 249
Blocher, H. 65, 240–270, 326
Bloesch, D. G. 135, 136, 148–151, 152, 159, 163, 165, 167, 169–170, 180, 329, 339
Boersma, H. 186, 209
Bonhoeffer, D. 257
Borg, M. 67
Boston, T. 240
Bowald, M. 171
Boyd, G. 55
Braaten, C. E. 291
Brakel, W. 249
Bray, G. 9, 19–40, 91, 114, 115
Bremmer, R. H. 238
Bright, B. 335
Brock, R. N. 194
Brown, A. W. 42, 45, 51
Brown, D. 67
Brown, R. E. 68, 82
Brunner, E. 57, 64, 330

Bucer, M. 235

Buchanan, J. 295

Buckley, J. J. 175

Bull, G. 115

Bultmann, R. 93, 157

Burgess, J. A. 301

Burman, F. 57

Burnett, R. 167

Calvin, J. 26, 29, 36, 52, 53, 60, 63, 109,
    114–115, 116–118, 119–120, 121, 122,
    134, 171, 178, 179, 180, 186, 188, 198,
    206, 208, 233, 235, 238, 240, 243,
    245–246, 247, 248, 250, 251, 260, 261,
    265, 266, 271, 276, 277–279, 282–287,
    291, 292, 298, 326, 328, 337, 339–340,
    350, 351–352

Cameron, C. M. 63

Camfield, F. W. 193

Campbell, J. M. 197

Cappadocians 22, 119

Carson, D. A. 242, 243, 322, 325, 333

Chafer, L. S. 241

Chalke, S. 201–204

Chambers, R. 164

Charry, E. 52, 53

Chedid, B. 335

Chemnitz, M. 62, 172

Cicero 339

Clark, D 135, 155, 160, 178

Clark, D. K. 128

Clark, S. B. 342

Clayton, P. 174

Clifford, A. C. 208

Clouse, R. B. 342

Clowney, E. P. 214, 222, 223, 224, 225,
    247, 248, 351

Cocceius, J. 57, 58, 241, 244

Cochrane, A. C. 339

Colson, C. 306, 335

Conn, H. 225, 235, 237

Crossan, J. D. 67

Crouch, A. 333

Cullmann, O. 57–58, 251, 338

Cyprian 184, 328, 329, 337

Cyril of Alexandria 108–109, 114

Dabney, R. L. 341

Davidson, D. 127, 153–156, 158, 160–162,
    170

Davies, W. D. 310

Dawn, M. 345

Demarest, B. 236

Dennison, J. T. 222

Dilthey, W. 159–160

Dittenberger, W. 84

Dummett, M. 126

Duncan, L. 350

Dunn, J. D. G. 68–69, 71, 309, 310,
    312–314, 315, 319, 333

Ebeling, G. 253

Edwards, J. 28, 36

Einstein, A. 160

Engel, M. P. 179

Erasmus, D. 235

Erickson, M. J. 92, 107–108, 129, 335

Farley, E. 133, 134

Fenner, D. 255

Ferguson, S. 227, 337, 350

Ferguson, S. B. 275

Fish, S. 160, 162

Fisher, G. P. 187

Foh, S. T. 342

Forsyth, P. T. 49, 192, 193

Foucault, M. 331

Frame, J. 10, 224, 225, 229, 344

Franke, J. R. 129, 146

Frege, G. 154

Frei, H. 127
Fuller, D. P. 252
Funk, R. W. 67

Gadamer, H.-G. 151
Gaffin, Jr, R. B. 12, 225, 226–227, 228, 229, 236, 238, 271–288
Gamble, R. C. 9, 211–239
Garcia, M. A. 284
Garlington, D. 325
Geertz, C. 142
Geisler, N. L. 306, 335
George, T. 306
Gerhard, J 62
Gerrish, B. 134, 178
Gill, J. 241
Gilson, E. 127
Godfrey, W. R. 303
Goldingay, J. 201
Gomarus, F. 235
Goulder, M. 93
Green, J. 200–201
Gregory the Great 185
Gregory Nazianzus 114
Gregory Palamas 22, 28
Grensted, L. W. 185
Grenz, S. J. 129, 135, 136, 143–147, 151, 152, 158, 163, 165, 167, 169–170, 180, 182
Grey, M. 194
Grudem, W. 236, 343
Gundry, R. H. 324
Gunton, C. E. 29, 51, 54, 58, 66, 94, 177, 178, 201

Habermas, J. 162, 169
Hadow, J. 240
Hamilton, I. 197
Hampson, D. 194–196
Harrison, G. S. 264

Hart, T. 135, 197
Hatch, E. 341
Hatch, N. 351
Hegel, G. W. F. 131
Helm, P. 102–103
Helseth, P. K. 335
Henry, C. F. H. 129, 149, 167, 168
Heyduck, R. 143
Hick, J. 67
Hilary 184
Hinlicky, P. R. 308
Hirsch, S. R. 151
Hodge, A. A. 190
Hodge, C. 36, 106, 114–116, 136–138, 139, 141, 154, 156, 158, 163, 167, 168, 207, 236, 251, 264, 265, 266, 269, 341
Holmer, P. 52
Honderich, T. 125
Hopkins, H. E. 44
Hort, F. J. A. 341
Horton, M. S. 56, 135
Hotchkiss, V. 339
Hull, G. G. 343
Hunsinger, G. 143
Hurley, J. B. 342
Husbands, M. 308
Hutchinson, J. H. 267

Irenaeus 58, 177–178, 185

Jacobsen, D. 41
Jellema, D. 207
Jenson, R. W. 291
Jewett, P. K. 244, 265
Jüngel, E. 253, 263

Kärkkäinen, V.-M. 21
Kaiser, Jr, W. C. 100–102, 231
Kent, T. 155, 160, 161, 162
Kermode, F. 58

Kingdon, D. 244–245, 247, 251, 265
Kline, M. G. 241, 268
Knight III, G. W. 214, 342
Kraus, J.-J. 134
Küng, H. 329, 330, 341
Kuyper, A. 60, 222, 223, 261–262, 339

Ladd, G. E. 75
Lampe, G. 93
Lane, A. N. S. 300, 302, 320
Lash, N. 48, 128
Lecerf, A. 250
Lehmann, K. 301–302
Leitch, J. W. 263
Leo XIII (Pope) 338
Letham, R. 120
Levinas, E. 130
Lewis, C. S. 203, 332
Lewis, G. 236
Lightfoot 341
Lillback, P. A. 188
Lindbeck, G. A. 59, 136, 142–143, 144, 155, 172
Lints, R. 135, 234, 236
Lloyd-Jones, M. 36
Locke, J. 152
Lossky, V. 28
Lusk, R. 286
Luther, M. 46–47, 53, 64, 172, 186, 233, 291, 292, 298, 315, 320

McClure, J. S. 182
McComiskey, T. 252
McCormack, B. L. 199, 209, 324
McCoy, C. S. 188
McGowan, A. T. B. 9, 13–18, 183–210, 240, 255, 257, 268
McGrath, A. 46, 135, 136, 138–142, 143, 151, 159, 163, 167, 173, 180, 299, 333
MacIntyre, A. 138

MacKenzie, R. E. 306, 335
McLaren, B. 134, 333
MacLeod, D. 112, 113–114, 122, 243, 341
Maimonides 339
Mallouhi, C. 335
Mann, A. 202
Marcel, P. C. 246, 247, 249, 250, 251, 252, 259
Marcion 185
Marsden, G. 351
Marsh, C. 194
Marshall, B. 127, 153, 156–158, 162–163, 170
Marshall, I. H. 59
Meek, D. 332
Melanchthon, P. 50, 62, 235, 291, 320
Metzger, B. M. 82, 83
Metzger, P. L. 291
Miller, E. 341
Moltmann, J. 29, 263
Moo, D. J. 252, 309
Morey, R. A. 344
Moucarry, C. 335
Moule, H. C. G. 108
Mueller, J. T. 280
Muller, R. A. 57, 128
Murphy, N. 129, 141, 155, 159
Murphy, T. A. 301
Murray, J. 105, 120–121, 191, 224, 227, 241, 255, 265, 271, 272, 273, 274–276, 279, 287, 334

Neuhaus, R. J. 306
Newbigin, L. 232
Newman, J. H. 182

Oden, T. C. 335
Olson, R. 150
Origen 184
Orr, J. 58, 244

Ott, C. 132
Owen, J. 57, 339

Packer, J. I. 189–193, 204–206, 208, 214, 236, 335
Pannenberg, W. 61, 159, 192, 301–302
Parker, T. H. L. 235
Parratt, J. 132
Pearson, W. 115
Pelagius 184
Pelikan, J. 335, 339, 350
Peter Martyr Vermigli 235
Peterson, D. 201
Pieper, F. 280
Pieper, J. 47
Pinnock, C. 55, 168
Piper, J. 324, 325, 343
Plato 339
Polanus, A. 235
Poole, D. 255
Porter, S. E. 51
Poythress, V. 241
Pratt, R. 214, 223, 224, 228, 231
Preus, R. D. 57, 301

Quine, W. V. O. 144, 154–155, 170

Räisänen, H. 333
Rahner, K. 61, 93
Rainey, D. 343
Ramm, B. 158
Raschke, C. 130–131
Ratzinger, J. (Pope Benedict XVI) 332, 340, 341, 347
Rausch, T. P. 306
Rendtorff, R. 242
Reumann, J. 301
Reymond, R. L. 10, 67–124, 107, 207, 231
Rhees, R. 52
Richard of St Victor 22, 28

Richardson, C. C. 337
Ricoeur, P. 126, 146
Ridderbos, H. 276, 279
Ritschl, O. 320
Robertson, O. P. 222, 252, 255, 260
Robertson, P. 335
Romerowski, S. 262
Rousseau, J. J. 337
Runia, K. 248
Rutherford, S. 36

Sailhamer, J. H. 217, 229, 230, 231
Sanders, E. P. 310–312, 313, 314, 315, 318, 321–322, 333
Sanders, J. 55
Saucy, R. L. 242
Schaeffer, F. 15
Schaff, P. 293–294, 297
Schilder, K. 250
Schillebeeckx, E. 93, 332
Schleiermacher, F. D. E. 19–20, 49, 128, 140, 329–330
Schmid, H. 280
Schnabel, E. 242, 248
Schoonenberg, P. 93
Schreiner, T. R. 309, 322
Schreiter, R. J. 132
Seeberg, R. 185
Seifrid, M. A. 291
Selby, P. 194
Sellars, W. 152
Servetus, M. 20
Sharp, G. 84
Siefrid, M. 307
Silva, M. 252
Simeon, C. 42–45, 51, 52, 55, 58, 59, 64
Smail, T. 201
Smeaton, J. M. 198–199
Smith, M. H. 121–122
Smith, S. 147

Socinus 190, 192
Spong, J. S. 67
Sproul, R. C. 306, 307, 308
Stendahl, K. 333
Stonehouse, N. B. 77
Storkey, E. 343
Stott, J. R. W. 209, 345
Strong, A. H. 187

Tanner, K. 194
Tanner, N. 46
Tappert, T. G. 292
Taschek, W. 153, 161
Taylor, C. 175
Taylor, J. 335
Taylor, V. 193
Tertullian 119, 184, 185
Thielman, F. 309
Thiering, B. 67
Thiselton, A. C. 233
Thomas Aquinas 28, 47, 153, 236, 238,
    328, 339
Thomas, D. 328–352
Thomasius, G. 106
Thornwell 341
Tillich, P. 93, 149
Torrance, T. F. 29
Tracy, D. 131
Travis, S. 201
Treir, D. J. 308
Triplett, T. 153
Trueman, C. R. 291, 331, 348
Tumin, M. 232
Turner, N. 83–84, 85
Turretin, F. 128, 190, 236, 238, 295

VanGemeren, W. 214
Van Ruler, A. A. 65
Van Til, C. 63, 215, 238, 239, 257
VanDrunen, D. 336

Vanhoozer, K. J. 10, 42, 51, 125–182
Venema, C. P. 289–327
Vidu, A. 170
Voetius, G. 236
Volf, M. 27, 134, 176
von Hase, K. A. 73
Von Rohr, J. 241
Vos, G. 72, 74, 75, 103, 211, 216, 217,
    222–223, 228, 229–231, 249, 251, 256,
    257

Wadell, P. 47
Walls, A. 180
Walther, J. A. 222
Warfield, B. B. 29, 69, 72–73, 74, 75,
    76–77, 80, 95, 102, 110–111, 112, 114,
    115, 116–120, 122, 123, 207, 208, 224,
    227, 347
Warren, M. 232
Waters, G. P. 309, 348
Webster, J. 134, 148, 165, 176
Webster, W. 335
Weir, D. A. 188
Welch, C. 234
Welker, M. 164
Wells, D. F. 104, 225, 226, 237, 345
Wellum, S. J. 145
Wendel, F. 292
Wesley, J. 44, 46
Westerholm, S. 309
Westphal, M. 152, 153
Whittaker, J. H. 52
Wiles, M. 92
Williams, G. 201
Williams, R. 174–175
Williams, S. N. 9, 10, 41–66, 173
Willis, D. 164
Wilson, A. N. 67
Witherow, T. 341
Witsius, H. 231, 241, 244, 246, 249, 251,

254, 255, 257, 258–259, 261, 266–269
Wittgenstein, L. 49, 52, 142
Wolterstorff, N. 129, 181
Wood, W. J. 153
Wright, N. T. 58, 309, 310, 314–318, 323, 333

Yarbrough, R. W. 57
Yeago, D. S. 175

Zenger, E. 242
Zizioulas, J. 28, 31
Zwingli, U. 233, 240

INDEX OF BIBLICAL REFERENCES

Genesis

1:1 88
1:26 26, 30, 34, 102, 220
1:26–27 342
1:31 257
2 – 3 258
2:16 188, 256
2:17 188
3:2 256
3:6 257
3:14–15 272
3:15 188, 254, 341
3:22 256
12 188
12:2–3 165
15 188
15:6 262
17 254
17:7 250, 265
17:18–21 265
17:23ff. 265
17:27 265
18 30

Exodus

3:14 31
19:6 247
34:6 263, 269

Leviticus

18 252
18:5 252, 254, 267, 268
24:11 78

Deuteronomy

7:8 264
9:4 254, 264
18:15 264
18:18 264
23:1 247
27:26 268
28:58 78
29:4 268
29:29 57
30:11ff. 264
30:12–14 254
32:9 272
32:34 260

Job

14:17 260

Psalms

16:9–11 101
32 244
35:23 81
38:15 81
38:21 81
45:4 85
45:6 85, 102
73:26 272
102:25–27 86
110 102
119:57 272

Isaiah

6:3 26

6:11–13 269
8:12ff. 81
8:14 81
30:27 78
45:22 76
53:5 198
53:12 107, 272
54:13 248
59:19 78
60:21 248

Jeremiah

10:16 272
31:34 248

Ezekiel

20:11 268
20:13 268

Daniel

7:13 72
12:7 269

Hosea

6:7 255
13:12 260

Joel

2:32 81

Habakkuk

2:4 254

Zechariah

1:4 *219*

7:7 *219*

7:12 *219*

Malachi

4:5–6 *219*

Matthew

1:1–17 *69*

3:17 *74, 198*

5:32 *338*

8:10 *70*

8:15 *343*

8:27 *69, 70*

9:1–8 *79*

9:2 *79*

9:6 *72*

9:14 *112*

9:27 *69*

9:36 *69*

11:4–5 *79*

11:25 *74, 75, 77*

11:25–27 *73–77*

11:27 *74, 75, 76, 77, 80, 97, 108*

11:28 *76*

12:8 *72*

13:38 *248*

13:41 *72*

14:14 *69*

16:13–16 *97*

16:13–19 *340, 341*

16:17 *75*

16:18 *341*

18:20 *80, 108*

19:21–22 *180*

21:12–13 *69*

21:16 *79*

21:37 *103*

21:41 *248*

21:43 *248*

22:44–45 *97*

24:30 *72*

24:36 *105*

26:37–38 *70*

26:39 *105*

26:42 *105*

26:53 *105*

26:64 *72*

26:72 *69*

26:74 *69*

27:55 *343*

28:8–10 *79*

28:16–20 *80*

28:18 *74, 80*

28:19 *37, 77–78*

28:20 *80, 108*

Mark

1:11 *74*

1:31 *343*

1:41 *69*

2:1–2 *79*

2:5 *79*

2:7 *73*

2:10 *72, 73*

2:28 *72, 73*

3:5 *69, 70*

4:37–38 *69*

6 *103*

6:6 *70*

10:14 *70*

10:21 *69*

10:47–48 *69*

11:15–17 *69*

13:25 *72*

13:32 *112*

14:34 *70*

14:71 *69*

15:4 *343*

15:39 *69*

Luke

1:5–10 *292*

2:1–2 *69*

3:1–2 *69*

3:22 *74*

3:23–37 *69*

4:39 *343*

5:17–26 *79*

5:20 *79*

5:24 *72*

6:5 *72*

7:9 *70*

7:13 *69*

7:22 *79*

7:48 *79*

8:3 *343*

10:21 *70*

10:21–22 *73*

10:22 *77*

10:40 *343*

17:13 *69*

19:45–46 *69*

20:13 *103*

21:27 *72*

22:20 *259*

23:4 *69*

23:6 *69*

23:14 *69*

23:47 *69*

24:13–35 *79*

24:34 *79*

24:36–43 *79*

24:44–52 *80*

John

1:1 *71, 79, 87–89, 88, 103*

1:2 *88, 89*

1:3   88, 89, 102
1:6   89
1:9   90
1:12   89
1:13   89
1:14   88, 89
1:17   236
1:18   71, 89
1:30   69
1:45   69
1:47   108, 112
1:48   80
2:11   79
2:14–16   69
2:19   101
2:25   108, 112
3:13   72, 78
3:16   204
4:6–7   69
4:29   69, 108, 112
5:12   69
5:17–18   96
5:18   31
5:21   80
5:26   105
5:27   72, 105
5:36   79
5:39   245
6:32   90
6:33   78
6:38   78, 102
6:42   69
6:45   248
6:46   78
6:50   78
6:53   72
6:58   78
6:62   72, 78
7:22   254, 263
7:27   69

7:31   97
7:46   69
8:23   78
8:24   94, 97
8:38   78
8:40   69
8:42   78
8:56   253
8:58   78
8:58–59   96
9:11   69
9:16   69
9:24   69
9:39   78
10:17   199
10:24–37   79
10:30   74
10:33   69, 96
10:36   78, 102
10:37–38   79
11:3   69, 112
11:5   69
11:6   112
11:11   112
11:11–14   108
11:14   112
11:25   176
11:26   176
11:36   69
11:47   69
12:2   343
12:27   69, 70, 105
12:46   78
14:1   79
14:6   75
14:11   79
14:13–14   79
14:16–23   37
14:18   274
14:20   272, 274

14:21   52
15   248
15:1   90
15:1–7   273
15:4–7   272
16:28   78, 102
16:30   112
17   210
17:1   105
17:3   90
17:5   78, 102
17:11   350
17:13   70
17:20–23   273
17:21   350
17:22   350
17:23   274, 350
17:24   78, 102
17:26   274
18:17   69
18:29   69
18:37   78
19:5   69
19:7   96
20:10–18   79
20:20–28   79
20:26–29   79
20:28   71, 79, 81, 87,
      94
20:31   82
21:1–22   79
21:14   79
21:17   112

Acts
1:4–9   80
2:22   69
2:24–31   101
2:30   101
2:31   101

2:40 *248*
2:47 *248*
6:3ff. *343*
7:38 *247*
7:55–56 *80*
8:12 *248*
9:3–5 *80*
9:10 *80*
13:34–35 *101*
17:31 *69*
22:6–8 *80*
22:17–18 *80*
24:14 *248*
26:12–15 *80*

Romans
1 – 3 *322*
1 – 4 *268*
1:3 *103, 105*
1:3–4 *56, 80*
1:7 *81*
1:16–17 *278, 315*
1:17 *295*
1:18 *213*
2 *268*
2 – 3 *296*
2:4 *87*
2:5 *260*
3:21–26 *315*
3:23 *323*
3:25 *260*
3:28 *298*
4 *254*
4:1–5 *253*
4:5 *296*
4:6–8 *253*
4:9–12 *254*
4:25 *307, 323*
5 *244*
5:1 *298*

5:8 *192*
5:9 *323*
5:12–19 *272, 273*
5:12–21 *295*
5:20 *254*
6:3 *349*
6:3–7 *272*
6:16 *87*
6:23 *296*
8:1 *272*
8:3 *103, 259*
8:9–10 *274*
8:13 *336*
8:17 *273*
8:29 *288*
8:29–30 *287*
8:32 *103*
8:33–34 *324*
9 – 11 *54, 244*
9:4 *262*
9:5 *71, 82–84, 85, 87*
9:8 *265*
9:22–23 *87*
9:31 – 10:6 *252*
9:32 *81*
9:33 *81*
10:5 *252, 254, 268*
10:6 *252*
10:6ff. *264*
10:6–8 *254*
10:9–13 *81*
10:12–13 *81*
11 *244, 248*
11:5ff. *248*
11:22–23 *87*
12 *336*
16:1 *343*
16:25–26 *273*

1 Corinthians
1:2 *81*
1:30 *327*
2:9 *273*
7:10 *338*
9:27 *43*
10:1–12 *248*
11:23 *338*
11:26 *350*
12 *336*
12:12ff. *273*
15 *80*
15:3 *278, 338, 346*
15:5 *79*
15:7 *80*
15:11 *99*
15:20–23 *272*
15:22 *259, 273*
15:45 *272, 274*
15:47 *272*

2 Corinthians
1:3 *83*
3 *252*
3:6 *240*
3:7 *268*
3:7–18 *269*
3:9 *268*
3:14 *240, 246*
3:17 *274*
3:18 *287*
5:21 *12, 32*
11:4 *337*
12:8–9 *81*

Galatians
1:3 *81*
1:6 *337*
2 *306*
2:15–16 *313*

2:16 298
2:20 193, 272, 274
2:21 323
3 268
3 – 4 244
3:7–9 253
3:10 268
3:10–14 313
3:11 254
3:12 252, 254, 268
3:13 192, 323
3:14 253
3:17ff. 253
3:21 259
3:23 253
3:24 269
3:27 279, 349
3:28 342
4 252, 269
4:4 103, 295
4:6 36
4:21–31 254
6:15 248
6:16 336

Ephesians
1:3 83
1:4 273, 274, 275
1:9 273
1:12 269
2:5–6 272
2:6 297
2:1ff. 336
2:19–22 273
2:20 129, 341
2:21 129
3:16–17 274
3:18–19 273
4 336
4:12 342

4:13–16 334
5:25ff. 336
5:32 273

Philippians
2:5ff. 295
2:6–7 107
2:7 106
2:8 93
2:12–13 336
3:9 256

Colossians
1 336
1:13 199
1:15–20 90
1:16 102
1:16–17 103
1:18 337
1:26–27 273
1:27 274
2:2 273
2:6 338
2:9 90
3:1–4 272
3:3 274

1 Thessalonians
1:1–2 81

2 Thessalonians
2:15 338
3:6 338

1 Timothy
1:10 10
3:11 343

2 Timothy
4:3 10

Titus
1:9 10
2:1 10
2:13 71, 83, 84, 86, 87

Hebrews
1:2 86, 103
1:3 86
1:6 86
1:7 85
1:8 71, 85–86, 87
1:8–9 86
1:10 86
1:10–12 86
1:11–12 86
1:13 86
2 247
2:14 69
2:14–17 93
2:17 69
3 268
4:2 245
4:9 263
4:12 176
5:5 86
5:7–9 105
7:12ff. 246
7:16 269
7:18 253
7:21 86
8 252
8 – 10 244
8:6–7 240
8:7 263
8:13 240, 263
9 269
9:9ff. 246
9:10 269
9:11 260
9:13 269

9:15 *260*

10:20 *269*

11 *253, 254*

11 – 12 *244*

11:40 *253*

12:14 *287*

12:18 *268*

12:18–22 *268*

12:22 *268*

13:8 *86*

1 Peter

1:3 *86*

2:5 *273*

2:9 *247*

3:14–15 *81*

2 Peter

1:1 *86, 87*

1:11 *86, 87*

2:1 *71*

2:19 *87*

2:20 *86, 87*

3:2 *86*

3:4 *87*

3:15 *87*

3:16 *87*

3:18 *86, 87*

1 John

1:2 *88, 90, 103*

1:7 *105*

2:8 *90*

2:19 *248*

2:28 *272*

5:20 *71, 89–90, 90*

Revelation

1:9–17 *80*

3:7 *90*

3:14 *90, 103*

6:10 *90*

13:8 *260*

17:8 *260*

19:7ff. *336*

19:11 *90*

22:2 *256*